Monetary and Banking History

Forrest Capie is an eminent economic historian who has published extensively on a wide range of topics, with an emphasis on banking and monetary history, particularly in the nineteenth and twentieth centuries, but also in other areas such as tariffs and the interwar economy. He is also a former editor of the *Economic History Review*, one of the leading academic journals in this discipline.

This book comprises a collection of papers by eminent scholars in the fields of historiography, banking, monetary economics both domestic and international, and tariff theory and policy, all areas to which Forrest Capie, in whose honour this book was produced, has made major contributions. Under the editorship of Geoffrey Wood, Terence C. Mills and Nicholas Crafts, this book brings together a stellar line of contributors – including Charles Goodhart, Harold James, Michael Bordo, Barry Eichengreen and Charles Calomiris. The book analyses many of the mainstream themes in economic and financial history – monetary policy, international financial regulation, economic performance, exchange rate systems, international trade, banking and financial markets – where historical perspectives are considered important. The current wave of globalisation has stimulated interest in many of these areas as 'lessons of history' are sought. These themes also reflect the breadth of Capie's work in terms of time periods and topics.

This expertly written book contains original scholarly work, often with new empirical results, and will be of interest to economics postgraduates and researchers, particularly those focusing on monetary economics, banking and economic history, as well as to central bankers and trade negotiators.

Geoffrey Wood is Professor of Economics at City University, London, UK. **Terence C. Mills** is Professor of Applied Statistics and Econometrics at Loughborough University, UK. **Nicholas Crafts** is Professor of Economic History at Warwick University, UK.

Routledge international studies in money and banking

1 **Private Banking in Europe**
Lynn Bicker

2 **Bank Deregulation and Monetary Order**
George Selgin

3 **Money in Islam**
A study in Islamic political economy
Masudul Alam Choudhury

4 **The Future of European Financial Centres**
Kirsten Bindemann

5 **Payment Systems in Global Perspective**
Maxwell J. Fry, Isaak Kilato, Sandra Roger, Krzysztof Senderowicz, David Sheppard, Francisco Solis and John Trundle

6 **What is Money?**
John Smithin

7 **Finance**
A characteristics approach
Edited by David Blake

8 **Organisational Change and Retail Finance**
An ethnographic perspective
Richard Harper, Dave Randall and Mark Rouncefield

9 **The History of the Bundesbank**
Lessons for the European Central Bank
Jakob de Haan

10 **The Euro**
A challenge and opportunity for financial markets
Published on behalf of Société Universitaire Européenne de Recherches Financières (SUERF)
Edited by Michael Artis, Axel Weber and Elizabeth Hennessy

11 **Central Banking in Eastern Europe**
Edited by Nigel Healey and Barry Harrison

12 **Money, Credit and Prices Stability**
Paul Dalziel

13 **Monetary Policy, Capital Flows and Exchange Rates**
Essays in memory of Maxwell Fry
Edited by William Allen and David Dickinson

14 **Adapting to Financial Globalisation**
Published on behalf of Société Universitaire Européenne de Recherches Financières (SUERF)
Edited by Morten Balling, Eduard H. Hochreiter and Elizabeth Hennessy

15 **Monetary Macroeconomics**
A new approach
Alvaro Cencini

16 **Monetary Stability in Europe**
Stefan Collignon

17 **Technology and Finance**
Challenges for financial markets, business strategies and policy makers
Published on behalf of Société Universitaire Européenne de Recherches Financières (SUERF)
Edited by Morten Balling, Frank Lierman and Andrew Mullineux

18 **Monetary Unions**
Theory, history, public choice
Edited by Forrest H. Capie and Geoffrey E. Wood

19 **HRM and Occupational Health and Safety**
Carol Boyd

20 **Central Banking Systems Compared**
The ECB, the pre-Euro Bundesbank and the Federal Reserve System
Emmanuel Apel

21 **A History of Monetary Unions**
John Chown

22 **Dollarization**
Lessons from Europe and the Americas
Edited by Louis-Philippe Rochon and Mario Seccareccia

23 **Islamic Economics and Finance: A Glossary, 2nd Edition**
Muhammad Akram Khan

24 **Financial Market Risk**
Measurement and analysis
Cornelis A. Los

25 **Financial Geography**
A Banker's view
Risto Laulajainen

26 **Money Doctors**
The experience of international financial advising 1850–2000
Edited by Marc Flandreau

27 **Exchange Rate Dynamics**
A new open economy macroeconomics perspective
Edited by Jean-Oliver Hairault and Thepthida Sopraseuth

28 **Fixing Financial Crises in the 21st Century**
Edited by Andrew G. Haldane

29 **Monetary Policy and Unemployment**
The U.S., Euro-area and Japan
Edited by Willi Semmler

30 **Exchange Rates, Capital Flows and Policy**
Edited by Peter Sinclair, Rebecca Driver and Christoph Thoenissen

31 **Great Architects of International Finance**
The Bretton Woods era
Anthony M. Endres

32 **The Means to Prosperity**
Fiscal policy reconsidered
Edited by Per Gunnar Berglund and Matias Vernengo

33 **Competition and Profitability in European Financial Services**
Strategic, systemic and policy issues
Edited by Morten Balling, Frank Lierman and Andy Mullineux

34 **Tax Systems and Tax Reforms in South and East Asia**
Edited by Luigi Bernardi, Angela Fraschini and Parthasarathi Shome

35 **Institutional Change in the Payments System and Monetary Policy**
Edited by Stefan W. Schmitz and Geoffrey E. Wood

36 **The Lender of Last Resort**
Edited by F.H. Capie and G.E. Wood

37 **The Structure of Financial Regulation**
Edited by David G. Mayes and Geoffrey E. Wood

38 **Monetary Policy in Central Europe**
Miroslav Beblavý

39 **Money and Payments in Theory and Practice**
Sergio Rossi

40 **Open Market Operations and Financial Markets**
Edited by David G. Mayes and Jan Toporowski

41 **Banking in Central and Eastern Europe 1980–2006**
A comprehensive analysis of banking sector transformation in the former Soviet Union, Czechoslovakia, East Germany, Yugoslavia, Belarus, Bulgaria, Croatia, the Czech Republic, Hungary, Kazakhstan, Poland, Romania, the Russian Federation, Serbia and Montenegro, Slovakia, Ukraine and Uzbekistan
Stephan Barisitz

42 **Debt, Risk and Liquidity in Futures Markets**
Edited by Barry A. Goss

43 **The Future of Payment Systems**
Edited by Stephen Millard, Andrew G. Haldane and Victoria Saporta

44 **Credit and Collateral**
Vania Sena

45 **Tax Systems and Tax Reforms in Latin America**
Edited by Luigi Bernardi, Alberto Barreix, Anna Marenzi and Paola Profeta

46 **The Dynamics of Organizational Collapse**
The case of Barings Bank
Helga Drummond

47 **International Financial Co-operation**
Political economics of compliance with the 1988 Basel Accord
Bryce Quillin

48 **Bank Performance**
A theoretical and empirical framework for the analysis of profitability, competition and efficiency
Jacob Bikker and Jaap W.B. Bos

49 **Monetary Growth Theory**
Money, interest, prices, capital, knowledge and economic structure over time and space
Wei-Bin Zhang

50 **Money, Uncertainty and Time**
Giuseppe Fontana

51 **Central Banking, Asset Prices and Financial Fragility**
Éric Tymoigne

52 **Financial Markets and the Macroeconomy**
Willi Semmler, Peter Flaschel, Carl Chiarella and Reiner Franke

53 **Inflation Theory in Economics**
Welfare, velocity, growth and business cycles
Max Gillman

54 **Monetary Policy Over Fifty Years**
Heinz Herrman (Deutsche Bundesbank)

55 **Designing Central Banks**
David Mayes and Geoffrey Wood

56 **Inflation Expectations**
Peter J.N. Sinclair

57 **The New International Monetary System**
Essays in honour of Alexander Swoboda
Edited by Charles Wyplosz

58 **Taxation and Gender Equity**
A comparative analysis of direct and indirect taxes in developing and developed countries
Edited by Caren Grown and Imraan Valodia

59 **Developing Alternative Frameworks for Explaining Tax Compliance**
Edited by James Alm, Jorge Martinez-Vazquez and Benno Torgler

60 **International Tax Coordination**
An Interdisciplinary Perspective on Virtues and Pitfalls
Edited by Martin Zagler

61 **The Capital Needs of Central Banks**
Edited by Sue Milton and Peter Sinclair

62 **Monetary and Banking History**
Edited by Geoffrey Wood, Terence C. Mills and Nicholas Crafts

Monetary and Banking History

Essays in honour of Forrest Capie

Edited by Geoffrey Wood, Terence C. Mills and Nicholas Crafts

Routledge
Taylor & Francis Group
LONDON AND NEW YORK

First published 2011
by Routledge
4 Park Square, Milton Park, Abingdon, Oxon OX14 4RN

Simultaneously published in the USA and Canada
by Routledge
605 Third Avenue, New York, NY 10017

Routledge is an imprint of the Taylor & Francis Group, an informa business

Typeset in Times by Wearset Ltd, Boldon, Tyne and Wear

British Library Cataloguing in Publication Data
A catalogue record for this book is available from the British Library

Library of Congress Cataloging in Publication Data
Monetary and banking history: essays in honour of Forrest Capie/edited by Geoffrey Wood, Terence C. Mills, and Nicholas Crafts.
p. cm.
Includes bibliographical references and index.
1. Money–History. 2. Banks and banking–History. I. Capie, Forrest. II. Wood, Geoffrey 1945– III. Mills, Terence C. IV. Crafts, N. F. R.
G231.M576 2010
332.109–dc22

2010031715

ISBN 978-0-415-74994-7 (pbk)
ISBN 978-0-415-45146-8 (hbk)
ISBN 978-0-203-83229-5 (ebk)

First issued in paperback 2013

Contents

Figures

Tables

Contributors

Mae Baker holds a first degree in Economics from the University of Manchester, a Master's degree in Economics and PhD in Finance both from the University of Leeds, and a Diploma in Education from the University of Sheffield. Mae's main focus of research interest lies in two lines of financial history: the development of the UK commercial banking sector; and the development of accounting information systems and financial management in the non-profit sector. Previous research has examined the investment decisions of fund managers and the interface between the City and the corporate sector.

Peter Basile received his bachelor's degree from Dartmouth College and Master's degree in Economics from Rutgers University. He has been working in the telecommunications industry for the last 20 years. He has held positions in marketing, market research and, most recently, financial analysis.

Michael Bordo is Professor of Economics and Director of the Center for Monetary and Financial History at Rutgers University. During the academic year 2006–7, he was Pitt Professor of American History and Institutions at Cambridge University. He has held previous academic positions at the University of South Carolina and Carleton University in Ottawa, Canada. He has been a visiting professor at the University of California Los Angeles, Carnegie Mellon University, Princeton University, Harvard University, Cambridge University and a Visiting Scholar at the IMF, Federal Reserve Banks of St Louis and Cleveland, the Federal Reserve Board of Governors, the Bank of Canada, the Bank of England and the Bank for International Settlement. He also is a Research Associate of the National Bureau of Economic Research, Cambridge, Massachusetts. He has a BA degree from McGill University, an MSc (Econ) from the London School of Economics and he received his PhD at the University of Chicago in 1972. He has published many articles in leading journals and ten books on monetary economics and monetary history. He is editor of a series of books for Cambridge University Press: *Studies in Macroeconomic History*. Recent publications include: with Barry Eichengreen, *A Retrospective on the Bretton Woods International Monetary System*, University of Chicago Press, 1993; with Claudia Goldin and Eugene White,

The Defining Moment: The Great Depression and the American Economy in the Twentieth Century, University of Chicago Press, 1998; *Essays on the Gold Standard and Related Regimes*, Cambridge University Press, 1999; with Alan Taylor and Jeffery Williamson, *Globalization in Historical Perspective*, University of Chicago Press, 2003.

Stephen Broadberry is Professor of Economic History at the University of Warwick and a Coordinator of the Economic History Initiative at CEPR. He has also taught at the Universities of Oxford, Cardiff and British Columbia and held visiting positions at the University of California, Berkeley; Humboldt University, Berlin and UPF Barcelona. His research interests include sectoral aspects of the comparative growth and productivity performance of Britain, the United States and Germany during the nineteenth and twentieth centuries; productivity in services, development of the European economy since 1000; the Great Divergence of productivity and living standards between Europe and Asia. He has been a managing editor of the *European Review of Economic History* and served on the editorial boards of the *Journal of Economic History*, *Explorations in Economic History*, *Structural Change and Economic Dynamics* and *Cliometrica.* He is a Trustee of the European Historical Economics Society and the Cliometrics Society and a Council Member of the Economic History Society. His previous books include *The Productivity Race: British Manufacturing in International Perspective* (1997), *Market Services and the Productivity Race: British Performance in International Perspective* (2006) and, as co-editor with Mark Harrison, *The Economics of World War I* (2005).

Charles W. Calomiris is one of the country's leading authorities on financial institutions. His research spans the areas of banking, corporate finance, financial history and monetary economics. He has advised numerous firms, agencies and governments on the performance and regulation of financial institutions. Calomiris is a research associate at the National Bureau of Economic Research and directs the American Enterprise Institute's project on financial regulation. He teaches international banking and a case course on business and finance in emerging market economies.

Alec Chrystal joined City University in 1988 after being Professor of Economics at Sheffield University. During 1997–2001 he was a senior adviser in the monetary analysis wing of the Bank of England. Duties during this time included drafting the Bank's quarterly Inflation Report, editing the Bank of England Quarterly Bulletin, editing the Bank's working paper series and writing briefing material for the Monetary Policy Committee. Alec returned to Cass Business School in September 2001 to become Head of a newly merged Finance Faculty, a post he occupied until January 2009. He has research interests in monetary economics, international finance, political economy and household debt. Several books have been authored or co-authored, including the latest five editions of a famous economics textbook with Richard G.

Lipsey, and *Controversies in Macroeconomics* (with Simon Price). He is a committee member of the Money, Macro and Finance Study Group, and a Vice-President of the British Association for the Advancement of Science Section F (Economics).

Michael Collins' research has been largely concerned with the nineteenth and twentieth centuries and has ranged across a spectrum of issues: from banking stability, financial crises, central bank performance, bank governance, mergers and acquisitions, the performance of financial institutions' investment portfolios, governance and auditing structures in the not-for-profit sector, and governance issues affecting nineteenth-century football teams. The research has made a major contribution to the understanding of the scale and nature of financial provision made to the business sector by British banks.

Nicholas Crafts is Professor of Economics and Economic History at the University of Warwick, a post he has held since 2005. Previously he was a Professor of Economic History at London School of Economics and Political Science (LSE) between 1995–2005. He also teaches for the TRIUM Global Executive MBA Program, an alliance of NYU Stern, the LSE and HEC School of Management. His main fields of interest are the British economy in the last 200 years, European economic growth, historical data on the British economy, the Industrial Revolution and international income distribution, especially with reference to the Human Development Index. He has produced a substantial body of papers for academic journals, the British government and international institutions such as the International Monetary Fund. During the 1980s Crafts argued that during the Industrial Revolution an abnormally high (compared to countries which industrialised later) proportion of the British economy came to be devoted to industry and international trade, and that the British economy always tended to grow slowly. When Britain was overtaken by Germany and the USA – both larger countries – in the late nineteenth century, this was not because of any deceleration of British performance.

Barry Eichengreen is the George C. Pardee and Helen N. Pardee Professor of Economics and Professor of Political Science at the University of California, Berkeley, where he has taught since 1987. He is a Research Associate of the National Bureau of Economic Research (Cambridge, Massachusetts) and Research Fellow of the Centre for Economic Policy Research (London, England). Professor Eichengreen is a fellow of the American Academy of Arts and Sciences (class of 1997). He is the convener of the Bellagio Group of academics and economic officials and chairs the Academic Advisory Committee of the Peterson Institute of International Economics. He is a regular monthly columnist for Project Syndicate. His books include *Golden Fetters: The Gold Standard and the Great Depression* (1992), *Globalizing Capital: A History of the International Monetary System* (second edition 2008) and *The European Economy since 1945: Coordinated Capitalism and Beyond* (paperback edition 2008).

Charles Goodhart, CBE, FBA is a member of the Financial Markets Group at the London School of Economics, having previously been its Deputy Director (1987–2005). Until his retirement in 2002, he had been the Norman Sosnow Professor of Banking and Finance at LSE since 1985. Before then, he had worked at the Bank of England for 17 years as a monetary adviser, becoming a Chief Adviser in 1980. In 1997 he was appointed one of the outside independent members of the Bank of England's new Monetary Policy Committee until May 2000. Earlier he had taught at Cambridge and LSE. Besides numerous articles, he has written a couple of books on monetary history; a graduate monetary textbook, *Money, Information and Uncertainty* (second edition 1989); two collections of papers on monetary policy, *Monetary Theory and Practice* (1984) and *The Central Bank and The Financial System* (1995); and a number of books and articles on financial stability, on which subject he was Adviser to the Governor of the Bank of England, 2002–4, and numerous other studies relating to financial markets and to monetary policy and history. In his spare time he is a sheep farmer (loss-making).

Harold James, who holds a joint appointment as Professor of International Affairs in the Woodrow Wilson School, studies economic and financial history and modern German history. He was educated at Cambridge University (PhD in 1982) and was a Fellow of Peterhouse for eight years before coming to Princeton University in 1986. His books include a study of the interwar depression in Germany, *The German Slump* (1986); an analysis of the changing character of national identity in Germany, *A German Identity 1770–1990* (1989) (both books are also available in German); and *International Monetary Cooperation Since Bretton Woods* (1996). He was also co-author of a history of Deutsche Bank (1995), which won the Financial Times Global Business Book Award in 1996, and he wrote *The Deutsche Bank and the Nazi Economic War Against the Jews* (2001). Recent works include *The End of Globalization: Lessons from the Great Depression* (2001), which is also available in Chinese, German, Greek, Japanese, Korean and Spanish, and *Europe Reborn: A History 1914–2000* (2003); *The Roman Predicament: How the Rules of International Order Create the Politics of Empire* (2006); *Family Capitalism: Wendels, Haniels and Falcks* (2006; also available in German, Italian and Chinese) and *The Creation and Destruction of Value: The Globalization Cycle* (2009). In 2004 he was awarded the Helmut Schmidt Prize for Economic History, and in 2005 the Ludwig Erhard Prize for writing about economics. He is also Marie Curie Visiting Professor at the European University Institute.

Lars Jonung joined DG ECFIN of the European Commission in Brussels as a research adviser in September 2000. He holds a PhD in Economics from the University of California, Los Angeles. Jonung was previously Professor of Economics at the Stockholm School of Economics. His research interests include monetary economics, monetary and financial history, the euro, European integration, inflationary expectations and the economics of Knut

Wicksell. He has published books and articles in English and Swedish and is co-author of the leading macroeconomic textbook in Swedish. Jonung served as chief economic adviser to Prime Minister Carl Bildt in 1992–4. He has been on the board of listed Swedish companies and has served as economic adviser to the Skandinaviska Enskilda Banken. He has made several contributions to the history of the Riksbank. He is co-editor of *The Great Financial Crisis in Finland and Sweden: The Nordic Experience of Financial Liberalization* (2009). Presently he is a columnist for *Dagens Nyheter*, the largest circulation morning newspaper in Sweden.

John Landon-Lane is an Associate Professor of Economics at Rutgers University, where he teaches econometrics at the undergraduate and graduate levels. He has published numerous papers in the areas of econometrics (time series, forecasting and Bayesian methods), macroeconomics (real business cycles and growth) and macroeconomic history.

Agnieszka Markiewcz is Assistant Professor at the Erasmus University, Rotterdam. Her main field of research is exchange rate economics. She has worked on questions of the choice of exchange rate regimes, and currency and fiscal unions applied to the European context. Her current research focuses on the exchange rate dynamics generated by learning mechanisms. Professor Markiewicz is a member of CESifo and ERIM. She received her Master's in International Economics at the Institut d'Etudes Politiques in Paris and her PhD from the University of Leuven in 2008.

Terence C. Mills, Professor of Applied Statistics and Econometrics at Loughborough University, has also formally held professorial appointments at Cass Business School and the University of Hull. Publications include the books *Time Series Techniques for Economists* and *The Econometric Modelling of Financial Time Series* (both published by Cambridge University Press), *Modelling Trends and Cycles in Economic Time Series* (Palgrave Macmillan) and the edited volumes *Economic Forecasting* and *Forecasting Financial Markets* (Edward Elgar) and *The Palgrave Handbook of Econometrics*. He has also published over 180 articles in journals and edited volumes across a range of fields spanning economic history, economics, finance, climatology and meteorology. These include articles in journals ranging from the *Journal of Economic History*, through to the *Economic Journal*, the *American Economic Review* and the *Journal of Econometrics*, to *Physica A*, the *International Journal of Climatology* and the *Journal of Climate*.

Paul Mizen has been a member of staff in the School of Economics at Nottingham since 1992. His research field is monetary economics and the transmission mechanism of monetary policy. This covers research into the demand for monetary and credit aggregates, the financial behaviour of the corporate and household sectors of the UK economy, and the relation between financial asset flows and real expenditure.

Hugh Rockoff has been a Professor of Economics since 1971 at Rutgers University and a Research Associate of the National Bureau of Economic Research. He has a BA from Earlham College and a PhD from the University of Chicago. His research focuses on the monetary and banking policies of the United States in the nineteenth and twentieth centuries, and on wartime price and production controls in the United States. He is the author with Gary Walton of a textbook: *History of the American Economy*.

Eugene N. White is Professor of Economics at Rutgers University and a Research Associate of the National Bureau of Economic Research. At Rutgers, he has been Chair of the Economics Department and Graduate Director. He was recently editor of *Explorations in Economic History*. His research focuses on financial architecture, the microstructure of securities markets, war finance, conflicts of interest, asset bubbles, banking crises and deposit insurance. He is author of over 50 articles and books on these topics. Most recently, he co-authored (with A. Crockett, T. Harris and F. Mishkin) *Conflicts of Interest in the Financial Services Industry: What Should We Do About Them?* (2004).

Geoffrey Wood went to the University of Warwick in 1968 as Lecturer in Economics and then spent two years as Visiting Economist with the Bank of England, where he was, from 1994 to 2004, a Special Advisor on Financial Stability. In 1975, he joined City University. He was Visiting Scholar at the Federal Reserve Bank of St Louis from 1977 to 1978, has also advised the New Zealand Treasury on a wide range of issues, and has also been a visiting scholar at the Federal Reserve Bank of New York and served as research adviser at the Bank of Finland. Geoffrey Wood is also a visiting Professorial Fellow in the Centre for Commercial Law Studies at Queen Mary and Westfield College, University of London and has been a visiting professor at the University of Athens. In the academic year 2004–5 he was Visiting Professor at the University of Oxford. He is on the editorial boards of the *Greek Economic Review*, the *Journal of Financial Education*, and the *European Journal of Political Economy*, and is a General Editor of the *Journal of Financial Regulation*.

Preface

Mervyn King

The economics profession, central bankers and the Bank of England in particular have been lucky to benefit from the insights of Forrest Capie over a long and distinguished career.

At a conference at the Bank of England in 2009, in the wake of the financial crisis, Forrest remarked that, 'There are few, if any, simple lessons that can be drawn from historical experience; there is no manual to which one can refer. History is better used when the patterns or the rhythms of the past are understood and absorbed.' And he pointed to a practical example: 'When something goes wrong, it is not necessarily a good thing to identify it and then disallow it in the future. Regulation is not necessarily the solution; it is just as likely to be the problem.'

But we must work hard to learn the lessons that history has to offer if we are to avoid making the same mistakes in the future. It is frustrating that many features of the financial crisis of 2008 and 2009 were observed in the past. But, as has so often been the case, at that 2009 conference Forrest was the person who drew the parallels for us. He focused on 1825, 1836/7, 1847, 1857 and 1866. In many ways, it was the failure to look back to those periods and appreciate their lessons that led to the problems we observed during 2008 and 2009. Far too many people, in the run-up to the crisis, were willing to place almost exclusive weight on the insights that could be gained from a short sample of data, often covering little more than a short period after the Second World War. And they had only a limited appreciation of the underlying drivers of even those short spans of data. That left us having to bear the pain of rediscovering lessons that we had learnt in earlier times. At this same conference, Forrest said, commenting on the period of unusual calm following 1866: 'The lessons were that the banks had to learn what shape their balance sheet should have. They did and stuck to it.' This lesson may well be the one that has to be relearned. And the pain suffered will be the same as Forrest noted was endured before: the 'abuse for the next 100 years for being too conservative'.

But uncovering these lessons is not straightforward. It is never the case that things repeat themselves exactly, but there are common components to events that, if we can uncover, we can learn from. It requires an unusual combination of objective analysis from an informed researcher and a dedication to leave no stone unturned to find every piece of relevant information. This must then be complemented by an ability to interpret that information in a dispassionate way, and a willingness to look behind the facts to see the underlying economic and social forces that drove the outcomes. Forrest is instilled with these qualities, and has made the most of them throughout his outstanding career.

Forrest is always honest in his assessments. In 1986, he wrote, in his paper 'What Happened in 1931?' with Terry Mills and Geoffrey Wood, that 'the world saw the consequences of central bankers not understanding central banking' during the Great Depression. In earlier work, he had already analysed the compounding effects of other policy measures, such as the imposition of tariffs. And he has done as much as anyone to assist researchers in understanding the importance of money and banking in the UK. It is only through such sage warnings and valuable insights drawn from an appreciation of the past, coupled with the example that Forrest sets to us all in terms of how to approach policy questions, that we will be able to avoid a similar fate in the future.

It is precisely for this reason that, when the Bank of England was considering who it should engage to write the latest instalment of its own history, Forrest was the natural choice. We are confident that in due course, Forrest's history of the Bank will become another highlight in an already glittering career. But not only are we confident of the quality of the insights that that history will include, we are grateful to Forrest for the way that he has carried out his research. Everyone who has dealt with Forrest during his time in the Bank holds him in the highest esteem, has valued his insights and enjoyed the experience of interacting with him. He has been extremely generous with his time, and the institution is enormously richer as a result. This Festschrift, with contributions from many leading thinkers, is a very fitting tribute to him.

Introduction

Nicholas Crafts, Terence C. Mills and Geoffrey Wood[1]

This book comprises a collection of papers presented to Forrest Capie not on his retirement but on the completion of his latest major project, the official history of the Bank of England from the 1950s to 1979. This official history is an addition to only one aspect of his work. Not only has he researched and published extensively in monetary and banking history; inspection of his list of publications (which is on pages 301 to 308 of this present book) shows that he has also written on international trade, unemployment, international finance, business cycles, growth, inflation (including hyperinflations) and deflation and the history of economic thought. In addition, he guided and worked on a project which led to major refinements and extensions to British monetary and banking data.

The chapters in this volume are all prompted by different aspects of his work, either developing prior work of his or contributing to the further development of areas he has studied. In addition, more than one makes use of the extensive data he collected and published in Forrest Capie and Alan Webber, *A Monetary History of the United Kingdom, 1870–1982: Data Sources & Methods* (1985). This short chapter briefly reviews these other chapters, places them in the context of present-day scholarship, and, in emulation of Forrest's admirable custom of relating his historical studies to present-day problems, tries to draw some policy implications.

Writing history

Forrest Capie is the fourth commissioned historian of the Bank of England. He follows John Clapham, who covered 1694 to 1914 in two volumes published in 1944; Richard Sayers, whose period was 1891 to 1944, produced a three-volume study in 1976; and John Fforde, who dealt with 1941 to 1958 in his 1992 study. In his contribution to this volume, Charles Goodhart considers these three earlier histories. He applauds the wealth of detail that can be found in each of them but is disappointed that they are not more substantive contributions to monetary history. In particular, Goodhart notes that none of them was really successful in placing the actions and role of the Bank in the context of either the economic environment or the history of economic thought. Goodhart looks forward to Capie's history and anticipates that, as a more focused monetary historian, Capie is better placed to produce a volume that locates the Bank of England's activities squarely in the context of macroeconomic history and the evolution of British macroeconomic policy.

In his final paragraph, Goodhart notes that a satisfactory monetary history of the UK has still to be written. Capie and Webber (1985) provided important ingredients in the form of long time series of the monetary aggregates which, along with a framework based on the quantity theory of money, were central to the classic study by Milton Friedman and Anna Schwartz, *A Monetary History of the United States, 1867–1960* (1963). In 1985 this approach might have been the basis for a monetary history of the UK. However, the implication of Barry Eichengreen's chapter is that this genre has been superseded by a more ambitious approach, which he calls 'the new monetary and financial history', such that a modern panorama would have to pay much greater attention to the analysis of financial markets.

Eichengreen points to a synthesis between the tradition of Friedman and Schwartz and that represented by Charles Kindleberger, notably in his classic *The World in Depression, 1929–1939* (1973). This synthesis entails quantitative historical investigation of both money and finance, together with a recognition of the implications of asymmetric information in financial markets. Eichengreen sees Ben Bernanke's 1983 article on the role of bank failures in magnifying the impact of monetary contraction on the real economy in the United States in the early 1930s as a landmark in the move to the new monetary and financial history.

Certainly, as the literature has built on Bernanke's contribution, it has become possible to look at the American Great Depression as a financial crisis and there is a much deeper understanding of the reasons for bank failures and their role in the monetary transmission mechanism. This goes beyond the scope of Friedman and Schwartz (1963) and not only offers a fuller understanding of why monetary policy errors proved so damaging but also provides a richer menu of policy lessons for financial regulators. At the same time, it is now possible to develop Kindleberger's insights in a more formal and quantifiable way.

Of course, the scope of the new monetary and financial history extends far beyond revisiting the Great Depression. Much attention has been paid to international capital flows and to analysis of government-bond markets as impressive new databases have been constructed, notably for the pre-First World War era of globalising capital. For example, the roles of the financial markets and international monetary regimes in providing discipline on sovereign borrowers, especially in emerging markets, have been explored in considerable detail. Again, this promises a rich resource of lessons relevant to the current crises.

Crisis management

For some years Forrest's work in monetary economics and banking has paid particular attention to banking crises. Three chapters in this collection reflect that focus – those by Mae Baker and Michael Collins, by Charles Calomiris and by

Eugene White. The chapters deal with central issues in the study of banking crises. The failure of an individual bank or of a group of banks can threaten the entire banking system if that failure, due to absence or asymmetry of information, creates fears and panic about the stability of the rest of the system. Baker and Collins deal with information. In the absence of information, lender of last resort action can stop panic. White deals with lender of last resort action in France; Calomiris, meanwhile, carries out an extensive historical review to identify the circumstances in which financial crises are particularly likely to occur.

Baker and Collins look at a period before the date when the Bank of England emerged as a fully fledged Central Bank by adding the role of lender of last resort to its responsibility for maintaining the monetary standard. They draw on the correspondence between George Carr Lynn, Senior Partner in the London bank, Glyn, Halifax, Mills & Co., and Joseph Langton, who had been deputy agent at the Bank of England's Liverpool office before becoming manager of the Bank of Liverpool on its formation in 1831.

In the 1830s there was a boom in bank shares and in the creation of new banks. Fifty-one new banking companies were created in the first half of 1836 alone, before the boom came to an end with a tightening of monetary conditions. These new banks outside London could issue their own notes, and the majority did so. The Bank feared that the changes created a threat to monetary stability since the Bank was a source of liquidity for other money market institutions which could draw on the balances they held at the Bank whenever they wished. The quality of the new banks was thus of keen interest to the Bank, and also, of course, to the established banks which would, were a run to start, be threatened by it.

Baker and Collins show what kind of information was monitored, how it was exchanged among banks, how confidential information was shared, and how credit was assessed by a mixture of accounting data and judgements of character – which latter they characterise as 'from a 21st century perspective … unscientific and subjective on occasions'. A twenty-first-century perspective might well lead an observer of the banking difficulties which occurred towards the end of the first decade of that century to wish that such judgements had not gone out of fashion.

The chapter by Baker and Collins shows how history skilfully applied can have important lessons long after the period of the data used for the historical study. White's paper leads to a similar conclusion. His starting point is the massive expansion of the Federal Reserve's operations in 2008. Many of the problems of that year arose in derivative markets and, in consequence of that, it has been argued, Bagehot's rules for containing and then ending a financial crisis, focused as they are on the banking sector, were then and have become henceforward too restrictive. In an elegantly structured chapter, drawing on experience of the Banque de France in the nineteenth century, White shows this to be incorrect. He does this first by showing how Bagehot's rules were implemented in Britain, noting that Bagehot's recommendation for how to 'stay' a panic can be succinctly stated as freely offering advances with the provisos:

> First. That these loans should only be made at a very high rate of interest. This will operate as a heavy fine on unreasonable timidity, and will prevent the greatest number of applications by persons who do not require it. The rate should be raised early in the panic, so that the fine may be paid early; that no one may borrow out of idle precaution without paying well for it; that the Banking reserve may be protected as far as possible. Secondly. That at this rate these advances should be made on all good banking securities, and as largely as the public ask for them.
>
> (Bagehot, 1873, pp. 96–7)

White goes on to point out that these rules were devised and (very effectively) implemented in a setting where there did not have to be consideration of how to operate when contracts for future delivery were important. The Banque de France, in contrast, did have to operate in such a world; White discusses how it coped, and what lessons can be learnt for today. He shows first that it did not deviate from its principles and always insisted on good collateral substantially discounted. This was not forthcoming when the Lyon Bourse got into difficulties in 1882 due to customers being unable to meet their losses, so the Banque did not lend and the Lyon exchange was declared insolvent in January of that year. In contrast, liquidity went to the Paris Bourse when, via its bankers, collateral of satisfactory quality was offered. A similar course was followed in 1896 – again, those who could offer good security got funds and those who could not did not.

In sum, then, the Banque de France precedent suggests that it is still possible, in a world with many and complex derivative contracts, to demand good collateral and let those who were insolvent fail, without disastrous consequences.

Finally, there is the chapter by Charles Calomiris. In the wake of the crisis of 2008 and onwards, it has become fashionable to return to the work of Hyman Minsky and Charles Kindleberger, and cite them as showing the ubiquity of crises, how they are an inevitable result of human nature, and how they have therefore to be carefully and thoroughly regulated against. Charles Calomiris considers this view, first clearly distinguishing between financial crises and banking crises. This distinction, made by Anna Schwartz in her classic 'Real and Pseudo Financial Crises' (1986), is essential, as the evidence shows that only when financial sector problems spread to the banking system is the economy as a whole threatened and policy response conceivably useful.

The chapter demonstrates that, while financial crises broadly defined may well be common and an inevitable feature of human behaviour, banking crises are not. Such crises, his examination of data from all round the world and from the start of the nineteenth century shows, do not occur regularly, but require precipitating events. In particular, they follow when the 'rules of the banking game' have been changed in a way such as to promote risk.[2] Examples are guarantees for mortgage lending in Argentina in the 1880s; restrictions on banks which make them vulnerable to shocks, such as restrictions on branch banking; and, of course, recently the encouragement of lending on subprime mortgages. In contrast, other changes can be stabilising – the most notable example is the central bank accepting lender of last resort responsibilities.

The points made in this chapter are important for understanding relatively distant history, for understanding the first banking crisis of the twenty-first century, and for avoiding errors from the rush to regulation that generally follows crises. For, again to quote Calomiris, 'Regulatory policy often responds to banking crises, but not often wisely.' His chapter contains an abundance of examples of such unwise responses.

Money and interest rates

The links between monetary aggregates and regimes, real and nominal interest rates, and prices and inflation have been at the core of Forrest's research throughout his career. Three chapters in the collection, by Terence C. Mills and Geoffrey Wood, by Peter Basile, John Landon-Lane and Hugh Rockoff, and by Alec Chrystal and Paul Mizen, consider these links over three different historical periods.

In the first of these chapters, Mills and Wood use recently published data and modern time series techniques to examine the relationship between interest rates, prices and inflation in Britain across the two-and-a-half centuries, from 1750 to 2006, for which reliable data is available. Particular attention is paid to changes in monetary regimes as these often lead to associated shifts in the empirical behaviour of interest rates and prices, most notably in the movements on and off the gold standard. For example, they find that when Britain was on the gold standard the 'Gibson Paradox', a positive relationship between nominal interest rates and the price level and regarded by Keynes as 'one of the most completely established facts in the whole field of quantitative economics', did indeed hold, at least before 1914. When the gold standard was suspended the relationship turned negative, however, and, after 1914, disappeared altogether. Interestingly, the only time that a relationship between interest rates and inflation is uncovered is during 1965 to 1997, which began with stagflation and ended with Bank of England independence.

Mills and Wood also modelled the real interest rate, which they found to be stationary (mean reverting) even though the nominal rate was non-stationary, this being a consequence of the excessive volatility of stationary inflation swamping the volatility of non-stationary nominal rates. Although the expected real rate is very stable across the entire period, at just under 3 per cent, from 1915 to 1964 it was about 1 per cent lower, and it also exhibited extreme and asymmetric volatility during the eighteenth and nineteenth centuries, with increases in volatility being more rapid than falls, with volatility generally declining during the twentieth century.

Basile, Landon-Lane and Rockoff focus on the behaviour of interest rates and money in the United States during the Great Depression and re-examine the debate over whether the US economy fell into a liquidity trap during the 1930s. They contrast the belief of the early American Keynesians that this was the case because yields on short-term government bonds were near zero for most of the decade with that of the alternative school of thought (which included Keynes!) who argued that, even though these rates were near zero, a liquidity trap had not occurred because the full spectrum of rates across the term structure had not reached low sticking points. Using both descriptive, historical analysis and vector autoregression econometrics, Basile *et al.* find that rates longer than short-term government bonds did appear to have been sensitive to changes in monetary policy, although mortgage rates were an exception. Although they are at pains to point out that their findings are not conclusive and are hardly likely to end the debate over whether there was a liquidity trap in the 1930s, they are able to address a wider question concerning the question of the monetary transmission mechanism: if lower interest rates are desired, can reliance be put on general increases in the stock of money to create 'tsunamis' throughout the whole spectrum of rates or does lowering rates in a depression require specific measures tied to specific markets?

A major intellectual achievement of Forrest was the construction, with Alan Webber, of historical money stock data for the United Kingdom. Alec Chrystal and Paul Mizen use an updated version of the Capie and Webber annual data set to revisit the demand for money, a topic that was of major importance during the 1960s and 1970s, when Forrest was just embarking upon his long career as a monetary historian, but which, over the last quarter of a century, has disappeared from academic debate as monetary innovation and problems with the interpretation of money stock data appeared to reduce the relevance of this function for policy analysis. The recent quantitative easing policy adopted by the Monetary Policy Committee of the Bank of England, which has the intermediate goal of substantially increasing the money stock, argue Chrystal and Mizen, warrants a revisiting of the monetary aggregates to 'see if they really should have been neglected or if some of the relationships which monetarists once espoused do continue to be evident in the data'.

Chrystal and Mizen show that there is indeed a stable relationship between inverse velocity and long interest rates over the period from 1870 to 2008 and are able to identify a long-run demand function for real money balances which has parameter values very close to those that would have been predicted from both monetary theory and empirical research up until the 1980s. In the long run there is proportionality between money and prices and in the short run there is two-way causality between money growth and inflation and between the output gap and inflation. They are thus able to conclude that their findings 'are very clear and reassuring for those of us who learned our macroeconomics in the 1960s and 1970s'.

Implications of economic integration

This section contains two chapters about protectionism and two about the euro. EMU can be viewed through the lens of monetary history but also can be thought of as a currency union which reduces barriers to international trade. Forrest has written a good deal about the euro in recent years while in his early career he made notable contributions to tariff history and so these contributions relate to topics which matter to him.

The chapter by Stephen Broadberry and Nicholas Crafts looks at the long-run experience of the British economy and argues that economic historians have generally tended to underestimate the importance of openness and relatively free trade for growth and productivity outcomes. They stress the advantages of free trade before the First World War for income levels through the absence of a large, low-productivity agricultural sector, while the era of protectionism from the 1930s through the 1960s was the period when British relative economic decline was most acute. They argue that tariffs, originally implemented as part of the 'managed-economy' strategy to address the macroeconomic problems of the depression years, had adverse rather than positive effects on long-run productivity performance while also proving hard to eliminate once in place.

Insofar as there were negative impacts on productivity from tariffs, a major reason is that they undermined competition in product markets. This aspect is explored by Crafts and Mills, who present estimates of trends in market power in the UK over the long run, as reflected in the markup of prices over costs. They find that price–cost margins were high in the early post-Second World War period and then fell sharply in the 1970s, especially in manufacturing, when trade costs fell steeply as a result of GATT agreements and entry into the European Economic Community. Given that there is strong evidence for the post-war period that strengthening competition had favourable productivity effects, this suggests that British reluctance to liberalise trade policies in the early post-war years was an important reason for relative economic decline. It is greatly to be hoped that the 2007–9 crisis does not give rise to a retreat from the policies of openness that have served the UK well during the past 30 years.

As noted earlier, the euro has frequently been viewed as part of a strategy to promote economic integration through the Single European Market programme. This seems plausible given the evidence that belonging to a currency union increases the volume of trade.[3] However, it is easy to put two and two together here and make five. In his chapter, Harold James presents results of detailed archival research which explores the history of the emergence of the euro, especially with regard to the mysterious absence of the state. He produces evidence that points to the key role of central banks and their search for ways to deal with currency volatility rather than an economic-integration agenda.

If the euro is to make a sustained contribution to economic integration, then it has to be viable in terms of delivering the goods in terms of macroeconomic outcomes, an issue about which Forrest has expressed scepticism in the past. In this context, it is generally accepted that spillover effects imply the need for mechanisms to ensure fiscal discipline is maintained in individual member countries which, in the absence of political union, retain control of fiscal policy. This draws attention to the issue of whether the fiscal aspects of the design of EMU are appropriate.

This question is examined by Michael Bordo, Lars Jonung and Agnieszka Markiewicz, who consider the lessons from the historical experience of six countries that have practised fiscal federalism – four (Canada, Germany, Switzerland, United States) successfully and two (Argentina and Brazil) not. They conclude that there are three conditions for a fiscal union to function well, namely, a credible commitment to a no-bailout rule for member governments, state autonomy over tax and spending decisions to allow local political preferences to be satisfied, and a capacity to learn from past mistakes and adapt to new circumstances. On this basis, Bordo *et al.* argue that the euro already has the fiscal union that it needs well incorporated in the rules of the Maastricht Treaty and the Stability and Growth Pact. However, they note that the current financial crisis may require these views to be revised and recent interventions by the EU in Greece together with pressing fiscal problems in other euro countries suggest that this is an important caveat.

Conclusion

These chapters were first presented and discussed at a conference held at Cass Business School, in London, in Forrest's honour. Forrest has worked there since 1979, since before, in fact, it became Cass Business School, and was known as City University Business School. It may seem slightly anomalous that an economic historian, albeit one with a strong interest in policy, worked for so long at a business school. This situation came about by accident. Forrest came to City University, London, to work in the recently created Department of Banking and Finance on the project that department was just starting when he came, a study of the monetary history of the UK. (That project led to the publication of a very large amount of research, as examination of Forrest's list of publications makes clear.) In the course of the life of the project, the Department of Banking and Finance became part of City University's business school. It would be reasonable to say, though, that a situation where an economic historian worked in a business school, although it came about by accident, was shown by the financial crisis at the end of the first decade of the twenty-first century to be a most desirable one.

Everyone who spoke at the conference is a friend or co-author (frequently both) of Forrest's. That so many from so many parts of the world fall into these groups is in itself a tribute to him. That they were all willing to write a chapter for this book, and often travel some way to present it, is a tribute to his engaging personality. Among his many attributes he has never confused intellectual with personal disagreement.

Notes

1 We gratefully acknowledge financial support for the conference in honour of Forrest Capie from the Bank of England and Cass Business School.

2 Clearly, such problems are sometimes exacerbated by monetary policy errors, as in the United States during the Great Depression.

3 Claims that these effects were massive, made originally by Rose (2000), no longer seem tenable. Even so, Baldwin (2006) concludes that the evidence points to a long-run increase in the volume of trade for euro members in the range 10–20 per cent.

References

Bagehot, W. (1873), *Lombard Street*, London: Henry King.

Baldwin, R. (2006), 'The Euro's Trade Effects', European Central Bank Working Paper No. 594.

Bernanke, B. (1983), 'Non-Monetary Effects of the Financial Crisis in the Propagation of the Great Depression', *American Economic Review*, 73, 257–276.

Capie, F. and Webber, A. (1985), *A Monetary History of the United Kingdom, 1870–1982*, London: Allen and Unwin.

Friedman, M. and Schwartz, A. (1963), *A Monetary History of the United States, 1867–1960*, Princeton: Princeton University Press.

Kindleberger, C. (1973), *The World in Depression, 1929–1939*, Berkeley: University of California Press.

Rose, A. (2000), 'One Money, One Market: the Effect of Common Currencies on Trade', *Economic Policy*, 15, 7–46.

Schwartz, A. (1986), 'Real and Pseudo Financial Crises', in F. Capie and G. Wood (eds), *Financial Crises and the World Banking System*, Macmillan: Basingstoke and London.

Part I

Writing history

1 The commissioned historians of the Bank of England

Charles Goodhart

1.1 Introduction and background

The Governor of the Bank of England, Montagu Norman (Governor, 1920–44), envisaged commissioning a history of the Bank as early as 1929. 'At the end of the year 1929 the Governor stated that he wished a history of the Bank of England's policy to be compiled currently and carried back, as occasion served, to the beginning of the post war period' (Bank of England, file G15/49). John Osborne, then working as Principal in the Chief Cashier's Office, was put to work on the exercise.[1] Part of its purpose was to provide background for the Bank in its evidence to the Macmillan Committee, 1929–31 (Sayers, 1976, Vol. 1, Chapter 16). In the event some of the material was felt to be too sensitive to put forward as evidence.[2] In the light of that experience, a bank official noted (ibid.), 'History, to be well written, need not, probably should not, be written concurrently with the events it records.'

But the Governor clearly felt that the Bank should have its history properly delineated. W. Marston Acres, 'History of the Bank from Within', had not had access to the files and was insufficiently policy oriented. Andreades was dismissed as 'dry as dust'. The next obvious occasion was 1944, simultaneously the 250th Anniversary of the Bank, and the 100th Anniversary of the Bank Chapter Act of 1844. In 1938 Henry Clay wrote to the then Deputy Governor, B.G. Catterns (Deputy Governor, 1936–45), proposing that J.H. Clapham be approached to do the job. No other name was put forward. As noted later, Clapham was the leading economic historian of the day. Moreover, 'that he is not primarily a monetary theorist is an advantage, since he would not be tempted to subordinate research to the support of preconceived monetary theories,' Clay to Catterns (Bank of England, file M12401: Histories of the Bank: Sir John Clapham).

Since then there have been only four commissioned histories,[3] with Richard Sayers, John Fforde and now Forrest Capie following Clapham, though there have been many other histories of part, or all, of the Bank's history (I did one such short account for the *New Palgrave*). Note should be taken of the distinction between a commissioned and an official history, since the latter implies that the institution has not only commissioned but has also checked and agreed the contents.[4] Clapham's history was published by Cambridge University Press, because of war-time exigencies; otherwise the Bank would have printed it themselves. But the Bank paid for it. In the CUP Catalogue, the blurb stated, “The book was, however, allowed to be wholly its author’s child – and the choice of material and expression of opinion are purposely made entirely at his own discretion.” As reported in several notes to the Bank’s Committee of Treasury then, the decision *not* to make these histories an *official* account could serve as protection for the Bank, for example against accusations of self-seeking bias. This distinction became, however, forgotten, or abandoned, by the time Fforde wrote; this history is now described as ‘official’ both in the opening blurb and in Fforde’s preface. Perhaps this was because by then it was taken for granted that each author would be expressing his own general judgement.

Clapham’s history is in two volumes, covering the years 1694–1914 (Vol. I, 1694–1797; Vol. II 1797–1914), though there is a brief Epilogue on ‘The Bank as it is’ (Clapham, 1944 pp. 417–427), briefly discussing subsequent changes. There was also an abortive Volume III, commissioned by the Bank’s Committee of Treasury after the first two volumes were completed, to cover the years 1914–31; I shall note its fate later (Bank of England files M12401 and CT.146.01: Books about the Bank, Vol. I: 1938–68). It was initially expected that writing this book would take just one year, and a fee of £1000 was proposed. Sir John’s prior commitments on the history of King’s College, Cambridge, where he was Vice Provost, and his work for the *Cambridge Economic History* slowed that down; and then the Second World War ensued. He worked part time, at fees ranging from £250 to £500 per annum. By August 1940 he had done Volume I; ‘Also if a bomb fell on me at the Bank it would be pleasant to have the 18th century (for which the new MS material is more valuable than for the 19th) set up in type’ (Clapham to Clay, M12401). Besides Clay, Clapham’s two main interlocutors at the Bank were Edward Holland-Martin and Humphrey Mynors (then the Bank’s Secretary).

Clapham died suddenly in 1946. His proposed Volume III was in typescript, but not revised for publication, and its sources were ‘narrowly restricted’[5] (Sayers, 1976, Preface, p. xii). Moreover (as noted in file CT.146.01), since he was an economic, and not a monetary, historian, ‘his unpublished “Volume III” gives too little prominence to technical problems and developments and is now thought unsuitable for publication.’ Instead Sir Theodore Gregory was asked in 1964 to prepare a survey of material and, very likely at Gregory’s suggestion, in 1967 the then Governor, L.K. O’Brien, approached Richard Sayers to take forward the Bank’s history. This was published in 1976, comprising two volumes of text, and a third of Appendices. It covered the period 1891–1944, with a considerable overlap.[6] The third commissioned history was undertaken by John Fforde. Lord Cobbold had written to Jasper Hollom (then Deputy Governor of the Bank) in 1979 urging the Bank to press forward with the next stage of the history as being in the long-term interest of the Bank as well as having a wider historical advantage. He admonished that the next Bank historian should be got to work ‘before any more of the main characters of the period die or go gaga’ (Cobbold to Hollom, file M12401).

After Fforde retired as Executive Director for Home Affairs in 1982, he remained in the Bank then as an Adviser for two years, focusing on preparations for writing the next stage of the history. He presumably wanted to do this; and as a close colleague of the Governors it might have been hard for them to deny him. I do not know whether there was much, or any, consideration of the pros and cons of having an internal senior official write up the Bank's history, though he himself had played little, or no role in the historical period that he covered; He joined the Bank in 1957 and his History ends in 1958. Anyhow, once he had retired from the Bank in 1984, he was asked by the Governors (Robin Leigh-Pemberton and his Deputy, Kit McMahon) to continue the official history of the Bank for the years 1941–58. There was much less overlap in this case. Fforde did not deal with war finance, and only went back to 1941 in so far as it was necessary to cover the discussions leading up to Bretton Woods, the Anglo-American Loan, and the establishment of the post-war international monetary regime, especially in Chapter 2. The history ends in 1958, prior to the publication of the Radcliffe Report.[7]

Forrest Capie, the fourth and latest commissioned historian, was asked by the Governor, Mervyn King, in May 2004, to take the official history on a further 20 years. The main starting point was necessarily the Radcliffe Committee Report (hearings started 1957, published 1959), but Forrest needed to go back to the mid 1950s to review the antecedents of this. The closing date was 1979, partly because of the Bank's 30-year rule on disclosure, partly because 1979 represented a major watershed between the Keynesian-style macro-policies of previous governments and the attempts of the subsequent Conservative government(s) to introduce new, and initially more 'monetarist', regimes.

1.2 The historians

1.2.1 Clapham

A rationale for presenting this particular paper is that I am one of the very few people to have known three of these four historians personally, and in each case, quite closely, at least for a few years[8] (and as a history specialist at school, and then as an economist undergraduate, I read Clapham's *Economic History of Modern Britain* [1930, 1932, 1938] and his *Economic Development of France and Germany, 1815–1914* [1921]). I was also privileged to review both the Sayers and Fforde histories, and have every intention of doing the same with Forrest Capie's forthcoming history. As you might expect, I did not review Clapham's History; but M. Anson of the Bank of England unearthed six reviews of this for me; the best two are by Lloyd Mints (1946) and by Sayers (1947).

Although Sir John Clapham is billed as an economic historian, he was an historian first and foremost, and not much of an economist. As Sayers' quote in note 6 suggests, Clapham had little interest in economic theory. His most famous paper, 'Of empty economic boxes' (1922), 'accused the theorists of operating with concepts which were empty and irrelevant', notably whether particular industries were operating under conditions of increasing, decreasing, or constant returns. Despite having a disdain for theoretical economics, he was at that time not only the leading historian of economic development, though he had had no particular expertise in monetary or financial history, but he was also an establishment figure. He was a protégé of Alfred Marshall, elected to the newly created Chair of Economic History at Cambridge in 1928 (held until retirement in 1938), and Fellow and then Vice-Provost of King's College (1933–43), and elected President of the British Academy in 1940. He was a safe choice as historian of the Bank, even if unlikely to be particularly original or perceptive on the monetary debates in which the Bank was embroiled in the nineteenth century.

1.2.2 Sayers

It is difficult after this lapse of time to recall how commanding a position Richard Sayers had in the 1950s and 1960s in the field of money and banking in the UK. This was partly because this field, which was then treated at LSE, and perhaps at several other UK universities, as quite separate from general macro-theory, was held to require a profound knowledge of both monetary history and institutional detail. Richard Sayers had both. His early work on *Bank of England Operations, 1890–1914* (1936), in which he shows how the Bank used open market operations to make its official Bank Rate effective, remains a classic. He also wrote histories of Lloyds Bank (1957) and Gilletts, a discount house (1968). During the war he served in the Ministry of Supply and then became deputy director of the economic section of the Cabinet Office, an experience which served him well when he came to write the history of *Financial Policy, 1939–45*.

But his main role was not as an historian, but as an analyst and recorder of current banking practices, especially in the UK, but much more widely; thus he edited *Banking in the British Commonwealth* (1952) and *Banking in Western Europe* (1962). His main claim to fame was his book *Modern Banking*, first published in 1938, but which went through innumerable editions thereafter (the seventh, 1976, being the last on my own shelves). This was the authorised text which all British students of the subject were required to read, at least until the 1970s; from 1938 until around the early 1970s it dominated the scene.

Besides his historical work, his main innovations and original ideas were, first, to switch analysis of the fulcrum for the determination of the supply of money from the cash ratio to the liquid assets ratio and, second, to emphasise the ease of substitution among, and between, bank deposits and other liquid instruments. Thus the emphasis on 'Liquidity' in the Radcliffe Report, on which Committee he and Alec Cairncross were the key participants, was very much his doing. While he was correct to realise that the Bank had to make such cash available to the banks as they needed, in order to keep market rates in line with the Bank Rate, he was mistaken in believing that the liquid assets ratio was any less porous; he wrote just as concern about controlling bank liquidity began to be abandoned in favour of a narrow focus on bank capital adequacy.

Sayers' doubts on the stability of the relationship between (any definition of) money and nominal incomes has stood the test of time much better, but he was unfortunate in the timing of the Radcliffe Report. This occurred just as the early econometric studies were proclaiming that the demand for money function was stable (though they all, then and later, soon thereafter 'broke down'). Moreover, the emerging US monetarists, led by Milton Friedman, were using improved (mathematical) techniques to integrate monetary and macro-theories in a way that left the more institutional approach of Sayers looking old-fashioned and fuddy-duddy. The Radcliffe Report was criticised in the UK, and ignored and dismissed in the USA, which embittered Sayers. Perhaps this unhappy experience may have led him to focus his energies more on his historical work, especially his history of the Bank of England.

1.2.3 Fforde

Three of the four authors of these commissioned histories have been professional (economic) historians. The (partial) exception is John Fforde. It is only partial because in the early 1950s he wrote a history of *The Federal Reserve System, 1945–1949.* After getting a First in PPE at Oxford, he became a student (1949–51) and then a Fellow of Nuffield College (1953–57), with a stint in Churchill's Prime Ministerial statistical branch, in practice his think tank, in between. Thus in his earlier years he did train as an academic and/or economic historian.

But by the time that I came to know him, especially in the 1970s, he would vociferously deny that he had any residual capacity as an academic economist, or indeed as an economist of any stripe. But he protested too much. He was always academic in intellectual character, with a strong desire to search out the truth, and a willingness to try out all the byways and alternatives. As Kit McMahon wrote in the ODNB, 'he was never comfortable adopting the easy or consensus view. Indeed he seemed sometimes to have a positive preference for difficult positions reached the hard way'; and as I wrote in my obituary, 'he had the academic skills of an historian, despite being slightly impatient with references and cross-references. His drafting skills and command over English were superb.' Perhaps because it covers the most recent period, Fforde's book is, I believe, the most readable so far, though perhaps not as technically good a history as Richard Sayers.

1.2.4 Capie

And that brings us to Forrest. Forrest is the most focused monetary historian in the whole group. Clapham was a general historian, with no expertise in money and banking. Fforde was hardly a professional historian at all. The nearest comparison is with Sayers. Forrest has covered a larger and wider range of work on British monetary, banking and Central Banking histories than Sayers. On the other hand, Sayers was more prominent in the analysis and study of current monetary issues. But as a monetary historian Forrest is better placed than any of his predecessors, perhaps excepting Sayers, to take the history forward. And Forrest's qualities of attention to detail, of open-mindedness, of theoretical understanding, and of deep concern with getting to the heart of the subject will have stood him, and us, his future readers, in good stead.

Let me now turn from the historians to their books.

1.3 The contents of the books

1.3.1 Clapham's history

Clapham's mission was to cover 220 years, as compared with 55 for Sayers, 15 for Fforde and now 20 for Capie. He was also working under the pressures of war-time (real war, not just a financial crisis) in bombed London, and under time pressure to publish in 1944. Under these circumstances he did what many others would have done, which is to narrow down his remit to a manageable exercise. That is to say that he interpreted his mission to be to report what the main dramatis personae in the Bank said, and did, without much reference to the wider scene in which the Bank played a role. Thus there is almost nothing about the influence of the Bank on government financing, on the developing structures of the bond and capital markets, on the developing structures of the banking and financial systems, or on the Bank's role in the wider economic development of Britain.

The nineteenth century was a period that contained some of the greatest debates about monetary matters, and great writers, especially Henry Thornton. But Clapham's approach to them is quite cursory, and at times seemingly to me a bit prejudiced; he sides overwhelmingly with the Bank in the Bullionist debate, and barely mentions the debate between the Currency and Banking schools (apart from Clapham, 1944, pp. 181–182). There is little, or no, discussion of the way in which the international Gold Standard worked, or of the Bank's central role in that. His antipathy to economic theory, and to the attempts of economists to impose generalisations over an uncomfortably idiosyncratic world, surfaces from time to time, notably in his section on Crisis Theory, Vol. I, pp. 225–226.

Clapham was an excellent historian, and what he did, in recording what was said and done by the top officials in the Bank, was, I am sure, well done. But for any wider appreciation of the importance and role of the Bank it is, perhaps, viewed as a good starting point, rather than the finished, completed version. As perhaps was implied by Sayers' negative comments on Clapham's work on the late nineteenth century, and from the decision not to publish Volume III, in this latter wider respect Clapham's History is something of a disappointment. I wonder whether there is a case for the Bank to commission a prequel, to have Forrest return to the history of the Bank in the nineteenth century, with the precise aim of placing the role of the Bank in the wider context of the development of both monetary thought and of the UK's financial system in that century.

1.3.2 Sayers' history

I have written reviews of both Sayers' and Fforde's histories, and these represent a much more considered and careful view than I have had time to revisit on this occasion. Nevertheless I have taken the opportunity to look at these two histories briefly again. While Sayers' history is, to my mind, both better analysed and better informed, and both wider and more detailed in scope and coverage than Clapham's, he does emphasise 'that this is not a monetary history of Britain in this period'.

> It cannot satisfy economists, partly because the source material does not allow the kind of statistical analysis many of them would deem essential, but also because the story as it has unfolded itself to me has seemed to turn on comparatively few and rounded figures.
>
> (Sayers, 1976, Preface, p. xii)

This is illustrated by the fact that there are virtually no Tables, Figures or Charts in the first two Volumes of text, and that the only Tables in Volume 3 cover (i) 'The Bank's Profit Position, 1890–1939', Appendix 35; (ii) 'Bank Rate Changes, 1890–1939', Appendix 36; (iii) 'Gold and Foreign Exchange Holdings', Appendix 37; and (iv) 'Changes in the Bank's Fiduciary Issue, 1844–1946', Appendix 38.

While it is true that monetary historical time series have been considerably improved since Sayers' time by the work of several scholars, including Forrest himself, the basic data from the monthly reports of the London Clearing Banks and the Bank of England's own note issue was readily to hand. Yet Sayers makes no effort to use them himself. He decries the failure of the Bank in general, or of Montagu Norman in particular, to develop any concept, or theory, of how best to manage domestic monetary policies, see for example pp. 493 and 499 in Volume 2, but Sayers himself provides no yardstick for doing so. Sayers records that the Bank did not believe that its monetary policies bore much responsibility for the interwar depression (often blaming fiscal policy instead), but offers no judgement of his own on the subject. Although Sayers' work was much better than that of Clapham, it was still written in something of a theoretical void. Is that a good thing, since it reduces any tendency to bias and subjectivity, or a bad thing, since it makes it that much harder to give a structure for analysis and assessment?

Let me turn next to three minor details that a reread of Sayers' History has provoked.

1 Sayers' title promises a History until 1944. In practice, he does not take his account beyond 1939, possibly because he felt that he had already covered this in his 1956 book on *Financial Policy, 1939–45*. Per contra, Fforde's History promises to start in 1941, but in practice opens in 1945. Thus what appears to be an overlap of two authors for the years 1941–44, turns out to be an underlap since neither cover the historical role of the Bank during the war years, 1939–45.

2 I had earlier failed to appreciate properly Sayers' dry and even wicked wit. Two examples will suffice. First, from footnote 2, p. 440:

> The exact timing of the announcement was dictated by the necessity of having both disclosure to the Cabinet and announcement to the House after the closure of markets. The Cabinet included J.H. Thomas.

Second, from p. 74: The Governor

> did not want to be beholden to the overweening ambition of a certain commercial banker.

For those few who at this greater distance of time fail to recognise this play on words, Edward Holden of the Midland Bank was a famously ambitious and powerful banker.

3 It is often stated, mistakenly, that the last run on a bank was at Overend Gurney in 1866. It is, perhaps, worth remembering that there was a run *at*, though not *on*, the Bank of England in August 1914. Thus Sayers, 1976, p. 71 (also see Appendix 3, p. 33),

> At this holiday date the public had little use for five-pound notes (the smaller denomination issued) and went to the Bank of England for sovereigns, queueing at Threadneedle Street to the delight of newspaper reporters.

If only the BBC and Robert Peston had been on hand in those days, the queue might have stretched all the way to Liverpool Street.

1.3.3 Fforde's history

John Fforde was more truly academic by temperament than almost all professional academics. He liked to tease out problems, worrying away after the truth, often from first principles. He would rarely accept the consensus, or the convention, as an excuse for thought. He was idiosyncratic in many ways, and altogether delightful as a person. These qualities all show up in his book. He describes himself, in his preface, as an 'amateur historian', and makes little attempt to abide by the tiresome conventions of professional historians, in the guise of giving references, etc.

On my necessarily brief rereading of his book (Fforde, 1992), my supposition is that Fforde primarily set himself the task of discovering how his immediate predecessors, and often subsequently colleagues, came to reach their key strategic decisions. He was superbly well placed to do so, knowing from the inside how the Bank worked and knowing many of the dramatis personae personally. He would also have imbibed, consciously or not, a thorough understanding of the wider history of the time. Perhaps he knew, or assumed that his readers knew, too much, since there is very little background of the wider economic or political scene given to a reader who might be unfamiliar with UK economic developments in these years. Younger readers could find this a difficult book even though it is a unique and unrivalled, and superbly written, account of the Bank's decision-making processes at the time – in this, quite narrow, respect far the best History yet.

In order to discover how, and why, his immediate predecessors did reach their decisions, the new material that Fforde needed were their own internal papers, and such official papers that came their way from the Treasury, and a few other foreign official sources, plus some recollections and memoirs of a few key players, e.g., Cobbold, Jacobsson, Keynes, Norman. There are relatively few statistics, just the key ones on which Bank officials focussed when they had to take a decision.

Fforde provides even fewer Tables of data than Sayers; just one, Table 3.1 on p. 91, on Sterling Liabilities in 1945, and no Figures or Charts. On the other hand the text is relieved by numerous photographs and some cartoons. While the available database was much more limited in those days, and econometrics, forecasting models and computer printouts unheard of, the absence of any wider statistical background is perhaps a surprise (and a shortcoming). But then Fforde was focusing on how, and why, Bank officials took their key strategic decisions, not so much, if at all, on the effect of such decisions on the wider economy. For the latter economic time series would be necessary; for the former internal documentation would suffice.

By the same token, Fforde discusses at some length such economic analysis as the Bank could assemble *internally*, notably on domestic monetary questions, for example the role of Lucius Thompson-McCausland, pp. 322–324. Lucius was not a professional economist, but sought to adopt that role in the Bank on domestic monetary matters, perhaps in part because those with more economic training, Clay, Mynors and later Maurice Allen, had little to offer on that subject. But Fforde hardly ever refers to *outside* economic academic or commentary writing. Manning Dacey gets one mention and Wilfred King five; *The Banker* gets eight passing mentions, as does *The Economist*. I saw on my brief reread no mention of *any* academic writing, whether in a journal or a book. There is no discussion of whether, and how, if at all, the changing patterns of economic thought were influencing the Bank. Fforde seems happiest with those aspects of policy which were shaped by the Bank's practical experience, e.g., market management in the gilt-edged market, especially pp. 648–649, rather than by abstract theory.

In short, the book had a quite limited objective, to explain how, and why, senior Bank officials took their key decisions. Within that limited confine, his History succeeds brilliantly. But there are wider issues, left largely unexplored.

1.3.4 Capie's history

Forrest Capie's History was published in the early autumn of 2010. I saw early drafts of some three, or four, chapters, and participated in his collection of oral history, one of the innovative features of his work. While I much admired the draft chapters that I saw, I wrote this text before I could see the complete book. I shall have to leave a comprehensive account of that to his reviewers and, above all, to his readers.

1.4 Conclusions

My quick reread of the first three commissioned histories has led me to the view that all of them, when faced with the mass of documentation before them, came to interpret their remit quite narrowly. They focused on what the Bank and its senior officials did, and to a varying degree why they chose that line of action, most brilliantly in the case of Fforde, least so with Clapham.

But what none of them really achieved was to place the actions and role of the Bank either in the context of the wider economic and financial development of the UK (and world) economy, or of the history of economic thought. Sayers is, perhaps, slightly less culpable in this respect than either Clapham or Fforde. But he, Sayers, was correct in his appreciation that his work was not a fully rounded monetary history. And none of the three authors deployed an over-arching theoretical structure against which current developments could be assessed.

So, a satisfactory Monetary History of the UK remains to be written. At an earlier stage, several decades ago, I had hoped that Forrest and Geoffrey Wood might also do that. But as we all grow older, that task will have to pass to younger generations. But I am confident that Forrest's History of the Bank will be, not only excellent on its own terms, but a worthy and massive contribution to any such more comprehensive history.

Notes

1 Osborne later briefly became Secretary of the Bank, 1934–35, before becoming Deputy Governor of the Bank of Canada (Sayers, 1976, vol. 2, pp. 515, 625).

2 Whether any has survived I do not know. Sayers mentions 'studying "internal" histories he wrote', Acknowledgements, p. xix, and refers to some Osborne notes in Chapter 13, p. 389, and did interview him personally, pp. xix and 389.

3 Or, arguably, five. Fforde found that he did not have the time, nor probably the inclination, to cover the 'administration of the Bank as well as of its participation in public affairs', Preface, p. xiii. Accordingly that role was given to Elizabeth Hennessey, whose commissioned book, *A Domestic History of the Bank of England, 1930–1960*, was published in 1992.

4 This is emphasised in the Preface to Clapham's history, where it is written (p. ix) 'As this is not an official history.…' Interestingly this phrase was not in the initial preface submitted to the Bank, and so was presumably added later at the Bank's behest.

5 Sayers, however, found Clapham's account of the August 1914 financial crisis "attractive" (ibid.), and reproduced this as Appendix 3 in his third Volume of Appendices, pp. 31–45.

6 In his Preface (p. xi) Sayers wrote:

> Sir John Clapham's two volumes, *The Bank of England*, published in 1944, did enter upon the twentieth century, but had little beyond 1890 to interest economic historians. It so happens that events in 1890–93 strongly coloured the Bank's development through the next twenty years, and this therefore was a fair starting post for a survey of the Bank's ways in the last pre-war generation, the subject of my first four chapters.

7 Fforde wrote in his Preface (p. xiv) that:

> If the book often begins during the war, where does it end and why? The Bank's observance of the thirty-year rule governing public access to official documents, together with intended publication in 1991, suggested at first that I should take the story up to the end of Lord Cobbold's Governorship in June 1961. I later concluded, however, that the completion of various phases of policy in 1958 was more important than the change of Governor in 1961. The final resumption of sterling's non-resident convertibility, at the end of 1958, was one such completion. The termination of the 1950s 'credit squeeze' and the introduction of Special Deposits in July 1958 was another. Furthermore, within the Bank's relationships with the financial community, 1958 saw the end of the Bank's first attempts to solve the supervisory and credit-control problems thrown up by the newly emerging secondary banks. The book therefore finishes with these and other completions. It does not, for example, deal more than tangentially with the Radcliffe Committee and its Report, which belong more properly to subsequent history.

8 Richard Sayers was my Professor when I was a Lecturer in Money and Banking at LSE, 1966–68; John Fforde was the Chief Cashier and the Director of Home Finance

when I was an Advisor at the Bank, 1968–82; Forrest Capie has been a colleague since 1992, and a co-author of a book on *The Future of Central Banking* (1995), commissioned to mark the Bank's tercentenary.

Bibliography

Acres, W. Marston (1931), *The Bank of England from Within 1694–1900*, Oxford University Press/Franklin Library.

Cairncross, A. (2004–9), 'Sayers, Richard Sidney', *Oxford Dictionary of National Biography, Oxford University Press.*

Capie, F. (2010), *The Bank of England, 1959–1979.*

Capie, F., Fischer, S., Goodhart, C., and Schnadt, N. (1995), *The Future of Central Banking: The Tercentenary Symposium of the Bank of England*, Cambridge University Press.

Clapham, J. (1921), *The Economic Development of France and Germany, 1815–1914*, The University Press.

Clapham, J. (1922), 'Of empty economic boxes', *Economic Journal*, Vol. 32, pp. 305–14 (September).

Clapham, J. (1930, 1932, 1938), *An Economic History of Modern Britain: The Early Railway Age 1820–1850: Volume 1* (1930); *An Economic History of Modern Britain: Free Trade and Steel 1850–1886: Volume 2* (1932); *and An Economic History of Modern Britain: Machines and National Rivalries (1887–1914) with an Epilogue (1914–1929): Machines and National Rivalries: Volume 3* (1938), Cambridge University Press.

Clapham, J. (1944), *The Bank of England*, Cambridge University Press.

Cramp, A.B. (1987), 'Sayers, Richard Sidney', *The New Palgrave: A Dictionary of Economics*, edited by J. Eatwell, M. Milgate and P. Newman, The Macmillan Press Limited.

Daunton, M. (2004–9) 'Clapham, Sir John Harold', *Oxford Dictionary of National Biography*, Oxford University Press.

Dean, P. (1987), 'Clapham, John Harold', *The New Palgrave: A Dictionary of Economics*, edited by J. Eatwell, M. Milgate and P. Newman, The Macmillan Press Limited.

Fforde, J. (1954), *The Federal Reserve System, 1945–1949*, Clarendon Press.

Fforde, J. (1992), *The Bank of England and Public Policy, 1941–1958*, Cambridge University Press.

Hennessey, E. (1992), *A Domestic History of the Bank of England, 1930–1960*, Cambridge University Press.

McMahon, K. (2004–9), 'Fforde, John Standish', *Oxford Dictionary of National Biography*, Oxford University Press.

Mints, L. (1946), Book review of *The Bank of England: A History*, by Sir John Clapham, *American Economic Review*, Vol. 36, 4 (Part 1), pp. 689–693 (September).

Radcliffe Report, (1959), also known as *Committee on the Working of the Monetary System Report*, Cmnd. 827, Her Majesty's Stationery Office (August).

Sayers, R.S. (1936), *Bank of England Operations, 1890–1914*, P.S. King & Son Ltd.

Sayers, R.S. (1938), *Modern Banking*, Oxford University Press.

Sayers, R.S. (1947), Book review of *The Bank of England: A History*, by Sir John Clapham, *English Historical Review*, Vol. 62, 242, pp. 106–107 (January).

Sayers, R.S. (ed.), (1952), *Banking in the British Commonwealth*, Oxford: Clarendon Press.

Sayers, R.S. (1956), *Financial Policy, 1939–45*, H.M.S.O.; Longmans, Green.
Sayers, R.S. (1957), *Lloyds Bank in the History of English Banking*, Oxford University Press.
Sayers, R.S. (ed.), (1962), *Banking in Western Europe*, Oxford: Clarendon Press.
Sayers, R.S. (1968), *Gilletts in the London Money Market, 1867–1967*, Oxford University Press.
Sayers, R.S. (1976), *The Bank of England 1891–1944: Volume 1, Volume 2,* and *Appendixes*, Cambridge University Press.

2 The new monetary and financial history

Barry Eichengreen

When I was introduced in graduate school to the literature on the history of financial markets and monetary policy, the state of the art was two books, Friedman and Schwartz's *Monetary History of the United States* and Kindleberger's *The World in Depression*. Friedman and Schwartz organized their analysis around carefully constructed time series for the principal monetary aggregates.[1] They anticipated and, to a very considerable extent provoked, the subsequent literature documenting the association of monetary stability with macroeconomic stability and showed how this focus could illuminate the development of monetary and financial policies. They demonstrated how a parsimonious set of money supply measures could provide a rigorous framework for historical analysis.

Two things were missing from Friedman and Schwartz's analysis. One was the financial market micro-structure providing the transmission belt from money to output. The banking system and bank failures were there but only in the aggregate. And the financial system more broadly was underspecified. Also missing was an encompassing analysis of how monetary policies in one country interacted with those of the rest of the world. Friedman and Schwartz's monetary history was US monetary history by design.

Kindleberger, in contrast, provided a detailed financial history of the interwar years.[2] The workings of financial markets giving rise to speculative dynamics and problems of liquidity and confidence were at the center of his analysis. A lively narrative showed how financial disturbances arose and how the structure of financial markets shaped their effects. Kindleberger gave center stage to investor dynamics as a source of shocks and to financial-market micro-structure as a transmission belt. His focus on financial spillovers led him to emphasize international linkages and to adopt a global perspective.[3]

But Kindleberger's temporal coverage was limited to the 1920s and 1930s. His analysis lacked a unified set of statistical indicators of the state and structure of financial markets analogous to Friedman and Schwartz's monetary aggregates. His characterization of financial dynamics rested on his skill at portraiture and narrative. By comparison with Friedman and Schwartz, it was less obvious how subsequent scholars could build on his work.

While neither set of authors was working in isolation – both had both intellectual forbearers and colleagues working along similar lines – their books were unusually influential.[4] Friedman and Schwartz's influence was reflected in a series of national monetary histories emphasizing the importance of monetary policy and organized around estimates of national monetary aggregates.[5] Kindleberger's was reflected, with a longer lag, in scholarship concerned with financial structure and with the origin and impact of financial disturbances at the national and international levels.[6]

The task thus became to close the gap between these approaches. Several decades later it is now possible to point to something resembling a synthesis, what might be called "the new monetary and financial history." The new monetary and financial history analyzes macroeconomic fluctuations in terms of not just monetary aggregates but also the structure and dynamics of financial markets. It explains how the impact of central bank policy is shaped by the structure of the financial markets transmitting monetary impulses to the economy and how financial outcomes are in turn shaped by the monetary policy regime. It applies quantitative measurement to both money and finance. It looks beyond national borders when doing so is necessary. It applies recent developments in economic theory – on the credit channel for the transmission of monetary policy and the role of asymmetric information in the operation of financial markets, for example – and makes use of advances in computing that have facilitated gathering and analyzing micro-data on banks and securities markets. The result has been to better integrate monetary and financial history.

A marker in the development of this synthesis is Bernanke's "Nonmonetary Effects of the Financial Crisis in the Propagation of the Great Depression."[7] Bernanke focused on the 1930s, at some level the ultimate testing ground for theories of macroeconomic fluctuations, an episode that had similarly been Kindleberger's subject in *The World in Depression* and one to which Friedman and Schwartz had devoted 100-plus pages of their *Monetary History*. He drew on Barro (1978) and others who had used nonstructural time series models to analyze the connections between money and output. The portion of his analysis that drew most attention was where Bernanke added the lagged deposits of failed banks to lagged monetary aggregates in an equation designed to explain post-1929 output fluctuations, finding that bank failures had a significant impact on output even after controlling for movements in the money supply and that adding them helped to account for the persistence of the output collapse.[8] His interpretation was that the financial crisis destroyed information capital, reducing the efficiency with which savings were directed into investment by the banking system.[9] Because the market for financial claims is incomplete, intermediation between borrowers and lenders entails nontrivial market-making and information-gathering services. These services being provided by banks, bank failures can curtail their supply. This explains the persistent negative influence of bank failures on output. By implication, the crisis in the financial system mattered over and above its impact on the money supply, the channel emphasized by Friedman and Schwartz.

While Bernanke's proxy for financial disruptions, namely the value of deposits in failed banks, may have begun to capture the working of the banking system, it said nothing about what went on in securities markets. For firms that could borrow on bond markets the destruction of bank relationships and decline in bank credit presumably mattered less. In addition, bank failures could have been capturing not just the decline in the efficiency of financial intermediation but also other factors, shocks to confidence for example. It was not clear, in other words, whether the correlation between the value of deposits in failed banks and the subsequent output fall reflected rising uncertainty about the future and consequent reluctance to spend – changes in credit demand, in other words – or the declining willingness and ability of the banking system to lend – changes in credit supply in this case. Here the debate paralleled the debate over Friedman and Schwartz's results, where skeptics had questioned whether causality ran from money to output or the other way around.[10]

The working paper version of Bernanke's essay sought to address these concerns by substituting the spread between the Baa corporate and treasury bond rates as a measure of the efficiency of financial intermediation, there being no obvious reason why a shock to confidence should affect different interest rates differently and it being plausible that the spread between risky and riskless lending rates captured the cost and efficiency of intermediation.[11] But those tests were dropped from the article as published. Referees may have objected that bond spreads could be capturing not just the greater difficulty of distinguishing borrowers subject to high default risk when the banking system is impaired but also the rise in default risk itself owing to the severity of the economic downturn. Specifically, bond spreads might reflect the destruction of borrowers' collateral and the increase in their indebtedness owing to the fall in the price level. Another objection derived from the imperfect substitutability of bank loans and bonds. Only large firms were generally able to access the bond market while small firms depended on bank loans for external finance.[12]

In response, presumably, to such objections, the published version of the article dropped the analysis of spreads and, in addition, attempted to rehabilitate Irving Fisher's (1933) debt-deflation theory of the Great Depression, restating it in terms of the impact on collateral and hence on the creditworthiness of potential borrowers. But this separate collateral or debt-deflation channel was not integrated with the time series analysis. As a result it was not taken up by many subsequent investigators.

As a demonstration of how events in financial markets could be added to an otherwise conventional analysis of the impact of monetary policy on output, Bernake's article was widely cited and built upon. Anari, Kolari and Mason (2005) developed an alternative measure of the disruption of the banking system, deposits in banks in the process of liquidation, and showed how this did a better job than deposits in failed banks of predicting output fluctuations. Their result suggested that bank failures may have mattered by impairing the ability of households and firms to draw on the funds needed to finance consumption and investment more than by impairing their delegated-monitoring and information-mediation functions. Haubrich (1990) compared the U.S. with Canada, whose banking system was more heavily concentrated, where banks were more widely branched, and where financial failures were fewer. His results supported Bernanke by counterexample: since bank failures never attained the same prominence in Canada, the nonmonetary channel was less influential there. Calomiris and Hubbard (1989) estimated a Bernanke-style model for the United States before World War I.[13] Focusing on the spread between interest rates on high- and low-risk assets as a measure of financial-system disruption, much as had Bernanke in his working paper, they found a strong correlation with their monthly measure of economic activity. Grossman (1993) similarly focused on the pre-WWI period in the U.S., distinguishing the impact of bank failures on the money supply operating through the substitution of currency for deposits, which shifted the LM curve, from nonmonetary effects operating through crisis or spending, which shifted the IS curve.[14] Eichengreen and Grossman (1997) included both the spread between risky and risk-free assets and a measure of the incidence of bank failures in equations for output, interpreting the two coefficients as picking up the effects of debt-deflation and financial-market disruptions, respectively.[15] Ramirez and Shively (2006) constructed state-level indicators of bank failures and output for the U.S. in the period 1900–1931 and found evidence of both a reduction in consumption and investment demand as bank failures immobilized deposits and a reduction in the supply of credit as a result of disintermediation. The extent of these disruptions depended on the extent of branching within the state and the existence of state-sponsored deposit insurance – that is, on the structure and regulation of the financial system.

Thus, Bernanke used an important historical episode to demonstrate the compatibility of explanations for macroeconomic fluctuations emphasizing monetary and financial factors. He showed how the financial channel could be analyzed using methods analogous to those used to analyze the monetary channel. The subsequent literature showed how disruptions affecting the financial channel could influence economic activity both by reducing the efficiency of financial intermediation, thereby depressing aggregate supply, and by destroying or immobilizing savings and wealth, thereby depressing aggregate demand.

Bernanke had taken the spread between corporate and treasury bonds as a measure of the riskiness of the financial environment. This spread was seen as reflecting the additional costs of lending to firms subject to default risk and the greater difficulty of distinguishing high- and low-risk borrowers when the economy and its financial system are impaired. Often this was referred to as the spread over the risk-free rate, where the assumption was that treasury bonds were free of default risk. This interpretation may have been reasonable for the U.S. in the late nineteenth and twentieth centuries, where the federal debt was serviced continuously. But it was not equally reasonable for other times and places. Indeed, there already existed a large literature on sovereign debt and default in histories of international financial markets.[16]

The debt crisis of the 1980s and the resumption of sovereign lending in the 1990s prompted a reassessment of that experience. A marker in the development of this literature was Flandreau, Le Cacheux and Zumer (1998).[17] They asked whether the costs of borrowing on foreign financial markets rose with the level of indebtedness, disciplining otherwise profligate governments and averting problems of debt sustainability.[18] Thus, financial markets as a source of market discipline were central to their story, although the independence of central banks and the operation of the international gold standard (Friedman and Schwartz's monetary factors, in other words) figured in their analysis as alternative hypotheses. The impact of this article derived (in part) from its demonstration of the feasibility of gathering historical data on spreads on sovereign bonds and levels of government indebtedness for a considerable number of European countries.[19] These were used to analyze the determinants of the return on government bonds relative to the return on British consols.[20] The key explanatory variable was the debt/GDP ratio.[21] The authors estimated linear and nonlinear relationships between this variable and interest rate spreads, the advantage of the nonlinear formulation being its pointing to a threshold debt/GDP ratio where spreads first begin responding to the level of indebtedness. The results confirmed the existence of a positive relationship between indebtedness and interest rates.

The specification preferred by the authors on statistical grounds indicated that interest rates began rising only when the debt/GDP ratio exceeded 100 per cent. The question pursued in the subsequent literature was whether this high threshold reflected an unusual commitment on the part of nineteenth-century governments to servicing their debts (perhaps because governments could carry more debt owing to the limited extent of the franchise, which discouraged populist policies that might culminate in debt default) or, alternatively, the imperfect and episodic nature of market discipline. And if market discipline was uneven, the further question was what accounted for this fact.

Among the control variables included in the authors' analysis was whether a country was on or off the gold standard. Here they followed Bordo and Rockoff (1996) in arguing that a commitment to gold-standard rules required monetary and fiscal discipline to prevent unpleasant monetarist arithmetic from undermining the exchange rate commitment.[22] Bordo and Rockoff had found that adherence to the gold standard was associated with lower sovereign spreads but that deficits and debt did not show up as significant determinants of interest rates. In contrast, Flandreau, Le Cacheux and Zumer, using a different country sample, found that indebtedness was consistently significant but that the gold standard mattered only in a linear specification otherwise rejected by the data.

This suggested further research questions. Did adherence to the gold standard have a uniformly positive impact on policy credibility and hence on terms of financial market access? Or was the effect less uniform, perhaps because some countries at some times were prepared to devalue their currencies? And if gold convertibility was contingent, was its credibility less than complete? Was it important therefore to model the decision to adopt or abandon the monetary regime?

Some of these questions were pursued by Ferguson and Schularick (2006), who considered the impact of gold convertibility on spreads in a larger sample of countries, finding less evidence of the gold standard effect in their expanded sample.[23] Obstfeld and Taylor (2003) reconsidered it in different periods, finding that the gold standard had an even weaker impact on interest rates in 1925–1931 than before 1914, when political circumstances were different.[24] Clemens and Williamson (2004) analyzed capital flows to different destinations instead of spreads, similarly finding evidence of a gold standard effect (countries on the gold standard having received larger flows, other things equal). Meissner (2005) analyzed the decision to go onto the gold standard, while Wandschneider (2004) and Wolf and Yousef (2007) considered the decision to abandon it.

Insofar as evidence for gold-standard discipline was uneven, investigators returned to the alternative of market discipline and thus to the functioning of financial markets. Attention to these issues encouraged research on the microstructure of the markets and specifically on their information-gathering and delegated-monitoring functions.

Flandreau (2003a), in a case study, focused on the *Service des Etudes Financieres* of Credit Lyonnais. This service, essentially a research department within the bank, assembled information on the creditworthiness of sovereign borrowers, gathering many of the same indicators used in late twentieth-century analyses of sovereign creditworthiness such as debt-to-output and debt-service-to-export ratios. When debt-servicing problems arose, as in the early 1890s, Credit Lyonnais allocated additional resources to its intelligence unit, signaling the perceived value of the function. Another such indication was the tendency for other investment banks to hire specialists with similar expertise. These observations are consistent with the emphasis in recent research on the delegated-monitoring and information-gathering role of financial intermediaries. At the same time the gradual development and slow diffusion of the functional form may help to explain why market discipline remained uneven.

The literature then goes on to describe other mechanisms useful for acquiring and processing information on foreign borrowers. These included standing committees of bondholders such as the British Corporation of Foreign Bondholders, which assembled a research library to which bankers, bondholders and others referred and which disseminated information to its members through meetings and reports. They included rating agencies like Moody's and Standard & Poor's and commercial publications targeted at investors.

These relationships between banks and governments developed in the context of imperfectly competitive markets. In some cases like Brazil in the 1880s, one bank might entirely dominate the market for bond flotations, while in others, such as Argentina, the lead bank might have to compete with a bevy of smaller rivals or, alternatively, form a syndicate.[25] Borrowers retained some room for maneuver; Flandreau describes how the Portuguese government, dissatisfied by terms in 1876, jeopardized its relationship with Baring Bros. in order to solicit a loan from Credit Lyonnais. Flores (2007) argues that these competitive dynamics figured importantly in the Argentine-Baring crisis. Being concerned to maintain its relationship with Argentina and to defend its share of that country's bond market, Baring Bros. continued offering the same favorable spreads to the government even as Argentina's economic and financial position deteriorated. It absorbed a growing fraction of the new debt in the face of reluctance on the part of other investors. Once the deterioration in fundamentals grew serious, individual investors withdrew from the market, leaving the underwriter unable to place the bonds it had guaranteed and forcing the Bank of England to organize a rescue. Here, then, we have an explanation for how the reluctance of an intermediary that had a sunk investment in its relationship with the government to allow erosion of its market share, together with a too-big-to-fail guarantee, weakened market discipline.

A broader question is what encouraged governments to repay given that sovereign immunity rendered legal recourse ineffectual. The answers in the modern literature are sanctions (trade retaliation, seizure of assets, etc., the factor emphasized by Bulow and Rogoff 1989) and reputation (the greater difficulty that a country with a record of defaulting faces in borrowing subsequently, as emphasized by Kletzer and Wright 2000). Mitchener and Weidenmier (2005a) analyze the sanctions. They ask first whether there was a loss of trade following a country's default. In contrast to modern studies, nineteenth century data finds little evidence of this.[26] While it may be that the connections between trade and finance were less intimate in the nineteenth century, it also may be, as Mitchener and Weidenmier suggest, that creditor countries did not resort to trade retaliation because they could apply more direct and powerful sanctions in the form of gunboat diplomacy (seizing the customs house and imposing direct administrative restrictions on the debtor's freedom to borrow).[27] The authors identify these "supersanctions" in 12 pre-1913 instances of sovereign default. They show that they were associated with a fall in *ex ante* default probabilities on new debt by more than 60 per cent, a decline in yield spreads by 800 basis points, and a reduction of time in default by a half.

That outcomes were affected by overwhelming force applied against small countries with little capacity to defend themselves is not surprising. More startling is Mitchener and Weidenmier's assertion that such intervention was used regularly as a contract-enforcement mechanism.[28] Given that the authors identify exactly 12 instances of supersanctions in nearly four-score sovereign defaults in the period 1870–1913, the point can be presumably argued either way. In addition, most of Mitchener and Weidenmier's cases are of small countries (Costa Rica, Guatemala, Nicaragua, Santo Domingo, Serbia, etc.) and instances where default arguably provided a pretext for intervention desired on other grounds. Skeptics will question, in other words, whether sanctions were an enforcement mechanism or incidental to the lending process.

It might be argued that sanctions had generalized effects even if they were most frequently applied to small countries, because other governments saw them as a shot across the bow. Mitchener and Weidenmier (2005b) explore this hypothesis in the context of President Roosevelt's 1904 announcement that the

U.S. was prepared to intervene in the affairs of Central American and Caribbean countries that were unstable and did not pay their debts. They find that sovereign debt prices rose by nearly 75 per cent in countries in the U.S. sphere of influence following announcement of the Roosevelt doctrine. The effect is evident not just in countries where intervention took place but also elsewhere, consistent with the idea that making an example of a few could affect the behavior of many.

But the countries concerned were still all relatively small, and they were of concern to U.S. politicians, diplomats and military planners for reasons beyond their management of debts.[29] One may still question, in other words, how military action against them might have affected the expectations and behavior of larger countries where circumstances were not the same.

Alternatively, it is possible to appeal to reputation and to the negative impact of default on governments' subsequent ability to borrow to explain why sovereigns repaid. The theoretical literature questions this mechanism on the grounds that the immediate saving in debt-service costs may dominate the costs to the country of diminished capital market access and that prohibiting future borrowing may be difficult in a decentralized market.[30] Flandreau and Zumer (2004) analyze the impact of default on interest rates prior to 1913, finding that spreads over British consols rose by 500 basis points upon default, but that this effect fell to less than 100 basis points after a year and essentially disappeared after ten years. They conclude that the interest rate penalty was smaller than the savings associated with the elimination of service obligations on the defaulted debt, consistent with Bulow and Rogoff's skepticism regarding the efficacy of the reputational mechanism.[31]

Another question for the reputational story is what enabled a decentralized market to effectively prevent the defaulting sovereign from borrowing. While some creditors might have wished to see the defaulting government punished, others, recognizing that the repudiation of old debts had enhanced the government's capacity to service new ones, may have been tempted to lend. The question is how the structure and operation of financial markets enforced the embargo.

One answer is collective organization by bondholders. Committees representing the creditors worked in concert with the issue houses and stock exchange to prohibit the issuance of new debt until the borrower had settled. Research on this topic has focused on the British Corporation of Foreign Bondholders (CFB), the most prominent such organization (see, e.g., Eichengreen and Portes 1989; Mauro and Yafeh 2003). The CFB had well-developed relations with the investment banks and stock exchange. The latter relied on the CFB for information when deciding whether to apply its rule of refusing quotation to new loans to governments whose debts were in default and that had refused to negotiate in good faith. But even the CFB had difficulty enforcing sanctions. Bondholders in other countries formed competing committees, and inter-committee coordination was less than complete. Hence, it still might be possible for the debtor to borrow in another market. In addition, the management of the CFB and other committees may have had mixed motives. The CFB was a creation of the investment houses and loan brokers. Its governing board initially included representatives of the issue houses.[32] The issue houses may have been anxious to see a settlement so that new loans could be floated, generating new commissions, whereas the bondholders may have preferred to see sanctions maintained until the debtor made a more generous offer.

Esteves (2007) investigates these questions for 57 bonds in default between 1870 and 1913. For each issue he determines whether the bondholders were represented by a standing committee, an ad hoc committee, or a committee organized by the banks and whether there were one or several competing committees. His results suggest that when the bondholders were represented by a committee organized by the banks they realized lower returns. The presence of several types of bondholders' committees also appears to have slowed the resolution of defaults and reduced the rate of return. On balance this is consistent with the presumption that the form of committee representation and more generally the way in which financial markets and their participants were organized mattered for outcomes.

An obvious direction for research was to extend these pilot studies that had established the feasibility of analyzing issue and yield data by building a comprehensive database of international bonds issued in the four decades prior to 1913 and comparing the behavior and dynamics with those of bonds issued when securities markets were again the dominant vehicle for cross-border portfolio finance, after 1990. This was undertaken by Mauro, Sussman and Yafeh (2002), who gathered monthly observations spanning 1870–1913 for secondary market yields on sovereign bonds denominated in British pounds and issued by Argentina, Brazil, China, Egypt, Japan, Portugal, Queensland, Russia, Sweden and Turkey.[33] They found that sharp increases in spreads, what might be referred to as financial crises or periods of financial distress, were less common before 1914. This is similar to the conclusion of Eichengreen and Bordo (2003), who use modern indicators of the incidence of currency and banking crises in comparing the late nineteenth century and today.[34] It is also consistent with the conclusion of studies of aggregate capital flows and of instances where these were interrupted, such as Adalet and Eichengreen (2007). These studies suggest that such problems had less of a tendency to spill contagiously across borders in the earlier period. The proportion of the variance of emerging market spreads accounted for by the first principal component was only about half as large before 1914 as after 1990. The diversification benefits from investing in several emerging markets rather than one were thus higher historically than today. And structural breaks in the historical spread series were typically related to country-specific economic and political events, whereas in the 1990s many such breaks seem to have been related to global economic and financial shocks.

The question is whether the lower co-movement of spreads in the earlier period was due to the lower co-movement of fundamentals or differences in investor behavior. Fundamentals are hard to measure: Mauro *et al.* look at the cross-country co-movement of the annual rate of change of exports in pound sterling (and U.S. dollars in the late twentieth century); they find that the first principal component accounts for 29 per cent of the variation in the growth of exports before 1914 but fully 54 per cent after 1965. They suggest that lower co-movements in the earlier period may reflect larger cross-country differences in economic structure.[35] Perhaps, but to the extent that exports co-varied less in the earlier period, this may have simply reflected the extent to which interruptions to capital flows co-varied less, making for fewer coincident interruptions in the availability of trade credit.

Mauro *et al.* argue that improvements in information cannot explain the increase in the cross-country co-movement of spreads between the two periods because the information environment was already sophisticated a century ago. To be sure, the trans-oceanic telegraph, specialized investor services like that of Credit Lyonnais and a variety of specialized investor publications may have meant that information on events affecting returns on overseas bonds became available to late-nineteenth-century investors relatively quickly. But it is hard to deny that information flows even more quickly in our twenty-first-century world.[36] And to the extent that herd behavior reflects incomplete information encouraging investors to infer that negative information about one country implies similar problems elsewhere, improvements in the information environment should have led to a decline in cross-country co-movements in yields, not to the observed increase. One might argue that the very proliferation of information has made it more difficult for investors to extract the bits relevant for forecasting yields.[37] But those arguing that changes in the information environment and investor behavior account for the greater prevalence of contagion today have an uphill fight.

Alternatively, one can challenge the contention that the common-creditor channel for contagion was less prevalent a century ago.[38] Triner and Wandschneider (2005) draw a distinction between instances when there were disruptions in the financial center that interrupted capital flows to several borrowing countries at once from episodes when shocks in one borrowing country did not infect the center or spread to other debtors – when the common-creditor channel for contagion did not operate, in other words. Applying their model to capital flows to Brazil following the Argentina-Baring crisis, they show that the disruption to the London market resulted in negative consequences for the Brazilian exchange rate, for the spread on Brazilian sovereign debt and for the volume of capital inflows.[39] Recent literature on contagion has stressed trade linkages and herd behavior by investors in addition to the common-creditor channel. To the extent that this recent work suggests the dominance of the common-creditor channel, it further underscores the value of close historical investigation.

Another fertile field for tests of contagion is the 1930s, when problems in the financial center were acute. Bordo and Murshid (2001) report increases in the cross-country correlation of bond prices and yields during the turbulence surrounding the 1929 stock market crash, the 1931 sterling crisis and the 1933 devaluation of the dollar.[40] But their study focuses on the advanced countries, which may not have been the main victims of financial contagion.[41] More likely candidates might include the emerging markets of Central Europe, such as Hungary, Czechoslovakia and Poland, which imported capital from Vienna, Berlin and London. Wandschneider (2004) considers their experience using weekly data on government bonds and finds contagion running from Austria to the other countries following the Credit Anstalt collapse in 1931.

The effects of these interruptions to capital flows were often heightened by foreign currency-denominated debt and debt with clauses guaranteeing payment in currency of constant gold content. In countries unable to prevent their currencies from depreciating when capital flows dried up, the greater domestic-currency cost of servicing such debt dealt an extra blow to creditworthiness. Using data for 30 countries in the period 1880–1913, Bordo and Meissner (2006) document this association between debt denominated in foreign currency or with gold clauses and the risk of debt and banking crises. They show that it is not enough to know the debt/GDP and debt service/export ratios, à la Flandreau and Zumer, in order to predict the likelihood of financial distress. In addition, it is necessary to incorporate information on the contractual attributes of the liability.

The question then becomes how countries acquired the capacity to issue and market domestic-currency debt. Bordo, Meissner and Redish (2005) point to the development of economic, financial and political institutions protecting creditor rights and reassuring foreign investors that they would not suffer from opportunistic manipulation of the currency. Flandreau and Sussman (2005) emphasize the development of a liquid financial market that made participation attractive for foreign investors, something on which early industrializers and large countries had a head start.

Although a significant portion of the new monetary and financial history focuses on securities markets, the same methodological innovations using insights from the theoretical literature on asymmetric information and enlisting improvements in computing power appear in the recent literature on financial institutions and monetary policy. A number of recent studies of monetary transmission and stability, for example, have used balance-sheet data for individual banks and firms. Fohlin (1998) uses bank- and firm-level data for Germany in the late-nineteenth and early twentieth centuries to trace the development of long-term relationships as captured by interlocking directorates. She finds little evidence that investment was less sensitive to retained earnings in firms with such relationships, casting doubt on the importance of the credit channel for monetary policy.[42] It may be that interlocking directorates were late in developing, which meant that bank-firm relationships had not yet matured by the end of the nineteenth century into the kind of sophisticated information-gathering mechanisms posited in models of delegated monitoring.[43] Or the development of securities markets may have provided large firms with other ways of relaxing credit constraints.[44] Or perhaps the interlocking directorates that famously characterized the German corporate and financial sectors in this period were more important for enforcing collusive relationships than relaxing credit constraints.[45]

Other research has used bank-level data to reconsider the causes of bank failures.[46] The results have pointed up the importance of both lender-of-last resort intervention and banking-sector structure and regulation. Richardson and Troost (2006) use bank-level data for Mississippi, which was divided between the 6th and 8th Federal Reserve Districts. The Atlanta Fed, which oversaw the 6th District, championed the extension of credit to troubled banks, while the St. Louis Fed, responsible for the 8th District, adhered to the real bills doctrine and eschewed such initiatives. The authors show that outcomes differed significantly across districts, with banks failing at lower rates in the 6th District in the crisis of 1930. Their results confirm that Fed policy mattered critically for the incidence of financial instability in the Great Depression.[47]

Banking system structure and regulation figure in this debate insofar as they translated into levels of concentration and branching. Studies using state-level data on failure rates (Wheelock 1995; Mitchener 2005) show that states allowing branch banking had lower failure rates than states allowing only unit or single office banking in the early 1930s, reflecting their greater capacity to achieve geographical and financial diversification.[48] Yet studies using data for individual banks (e.g., Calomiris and Mason 2001; Carlson 2004) find that branch banks were more likely to fail than unit banks because they pursued strategies of reducing their reserves rather than diversifying their portfolios. In addition, Carlson (2004) shows that branch banks' portfolios were *ex post* riskier than those of unit banks in the circumstances of the early 1930s.

Carlson and Mitchener (2009) attempt to reconcile these contradictory findings. They show that marginally profitable banks, faced with heightened competition, were forced out through merger or liquidation. As weaker banks closed and the sector underwent consolidation, systemic stability improved. Insofar as branching served as a mechanism for heightening competition, it ultimately exerted this stabilizing influence. But this did not mean that branched banks were the strongest or most stable. Insofar as they reduced their reserves in the belief, mistaken in the circumstances of the Great Depression, that geographical diversification conferred economic and financial diversification, they had a greater tendency to fail.[49]

Analogous work is now under way for other countries. Adalet (2005) shows for Germany that universal banks were unusually susceptible to failing in the early stages of the Great Depression, reflecting their close connections to industry and the impact on their solvency of the fall of industrial production. Foreign deposit exposure also appears to have increased the probability of bank failure. Here too the story is complex. Adalet (2005) shows that bank balance sheets had been weakened significantly by World War I and the post-war hyperinflation but that this weakness had been papered over by foreign capital inflows attracted by the prevailing high level of interest rates, by Germany's return to the gold standard which investors assumed eliminated the currency risk of reichsmark deposits, and by the too-big-to-fail guarantee enjoyed by the large banks. With the erosion of the belief that the banks and currency were stable, capital flows turned around, and the house of cards came crashing down.

The question is what precipitated the capital-flow reversal – whether Germany's crisis started as a bank run that ultimately undermined the stability of the currency or as run on the currency that undermined the stability of the banks. Recent scholarship, influenced by studies of the post-1970 period showing that banking crises typically precede currency crises (see, e.g., Kaminsky and Reinhart 1999), has tended to privilege problems in the banking system. Adalet (2005), using a sample of bank balance sheets, shows that the banks did little to put their financial house in order between the Dawes Plan in 1924 and the onset of the Depression in 1929. Schnabel (2004) attributes this reluctance to restructure and the riskiness of subsequent investments to the belief that the banks were too big to fail; she concludes that the 1931 crisis would not have occurred had the banks "acted with caution" in the 1920s.

The contrary view, that this episode was first and foremost a run on the currency, is advanced by Ferguson and Temin (2003). They emphasize political events in the spring and summer of 1931, above all declining public support for the austerity measures that were Chancellor Bruning's response to Germany's fiscal problems. These fanned fears that the country's fiscal crisis would run out of control, forcing the central bank to monetize deficits and leading either to currency depreciation or capital controls. As capital flowed out, financial conditions tightened and the economic situation deteriorated further, undermining bank balance sheets. But with German reluctance to abandon the gold standard (unavoidable given memories of the 1923 hyperinflation) and the delay in applying capital controls (whose imposition was similarly inconsistent with gold-standard orthodoxy), the Reichsbank had limited capacity to intervene. Indeed, to the extent that it did so, its intervention further undermined confidence in its exchange rate commitment, reinforcing the currency crisis and through that channel compounding the problems of the banks.

The authors' evidence in support of the currency-crisis view includes a detailed analysis of German politics and of how political constraints hamstrung the efforts of the Bruning government to resolve the fiscal crisis. Their main evidence against the banking-crisis interpretation is that the deposit/currency ratio was relatively stable in the first half of 1931. There was no sharp increase in this ratio like that associated with the banking crisis in the United States.[50] In May, total deposits fell by only 5 per cent, hardly indicative of a run on the banking system.

But Reichsbank reserves as a share of the note issue actually rose that same month, which is hardly indicative of a run on the currency. Measured by the behavior of these variables, there was neither a full-blown currency crisis nor a banking crisis in May 1931. Thus, the failure of deposits to move is not obviously evidence one way or the other, since none of the relevant variables had yet begun to move significantly. And once they began moving, in June, they all moved together. Deposits fell by a larger proportionate amount in June than in May, and the Reichsbank's gold cover fell by an even larger fraction, dipping below the 40 per cent mandatory minimum by month's end. Evidently, none of the evidence invoked in this debate really makes the case one way or the other.

I have some sympathy for the view that lack of political support for policies of austerity undermined confidence in the reichsmark, since this is the story I have told for the sterling crisis of September 1931 (Eichengreen and Jeanne 2000). In the British case this story can be told without reference to banking problems.[51] But this does not mean that their role was negligible in Germany. There was extensive contemporary commentary about the problems of the German banks. Investors may have grown skeptical that the authorities had the stomach to leave the symptoms untreated. Realizing that intervention would require further liquidity injections and either a decline in the gold cover or the imposition of capital controls, they had good reason to get their money out of the banks and the country before their deposits lost liquidity or value. In this view, the events of June 1931 in Germany were both a currency crisis and a banking crisis. If so, attempting to prioritize one over the other makes little sense.

As these examples make clear, the last two decades have seen the development of a new monetary and financial history. This new literature has bridged the gap between the earlier money- and finance-focused literatures. While still acknowledging the importance of central bank policy, it has placed more emphasis on the financial markets and institutions transmitting monetary impulses to the economy. It takes financial markets as well as monetary policy as a source of disturbances. It builds on theoretical work acknowledging the incompleteness of information used by investors and depositors to make decisions. It suggests how financial markets and institutions attenuate these problems. It utilizes advances in computing power to process historical microdata on individual banks and securities as a way of shedding light on the operation of those markets.

Any survey of so vast a field is necessarily selective. I am conscious of having neglected the large literature on central banking and financial systems outside a few Western European and North American countries as well as problems of monetary and financial instability before the mid-nineteenth and after the mid-twentieth centuries. As I write, policy makers are grappling with a global credit crisis emanating from the subprime mortgage market in the United States (but ramifying much further). This has prompted two debates.

First, to what extent was the stage for the crisis set by overtrading and speculation, incentive problems in financial institutions, and lax supervision and regulation, on the one hand, versus loose monetary policy in the United States and capital inflows from emerging markets, on the other? One suspects that both monetary and financial factors played a role and that an adequate analysis of the crisis will require future historians to address both aspects, and their interaction.

The second debate is whether the response of central banks and supervisors to the crisis has done more to aggravate than contain it. To this question the only reasonable answer is that time will tell. Our age of abundance, as it were, will surely produce no shortage of raw material for future monetary and financial historians.

Notes

1 See Friedman and Schwartz (1963).

2 This distinction between monetary and financial history was made explicit in the author's subsequent financial history of Europe, expressly advanced as an alternative to Friedman and Schwartz's approach (Kindleberger 1981).

3 Even though his book had originally been commissioned as one in a series on the American economy.

4 The likes of Philip Cagan in the case of Friedman and Schwartz and Hyman Minsky in the case of Kindleberger.

5 Capie and Webber (1985) is an early and influential example of the genre.

6 See for example White (1990) and Capie and Wood (1997).

7 See Bernanke (1983a). As is almost always the case, it is clear that the author was not working in a vacuum. Bernanke's graduate school classmate Frederic Mishkin had already published in the *Journal of Economic History* an account of the Great Depression emphasizing consumer finances (the household balance sheet). See Mishkin (1978). And as a graduate student at MIT, Bernanke would have been exposed to the work of Friedman and Schwartz via Temin and Kindleberger.

8 Following the fashion of the time, his measures of monetary impulses distinguished their predictable and unpredictable ("anticipated" and "unanticipated") components.

9 This interpretation built on work on the financial accelerator by, inter alia, Bernanke and Gertler (1987) – that is, on how changes in financial conditions affected investment and thereby business cycle fluctuations.

10 See Temin (1976) and Gordon and Wilcox (1981).

11 See Bernanke (1983b).

12 Large and small firms were also affected differentially by the post-1929 downturn independently of what went on in financial markets, rendering spreads constructed from bond market data less than indicative of what was happening in the banking system.

13 Given the existence of time series on the number of bank failures and the frequency of banking crises in this period (Sprague 1910), the pre-war period quickly became a popular testing ground for this class of theories.

14 He reported evidence of the operation of both channels.

15 The idea was that bank failures picked up the destruction of information capital and the decline in the efficiency of financial intermediation per se, à la Bernanke, while the effects of the interest rate spread, after controlling for the effects of bank failures, now picked up the residual influence of other channels, such as debt deflation. They too found some evidence of the operation of both channels.

16 See for example Wynne (1951).

17 Again, it is clear that these authors were not working in a vacuum. They were aware, for example, of Bordo and Rockoff (1996), which was less concerned with the internal workings of financial markets per se but utilized a similar methodology (see below).

18 This question was inspired by the debate in Europe during the run-up to monetary union about the need for a Stability and Growth Pact (hence their title). Officials argued that transnational oversight was needed to prevent governments from overborrowing, but independent observers suggested that market discipline could substitute adequately for such administrative procedures (Bayoumi, Goldstein and Woglom 1995).

19 Previous studies had undertaken a similar analysis for the interwar period (Eichengreen 1989) but not for the late nineteenth century, at least that I am aware.

20 Where the latter proxied for the risk-free rate.

21 Controls included the export-GDP ratio, per capita GDP as a measure of economic and financial development, and a number of institutional variables.

22 This work built on previous research in economics and economic history on problems of credibility and time consistency and on the role of fixed exchange rate regimes such as the gold standard as commitment mechanisms (Bordo and Kydland 1995).

23 Bordo and Rockoff's original study had considered ten countries. Ferguson and Schularick considered some 60 independent countries, colonies and self-governing parts of the British Empire. The two samples differing mainly by the presence of a large number of developing economies in the expanded sample, Ferguson and Schularick argue that gold convertibility mattered for credibility in the advanced center but not the poor periphery, where conditions were too volatile for it to stick. The authors then conclude that membership of the British Empire was a more important no-default guarantee than adherence to the gold standard for bonds floated on the London market.

24 Contrary to Ferguson and Schularick they find that public debt and British Empire membership were important determinants of spreads after World War I but not before.

25 In the second half of the 1880s, Baring lost one Argentine loan to a syndicate made up of Disconto Gesellschaft, Norddeutsche Bank, Oppenheim and Banque d'Anvers, and formed a syndicate with Deutsche Bank and a number of smaller participants to underwrite another. See Flores (2007) and below.

26 Tomz (2004) uses a collection of case studies to test the same hypothesis and reaches the same conclusion.

27 In modern studies (e.g., Rose 2005) trade appears to decline not because of the imposition of retaliatory tariffs or quotas but because the interruption of financial flows, including trade credits, disrupts the supply of exports and the ability to finance imports. "For most of modern history," in contrast, in the words of Tomz (2004), trade credits were supplied not by bondholders but by separate actors "with distinct and often opposing interests."

28 In other words, that supersanctions were the rule rather than the exception before 1913. Previous investigators such as Lindert and Morton (1989) and Eichengreen and Portes (1989) had argued that instances of gunboat diplomacy were few and far between, governments generally leaving bondholders to fend for themselves.

29 They stood astride the isthmus spanned by the Panama Canal, and their economic policies were of particular concern to influential corporations like the United Fruit Company.

30 Studies of twentieth-century experience similarly offer mixed evidence of whether default hinders capital market access and significantly raises the cost of borrowing. See Eichengreen (1989), Cardoso and Dornbusch (1989), Jorgensen and Sachs (1989) and Ozler (1993).

31 The most extensive study of reputation is Tomz (2007). The author gathers data on issues and yields for a number of sovereign bonds floated in Amsterdam in the late eighteenth and early nineteenth centuries and in London in the late nineteenth and early twentieth. He suggests that countries that paid faithfully for a number of years saw their risk premia decline relative to those charged to unproven borrowers, while countries that defaulted found it more difficult to raise new capital until they reached a settlement acceptable to their creditors. The strength of this analysis is the long period covered, which allows the author to track how the "seasoning" of borrowers affected interest rates. Its weaknesses are the relatively small number of bonds that provide the basis for the analysis and its failure to address the limitations of the reputational mechanism emphasized by Bulow and Rogoff.

32 It did so until 1898, at which point these representatives were removed and the Council was expanded to include representatives of the British Bankers' Association and the London Chamber of Commerce, along with miscellaneous members at least six of whom were substantial bondholders. Eventually these miscellaneous members came to include the Association of Investment Trusts, the British Insurance Association as representatives of institutional investors, along with the Bank of England and the London Stock Exchange.

33 They computed spreads by subtracting the yield on British consols. Their modern comparison was with the secondary market spread on Brady bonds, the benchmark emerging market debt instrument in the 1990s, Brady bonds being denominated in U.S. dollars, and spreads are computed relative to yields on U.S. treasury bonds.
34 Bordo and Eichengreen compare slightly different periods: 1880–1913 and 1973–1998.
35 This is far from self-evident: emerging markets today produce both industrial goods and primary products, whereas before 1913 capital importing countries produced almost entirely primary products, albeit different primary products in different countries.
36 This is the conclusion of the comparison of the information environment in the two periods in Bordo, Eichengreen and Irwin (1999).
37 Or one might suggest, like Mauro *et al.*, that the institutional investors dominating the market today have a greater tendency to herd than the individual investors who dominated the market a century ago.
38 On common-creditor theories of contagion, see Kaminsky, Reinhart and Vegh (2003).
39 Still to be established is the generality of the effect – does it show up to the same extent in other capital-importing countries, Australia for example, and other periods of generalized distress, such as 1893 and 1907? Evidence in Bordo and Murshid (2001) suggests a sympathetic increase in spreads on Chilean bonds, but overall the evidence of generalized contagion is weak. They also find less evidence of an increase in spreads following public disclosure of Baring's difficulties, as opposed to news of problems in Argentina.
40 Although not all of these increases are statistically significant.
41 Admittedly, they consider also Argentina, Brazil and Chile.
42 Fohlin (2000) has used data on the British, German and U.S. banking industries to cast doubt more generally on the importance of universality (the combination of commercial and investment banking services in one institution) for concentration, levels of market power and financial performance.
43 This is what is suggested by the author's own subsequent work (Fohlin 1999).
44 For this argument see Rajan and Zingales (2003).
45 See Webb (1980).
46 Earlier work had proceeded through cross-country comparisons (Grossman 1994; Bernanke and James 1991) and detailed case studies (Wicker 1996).
47 They also suggest that it may be anachronistic to speak of "Fed policy" – that multiple policies were in fact pursued by the System's constituent reserve banks.
48 It might be objected that this finding is contaminated by the omission of unobserved characteristics of individual states and the relatively limited number of observations. However, Mitchener (2001) undertakes essentially the same exercise for a matched sample of some 3,000 county observations (using the matching to control for unobservables), and obtains essentially the same result.
49 An interesting question is why we don't see branch banks in Canada reducing reserves and taking on additional risk to an extent that translated into widespread bank failures. To my knowledge this aspect of the U.S.-Canadian comparison has not been pursued.
50 The authors also invoke the different behavior of demand and time deposits in support of their view. They observe that the episode did not commence with the withdrawal of demand deposits, as one would expect in a classic banking panic, although there was a sharp decline in time deposits and thus in total deposits in June 1931, consistent with the banking-crisis view. It is not so clear to me that the differential reaction of demand and time deposits necessarily supports one interpretation over another. Ferguson and Temin also observe that the sharp fall in time deposits in June was limited to the six big banks, as if there was no sign of the contagion to other banks "that is the hallmark of a general banking crisis." In fact, their data suggests otherwise; these show time deposits falling in June across all types of financial institutions.
51 See however James (2001) and Accominetti (2009).

References

Accominotti, Olivier (2009), "London Merchant Banks, the Central European Panic and the Sterling Crisis of 1931," unpublished manuscript, Sciences-Po and University of California, Berkeley (July).

Adalet, Muge (2005), "Fundamentals, Capital Flows and Capital Flight: The German Banking Crisis of 1931," unpublished manuscript, School of Economics and Finance, Victoria University of Wellington, New Zealand (July).

Adalet, Muge and Barry Eichengreen (2007), "Current Account Reversals: Always a Problem?" in Richard Clarida (ed.), *G7 Current Account Imbalances: Sustainability and Adjustment*, Chicago: University of Chicago Press, pp. 205–246.

Anari, Ali, James Kolari and Joseph Mason (2005), "Bank Asset Liquidation and the Propagation of the Great Depression," *Journal of Money, Credit, and Banking* 37, pp. 753–773.

Barro, Robert (1978), "Unanticipated Money, Output, and the Price Level in the United States," *Journal of Political Economy* 86, pp. 549–580.

Bayoumi, Tamim, Morris Goldstein and Geoffrey Woglom (1995), "Do Credit Markets Discipline Sovereign Borrowers: Evidence from the U.S. States," *Journal of Money, Credit and Banking* 27, pp. 1046–1059.

Bernanke, Ben (1983a), "Nonmonetary Effects of the Financial Crisis in the Propagation of the Great Depression," *American Economic Review* 73, pp. 257–276.

Bernanke, Ben (1983b), "Nonmonetary Effects of the Financial Crisis in the Propagation of the Great Depression," Working Paper, Graduate School of Business, Stanford University.

Bernanke, Ben and Mark Gertler (1987), "Financial Fragility and Economic Performance," *Quarterly Journal of Economics* 105, pp. 87–114.

Bernanke, Ben and Harold James (1991), "The Gold Standard, Deflation and Financial Crisis in the Great Depression: An International Comparison," in R. Glenn Hubbard (ed.), *Financial Markets and Financial Crises*, Chicago: University of Chicago Press, pp. 33–68.

Bordo, Michael, Barry Eichengreen and Douglas Irwin (1999), "Is Globalization Today Really Different from Globalization a Hundred Years Ago?" *Brookings Trade Forum*, pp. 1–50.

Bordo, Michael and Finn Kydland (1995), "The Gold Standard as a Rule: An Essay in Exploration," *Explorations in Economic History* 32, pp. 423–464.

Bordo, Michael and Christopher M. Meissner (2006), "The Role of Foreign Currency Debt in Financial Crises, 1818–1913 vs. 1972–1997," *Journal of Banking and Finance* 30, pp. 3299–3329.

Bordo, Michael, Christopher M. Meissner and Angela Redish (2005), "How Original Sin Was Overcome: The Evolution of External Debt Denominated in Domestic Currencies in the United States and the British Dominions, 1800–2000," in Barry Eichengreen and Ricardo Hausmann (eds.), *Other People's Money: Debt Denomination and Financial Instability in Emerging Market Economies*, Chicago: University of Chicago Press, pp. 122–153.

Bordo, Michael and Antu Murshid (2001), "Are Financial Crises Becoming Increasingly More Contagious?" in Stijn Claessens and Kristen Forbes (eds.), *International Financial Contagion*, Dordrecht: Kluwer Academic, pp. 367–403.

Bordo, Michael and Hugh Rockoff (1996), "The Gold Standard as a Good Housekeeping Seal of Approval," *Journal of Economic History* 60, pp. 389–428.

Bulow, Jeremy and Kenneth Rogoff (1989), "Sovereign Debt: Is to Forgive to Forget?" *American Economic Review* 79, pp. 43–50.
Calomiris, Charles and Glenn Hubbard (1989), "Price Flexibility, Credit Availability, and Economic Fluctuations: Evidence from the United States, 1894–1909," *Quarterly Journal of Economics* 104, pp. 429–452.
Calomiris, Charles and Joseph Mason (2001), "Causes of U.S. Bank Distress During the Depression," *Proceedings of the Federal Reserve Bank of Chicago*, pp. 530–554.
Capie, Forrest and Alan Webber (1985), *A Monetary History of the United Kingdom, 1870–1982*, London: Allen & Unwin.
Capie, Forrest and Geoffrey Wood (eds.), (1997), *Asset Prices and the Real Economy*, London: Macmillan.
Cardoso, Eliana and Rudiger Dornbusch (1989), "Brazilian Debt Crises: Past and Present," in Barry Eichengreen and Peter Lindert (eds.), *The International Debt Crisis in Historical Perspective*, Cambridge, MA: MIT Press, pp. 106–139.
Carlson, Mark (2004), "Are Branch Banks Better Survivors? Evidence from the Depression Era," *Economic Inquiry* 42, pp. 111–126.
Carlson, Mark and Kris Mitchener (2009), "Branch Banking as a Device for Discipline: Competition and Survivorship During the Great Depression," *Journal of Political Economy* 117, pp. 165–210.
Clemens, Michael A. and Jeffrey G. Williamson (2004), "Wealth Bias in the First Global Capital Market Boom, 1870–1913," *Economic Journal* 114, pp. 304–447.
Eichengreen, Barry (1989), "The U.S. Capital Market and Foreign Lending, 1920–1955," in Jeffrey Sachs (ed.), *Developing Country Debt and Economic Performance: The International Financial System*, Chicago: University of Chicago Press, pp. 107–158.
Eichengreen, Barry and Michael Bordo (2003), "Crises Now and Then: What Lessons for the Last Age of Financial Globalization," in Paul Mizen (ed.), *Monetary History, Exchange Rates and Financial Markets*, Cheltenham: Edward Elgar. pp. 52–92.
Eichengreen, Barry and Richard Grossman (1997), "Debt Deflation and Financial Instability: Two Historical Explorations," in Forrest Capie and Geoffrey Wood (eds.), *Asset Prices and the Real Economy*, London: Macmillan, pp. 65–105.
Eichengreen, Barry and Olivier Jeanne (2000), "Currency Crisis and Unemployment: Sterling in 1931," in Paul Krugman (ed.), *Currency Crises*, Chicago: University of Chicago Press, pp. 7–46.
Eichengreen, Barry and Richard Portes (1989), "After the Deluge: Default, Negotiation and Readjustment during the Interwar Years," in Barry Eichengreen and Peter Lindert (eds.), *The International Debt Crisis in Historical Perspective*, Cambridge, MA: MIT Press, pp. 12–48.
Esteves, Rui Pedro (2007), "Quis Custodiet Quem? Sovereign Debt and Bondholders' Protection Before 1914," Economics Series Working Paper no. 323, University of Oxford, Department of Economics, April.
Ferguson, Niall and Moritz Schularick (2006), "The Empire Effect: The Determinants of Country Risk in the First Age of Globalization," *Journal of Economic History* 66, pp. 283–312.
Ferguson, Thomas and Peter Temin (2003), "Made in Germany: The German Currency Crisis of July 1931," *Research in Economic History* 21, pp. 1–53.
Fisher, Irving (1933), "The Debt Deflation Theory of Great Depressions," *Econometrica* 1, pp. 337–357.
Flandreau, Marc (2003a), "Caveat Emptor: Coping with Sovereign Risk under the International Gold Standard," in Marc Flandreau, Carl-Ludwig Holtfrerich and Harold

James (eds.), *International Financial History in the Twentieth Century: System and Anarchy*, Cambridge: Cambridge University Press, pp. 17–50.

Flandreau, Marc (2003b), "Crises and Punishment: Moral Hazard and the Pre-1914 International Financial Architecture," CEPR Discussion Paper no. 3742 (February).

Flandreau, Marc, Jacques Le Cacheux and Frederic Zumer (1998), "Stability without a Pact? Lessons from the European Gold Standard, 1880–1914," *Economic Policy* 26, pp. 115–163.

Flandreau, Marc and Nathan Sussman (2005), "Old Sins: Exchange Clauses and European Foreign Lending in the 19th Century," in Barry Eichengreen and Ricardo Hausmann (eds.), *Other People's Money: Debt Denomination and Financial Instability in Emerging Market Economies*, Chicago: University of Chicago Press, pp. 143–189.

Flandreau, Marc and Frederic Zumer (2004), *The Making of Global Finance, 1880–1913*, Paris: OECD.

Flores, Juan-Huitzi (2007), "Information Asymmetries and Financial Intermediation during the Baring Crisis, 1880–1890," Working Paper in Economic History 07–16, Universidad Carlos III de Madrid, October.

Fohlin, Caroline (1998), "Relationship Banking, Liquidity and Investment in German Industrialization," *Journal of Finance* 53, pp. 1737–1758.

Fohlin, Caroline (1999), "The Rise of Interlocking Directorates in Imperial Germany," *Economic History Review* LII, pp. 307–333.

Fohlin, Caroline (2000), "Banking Industry Structure, Competition, and Performance: Does Universality Matter?" Social Science Working Paper no. 1078, Division of the Humanities and Social Sciences, California Institute of Technology, March.

Friedman, Milton and Anna Schwartz (1963), *A Monetary History of the United States, 1863–1960*, Princeton: Princeton University Press.

Gordon, Robert J. and James Wilcox (1981), "Monetarist Interpretations of the Great Depression: An Evaluation and Critique," in Karl Brunner (ed.), *The Great Depression Revisited*, Dordrecht: Kluwer.

Grossman, Richard (1993), "The Macroeconomic Consequences of Bank Failures under the National Banking System," *Explorations in Economic History* 54, pp. 654–682.

Grossman, Richard (1994), "The Shoe that Didn't Drop: Explaining Banking Stability During the Great Depression," *Journal of Economic History* 54, pp. 654–682.

Haubrich, Joseph (1990), "Nonmonetary Effects of Financial Crises: Lessons from the Great Depression in Canada," *Journal of Monetary Economics* 25, pp. 223–252.

James, Harold (2001), *The End of Globalization*, Cambridge: Cambridge University Press.

Jorgensen, Erika and Jeffrey Sachs (1989), "Default and Renegotiation of Latin American Foreign Bonds in the Interwar Period," in Barry Eichengreen and Peter Lindert (eds.), *The International Debt Crisis in Historical Perspective*, Cambridge, MA: MIT Press, pp. 48–85.

Kaminksy, Graciela and Carmen Reinhart (1999), "The Twin Crises: The Causes of Banking and Balance of Payments Problems," *American Economic Review* 93, pp. 473–500.

Kaminsky, Graciela, Carmen Reinhart and Carlos Vegh (2003), "The Unholy Trinity of Financial Contagion," *Journal of Economic Perspectives* 17, pp. 51–74.

Kindleberger, Charles (1973), *The World in Depression 1919–1939*, Berkeley: University of California Press.

Kindleberger, Charles (1973), *The Financial History of Western Europe*, Oxford: Oxford University Press.

Kindleberger, Charles (1978), *Manias, Panics and Crashes*, New York: Basic Books.
Kindleberger, Charles (1981), *The Financial History of Western Europe*, Oxford: Oxford University Press.
Kindleberger, Charles (1984), *A Financial History of Western Europe*, Boston: Allen & Unwin.
Kletzer, Kenneth and Brian Wright (2000), "Sovereign Debt as Intertemporal Barter," *American Economic Review* 90, pp. 621–639.
Lindert, Peter and Peter Morton (1989), "How Sovereign Debt Worked," in Jeffrey Sachs (ed.), *Developing Country Debt and Economic Performance: The International Financial System*, Chicago: University of Chicago Press, pp. 39–106.
Mauro, Paolo, Nathan Sussman and Yishay Yafeh (2002), "Emerging Market Spreads: Then Versus Now," *Quarterly Journal of Economics* 117, pp. 695–733.
Mauro, Paolo and Yishay Yafeh (2003), "The Corporation of Foreign Bondholders," IMF Working Paper 03–107.
Meissner, Christopher (2005), "A New World Order: Explaining the Emergence of the Classical Gold Standard," *Journal of International Economics* 66, pp. 385–406.
Mishkin, Frederic (1978), "The Household Balance Sheet and the Great Depression," *Journal of Economic History* 38, pp. 918–937.
Mitchener, Kris James (2001), "Are Banking Supervision and Regulation Super or Regular? A Country-Level Analysis of Bank Failures in the Great Depression," Chapter 4 in *Supervision, Regulation, and Financial Instability: The Political Economy of Banking During the Great Depression*, unpublished Ph.D. dissertation, University of California, Berkeley.
Mitchener, Kris James (2005), "Bank Supervision, Regulation and Instability during the Great Depression," *Journal of Economic History* 65, pp. 152–185.
Mitchener, Kris James (2007), "Are Prudential Supervision and Regulation Pillars of Financial Stability? Evidence from the Great Depression," *Journal of Law and Economics* 50, pp. 273–302.
Mitchener, Kris James and Marc D. Weidenmier (2005a), "Supersanctions and Sovereign Debt Repayment," NBER Working Paper no. 11472.
Mitchener, Kris James and Marc D. Weidenmier (2005b), "Empire, Public Goods, and the Roosevelt Corollary," *Journal of Economic History* 65, pp. 658–692.
Obstfeld, Maurice and Alan Taylor (2003), "Sovereign Risk, Credibility and the Gold Standard: 1870–1913 versus 1925–31," *Economic Journal* 113, pp. 241–275.
Ozler, Sule (1993), "Have Commercial Banks Ignored History?" *American Economic Review* 83, pp. 608–620.
Rajan, Raghuram and Luigi Zingales (2003), "The Great Reversals: The Politics of Financial Development in the Twentieth Century," *Journal of Financial Economics* 69, pp. 5–50.
Ramirez, Carlos D. and Philip A. Shively (2006), "Do Bank Failures Affect Real Economic Activity? State-Level Evidence from the Pre-Depression Era," *Proceedings of the Federal Reserve Bank of Chicago*, pp. 461–474.
Richardson, Gary and William Troost (2006), "Monetary Intervention Mitigated Banking Panics during the Great Depression: Quasi-Experimental Evidence from the Federal Reserve District Border in Mississippi, 1929–1933," NBER Working Paper 12591 (October).
Rose, Andrew (2005), "One Reason Countries Pay Their Debts: Renegotiation and International Trade," *Journal of Development Economics* 77, pp. 189–206.
Schnabel, Isabel (2004), "The German Twin Crisis of 1931," *Journal of Economic History* 64, pp. 822–871.

Sprague, Otto (1910), *History of Banking Crises Under the National Banking System*, Washington, D.C.: GPO.

Temin, Peter (1976), *Did Monetary Forces Cause the Great Depression?* New York: Norton.

Tomz, Michael (2004), "Finance and Trade: Issue Linkage and the Enforcement of International Debt Contracts," unpublished manuscript, Stanford University.

Tomz, Michael (2007), *Reputation and International Cooperation: Sovereign Debt across Three Centuries*, Princeton: Princeton University Press.

Triner, Gail D. and Kirsten Wandschneider (2005), "The Baring Crisis and the Brazilian Encilhamento, 1889–1891: An Early Example of Contagion among Emerging Capital Markets," *Financial History Review* 12, pp. 199–225.

Wandschneider, Kirsten (2004), "Central Europe in the Inter-war Period: A Case for Contagion?" unpublished manuscript, Middlebury College.

Webb, Steven B. (1980), "Tariffs, Cartels, Technology and Growth in the German Steel Industry, 1879–1914," *Journal of Economic History* 40, pp. 309–340.

Wheelock, David (1995), "Regulation, Market Structure, and the Bank Failures of the Great Depression," *Federal Reserve Bank of St. Louis Review* 77, pp. 27–38.

White, Eugene (ed.) (1990), *Crashes and Panics: The Lessons from History*, New York: Dow Jones-Irwin.

Wicker, Elmus (1996), *The Banking Panics of the Great Depression*, Cambridge: Cambridge University Press.

Wolf, Holger and Tarik Yousef (2007), "Breaking the Fetters: Why Did Countries Exit the Interwar Gold Standard?" in Timothy J. Hatton, K.H. O'Rourke and A.M. Taylor (eds.), *The New Comparative Economic History: Essays in Honor of Jeffrey G. Williamson*, Cambridge, MA: MIT Press, pp. 241–266.

Wynne, William H. (1951), *State Insolvency and Foreign Bondholders*, New Haven: Yale University Press.

Part II

Crisis management

3 English financial markets in the 1830s

Information networks, risk assessment and banking crisis

Mae Baker and Michael Collins

3.1

The 1830s in Britain were exciting, vibrant and enterprising. The country was consolidating its position as the First Industrial Nation, beginning to enjoy the fruits of new technological developments in manufacturing, fuel production and transportation. Nor were the major changes confined to physical advances. Important innovations were also occurring in market organization, in communication systems and in the governance of the corporate sector, especially in the wider adoption of the joint-stock form of ownership and, most notably, as applied to steam railway enterprises and banking firms. It was a decade of strong population growth, sharply increased urbanization and increases in income and wealth. Internationally, Great Britain was becoming the single most important trader, with pride of place given to 'King Cotton' (with the raw material imported largely from the USA and with manufactured yarn and pieces becoming the country's staple exports). In this decade (as in many others in the early and mid-nineteenth century) there was also strong cyclical change, with an upswing in the economy from 1833 culminating in boom conditions in 1836 which, in turn, were sharply dissipated by a financial crisis in 1837, quickly followed by another in 1839, the latter marking the beginning of a recession which lasted into the early 1840s (Matthews, 1954).

The country's two most important commercial and financial centres at that time were London and Liverpool, and it is with the nature of financial information flows and inter-bank relations between the two cities that this chapter is concerned. In the chapter we use private, daily correspondence between George Carr Glyn and Joseph Langton to provide a fascinating insight into how money markets worked in the 1830s. George Carr Glyn was the senior partner in the London private bank, Glyn, Halifax, Mills & Co (hereafter referred to as 'Glyn's') (Fulford, 1953). In 1835 Glyn's stood at the centre of a network of fifty-seven banks throughout Britain for whom it acted as London agent. By the early 1840s it, and Barclays, were the largest of London's commercial banks. Glyn (1797–1873) was a free trade liberal, Chairman for fifteen years of the London & Birmingham Railway (known as the London & North Western from 1845), a Whig MP for Kendal, a close associate of John Horsley Palmer (Bank of England

Director from 1811 and Governor, 1830–33), and was raised to the peerage as Lord Wolverton by Gladstone in 1867. Glyn's correspondent was Joseph Langton (1793–1855) who had been deputy agent at the Bank of England's Liverpool office before his appointment as manager of the newly formed Bank of Liverpool in 1831. The Bank of Liverpool was the foremost joint-stock bank of the town with leading merchants prominent on the board (Chandler, 1964: 239–55). Many of the bank's early chairmen (most notably William Brown, Adam Hodgson, Joseph Hornby and George Holt) not only played active roles in commercial life and in the promotion of other new companies in the railroad and financial sectors, but also in public life as reformers in the slave trade and in educational provision. Both Glyn and Langton had been educated at Westminster School and in the 1830s both sent their sons to Dr Arnold's new school at Rugby. The correspondence reveals a meeting of minds on many of the banking issues of the day and it provides a frank insight into what made the money markets tick.

3.2

The significant economic changes that were occurring in the second quarter of the nineteenth century created both opportunities and challenges for participants in the market and for the existing control mechanisms, and this no more so than in financial markets. In the banking sector, adoption of the corporate structure gave rise to a company flotation mania by the middle of the decade. Reform legislation of 1826 removed the Bank of England's monopoly of partnerships of over six people in England and Wales and allowed all banks operating outside London to adopt a joint-stock ownership structure (with the issue of shares to numerous proprietors). Yet, at first, the uptake was slow, with only fourteen joint-stock banks created by the close of 1830 (Thomas, 1934, appendix M). But the pace soon quickened. Another forty-four of the new banking companies were formed during 1832–35 and, by mid-decade, the possibilities of the new banking structure had so fired the imagination of the stock market that a speculative boom in bank shares was in full swing. In fact, another fifty-nine banking companies were created in the first half of 1836 before tight monetary conditions led to the collapse of the boom. Lancashire was at the heart of this feverish pace of company promotions (and not just in banking). In Liverpool alone ten new banks with a nominal capital of £3.3 million were floated in the first half of 1836 (Collins, 1972a: 93). A flavour of the times can be gleaned from the prospectus of the so-called 'Accommodation Bank' that appeared in the *Liverpool Albion* of 29 February 1836, even if – it must be allowed – the authors may have had their tongues firmly planted in their cheeks when placing the advertisement. The bank's promoters promised that 'the liberality of [the new institution] shall be commensurate with the liberality of the Age…'. They proposed to issue their own notes (which was unknown in Liverpool at that time) and 'thus, Capital rendered unnecessary, will be merely nominal'. Bills were to be discounted 'in a liberal manner' and 'advances will be made … without security and without limit. Thus profits unprovoked by Capital will spontaneously and abundantly accumulate.'

The new provincial joint-stock banks were entitled to issue their own notes (at a minimum £5 denomination and convertible on demand to gold, or Bank of England notes, once the latter became legal tender in 1833); and the majority of the new companies did issue notes. In a similarly liberal vein, legislation placed no restriction on the number of offices a bank could operate and – in contrast to the established private banking partnerships – many of the new banks began to develop branching networks in their region of activity. Thus the new banks constituted a direct challenge to the Bank of England, as well as to the existing private banks. The challenge to the Bank was two-pronged. First, there was the commercial rivalry for banking business. The Bank of England at that time was not part of the public sector. It did manage the government's accounts, (from 1833) its notes were legal tender in England and Wales, de facto it held the country's gold reserves, and all the leading London bankers maintained accounts at the Bank, but it also conducted normal commercial banking activities (including discounting and lending) at the top end of the market. The Bank of England was privately owned and its bondholders expected to earn a reasonable dividend. Thus, no matter what 'public responsibilities' Bank directors and others may have supposed the Bank to carry in the 1830s, as the biggest bank in the kingdom it certainly competed in the market for banking business and its directors were aware of the need to maintain profitability. Indeed, the banking legislation of 1826 and 1833 added sharply to the potential for competitive strains between the Bank and other banks. In addition to permitting the formation of joint-stock banks outside London, the reforms of 1826 also encouraged the Bank to break with tradition and open branches of its own in the provinces. This it proceeded to do in the major cities of England and Wales. Most of the new joint-stock banks were of such a stature as not to be direct rivals for the sort of high quality commercial business conducted by the Bank but a sufficient number of the newcomers were founded by very respectable promoters and with large enough capital resources to cause the Bank (and existing private bankers) some discomfort. This was greatly increased on the occasion of the renewal of the Bank's charter in 1833 when joint-stock banks were allowed in London, provided they did not issue notes. The London and Westminster bank was formed in that year, and was quickly followed by the London Joint Stock Bank and the National Provincial Bank of England, and all three were to become major institutions operating with London head offices.

So developments in the banking market added a new competitive edge to Bank of England business. But in the eyes of the Bank the changes also constituted a different kind of challenge, by creating a potential threat to monetary stability. Of course, this alleged 'threat' to systemic welfare also provided a 'public interest' argument which could be used against the new banks. To understand this fully it needs to be seen in the context of the Bank's relationship with the money markets and the gold standard in the 1830s. Formally, the Bank of England had a legal obligation under the gold standard to maintain convertibility of its notes at the official parity rate of £3 17s 10d per standard ounce of gold. The commercial banks held very little gold themselves. This they were able to do partly because, as we have seen, from 1833 they could always use legal-tender Bank of England notes to meet demands for cash from customers, but mainly because they either maintained cash balances at the Bank itself or at other banks that had such balances. In this way, either directly or indirectly, money market institutions could draw on their balances at the Bank when needed. In normal money market conditions commercial bank balances at the Bank would operate as part of a clearing mechanism (though a separate London Clearing House had been established in 1773 and, in addition, by the 1830s a number of the large London banks acted as agents for many provincial banks for whom they routinely settled payments between their banking connections and those banks' customers). However, it was in less normal times, when pressure for cash was high (say, during a banking panic or external drain of gold) and the commercial banks were going to the Bank for loans and bill discounts and/or drawing down their cash balances at the Bank, that it became clear that it was the Bank which was, in effect, holding the specie reserve of the whole banking system. Thus, avoidance of such runs for cash, and of the causes of them, was in the interests of both the Bank and the banking system. Despite its private sector status the Bank did, on occasions, accept a 'public good' argument that it should shoulder such responsibility for avoiding severe adverse market conditions and/or threats to systemic stability, despite its private sector status. As we shall see, in the 1830s the exact perception of the 'public good' was open to interpretation but it could include measures to discourage speculation, attempts to regulate the issuing of bank notes (not surprisingly, Bank representatives tended to favour a monopoly Bank of England note issue), a responsiveness to take corrective action if a fall in the value of sterling on foreign exchange markets should threaten to provoke a loss of gold overseas (and, thus, endanger convertibility), and a preparedness to act as lender of last resort in an emergency. As we shall see, all these issues were matters of moment during the crisis of 1837.

Another 'challenging' development arose from innovation in the money markets. In the 1830s the bill of exchange was central to the expansion of credit in both the domestic and international markets and a description of the bill system operating in Liverpool gives a fair indication of the scale of the commercial credit system throughout the country (Collins, 1972a: 260–3). Bills were the common form of credit in both domestic and international trade. Commonly, a bill of exchange would be drawn by the vendor of goods (and creditor) on the purchaser (and debtor) and once 'accepted' by the latter (s)he was legally obliged to pay the creditor according to the terms specified in the bill. Most bills were payable in London but the period of credit granted and the customary rate of interest (usually expressed in the reciprocal as the rate of discount on the price for cash payments) varied from trade to trade. In the raw cotton trade, brokers/dealers paid the importers in three-month bills; and manufacturers (mainly based in the Lancashire hinterland) paid the brokers/dealers in two-month bills, after the expiry of two months' credit. In addition, in Lancashire it was normally possible to pay for goods with miscellaneous bills whose origins lay elsewhere than in the transaction at hand. Rather than hold such bills that came to them in the course of their business until they matured, it was common for business people to discount them at their bankers or to use them as a means of payment in other business transactions. The legal ownership of these bills was easily transferred through endorsement. Indeed, in Lancashire at this time merchants were in regular receipt of a miscellany of bills as media of exchange (Ashton, 1945). A third form of bill for paying for commercial transactions was the banker's draft. These were bills drawn by a local bank on the London bank with whom it had an account, and were available (at a commission) to regular banking clients for use in their own business transactions.

In addition to the direct creation of bankers' drafts, local banks were central to the commercial credit system in that the banks' willingness to discount bills provided the chief means by which merchants could encash bills. Banks discounted bills for regular and 'occasional' customers. In the former case, business firms had established arrangements with their bankers regarding the value and type of bills that would be routinely accepted and it was normal for the firms' current accounts to be credited for the full value of the bills less the current market rate of discount (i.e. the rate of interest charged). In the case of occasional discounters, the availability of the credit facility was not guaranteed and the bills presented would be judged and priced on their merits. For bankers, the business of bill discounting became more attractive in 1833 when bills of under three months' duration were exempted from the ceiling on interest rates imposed by the usury laws.

> The banker could do a number of things with a discounted bill. He could hold it till maturity; he could rediscount it; or, if not a contract banker with the Bank of England [see below], he could re-issue it. In the last case, [after endorsement by the bank] the bill would be paid out to a bank customer and could be used by him to finance commercial transactions ... in effect, the endorsement could transform a second or third class bill into a first class one.
>
> (Collins, 1972a: 262)

The banks also performed a critical remittance function. Daily, the banks sent bills, cash and documentation of all sorts to destinations throughout the country, by far the most important of which was London. Almost all bills of exchange were payable in the capital and it was there that the London bankers and the discount brokers provided the mainstay to the national bill market. By the 1830s the business of the four largest bill brokers – Overend, Gurney & Co., Sanderson & Co., Alexanders & Co., and James Bruce – was extensive as they routinely discounted and rediscounted bills that were sold to them, or bought from them, by bankers and others (King, 1936; Scammell, 1968). Another important development was the discount houses' willingness to pay interest on cash balances left with them for very short periods, thus providing the London bankers with a very convenient, interest-earning repository for their near-cash assets. The final piece in the jigsaw of the London money market was the Bank of England. The

London banks held balances (though no interest was paid in this case) at Threadneedle Street and the Bank was willing to discount first-class bills (though the Bank never rediscounted – i.e. it never sold them on to others with its own endorsement on such bills) and (less often) to provide advances on top class security to banks and discount houses.

Figure 3.1 tries to capture the main components of the network of credit relationships described above, and of which more detail is given in the rest of the chapter. Because of the subject matter of this chapter, a provincial bank, such as the Bank of Liverpool, is placed at the centre of the figure. The Bank of Liverpool provided bill discounting, overdraft and remittance facilities for local business people and, through its connections with London-based banks (such as Glyn's) and the London discount houses (such as Overend's), it was able to augment its own supplies of both credit and market intelligence to a significant extent. In addition, the Bank of Liverpool had an account at the local office of the Bank of England which provided the provincial bank with discount, lending and remittance facilities, and with a direct link to the Bank of England in London. The Bank of Liverpool also had links with many other provincial banks. Importantly, these various interconnections provided not only mutually supportive credit lines but also reciprocal sources of confidential intelligence on markets, securities and individual firms.

It is clear from this brief description alone that the bill credit system involved a mountain of bills drawn on many thousands of British and overseas firms. It also required a myriad of risk assessments and credit rating decisions being made every day, and this at a time when no established credit rating agencies

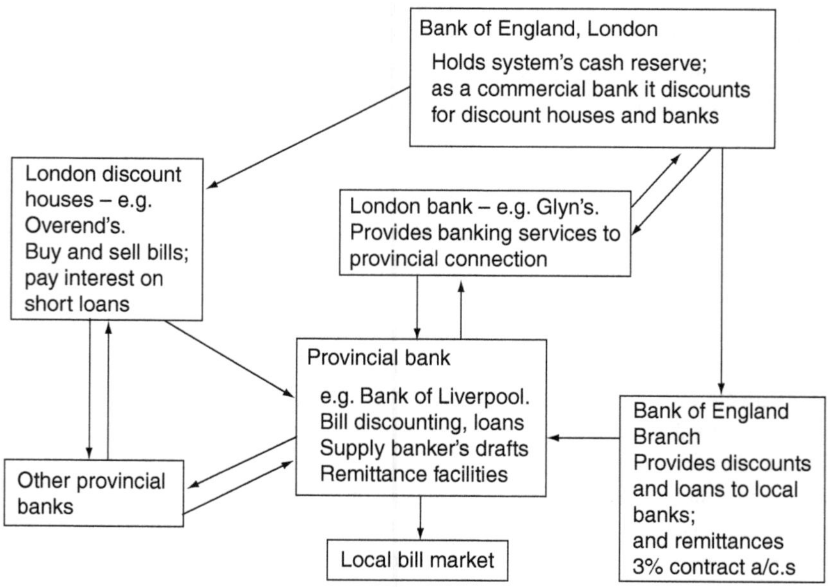

Figure 3.1 1830s bill credit system and institutional relations

existed. At the time, the viability of the credit system depended upon individual banks accumulating information on their own clients and on the preparedness of those banks to share that information with other banks in an information network based on trust and mutual interest. For provincial banks, they could share information with other provincial banks, with London discount houses and – if they were fortunate enough to have an account at one of its provincial branches – with the Bank of England, but the most important mutual exchange of information was that with their London banking agent. The rest of the chapter explores the type of relationships that existed in the 1830s between the largest joint-stock bank in Liverpool (the Bank of Liverpool) and other money market institutions.

3.3

The Bank of Liverpool started business in May 1831, appointing Glyn's as its London banking agent, opening an account at the Liverpool office of the Bank of England, and opening an account for the leading London discount broker, Overend, Gurney & Co. (Chandler, 1964: 256, 258) All three connections were to be important in the early success of the Liverpool bank. Important connections were also established with other provincial banks throughout Great Britain, including a close relationship with another pioneer of joint-stock banking, the Bank of Manchester.

'...London was always the financial centre, drawing together the independent banks, private and joint-stock alike, into a single banking system. The unity depended on the link ... between the country banker and his "London agent"...' (Sayers, 1957: 109). The chief role of London agents such as Glyn's was to facilitate the smooth operation of the provincial banks' dealings with the capital. They received remittances of cash and securities from the provincial bank, with the latter maintaining a cash balance with the London Bank and upon which the provincial bank could draw. The London agent paid off debts and received payments on behalf of the provincial bank (including those due on bills of the bank's clients and of the bank itself, and cheques drawn by and on the bank), transferred funds, handled the purchase and sale of various securities, and provided some banking services to the clients of the provincial bank when they were in London. Some London banks would redeem their provincial agent's notes (though in the case of the Liverpool banks there was no need for this service, as they used Bank of England notes and issued no notes of their own). The London bankers also acted on behalf of their client in the case of any difficulties over unpaid bills, dishonoured cheques, the validity of securities, the recovery of monies in default cases, and so on. In normal times the London bank handled the clearance of numerous payments between London and the provinces and for a large concern such as Glyn's it would be performing a significant inter-regional intermediary role as it was in receipt of an inflow of funds from some of their provincial bank connections and of an outflow of funds with others. On occasions – and, certainly, in emergencies – the London agent would allow the provincial bank to overdraw on the account (some collateral security would be deposited with the

London bank) which could be of great benefit to the provincial firm, although the expectation was that in usual times a credit balance be maintained on the account.

The early operation of the account between the Bank of Liverpool and Glyn's was considered highly satisfactory by both parties, not least because of the growing commercial success of the Liverpool bank. On 22 March 1833 (the reference for all such letters referred to hereafter is BLD Langton 1833, Barclays Bank Archive, Accession 25–265) George Carr Glyn wrote:

> We take the opportunity … to express the entire satisfaction which we feel, not only as to the manner on which the account of the Bank of Liverpool has been conducted thro' us, but also as to the principle of remuneration made to us for it … [However] the allowance of 2½ percent Interest on the floating cash balance is the only point which in the present state of the money market might require observation from us but the arrangements by which you regulate the cash receipts to meet your payments are so judiciously made to prevent a large balance that we refrain from proposing any alteration even on that point of possible loss to us.

On 27 March 1833, Glyn told Langton that:

> We are most desirous of meeting the wishes of the directors and accept in lieu of commission for three years the annual sum of £600, but allow us to add, that contemplating the certainty of a great and immediate increase in the business of the Company, as well from the powerful influence of its own connections, as from the gradual extension of the commercial relations of Liverpool, we trust the directors will feel no objection in the event of the amount exceeding two millions in any year, that an addition should be made to that sum at the rate of £200 for the succeeding million [which commission rate Langton, in the custom of the day, recorded at 4¾d per £100].

By 1836 (2 July 1836) Glyn was still expressing satisfaction although seeking an increase in the fee which by then was back to a fixed amount:

> We cannot enter upon the subject [of a review of the terms on the account] … without alluding to the great satisfaction which has been felt by us on our connection with the Bank of Liverpool, not only from the manner in which the business has been conducted with us by you but also from the great respectability of the parties with whom it has connected us. We may congratulate you on the rapid increase which has taken place in the business … and have only to propose the same arrangement should be continued … with the alteration of the annual remuneration from its present amount [£800] to £1000 per an. And requesting (a point which in fact is not material as a matter of profit to you, but is to us as a question of principle) that the rate of interest allowed on the working cash balance may be reduced from 2½ to 2 per Cent.

In addition to managing the financial arrangements between the banks, a fundamental aspect of a successful London-provincial bank relationship was the exchange of timely, accurate information, which through daily correspondence helped provide a regular update of market intelligence. In the absence of today's easy reference to credit rating agencies, the determination of acceptable credit limits for individuals and firms and the assessment of risk involved depended critically on acquiring information from a reliable source. In the normal course of business, all banks acquired inside information on their own clients and on firms and individuals with whom they had done business over a number of years. This they were prepared to share in a confidential manner with their banking connections and a major bank such as Glyn's stood at the centre of a national (and, on occasions, international) network of market information. Almost every piece of correspondence contained queries on, or answers to queries on, the creditworthiness of parties to bills, acceptances and other securities on which the bank may be considering providing credit. The assessments were subjective and qualitative, of course (no mathematical modelling in those days!), but they were based on what evidential information was available and on the judgement of experienced bankers. Typical of the replies to the Bank of Liverpool's queries are: 'I believe W & J are very respectable timber merchants – an old concern. We consider G H quite safe for that amount. They stick to their trade' (30 November 1837). 'Mr B B W is a very old person but quite safe when you get him on paper – he is a customer of ours as a stock broker' (28 December 1837). 'Mr J D F is reported as a very respectable man in character but considered not to have much property' (11 January 1838). On 2 September 1833, Glyn informed Langton that: 'We have made particular enquiries of the House named in your note ... and the answers we receive are so highly satisfactory and confirming our previous opinion that we should have no hesitation entrusting them to a considerable extent.' Understandably, the enquiries were more numerous at the commencement of the Bank of Liverpool's business, and the correspondence reveals how critical a well-informed London agent was to a new banking company. For instance, on 30 September 1831, in response to such a request, Glyn noted:

> ...your second note of enquiry, to which we reply by saying Nos 1,3,4,6,8,9 and 11 we should feel no difficulty in giving credit to, feeling assured that the acceptances would be founded on real transactions and backed by plenty of means. We have reason to think that a good deal of money has been lost in the cases of Nos 5 and 10 – Nos 2 and 7 are respectable but in a smaller way of business. The last firm is not known on the Corn Exchange.

Later in the same year (3 November 1831) Glyn was advising that:

> We believe Mr Smith to be a very respectable man and ... found him exceedingly regular in his transactions with us – the July advance which he asked of us, was upon bills of exchange of the most trustworthy description. [Moreover the firms that normally accept his bills] would not give their acceptance to any but bona fide transactions.

That last reference to *bona fide* bills is significant, for throughout the correspondence both banks express the view that bills that derived from real trade transactions – with goods being purchased – are among the soundest security on which bank credit should be advanced. Bills created for other purposes (such as raising credit to purchase stock market securities) were considered speculative, potentially damaging to systemic stability and were to be avoided.

The provision of information was reciprocal, with Glyn's enquiring about Liverpool, Lancashire or Irish firms of whom the Bank of Liverpool had more reliable information than the London bank. Thus, on 2 June 1836 Glyn was asking Langton: 'May Mulholland & Co. [a Liverpool merchant house] be trusted to the extent of £20000 or £25000 upon very regular mercantile transactions for twelve months [?] I should be glad to hear as soon as you can.' Earlier, on 8 November 1833, Glyn had written:

> I am not sure whether it is through the kind offices of your establishment that we are … indebted for an account opened with us by Mess Archibold Watson & Co but at any rate will you allow me to inquire of you in confidence about them, for it is a most satisfactory thing to us to be able at once to get at the proper standing of new connections…

The following extracts from two letters from Glyn to Langton bear out the importance of the exchange of confidential and trustworthy information. They concern the appearance in the spring of 1834 of large bills drawn in favour of the American merchant house of W & J Brown (predecessor of Brown, Shipley & Co., the US merchant bank), which was a major customer of the Bank of Liverpool and whose senior partners were prominent among the bank's directors – so, this was potentially a delicate matter.

> I feel it is a great advantage to be able to communicate with you confidentially and on that footing of asking for information upon any point which may attract notice – in the present instance pray remember that I should not presume to comment on any transactions between you and your friends, but apprehending that some remarks may be circulated in the money market upon the two large drafts on us, one due today and another for £40000 remitted to the same quarter, you would oblige me for the sake of both our establishments by giving me any information to counteract any surmises which might be thrown out…
>
> (27 March 1834)

Langton was able to reassure Glyn that the bills represented genuine trading transactions:

> Many thanks for your most satisfactory communication of the 29 Inst – the result of which is just as I had anticipated and under ordinary circumstances I should have been quite content to have replied to any remarks, by

> reference to the well established reputation of Mess W & J B & Co, but taking into consideration the present state of commercial matters in the United States and feeling that many might not be disinclined to draw unfavourable conclusions to the prejudice of both our establishments from transactions which on explanation would be most legitimate, I thought it better to produce [?] from you the conclusive authority which you have now given me – for these objects my friends have wished me to write to you though we all felt that as long as these large transactions passed through Mess^r Denison Co only, so no prejudice was likely to arise – I am also very glad to have received your communication and that thro Mess^r D from Mess^r W&JB & Co, as though unnecessary for our satisfaction, yet they have enabled me to speak confidently as to Mess^r B. Co's high standing (even in the present state of the United States) among our commercial community.
>
> (31 March 1834)

In addition to regular comments on the standing of individual business firms and securities, the letters also contain a routine exchange of assessments on the current state of markets, including the money market, the exchange rate market, the stock market (dominated by government securities and, to much lesser an extent, rail and banking stock) and the commodity markets. As early as 14 April 1836, Glyn was warning of the excesses in financial markets, including the large scale flotations of new joint-stock banks, that were leading to unstable boom conditions.

> I am really most seriously alarmed at all these schemes of every sort, in which Lancashire appears to be more prominently extravagant even than London if it is possible. We must all look out, luckily the Bank of England is in good [condition?] as to her bullion and there is every disposition there and in Downing St. and in Lombard St. also to act upon the warning notes.

On the flotation of new rail companies, Glyn was also privy to expert opinion. For instance, on the creation of the Great Western, he advised Langton that, 'I think the directors ... excellent men of business, disposed to take up the working of their Co. with energy and attention, and willing to make themselves masters of their new calling' (9 January 1836).

While well-informed, sensible and normally reliable, Glyn's judgement was not always correct. For instance, he was initially reassuring about the prospects for Esdaile's bank, in which his brother-in-law was involved:

> The confidential inquiry in your note of the 2nd. brings me to a subject which has caused me very great regret and annoyance. My brother in law is one of my oldest and best friends and the groundless loss of his connections has been most vexatious to me. Harris's of Bradford was the first to throw the stone & Backhouses' followed. The Birmingham Banking Company moved in consequence of some local misunderstanding between them and

> the Joint Stock Bank of Coventry with which Esdailes are connected. My own conviction is (founded upon the best information), that Esdailes are perfectly good and indeed possessing ready means to a considerable extent, that these surmises are entirely groundless and probably intentional.
>
> (4 July 1836)

However, Esdaile's ultimately proved to be unsound and had to be liquidated.

Also his position as a prominent City private banker, and as a close ally of the Bank of England, coloured his judgement on the new joint-stock banks that appeared in London in the 1830s (although, in contrast, he actively sought the business of the new provincial joint-stock banks). In his comments of 31 March 1834 he was unable to resist taking a dig at the new London & Westminster Bank: 'The New Banking Company is positively doing nothing – it will not get on.' In this he was wrong – the Westminster, of course, was destined to be one of the biggest banks in the world!

While the *raison d'être* for the banks' relationship was commercial, the bond between Glyn and Langton was personal, based on trust and a shared view of the world, and such a relationship obviously underpinned the reliability of frankness of the exchange of commercial information. Both men had been educated at Westminster School and their correspondence covers family affairs, health matters, politics and even the state of the weather. For instance, George Carr Glyn was a liberal and his letters provide a close account of the parliamentary elections in London which occurred after the death of the King in June 1837. He was disappointed that his friend and Bank of England director, John Horsley Palmer, was persuaded to stand as a Tory candidate for the City seat but, on 25 July 1837, he was able to report with some satisfaction that '...the Sheriffs have just announced the return to be, Wood, Crawford, Pattison and Grote, the latter beating Palmer by six only!!! I assure you the Conservatives have surprised us but are themselves disappointed having fully calculated on Palmers return.' Other letters comment on severe snowfalls, on cholera and influenza outbreaks with their adverse effects on the clerks' attendance at the bank's office. One disaster that suggested every cloud could have a silver lining was the fire that destroyed the Exchange in January 1838. For a year Glyn had been trying to sell the City offices of the failed Esdailes Bank, in which Glyn's brother-in-law had been a partner – 'good arises frequently out of mischief and the destruction of the offices of the Royal Exchange Insurance Company has enabled us to sell Esdailes house to that institution very well' (11 January 1838). The final illustration of the strong personal foundation of this particular inter-banker relationship is in the letters dealing with their sons' education. In the autumn of 1837 Glyn sent his eldest son to Rugby School where Langton already had his two sons, with all three sharing common accommodation. And Glyn was soon

> ...taking the earliest opportunity of thanking you and Mrs Langton for your kind consideration about my boy. Mrs Glyn and I placed him at Rugby on Saturday and left him under the care of your boys – sundry adornings are

talked of in their study – we were much pleased with all we saw and I was especially so with Dr Arnold. Mr Grenfell is a most excellent person. I expect my boy will find it hard work at first.

(5 September 1837)

Family concerns were the subject of comment again in the new year when Glyn reported: 'My Rugby boy has been very unwell, verging on a severe attack of jaundice – I guess the three eat too many sausages…' (5 January 1838). While this sort of personal exchange was peripheral to their main business, it is nonetheless indicative of the personal nature of intelligence-gathering at that time – based on trust, confidence in each other's ability to keep a secret when necessary. They were 'insiders' whose relationship enabled them to conduct prosperous businesses – and for Glyn's this type of network spread throughout the country and, indeed, overseas (the bank had particularly strong links with Canada).

3.4

For the Bank of Liverpool the other important sources of up-to-date information on the markets and the people and firms operating within them were the provincial bank's contacts with the London discount market, the Bank of England and with other provincial banks.

In addition to Glyn's the main supplier of London intelligence for the Merseyside bank was the leading discount house, Overend, Gurney & Co. The Bank of Liverpool, in common with other banks in the thriving port, normally received many more bills for discount than they had resources from deposits and capital to finance on their own, so they were heavily dependent on the London discount market for selling on (or rediscounting) bills. The intelligence provided by Overend's mainly concerned the drawers, endorsers and acceptors of bills, as well as on the general state of the money market and, in that sense, was of a similar nature to that from Glyn's. The following three letters from the senior partner, Samuel Gurney, are illustrative of the type of intelligence provided by the Quaker firm.

Esteemed Friend,

We have made particular enquiries respecting the parties written about.

B Barnwall stands very respectably at Lloyds and would find no difficulty in getting credit for one or two Thousand Pounds. Although this is the feeling at Lloyds and may be Depended upon yet upon the whole enquiries we have made have rather lowered the firm in our estimation so far as their being in possession of much property.

T J Lancaster has been much respected here – we are informed that his affairs are small – say about £65000 of which £20000 is due to two relatives.

About six weeks since the eldest son of the late clarke [sic] of the house of Lubbock & Co. [London bankers] circulated a very illnatured letter respecting his fathers affairs as connected with that house – this young man is a thorough scamp and the letter had not much effect in London although it did the firm no good – it reached Perfect & Co [provincial bank] and induced them to change their account. Their act has we regret to say been followed by Harding Smith & Co [provincial bank] of Burlington – they have both opened their accounts with Jones Loyd & Co. [London bank].

(Overend Gurney & Co, to Langton, 20 November 1833)

Esteemed Friend
We are very much obliged to thee for your private note. – Beglie & Young are undoubtedly good in our opinion.

We have nothing new here everything going on favourably. The exposure that took place sometime back between some in our line of business and a house here being a branch of a firm in Manchester, appears to wear an even worse aspect than at first – the amount of loss that will accrue is very large and highly discreditable – … from what we hear … the firm can stand the loss but nothing can stand a continuation of the same system of management.

(25 November 1833)

Esteemed Friend
We have pleasure in reducing our charge for discount on your remittance of this day to 2¾ Per Cent – Our market altogether wears a favourable aspect – the exchanges appear as if they would advance [i.e. the value of sterling rise against other currencies] and the pacific complexion of the King's speech has given increased confidence. For these reasons we anticipate a continuance of great facility in these markets.

(5 February 1834)

In reporting a rise in interest rates in the London money markets on 11 April 1834, Gurneys offered the following analysis:

Several causes have operated to produce this effects of which we may specify the gradual and large increase of the funds of the East India Comp[y] in the hands of the Bank [of England] – being an abstraction of so much of the circulating medium – the financial operations of Government have also the same tendency – Gradual sales have been made some time back of Savings Bk Stock the proceeds being lodged in the Bank – other financial proceedings have been taking place having the object of accumulating money to pay £3,000,000 to the Bank in August according to the terms of the renewal of the Charter – all this has also stongly operated to diminish the circulation – the Bank however has now under its consideration the best method of correcting the evil that has arisen. Of which we will write further so soon as we can with clearness.

In addition to Glyn's and Overend's, the Bank of Liverpool also had an account with the Bank of England (sometimes referred to as 'the Bank' below) at the latter's Liverpool office (Collins, 1972a, 1972b). The Bank of England opened a branch on Merseyside in 1827 and the newly formed Bank of Liverpool opened an account there in 1831. The Bank of England paid no interest on deposit balances but offered its provincial banking customers bill discounting services and (less commonly used) advances or loans. In this way the Bank of Liverpool was able to augment other, money market sources of credit. Thus, in addition to discounting with the London bill brokers, the Bank of Liverpool was able to finance part of its extensive commercial bill discounting business through the Bank of England. In fact, it was the Bank's two Lancashire offices, at Liverpool and Manchester, that were the largest discounters of bills (very often, even more than Threadneedle Street) but the Bank operated offices in all the major English towns including Birmingham, Leeds, Newcastle and Bristol. The Bank also permitted account holders to transfer funds between its offices (including London) for collection by third parties, with no commission charge if the parties also had a Bank of England account (as was the case with many of the banking fraternity, especially in the capital). Thus, provincial banks with an account at the Bank were able to transfer funds around the country and were able to obtain (as well as pay in) notes, coin and bullion in their locality, a facility that could be critical during the recurrent banking crises of the mid-nineteenth century. The ready supply of bank notes (legal tender from 1833) was particularly important to the Liverpool banks as they did not issue notes of their own. The Bank, of course, was keen to establish as big a circulation for its own notes (and, ideally, should have preferred to have an outright monopoly (Clapham 1944: 121–30)) and one incentive it offered to discourage banks from issuing their own notes was to provide a favourable contract discount account for non-issuing banks. The Bank of Liverpool was one of the local banks to take advantage of this facility and, in so doing, gained a guaranteed discount facility at a fixed rate of 3 per cent per annum up to a ceiling equivalent to two-thirds of its paid-up capital. Any bills discounted beyond that amount could be discounted at the Bank's normal rate. The advantage to the local bank can be gauged by the fact that for all but three-quarters, the average Bank rate on best bills was always in excess of 3 per cent, and was 4 per cent or over for most of the time, 1830–43.

However, it should be said that the Bank of England was very choosy about the bills it would discount, excluding some securities that would be readily acceptable to other banks and discount houses. For the Bank, bills could be of no more than ninety-six days duration, they needed to have respectable commercial originators who were known to the Bank, and they had to include two good British names (excluding that of the discounter) (Bank of England Liverpool branch correspondence, vol. 3, letters from head office dated 26 March 1832, p. 356; 14 April 1832, p. 376).

> But even the most secure bill would be rejected if the Bank suspected [that] its origin did not lie in a 'bona fide' trade transaction, in which goods were

> actually transferred … In 1831 J.H. Palmer wrote, 'to discount any other than *negotiated* bills would in fact be lending a Banker *capital* to lend to his customer, in other words helping him to create capital, rather than circulate capital already in existence – which latter alone is legitimate business.'
>
> (Collins 1972a: 42, quoting from Palmer's letter of 15 June 1831 in volume 3 of the Liverpool branch correspondence, p. 123)

From October 1830 at its branches the Bank of England was also prepared to make very short-period loans (of a few days) on bills and Exchequer bills presented to it by local banks (and other customers) for discount in London (the Bank exercising the option to discount them itself or pass them on to the discount brokers), those loans providing the provincial banks with immediate cash for bills, rather than having to wait on the time it would take to transmit the bills to London and await the return of cash. The other service the Bank branch performed for the Bank of Liverpool was the provision of intelligence on the state of the markets of a similar nature to that provided by Glyn's and Overend's, though admittedly less frequently. In a similar manner, the Bank of Liverpool, and other local banks from across the country, provided the Bank's local agents with market intelligence which was conveyed to Threadneedle Street on a daily basis. And, of course, the opening of branches meant that the Bank was in frequent contact with the cream of the provincial business communities. In this manner, after the establishment of its branches the Bank of England had its finger on the pulse of the local economies of the country's commercial and manufacturing areas, adding to the existing nationwide inter-bank intelligence network. The nascent Bank of Liverpool of the 1830s was particularly fortunate to benefit from the close relationship that existed between the Bank of England's agent, S. Turner, and its general manager, Joseph Langton, who had previously been the deputy-agent at the branch.

Supplementing the two-way flow of information with London, the Bank of Liverpool also had a network of connections with other provincial banks and, in the bank's early days, no provincial inter-bank relationship was stronger than that with the Bank of Manchester. Both banks were established by leading businessmen of their locality, they saw themselves as champions of joint-stock banking and both had Glyn's as their London agent. There are only 30 miles between Liverpool and Manchester, communications between the two were excellent, even more so after the opening of the steam railway in 1830, and the pre-eminence of the Lancashire cotton trade and manufacture created the closest commercial and financial ties between the two towns. The two banks were the leading joint-stock banks in their respective towns and there was cooperation at board level, with some common share ownerships, as well as between the two general managers, Langton and Burdekin. The letters reveal a relationship between the two banks of a similar nature to that between Glyn's and the Bank of Liverpool without, of course, the greater scale and importance of the London connection. They provided reciprocal banking services for each other. So, both provincial managers regularly exchanged views on the state of their respective commodity and money markets, they exchanged information on interest rates, shared their views on legislative or policy matters affecting banks, they acted as local agents on behalf of the other's customers (e.g. providing credits to such customers when they were visiting the other town) and, routinely, they answered each other's queries about the credit standing of business people in their own locality. Thus, on 24 July 1834 Burdekin advised, 'I consider Forths & Co to be perfectly Safe, and in a money making way, although perhaps not very rich.' The next day (25 July) he was asking Langton to 'Grant me to introduce to you Mr Robert Anderson who may probably have occasion to draw upon us during his stay in Liverpool, in which case I will thank you to honour his checks upon our account to the extent of two thousand pounds – say, £2,000/-.'

However, a discordant note entered the relationship between the two banks when, at the end of 1834, the Bank of Manchester took the decision to issue its own notes. This action was to put it on a collision course with the Bank of England and was to incur the disapproval of Glyn's, both of whom, as we have seen, were very close commercial partners of the Bank of Liverpool. Glyn's, in fact, were not prepared to provide the greater credit facilities required to cover the Bank of Manchester's note circulation and on 18 November 1834 they informed Langton that, 'It is with great satisfaction I find the Bank of Manchester has made an arrangement with Messrs Denison Co for its London agency … My conviction is … that no other course in justice to ourselves and our general business could have been taken by us and that separation was most advisable, though always generally speaking unwilling to lose a connection.' Burdekin, of course, strongly represented the Bank of Manchester's viewpoint and it was to take a personal visit from George Carr Glyn to the Bank of Liverpool board to smooth ruffled feathers and re-establish normal cordial relations between the London and Liverpool banks.

3.5

So far, it has been our intention to illustrate the extent of the intelligence network available to a new, successful bank in the 1830s. The various examples also provide insight into the depth of the information flows – as well as the type of banking services – provided by the different components of the network; by the London banking agent, by London discount houses, by the Bank of England branches, and by other provincial banks. As has already been noted, most information concerned comments on individual firms, people or securities, but a core element was also the provision of intelligence on the state of markets. Comment would range across the cotton trade, African trade, Irish conditions, the American trade, the exchange markets and, of course, the state of the money markets. On the last, Bank of England action and policy drew a great deal of comment and, as a London money market insider, George Carr Glyn's comments on the Bank are particularly well informed. In the 1830s the nascent central bank was struggling with two important, inter-related conflicting forces. The first was concerned with finding a means to reconcile the requirement to protect the (commercial) interests of its shareholders while fulfilling, what some considered to be, its 'public responsibilities'. Second, effective action in the developing financial crisis called for careful judgement in identifying 'deserving' cases for bailouts while avoiding giving succour to speculative practices. Three instances during 1836–37 highlight the approach taken by the Bank: the support for the Northern and Central Bank of England (N&CBoE); the rescue of Esdaile's bank; and reaction to the liquidity problems of the large Anglo-American merchants (Collins, 1972c).

Glyn's accounts of these episodes reveal a rather hesitant approach by the Bank of England to providing lender of last resort facilities. This, of course, is understandable in that the Bank had no such formal responsibility. However, in the 1830s the Bank's position was more complex and the letters show that the views of the Court's directors were deeply divided. The two main points of friction among the directors arose over protecting dividends even when systemic stability may be better served by taking action that might sacrifice some profitability; and over a strict application of Currency School (or monetarist) principles as opposed to a more pragmatic approach to supporting both individual banking and commercial firms and the credit system in general.

In December 1836 the money market was preoccupied with the affairs of the poorly managed N&CBoE, one of the newly created banks that had taken advantage of legislative reform to develop a branch network and to issue its own notes, both activities to which Glyn, and most at the Bank, were opposed. When the directors of the N&CBoE went cap in hand to the Bank of England for a bailout, the Bank consulted with the leading London bankers (including George Carr Glyn) who urged the Bank to provide emergency aid for the sake of systemic stability:

> The Governor, Deputy & Mr H Palmer immediately sent for Mr J Smith, Mr Lloyd and me [the top London bankers] and after a protracted discussion and upon our representation of the immensity of the mischief which must follow the suspension [of the Northern & Central] with its extended branches to the whole of the country and mercantile community, we stated our conviction to be the imperative necessity of the Bank of E departing from its general rules and provided the N&C would consent to withdraw its [bank note] circulation and suppress the branches, rendering full assistance to meet the demands upon them and to prevent any suspension of payment ... the crisis which would have followed this stoppage would have caused great evil...
>
> (30 November 1836)

Glyn remained full of praise for the Bank's decision to provide credit to the stricken bank in order to allow an orderly liquidation and, in so doing, avoid a more general commercial collapse. The more so, because of the Bank's well-known antagonism towards this particular banking concern which had an aggressive strategy of rapid note and branch expansion.

Glyn was more critical of the Bank over the rescue of the London bank, Esdaile's, in which his own brother-in-law was a partner (see Glyn's letters dated 9, 23, 30 January 1837). The difficulties that the bank was facing had been the subject of confidential discussion among a small group of leading London bankers (including Glyn) and the Bank of England for some months and although it was illiquid by January 1837, its ultimate solvency was not doubted by Glyn who was very familiar with Esdaile's books. For this reason he was disappointed with the Bank's refusal to provide enough funds to allow an orderly liquidation, especially as the bank had an extensive network of seventy-two banking correspondents and its failure could undermine confidence throughout the country. Glyn took a prominent role among a delegation of London banks that eventually persuaded the Bank to reverse its position by offering Esdaile's a loan of £150,000 on the security of a guarantee provided by ten of those banks.

A more serious threat to systemic stability arose from the deteriorating financial state of the leading mercantile firms engaged in the Anglo-American trade which was in a parlous state during 1837 (Temin, 1969: 141–3). The Bank, at the urging of most of the mercantile and banking community, had afforded extra lending to the affected merchant houses and under the guidance of its senior director, John Horsley Palmer (who had personal experience in operating in the American trade) this continued until mid-1837. By May of that year the three worst affected firms, Wilson's, Wildes' and Wiggin's (the '3 W's') were once more seeking extraordinary support from the Bank. But, much to Glyn's consternation, the Bank of England directors (by a bare majority of one, and against the advice of the Governor, his deputy and Palmer) decided to refuse further aid and allow the three firms to fail (3 June 1837). Nevertheless, constant lobbying by leading banks, including the Bank of Liverpool, and provision of their own financial support (including signing up to a guarantee list to provide the Bank of England with security for a loan of up to £300,000 for Brown's [7, 13, 14 & 21 June 1837; and letters from London to the Liverpool Bank of England agent, vol. 5, 15 & 19 June 1837 – Bank of England record office]) meant two other leading Anglo-American firms, Lizardi's and Brown's, continued to meet all their obligations. After the suspension of specie payments by the United States on 11 June 1837 had helped reduce somewhat the dangers of American commercial firms meeting due payments (for many transactions payment in the notes of leading US banks could now be used instead of precious coin), the Bank of England announced its willingness to advance on overdue bills in the hands of the American houses that had not yet folded, 'provided the directors are satisfied with the security of the parties applying for loans...' (22 June 1837). Glyn was relieved that the Bank directors were prepared to accept this limited responsibility towards the whole financial system although, overall, he remained critical of its hesitancy to act as a lender of last resort at critical junctures during the crisis.

3.6

We hope that the selective use of the correspondence of the Bank of Liverpool has provided some insight into the operation of the information network that was critical to the success of the commercial credit system that, in its turn, provided such a fundamental underpinning to the country's sustained economic growth. Commercial credit depended upon the continued health of the bill market. For a mercantile community in a thriving commercial centre such as Liverpool in the 1830s, the first resort for credit was the local bank. And the local bank's ability to meet clients' demands for credit depended not only upon the bank's success in attracting local savings in the form of deposits but also upon its access to the national pool of credit. The gateway to this pool was via ties with London banking agents, London discount houses, the Bank of England and other provincial banks. These were the intermediary channels through which credit could flow from those areas and individuals with surplus funds to the net borrowers. As the Bank of Liverpool's correspondence has demonstrated, the risks involved in such a credit system were rendered acceptable by the willingness of participating institutions to share confidential data. The daily exchange of correspondence was filled with such information and while, from a twenty-first-century perspective, it may seem rather cumbersome – and, certainly, unscientific and subjective on occasions – it did provide frank assessments of creditworthiness from informed insiders. The personal nature of the relationships of the members of the network helped instil trust and reliability, and these would grow stronger the longer a successful partnership survived. It is clear from the Bank of Liverpool's experience that being a member of an extensive network of commercial intelligence and support was critical to the success of a new banking enterprise in the 1830s.

References

The main archive material used is the correspondence of Joseph Langton, manager of the Bank of Liverpool, reference: BLD Langton 1833, Barclays Bank Archive, Accession 25–265. We are extremely grateful for permission from Barclays Bank plc to use the material and also for the kind assistance of Barclays archive staff under the leadership of Maria Sienkiewicz.

Ashton, T. S. (1945). 'Bills of exchange and private banks in Lancashire, 1790–1830', *Economic History Review*, XV (1): 25–35.

Chandler, G. (1964). *Four centuries of banking.* Vol. 1. Batsford, London.

Clapham, J. H. (1944). *The Bank of England. A history.* Vol. 2. Cambridge University Press, Cambridge.

Collins, M. (1972a). *The Bank of England and the Liverpool money market, 1825–1850.* Unpublished PhD, University of London.

Collins, M. (1972b). 'The Bank of England at Liverpool, 1827–44', *Business History*, 14: 144–65.

Collins, M. (1972c). 'The Langton papers: Banking and Bank of England policy in the 1830s', *Economica*, 39: 47–59.

Fulford, R. (1953). *Glyn's, 1753–1953. Six generations in Lombard Street.* Macmillan & Co., London.

King, W. T. C. (1936). *History of the London discount market.* London.
Matthews, R. C. O. (1954). *A study in trade cycle history. Economic fluctuations in Great Britain, 1833–42.* Cambridge University Press, Cambridge.
Sayers, R. S. (1957). *Lloyds in the history of English banking.* Oxford University Press, Oxford.
Scammell, W. M. (1968). *The London discount market.* St. Martin's Press, London.
Temin, P. (1969). *The Jacksonian economy.* Norton, New York.
Thomas, S. E. (1934). *The rise and growth of joint stock banking.* Pitman & Sons, London.

4 Implementing Bagehot's rule in a world of derivatives

The Banque de France as a lender of last resort in the nineteenth century

Eugene N. White

The expansion of the scope and size of the Federal Reserve's operations to halt the Meltdown of 2008 violated Bagehot's lender of last resort rules for central banks. In increasingly complex and diverse financial markets, where derivatives have a vital role, it was argued that Bagehot's traditional principles had to be jettisoned. Based on the experience of the nineteenth century Bank of England, it appeared that Bagehot had prescribed rules that were too narrowly focused on banking. History would appear to be no guide. However, across the channel, at the same time that Bagehot was writing, the Banque de France operated in a very different financial system. In France, shocks frequently emanated from the stock exchanges where the dominant instrument was a derivative – a forward contract. Crashes in asset values ignited waves of broker defaults on the Paris Bourse and other exchanges, threatening the settlement of contracts and producing a more general liquidity crisis. After recurrent crises, the Banque adopted policy rules that Bagehot would certainly have approved and successfully navigated severe liquidity shocks originating on the exchanges.

The Banque's regents were adamant that its principles should not be abandoned when providing liquidity to the markets, no matter how severe the crisis. By the last quarter of the nineteenth century, the Banque refused bailouts; instead, it freely provided liquidity against the highest quality collateral at a high interest rate. Thus in 1882, the solvent Bourse de Paris received an emergency loan to manage an extraordinarily difficult end-of-month settlement, but the insolvent Bourse de Lyon was allowed to fail. In the 1896 crash, individual brokers with good collateral received advances while those without were excluded and failed. On both occasions, many investors in the forward market were ruined by the collapse of equity prices, yet the liquidity of the exchanges was quickly restored. The long depression that followed the 1882 crash was not a consequence of damage to the capital and money markets but excessive investment in low quality assets during a long expansion.

Using the minutes of the Conseil Général of the Banque de France, this paper examines in detail how this central bank acted as a lender of last resort in an environment where shocks to the financial system came from rapid declines in asset values that caused customers to default on their derivatives contracts, leading to broker defaults on the exchanges and the over-the-counter markets.

Although the Bourse provided some protection to customers and brokers from defaulting brokers through the Common Fund, it was often insufficient and the moral hazard generated by this mutual guarantee may have amplified risk-taking. Losses on the stock market were strongly felt in the rest of the financial system because customers borrowed to carry forward contracts from one settlement date to the next, thereby tying the banks to the exchange's liquidity. During crises, the Banque was regularly confronted with demands from the stock exchange for loans to guarantee its liquidity on settlement days, with little time to evaluate the situation. After a long period of vacillation, uncertain of whether to provide and how much credit to deliver, the Banque de France moved to adhere to Bagehot's basic principles. This change in policy enabled the central bank to manage subsequent incipient liquidity crises arising on the exchanges and the over-the counter markets, preventing them from spilling over into the banking markets.

4.1 Implementing Bagehot's rule in Britain

In considering whether a central bank should follow Bagehot's rule when it intervenes in a financial crisis, one must first carefully define a financial crisis. While this term is often bandied about, Anna Schwartz (1986) gave it a precise definition as a liquidity crisis within the Friedman-Schwartz-Monetarist tradition as a threat to the stability of the money stock. If the public scrambles for liquidity by withdrawing deposits for cash or the banks scramble for liquidity to increase their reserves relative to their liabilities, then the money stock may fall precipitously and a credit contraction will begin. As a lender of last resort, a central bank can alleviate such a crisis by providing more high powered money in the form of currency or bank reserves. As Capie (1998) has pointed out, how this action is put into operation is a key issue. Should the central bank provide liquidity to the market as a whole, turning a blind eye to the fate of individual institutions? Or, should it provide liquidity to key banks and other financial institutions – deemed "Too Big to Fail" – that may or may not be solvent but whose demise could trigger a general collapse? The latter approach has the potential for creating incentive for reckless behavior because of moral hazard; furthermore, it is hard to resist because there are often strong political pressures to save firms and jobs.

Bagehot's rule was, of course, formulated within the context of the nineteenth century British financial system, when the core threat to the financial system came from a panic generated by bank runs, where the public sought to convert banknotes and deposits into coin – the exact sense of a crisis as defined by Schwartz. Bagehot's recommendations were designed to ensure that the Bank of England would simply provide liquidity to the general market and avoid the problem of deciding which institutions should be aided. The need for a lender of last resort had been recognized much earlier. In *An Enquiry into the nature and effects of Paper Credit* (1802), Henry Thornton had observed that if one bank fails a general run is likely to ensue, therefore, the Bank of England should increase its discounts but it should not assist individual failing banks: "The relief should neither be so prompt and liberal as to exempt those who misconduct their business from all the natural consequences of their fault, nor so scanty and slow as deeply to involve the general interests" (Thornton, 1802, p. 188). The problem with this qualitative rule is that it does not provide a mechanism to deny credit to those who "misconduct their business" and are presumably insolvent.

For the first half or perhaps three-quarters of the nineteenth century, the Bank of England did not behave consistently (Capie, 1998). Part of the problem was that the Bank had conflicting objectives, competing with other financial institutions for business. This conflict of interest was finally resolved when the Bank put its public responsibility ahead of its private profitability in the 1870s. Yet, even before this event, Bignon, Flandreau and Ugolini (2009) find that a Bagehot-like policy developed slowly after 1847 and may have been in place when Bagehot chastised the Banque for its inconsistency. In the early nineteenth century they provide evidence that the Bank often rationed credit during crisis. They identify the crisis of 1866 as most likely the turning point, after which the Bank followed Bagehot's prescription for a lender of last resort.

Bagehot's recommendation for how to "stay" a panic can be succinctly stated as freely offering advances with the provisos (Bagehot, 1873, pp. 96–97):

> First. That these loans should only be made at a very high rate of interest. This will operate as a heavy fine on unreasonable timidity, and will prevent the greatest number of applications by persons who do not require it. The rate should be raised early in the panic, so that the fine may be paid early; that no one may borrow out of idle precaution without paying well for it; that the Banking reserve may be protected as far as possible. Secondly. That at this rate these advances should be made on all good banking securities, and as largely as the public ask for them.

The Bank of England adopted this approach and became a full fledged lender of last resort through the buffer of the discount houses, indirectly channeling liquidity to British banks. This arrangement enabled the Bank to avoid the problem of deciding how much credit to provide to each borrower. Bagehot had little sympathy with the "unsound" banks, a "feeble minority," and wanted to deny them credit in a crisis. The problem then and now was the moral hazard problem. Among the institutions clamoring for advances would be "unsound" banks, and it would be difficult to sort out solvent and insolvent ones. If the Bank rescued all, it would encourage more risk-taking in the future. Bagehot's solution to avoid these perils was to discount only high quality paper regardless of its source via the discount houses. Capie (1998, p. 322) has argued that "it is possible that a crucial element in this story is that anonymity is of fundamental importance in the execution of the lender-of-last-resort function." The central bank simply discounts on good quality collateral and does not worry about the source. By following this procedure, the Bank prevented financial crises and let "bad" banks like the City of Glasgow Bank fail in 1878. It might even organize a lifeboat operation for a premiere British bank like Barings in 1890, but it would not bail out a bank.

Implementing Bagehot's rule in other countries in the nineteenth century and today has presented challenges that call into question whether following his rule was only possible in the nineteenth century British financial system. Other European countries and the United States did not have the deep market formed by the discount houses to provide a buffer of anonymity between the banks and the central bank. In the early years of the Federal Reserve, Schwartz (1992) discovered that by providing discounts directly, the Fed encouraged weak banks to borrow. These troubled institutions were kept afloat by what became long-term loans. This loss of anonymity may thus have made the lender of last resort task more difficult for other central banks. But did differences in financial systems render it impossible for all but the Bank of England to carry out its lender of last resort function without slipping into bailouts?

To complicate matters, liquidity crises may arise from shocks not only to the banking system but also to financial markets. In the late nineteenth century Anglo-American world, equities were largely traded with spot contracts on exchanges and over-the-counter markets, and formal futures markets were beginning to appear. Bagehot and officials at the Bank of England did not have to consider the special problems that result from a scramble for liquidity in a market where financial contracts are for future rather than immediate delivery. A stock market crash could quickly translate into a liquidity crisis when customers and brokers were uncertain who would be able to complete their contracts on settlement days. The demand for cash might start on an exchange but it would ultimately manifest itself in the banking system. In this world, how did the Banque de France operate?

4.2 Implementing Bagehot's rule in France

Established in 1800, the Banque de France was a private institution where the government exercised influence by its nomination of the governor and two subgovernors.[1] Management of the institution was controlled by the General Assembly of stockholders, which was limited to the largest 200 shareholders, each of whom had one vote. The General Assembly elected 12 Regents from its number and chose three Censers who served as auditors. The Regents, the Governors and the Sub-Governors formed the General Council of the Banque that was delegated authority over its policy. In turn, the General Council selected a Central Committee of three of its members who oversaw the daily operations.

Like the Bank of England, the Banque was a commercial institution whose interests could conflict with those of the Banque as a lender of last resort. But, unlike the Bank of England, most historians have not assigned a time during the nineteenth century when the Banque accepted its role as lender of last resort as paramount. Furthermore, there is a long tradition in French historiography that sees the state behind most of the policy decisions of the Banque. For example, Bouvier (1988, p. 80) states that "From 1852 to 1914 it was as a result of pressure put on it by the State that the Banque increased the number of its branches; that *all* [Bouvier's emphasis] the decreases in the rate of discount were decided."

For the period 1852–1870, Plessis (1980, p. 7) wrote that the Banque "was subject to frequent intervention amounting to a constant control, on the part of the Ministry of Finance in particular and the public authorities in general." This intervention might come in the form of an attempt to stimulate the economy by lowering the interest rate or by lending to the government. According to Bouvier (1988), pressure was also put on the Banque to aid a specific industry or rescue a financial institution. For example, he cites that the Banque was compelled in 1852 to accept railway bonds as collateral for its advances. When a crisis erupted in 1856 and the Regents were split over whether to suspend gold payments, the government forced the bank to maintain convertibility. Against its will, the Banque aided Crédit Mobilier in 1867, saved the Comptoir d'Escompte de Paris in 1889, and was forced to provide permanent advances to official "caisses" of Crédit Agricole in 1897.

Yet, these studies may overstate the case and may be colored by the Banque de France's twentieth century experience. Many of the examples that are cited come from the period of the autocratic Second Empire, rather than the more open and democratic regime of the Third Republic. The details of many of these interventions are not well known. However, a closer examination of some cases makes the Banque looks less like a pawn of the government and more like an independent central bank. In the case of the Comptoir d'Escompte, this bank was undermined when the president of the bank, without the approval of the board of directors, conspired with a metals company to try to corner the copper market by providing huge loans (Liesse, 1909). The president's suicide and resulting disclosure of the bank's position sparked a run on this leading financial institution. In response the Banque provided a collateralized 140 million franc loan, leading interest rates and its discount rate to spike, as seen in Figure 4.1. The Comptoir was liquidated and the Banque's loan fully repaid. Its bank capital was not exhausted and, apparently, its goodwill capital was sufficient that an issue of stock recapitalized a reorganized bank. Rather than a bailout, the Banque de France's action looks more like an intervention to prevent a general panic and allow the reorganization of a solvent institution. Examining the behavior of the Banque's discounting policy relative to market rates, Bignon, Flandreau and Ugolini (2009) find that after 1857, the Banque, like the Bank of England, began to act more like a lender of last resort, lending freely at a high rate rather than holding down its discount rate and rationing credit. Together this evidence suggests that the Banque de France shifted to operating as a lender of last resort about the time that the Bank of England did, even though it operated in a different financial system, where there was no British-style discount market to provide a buffer of anonymity and important liquidity shocks originated on the stock exchanges.

The Banque de France discount operations would have been familiar to any contemporary central banker. To anyone who had an account at the Banque – manufacturers and merchants as well as banks – it offered discounts on bills of exchange, bills to order, or warrants of less than three months maturity, with three signatures or two signatures if there was collateral of acceptable securities.

At least in ordinary times, only short-term paper of the highest quality could be discounted. Banks were an important participant in these operations, although the extent of their balances at the Banque are unknown. One estimate reported that about 70 percent of discounts had the signature of at least one bank as endorser. When interviewed by the U.S. National Monetary Commission (Aldrich, 1910, p. 207), the Governor of the Bank of France, M. Pallain was asked, "Does the amount and the character of credit granted to other banks depend on the amount and the character of their accounts at the Bank of France?" Pallain responded:

> There is no fixed rule, and although the balance of the account is not a matter of indifference, it is more especially the quality of the paper presented which fixes the extent of the credit. In periods of crisis in 1830, 1848, in 1870, in 1889, the general council of the Bank did not hesitate to come to the assistance of establishments which were in difficulties, but which held assets of unquestioned character and value, by extending to them the largest possible credits.

While the Banque officially maintained that it upheld a Bagehot rule by lending freely on only good collateral, minutes of the General Council offer more insight into the views of the Banque and the precise policies pursued in financial crises.

The source of liquidity risk that arises from derivatives markets is well known – especially after the Meltdown of 2008 – but it was equally understood as a threat in late nineteenth century France. The threat to the liquidity of the financial system in derivatives market occurs because of counterparty risk. In the nineteenth century French forward market, there was a risk of default on contractual obligations because of the time lag between the contract and delivery dates. A broker in such a market faced the risk that a customer would default when there was a decline in his or her net wealth. If the customer was unable to complete the contract on the settlement date and the collateral was insufficient, brokers typically absorbed the loss to make good to the counterparty broker and his customer. If the default was large enough or enough customers defaulted, the broker may not have been able to meet his commitments on the settlement date and he may have defaulted. The failure of one broker might then produce a cascade of defaults, as their positions to each other were revealed. Given the asymmetry of information on the ultimate ability of parties to make good on their obligations, there could be a scramble for liquidity beyond the market by customers and by banks that provided credit to customers to roll over their forward contract commitments from one settlement period to the next.

Trading in derivatives may be organized either by formal exchanges or in over-the-counter markets. On the exchanges, the integrity of exchange transactions is protected by a mutual guarantee fund, usually embedded in the exchange's clearinghouse and subscribed to by all the brokers. Counterparty risk is thus mutualized, ensuring the liquidity of the market by allowing customers to trade without concern about the creditworthiness of their brokers or their brokers' counterparties. Given the moral hazard involved in such an arrangement, the incentives to exploit it are managed by a mix of monitoring, margin, position, and capital requirements and price limits. Consequently, each brokers' activities have a relatively high degree of transparency to others on the exchange. If instead of an exchange, trading in derivatives is conducted in the over-the-counter market, the integrity of the transactions is guaranteed by the reputation of the brokers or their firms, often banks. A financial firm engaged in this activity must develop internal monitoring procedures and regulations to control risk-taking of its brokers. By effective policing, the banks or other financial institutions invest in their reputation to provide customers with the confidence that they will be able to meet their contractual obligations. Additional risk may arise if brokers or their banks take positions in the markets. On the French exchanges, brokers could only legally act as agents for their customers, eliminating this risk; but there was no similar constraint on brokers and banks operating in the over-the-counter markets.

The recent explosion of derivatives trading outside of the exchanges suggests that the controls implemented by the exchanges to control moral hazard, while successful, lowered the returns to trading on the exchange, leading to the growth of over-the-counter trading. In France, the failure to implement adequate internal controls led Sociéte Générale to suffer embarrassing losses by its rogue trader Jerôme Kervial; while in the United States the insurance giant AIG collapsed in large part because of its position in the market for credit default swaps. It is generally argued that both exchange-based and over-the-counter derivatives systems can manage idiosyncratic shocks; but what is in doubt is whether they can manage systemic shocks without a general crisis erupting. The fact that Sociéte Générale survived in otherwise calm times in spite of the massive losses while AIG failed when the market for mortgage securities foundered at the start of a severe recession suggests that systemic shocks present the same challenge to derivatives markets as they do to banking markets.

Until the 2007–2009 crisis, the threat to liquidity from counterparty risk received relatively little attention among economists.[2] No derivatives exchange in the United States had failed. Only a few professionals were aware of historical cases, such as the 1902 failure of one member of the Chicago Board of Trade that caused large widespread losses. It was these problems that led exchanges to create mutual guarantee funds with the associated rules to control counterparty risk (Moser, 1998). However, two of the few who studied the potential risk in the derivatives markets were Randall Kroszner and Ben Bernanke, a member of and the chairman of the Federal Reserve. Krozner's survey (1999, 2000) of American futures markets' mutualization of risk through the clearinghouses' guarantee funds led him to conclude that they had aligned their incentives to effectively manage the risk. However, by 1996 the rapid growth of the over-the-counter derivatives market gave it twice the notional amount of derivatives outstanding on the exchanges. The OTC market had adapted to trading of new, often tailor-made, non-standardized products, and clearing without a clearinghouse to monitor counterparties and provide mutual insurance.[3] Without these institutions, Kroszner (2006) saw potential for systemic risk in the event of a default by a large market participant in stressed market conditions.

Bernanke (1990) also emphasized the centrality of the exchanges' clearing-houses that ensure the completion of trades, fulfilling a "banking" role as part of a payments system, in addition to their role as an insurance company, protecting the exchange from the risks of members' defaults. Like Kroszner, Bernanke viewed the exchange-based trading system for derivatives as adequate to handle idiosyncratic shocks but not systemic shocks that could overwhelm the clearinghouses' capital and the member-assessment powers. Bernanke considered events during the October 1987 crash as particularly informative. When some members of the options exchanges appeared ready to default, the Fed flooded the market with liquidity and the Fed "persuaded" banks to lend freely to brokers. It singled out Continental Illinois, the parent company of First Options of Chicago, to ensure that the bank had sufficient funds to avoid a default that might have undermined the Chicago Board of Options. Three member firms of the exchange ultimately defaulted but the clearinghouse was able to assess its members to cover these losses. In light of this experience, Bernanke saw a role for the Fed as not only a lender of last resort but also as an "insurer of last resort." He concluded (1990, p. 146) that:

> When the financial system is conceived broadly to include the government as the "insurer of last resort" the current institutional setup seems satisfactorily robust to the threat of financial crisis.

The problem was that by 2008 most derivatives trading was over-the-counter by large interconnected firms where there was little monitoring. There appeared to be no alternative but to bail out or let fail the large individual firms. There was no anonymity and a considerable danger of moral hazard given that the immediate demand for liquidity from the Fed gave little time to assess the dangers or viability of a bank or insurance company, leading to difficult choices when faced with the collapse of Bear Stearns, Lehman Brothers and AIG. Bagehot's rule to lend freely at a high rate of interest but only on good collateral would seem to be impossible to implement in this environment. However, an examination of the experience of the Banque de France in three late nineteenth century crises shows how it managed to follow Bagehot's rule.

4.3 Crisis: 1851

Until the reforms that followed the Crash of 1882, defaults by brokers threatened the operation of the Paris Bourse on numerous occasions after sharp declines in asset values (Riva and White, 2010). Serious crises caused the Bourse to seek aid from the Banque de France or the Treasury to ensure its liquidity. Records show that assistance was provided in 1818, 1840 and 1848, while the Banque became increasingly concerned about the repeated demands for assistance.

The minutes of the General Council of the Banque de France report that on December 22, 1851, the Governor presented a request to the Council for assistance from the Paris Bourse. The Chambre Syndicale, the governing body of the exchange, feared that defaults by members resulting from the sharp market movement would wipe out the guarantee fund and leave the brokers with inadequate liquidity to proceed with their end-of-month settlement. The exchange wished to discount short-term government bonds, the Bons du Trésor. It offered to have them endorsed by the members of the Chambre Syndicale, in their role of its administrators, but offered no personal guarantee, as that would have involved greater liability for all the signers.

This request provoked a debate within the General Council over whether it was permissible to grant such a credit under the Banque's statutes. One regent pointed out that the Banque had suspended discount of these bonds after the crisis in 1848 when the government sought financial relief by delaying payment on these bonds for six months. To such members of the Council, the quality of the government's paper appeared to the Banque to be inferior to ordinary commercial paper. Perhaps even Bagehot would have been surprised by the strong stand they took on the question of "good collateral." Although the General Council and Censors approved of the discount, the Governor reminded the Bourse's head, or Syndic, that this type of collateral was less than desirable because of the payments suspension following the events of February 1848.

The loan enabled the Bourse to carry out its settlement, but the Banque was distressed by the frequency of requests for aid from the exchange. In the aftermath of the crisis, the minutes of the General Council record a disgruntled regent's complaint that the Bourse's request was made on the eve of the settlement with the threat of a liquidity crisis, giving the Banque little chance to consider the issue. Although they did not use the modern term moral hazard, the Council members' discussion of the pattern of lending to the Bourse shows signs of their impatience with the risk taken by the brokers.

4.4 Crisis: 1882

In comparison with 1851, the crisis of 1882 was far more serious (White, 2007), but the response of the Banque shows a greater agility and sophistication. Like the post-1870 Bank of England, the Banque de France showed little vacillation when confronted with the potential collapse of the Bourse de Lyon and the Bourse de Paris and appears to have adhered to its own strict rules – which mirrored Bagehot's thinking.

Given the magnitude of this crisis, its details are better known. The 1882 collapse brought an end to the long boom that followed the end of the Franco-Prussian War of 1870–1871 and the resolution of France's reparations to Germany. The reparations of 5 billion gold francs, the equivalent of 25 percent of one year's GDP, had been raised by two heavily over-subscribed bond issues in 1871 and 1872, permitting complete payment in 1873. The success of these issues helped to stimulate an investment and stock market boom, fueled by falling interest rates, as seen in Figure 4.1. The Banque de France lowered its discount rate from 6 to 2 percent by 1877, an historic low; and then remained within a band of 2 and 3 percent for the rest of the decade. After 1877, open market paper rates stayed below 3 percent, reaching lows of 1½ percent, and yields on the *rentes* dropped to 3½ percent.

In this favorable market, the French Treasury started to refinance one billion francs in debt in July 1881. Italy followed suit and subscriptions to its refinanced debt drew gold into Italy. In response, the Bank of England raised its discount rate, forcing the Banque de France to push up its rate to 4 percent in August 1881 and then 5 percent in October 1881. Although the stock boom continued for another two months, funding for carrying forward contracts over to the next settlement period, the *reports*, became very expensive. As risk in the market grew, the cost of *reports* for blue chip stocks climbed from 4 percent at the end of 1880 to 8 percent in the Spring of 1881, then 10 percent after the Banque increased the discount rate. These increases reflected the risk assessment of lenders who saw an increasing potential for a crash. One of the leading speculative stocks was l'Union Générale, an investment bank (*banque des affaires*). Founded in Lyon in 1878, it had rapidly built up a network of interlocking financial institutions focused on investments in the Balkans. This bank was a highly leveraged firm with purported capital of one billion francs. The price of this bank's stock had risen from 500 francs in 1879 to 3,000 francs in 1881, but was viewed as very risky, with *reports* in late 1881 costing 29 percent. When its investments soured and it was discovered that it had produced misleading accounts, l'Union's stock collapsed, leaving investors that had gambled on its steady rise in the forward market with huge potential losses on the upcoming settlement day. Then, when the Austrian government refused a concession to another new institution, the Banque de Lyon et de la Loire, shares plunged and a run shut the bank down, igniting runs on l'Union and other banks.

The Paris Bourse and the second most important exchange, the Lyon Bourse, were centers of the stock market boom and faced a potential disaster in January

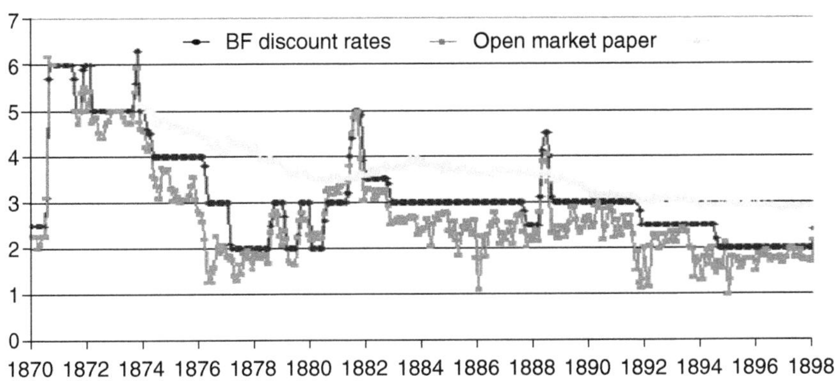

Figure 4.1 Interest rates 1870–1904 (source: NBER Macro History Data Base, Series 11021, 13013, and 13017, www.rber.org).

1882. On January 4, the spot price of l'Union Générale reached 3040 francs with forward prices for mid-January of 3020–3060 francs. By January 14, the spot price had fallen to 2800 francs. The brokers on the Lyon Bourse shut down the exchange on January 19, unable to cover the contracts of their ruined customers, sparking a scramble for liquidity, while the spot price eventually tumbled to 500 francs in Paris on January 30. As the end-of-month settlement loomed, many investors faced huge losses. It appeared that more than a few of the stock brokers on both exchanges would not be able to make good on their defaulting customers' forward contracts and the mutual guarantee funds would prove to be insufficient, provoking a wider liquidity crisis.

On January 23, 1882, a delegation from Lyon petitioned the Banque de France to provide a nine month advance of 125 million francs to enable the exchange to carry out an orderly settlement in the face of large losses. Against this credit, a syndicate of the leading bankers, financial institutions and capitalists pledged securities to indemnify the Banque against any losses up to 30 million francs. The following day the General Council considered the petition and turned it down, noting that the securities (bonds and stocks of industrials, mining and financial institutions) could not be used as collateral under the statutes of the Banque. To use these securities, the Governor admonished the Lyonnais "ce serait un précédent très dangereuse que de ne pas respecter les statuts." Instead, the Conseil was willing to consider a three month advance of 100 million francs if the members of the syndicate each gave their personal guarantee on the discounted securities. Faced with unknown losses, the Lyonnais declined and on January 28, the Tribunal de Commerce announced the liquidation of the Lyon exchange. It was insolvent. The Banque would not agree to a bailout or any loan without collateral on which it presumed there would be no possible loss.

In the meantime, the brokers of the Bourse met on January 25, 1882 and gave the Syndic the authority to contract an 80 million franc loan from the Banque. When this request came to the January 28 meeting of the Banque's General Council, the Governor quickly ceded the floor to the Baron de Rothschild. The premiere French banker opined that the Bourse de Paris, unlike Lyon, was not insolvent and that the 80 million francs was a "un temoignage de confiance" and a complement to existing resources for the "besoins spéciaux du moment." However, aid to the Bourse would have to follow the rules of the bank and the public must be persuaded that ordinary funds had not been diverted to the Bourse. To follow its rules, the loan was intermediated by a syndicate of banks because the Banque could only provide a loan upon collateral of bankable paper that the brokers lacked. The credit would be obtained indirectly, with Chambre Syndicale creating ten-year 5 percent bonds to deliver to the banks who would receive them and issue three-name, three-month paper that could be discounted at the Bank of France.

The syndicate included all major banks in France, with shares in the bonds parceled out approximately according to each bank's relative importance. The Rothschilds took 10 million francs and Crédit Foncier, the Comptoir d'Escompte, the Banque de Paris et des Pays Bas, Société Générale, Crédit Lyonnais and the Banque d'Escompte each taking 5 million francs. The remainder was apportioned to private and public banks: Heine, Gunzburg, Stern, Hensels, Camonds Vernes, Cohen, De Machy et Silliere, Gillet, Hottinguer, Marnard, Mallet frères, Hannadex, Péreire frères, Mirabad, Donon, Alberti, Crédit Foncier, the Comptoir d'Escompte, the Banque de Paris et des Pays Bas, Société Générale, Crédit Lyonnais, the Banque d'Escompte, the Société de Crédit, the Société de Depots et Comptes Courants, the Banque Hypothecaire, Crédit Mobilier, Crédit Moblier Espagnol, the Banque Ottomane, the Banque Franco-Egyptienne, Crédit General Francais and the Banque de Constantinople. Following the principles of this loan, Banque set up a syndicate for Lyon with a capital of 25 million, subscribed by leading banks to provide credit to banks and other financial institutions in need of liquidity.

With these resources in hand, the Paris Bourse opened the first day of the end-of-month January settlement. To complete their contractual obligations, 14 of the 60 brokers asked for 66.8 million francs in assistance. The remains of the 80 million francs plus the 7 million from the mutual fund were not enough to cover the needs of the second day of the end-of-month settlement. The Syndic then obtained a second 18 million loan from the Rothschilds. Once the liquidity crisis was over, the Rothschild loan and 50 million francs of the 80 million were quickly repaid. The Bourse was then left with a 30 million francs loss from defaulting brokers, which was covered by a joint assessment of the remaining brokers in October 1882. Seven brokers ultimately failed and gave up their seats on the exchange (White, 2007).

The action of the Banque de France permitted the Bourse de Paris to continue its operation, following the liquidity crisis; but none of the insolvent brokers or the insolvent Lyon exchange was bailed out. If the potential of aid from the Banque had tempted brokers to take risks, this episode should have disabused them of this idea. Pressure on the financial system was relieved when on February 2, 1882, a telegraph from London informed the Banque that the Bank of England had reduced its discount rate from 6 to 5 percent. In response the Banque reduced its discount rate from 5 to 4.5 percent and its rate on advances to 5.5 percent, followed by further reductions in March. The Banque had stuck to its rules that it would only discount a limited type of high quality collateral. Given the absence of this collateral in the hands of the brokers, the role that Rothschild played in providing a means to intermediate was crucial.

The actions of the Banque de France as a lender of last resort look very much like those of the Federal Reserve vis-à-vis the brokers of the Chicago Board of Options during the crash of 1987, except that the Banque organized a syndicate to channel liquidity rather than generally providing liquidity and pressing the banks to lend freely. However, the Banque, unlike the Fed, did not focus attention on any particular broker or firm. In a sense, the syndicate provided "anonymity" for the allocation of aid, enabling the Bourse to administer the credit and manage its defaulting brokers.

4.5 Crisis: 1896

In the years before the next stock market crash, the collapse of the Comptoir d'Escompte was managed by the Banque de France, freely providing credit but at a high rate of interest, as seen in Figure 4.1. The disruption was brief and interest rates again began to decline, contributing to a new bull market. It surged not on the Bourse, which had undergone major reforms, reducing risk-taking by brokers, but on the Coulisse or curb market. This less regulated market had no clearinghouse/mutual fund or close monitoring of its members (White, 2009; Riva and White, 2010). By the early 1890s, the Coulisse had become the dominant market, just as the over-the-counter market did in the United States in the 1990s. Although no volume data exists, a tax on transactions was introduced in 1893. For 1893–1895, the Ministry of Finance reported the revenue by source (Vidal, 1910, p. 233). The brokers on the Paris Bourse paid 11.8 million francs, those on other exchanges paid 1.7 million francs, but the coulissiers (brokers on the Coulisse) and the banks, which had begun to trade for their customers, delivered 22.1 million francs to the Treasury.

The boom began in 1894 in South African gold mining stocks, following their enthusiastic reception on the London exchange. These new foreign mining shares were traded on the Coulisse, as they were not listed on the Bourse, which signaled them to be high risk investments. By the end of 1895, there were 66 new gold, coal and colonial exploration companies added to the Coulisse's cash market and 32 to its forward market. The boom was facilitated by falling interest rates, with the Banque's discount rate reaching 2 percent for the first time since 1881, with both short-term rates and the yield on the *rentes* reaching historic lows.

The market for gold and allied stocks crashed in January 1896 when news arrived of the failure of the Jameson raid to provoke a British takeover of the Transvaal Republic. Although there was a scramble for liquidity with spiking interest rates, the Bourse did not appear to be threatened and no assistance was requested. But, many customers of the brokers on the Coulisse had been seduced by the gold stock boom and now could not complete their contractual operations, placing considerable strain on specific brokers.

The Banque de France managed this crisis by following its strict rules as a lender of last resort. Solvent but illiquid brokers who had accounts at the Banque were given direct assistance upon good collateral. Table 4.1 shows the direct advances provided to brokers during this crisis. With the exception of one individual, all are *agents de change* or an *associé d'agent de change*, that is, an official broker on the Bourse or one of their employees. On good collateral, brokers could apparently obtain credit up to three million francs. The one exception was Frank, a *courtier de change*, a foreign exchange broker; however, he was only granted a relatively modest credit of 372,000 francs. The Banque did not feel it needed to offer a blanket guarantee to the market. None of the official brokers failed, having avoided direct involvement in the gold bubble. The brokers who provided services to investors in this market did not have the access or the good quality collateral required, and they were left to fail.

Table 4.1 Assistance by the Banque de France to brokers (February 1896)

February 20: advances	
Couturier, *agent de change*	2,780,000 FF
Lecomte, *agent de change*	3,000,000 FF
Duverger, *agent de change*	3,000,000 FF
Frank, *agent de change*	372,000 FF
Lestibidois, *agent de change*	2,085,000 FF
February 27: advances	
Sargenton, *agent de change*	220,000 FF
Aube, *agent de change*	243,000 FF
Roblot, *agent de change*	600,000 FF
Hamilbourg, *agent de change*	1,463,000 FF
Margareles, *agent de change*	1,636,000 FF
Eonnel, *associe d'agent de change*	3,000,000 FF
Labarre, *associe d'agent de change*	3,000,000 FF
Chalupt, *associe d'agent de change*	3,000,000 FF
Dudorst, *associe d'agent de change*	3,000,000 FF
Roblot, *agent de change*	600,000 FF
Bacheler, *agent de change*	1,200,000 FF
Verneuil, *agent de change*	2,920,000 FF

Source: Banque de France Conseil Général Procès-verbaux 1895–1897.

The coulissiers suffered but there is no record of their losses, as they were not part of an exchange that would have chronicled their problems. The credits granted to the brokers and their employees on the Bourse totaled 30,493,000 francs. While this crash was smaller than the crash of 1882, it was still a substantial credit for the Banque to advance. The magnitude of losses for the coulissiers, banks and others can only be guessed at. But, with twice the volume of the Bourse and dominating trade in the speculative stocks, it is difficult to believe that their losses were not substantial. If their losses were on the order of the credits to the official brokers, then the losses would compare to those experienced by the Bourse in 1882. In the absence of data, this is speculative. On the other hand, given the consistent policy followed by the Banque, the coulissiers probably knew that they could not expect assistance from the Banque if they did not have accounts and if they did not have the appropriate collateral. Thus, they may have been more prudent than just suggested. While further research is needed to determine whether the strict Bagehot-like policy of the Banque de France deterred them from taking large risks, it is clear that the crisis was well contained.

4.6 Conclusion

The actions of the Federal Reserve in 2008 will continue to be debated, as the vast expansion of its balance sheet, purchase of illiquid assets and apparent extension of liquidity to the whole financial system has no precedent. The bailout, especially of the insolvent insurance company AIG, doomed by its position in the credit default swap market, has fueled popular outrage at Fed policies. Whether one believes that this was a necessary action or not, there is reasonable concern that it created substantial moral hazard that may result in more risk-taking in the future. Those who advocate the strict use of a Bagehot rule to counter this problem appear to their critics as supporters of a quaint policy that was specific to the period and cannot pass muster in a world of increasingly complex financial instruments and markets. Yet, the Banque de France faced crises that in many ways resemble the meltdown on modern derivatives markets. Following Bagehot's precepts, the Banque successfully managed these crises and restored liquidity to the market without costly and embarrassing bailouts, suggesting that a narrow Bagehot role for a lender of last resort may still be consistent with longer-term financial stability even in the presence of large, volatile derivative markets.

Notes

1 Although these top officials were removable at the pleasure of the government, it never exercised this sanction.
2 Clark and Perfect (1996) noted the potential for losses on the OTC derivatives market to create contagion and potentially systemic effects.
3 Some monitoring was provided by the rating agencies. Krozner (1999).

References

Aldrich, Nelson W., *Interviews on the Banking and Currency Systems of England, Scotland, France, Switzerland and Italy* (Washington: National Monetary Commission, 1910).

Bagehot, Walter, *Lombard Street, A Description of the Money Market* (London: Kegan Paul, 1873; reprinted, Homewood, IL: Richard D. Irwin, Inc., 1962).

Banque de France, Conseil Général, *Procès-verbaux* (various years).

Bernanke, Benjamin S., "Clearing and Settlement during the Crash," *Review of Financial Studies* Vol. 3, No. 1 (1990) pp. 133–151.

Bignon, Vincent, Marc Flandreau and Stefano Ugolini, "Bagehot for Beginners: The Making of Lending of Last Resort Operations in the Mid-19th Century," Norges Bank Working Paper No. 22 (2009).

Bouvier, Jean, "The Banque de France and the State from 1850 to the Present Day," in Gianni Toniolo, ed., *Central Banks' Independence in Historical Perspective* (Berlin: Walter de Gruyter, 1988), pp. 73–104.

Capie, Forrest, "Can There Be an International Lender-of-Last-Resort?" *International Finance* Vol. 1, No. 2 (1998), pp. 311–325.

Clark, Jeffrey A., and Steven B. Perfect, "The Economic Effects of Client Losses on OTC Bank Derivatives Dealers: Evidence from the Capital Markets," *Journal of Money, Credit and Banking* Part 2, Vol. 28, No. 3 (August 1996), pp. 527–545.

Kroszner, Randall S., "Can the Financial Markets Privately Regulate Risk," *Journal of Money Credit and Banking* Part 2, Vol. 3, No. 3 (1999), pp. 596–618.

Kroszner, Randall S., "Lessons from Financial Crises: the Role of the Clearinghouses," *Journal of Financial Services Research* Vol. 18, No. 2/3 (2000), pp. 157–171.

Kroszner, Randall S., "Central Counterparty Clearing: History, Innovation and Regulation," Federal Reserve Bank of Chicago, *Economic Perspectives* (4th Quarter, 2006), pp. 37–40.

Liesse, André, *Evolution of Credit and Banks in France* (Washington, D.C.: National Monetary Commission, 1909).

Meltzer, Allan H., "Policy Principles: Lessons from the Fed's Past," in John D. Ciorciari and John B. Taylor, *The Road Ahead for the Fed* (Stanford: Hoover Institution Press, 2009).

Moser, James T., "Contracting Innovations and the Evolution of Clearing and Settlement Methods at Futures Exchanges," Federal Reserve Bank of Chicago, Research Department Working Paper (1998, WP-98–26).

National Bureau of Economic Research, Macro History Data Base, www.nber.org.

Plessis, Alain, *Résumé de Thèse* (mimeo, 1980).

Riva, Angelo and Eugene N. White, "Danger on the Exchange: How Counterparty Risk Was Managed on the Paris Bourse in the Nineteenth Century," National Bureau of Economic Research, Working Paper 15634 (January 2010).

Schwartz, Anna J., "Real and Pseudo Financial Crises," in Forrest Capie and Geoffrey E. Wood (eds), *Financial Crises and the World Banking System* (London: Macmillan, 1986), pp. 11–31.

Schwartz, Anna J., "The Misuse of the Fed's Discount Window," *Federal Reserve Bank of St. Louis Review* (September/October 1992), pp. 58–69.

Thornton, Henry, *An Enquiry into the nature and effects of Paper Credit* (London: J. Hatchard, 1802, reprinted London: George Allen and Unwin, 1939).

Vidal, E., *History and Methods of the Paris Bourse* (Washington, D.C.: National Monetary Commission, 1910).

White, Eugene N., "The Crash of 1882 and the Bailout of the Paris Bourse," *Cliometrica* Vol. 1 (2007), pp. 115–144.

5 Banking crises and the rules of the game

Charles W. Calomiris

The author thanks conference participants, Allan Meltzer, and Joseph Mason, for helpbul comments on earlier drafts of this chapter.

5.1 Introduction

Pundits, policy makers, and macroeconomists often remind us that banking crises are nothing new, an observation sometimes used to argue that crises are inherent to the business cycle, or perhaps to human nature itself. Charles Kindleberger (1978) and Hyman Minsky (1975) were prominent and powerful advocates of the view that banking crises are part and parcel of the business cycle, and result from the propensities of market participants for irrational reactions and myopic foresight.

Some banking theorists, starting with Diamond and Dybvig (1983), have argued in a somewhat parallel vein that the structure of bank balance sheets is itself to blame for the existence of panics; in their canonical model, banks structure themselves to provide liquidity services to the market and thus create large liquidity risks for themselves, and also make themselves vulnerable to self-fulfilling market concerns about the adequacy of bank liquidity. The theoretical modeling of banking theorists, like the myopia theory of Minsky, is meant to explain prevalent banking fragility – a phenomenon that any blogger can now trace at least as far back as AD 33, when Tacitus (Book VI) tells us that the Roman Empire suffered a major banking panic, which was quelled by a large three-year interest-free loan to the banking system by Emperor Tiberius.[1]

There is, however, at least one obvious thing wrong with all these arguments that purport to show how myopia, business cycles, and inherent bank liquidity transformation can explain the historical constancy of banking crises: in fact, the propensity for banking crises has not been at all constant over time or across countries. Banking crises have not regularly and consistently accompanied business cycles. In fact, banking crises have been much more frequent in some eras than in others and much more frequent in some countries than in others. The differences across countries and across time are dramatic, as this paper will demonstrate.

This is, in fact, a central lesson of the history of banking crises, which economic historians should be emphasizing in their discussions with macroeconomists, theorists, and policy makers in the wake of the current global banking crisis: banking crises are not an historical constant, and therefore, the propensity for banking crises cannot possibly be said to be the result of factors that have been constant over time and across countries for hundreds of years, including business cycles, human nature, or the liquidity transformation inherent in bank balance sheets.

A second, related lesson of the history of banking crises, and the main point of this paper, is that the structure of the rules governing the banking system within a country – defined by the rules that govern the location, powers, and the operations of each of the banks, including government subsidies or special rights granted to favored participants in the banking system and the incentive consequences of those subsidies and rights – has been at the center of the explanation of the propensity for banking crises for the past two centuries. In times and places where politically determined microeconomic rules of the banking game have encouraged risky practices or prevented effective private measures to limit banking crisis risk, the risk of banking crises is high; conversely, the absence of such adverse political rules of the game have resulted in stable banking systems.

Some of this evidence is visible in the history of particular countries, not just in cross-country comparisons. When the political equilibrium governing the rules of the banking game changed for the better (worse) in a particular country, previously unstable (stable) banking systems became stable (unstable). The primary purpose of this paper is to review these experiences and consider their lessons for current policy reactions to the global banking crisis of 2007–2009. Specifically, Sections 2, 3, and 4: (1) review the experience of the United States in the nineteenth and early twentieth centuries in this regard, (2) compare and contrast the banking rules of the game of the highly stable pre-World War I period with those of the last thirty years' highly unstable banking experience, and (3) explain how Great Britain changed from suffering a highly unstable banking system during the first six decades of the nineteenth century to becoming a paragon of stability in the pre-World War I era.

This emphasis on the microeconomic rules of the banking game, and the political economy that gives rise to those rules, should not be interpreted as an argument for the irrelevance of macroeconomic considerations (monetary policy, the phases of business cycles, etc.) in understanding banking crises. Monetary policy and other macroeconomic considerations have indeed been an important source of financial crises, which include asset price bubbles, exchange rate collapses, and a host of other phenomena, as well as banking crises. It is also true that financial crises, broadly defined to include asset pricing booms and busts, have been a common feature of business cycles throughout time. But although monetary policy errors have often set the stage for banking crises (see Bordo 2007; Bordo and Wheelock 2007, 2009; Calomiris 2009a), monetary policy errors and business cycle swings more generally have not proven to be sufficient conditions for *banking* crises. Destabilizing monetary policy, or other macroeconomic considerations, only tend to produce banking crises alongside cyclical contractions when the microeconomic rules of the banking game are poorly designed.

Indeed, a third lesson from the history of banking instability is that the ability to derive useful lessons about banking crises depends on defining banking crises properly. Banking crises must be distinguished from the broader category of "financial crises," which include a variety of other phenomena (i.e., sovereign debt defaults, exchange rate depreciations, land price declines, and stock market declines), which may or may not be associated with banking distress. And banking problems, including significant declines in deposits for the system as a whole, or the failure of one or two banks, do not equate to a banking crisis.[2] What makes a banking problem into a banking crisis?

When defining banking crises it is important to distinguish between two different aspects of banking crises – waves of bank insolvency (episodes in which bank losses result in many failed banks), and banking panics (moments in which the banking system as a whole suffers from sudden, large withdrawals of deposits).[3] Sometimes these two aspects have coincided (as during some episodes in the U.S. in the 1830s and the 1930s, and many recent episodes), but often they have not coincided. The 1920s in the U.S. witnessed a severe wave of bank failures, but not panics. The U.S. experience between the Civil War and World War I witnessed several banking panics but no significant waves of bank failures. It is useful to recognize panic and insolvency as separate aspects of banking crises because these different aspects reflect separate causal influences. In my review of the history of banking crises, therefore, I take account of both panics and episodes of high insolvency. Nevertheless, the key insight of this paper – that politically driven rules of the banking game drive the presence or absence of crisis risk – applies to both the panic and insolvency aspects of banking crises; that is, poorly designed structures and incentives for the banking system explain both the propensity for banking panics and the propensity for severe waves of bank failures.

This review offers important insights for policy makers. The crisis of 2007–2009 has sharpened or redefined many public policy questions of central importance to prudential financial regulation (a means of preventing crises) and the proper role of government assistance policy (a means of mitigating the costs of crises). What do we learn from the policy responses to banking crises in the past about the appropriate reforms we should undertake in reaction to recent events? How should the past guide our current policy adaptations?

A fourth lesson from the history of banking crises concerns the circumstances that tend to produce effective learning in the policy responses to crises. In previous banking crises, reforms have often followed in the wake of crises, but the record of reform is uneven. One successful historical reform described in this paper – the mid-nineteenth century British reform of the Bank of England, reviewed in Section 4, which successfully eliminated lending rules that gave rise to the frequent panics that plagued Britain in the early nineteenth century – shows that meaningful structural reforms that reduce incentives to take on excessive risk can stabilize banking systems. On the other hand, policy responses sometimes make matters worse: the failure to re-charter a central bank in the U.S. in the 1830s reflected, in part, mistaken views about the Second Bank of the United States during the crises of 1819 and 1825; and the bank regulatory changes in the U.S. in 1933 reflected political deal making rather than a proper response to the root causes of banking instability.

After considering these historical perspectives on the origins of banking distress and the policy solutions to address it – which consist of a detailed analysis of U.S. banking crises in Section 2, a broader review of the global history of bank insolvency in Section 3, and the history of British panics in Section 4 – Section 5 reviews the causes of the financial crisis of 2007–2009 and considers prospects for reform today. Section 6 concludes.

5.2 The microeconomic foundations of U.S. banking crises: 1790–1933

The peculiar fragility of U.S. banks in the pre-Depression era

As many scholars have recognized for many years, U.S. banks were unusually vulnerable to systemic banking crises compared to banks in other countries (for reviews, see Bordo 1985, and Calomiris 2000). The U.S. was uniquely vulnerable to panics in the years between the Civil War and World War I. Sprague (1910) and Calomiris and Gorton (1991) identify six episodes of particularly severe banking panics in the United States between the Civil War and World War I. Prior to the Civil War, there were other nationwide banking crises in 1819, 1837, and 1857, in which both systemwide panic and many bank failures occurred. In the 1920s, the U.S. experienced waves of bank failures in agricultural states, which have always been identified with fundamental shocks to banks, and which did not give rise to national or regional panics.

Other countries, including the U.S.'s northern neighbor, Canada, did not suffer banking crises during these episodes of systemic U.S. banking distress. The key difference between the U.S. and other countries historically lay in the structure of the U.S. banking system. The U.S. system was mainly based on unit banking – geographically isolated single-office banks. Unit banking meant that banks could not enjoy diversification economies by pooling loan risks from different regions. Unit banking, which resulted in thousands, and sometimes tens of thousands of banks, also limited the ability of banks to pursue collective action by pooling resources during periods of adverse shocks. A system with tens of thousands of geographically distant banks simply could not organize appropriate collective action to stem financial crises.[4] Other countries did not choose the fragmented U.S. approach to banking, and no other country experienced the U.S. pattern of periodic banking panics prior to World War I, or the waves of agricultural bank failures that gripped the U.S. in the 1920s.

Canada's early decision to permit branch banking throughout the country ensured that banks were geographically diversified and thus resilient to large sectoral shocks (like those to agriculture in the 1920s and 1930s), able to compete through the establishment of branches in rural areas (because of low overhead costs of establishing additional branches), and able to coordinate the banking system's response in moments of confusion to avoid depositor runs (the number of banks was small, and assets were highly concentrated in several nationwide institutions). Coordination among banks facilitated systemic stability by allowing banks to manage incipient panic episodes to prevent widespread bank runs. In Canada, the Bank of Montreal occasionally would coordinate actions by the large Canadian banks to stop crises before the public was even aware of a possible threat (Calomiris 2000, Chapter 1).

The United States was unable to mimic this behavior on a national or regional scale, although during the antebellum period, a few southern branch banking states, and three Midwestern states that formed mutual guarantee systems with small numbers of members, were able to implement successful, stabilizing coalitions of banks at the state level for purposes of mutual protection during banking crises (Calomiris 1989, 1990, 2000; Calomiris and Schweikart 1991). But these were short-lived and isolated exceptions; U.S. law prohibited nationwide branching, and most states prohibited or limited within-state branching. U.S. banks were numerous (e.g., numbering more than 29,000 in 1920), undiversified, insulated from competition, and geographically isolated from one another, and thus were unable to diversify adequately or to coordinate their response to panics (U.S. banks did establish clearing houses in cities, which facilitated local responses to panics beginning in the 1850s, as emphasized by Timberlake 1984 and Gorton 1985).

The fragmented structure of U.S. banking explains why the United States uniquely suffered banking panics in the years between the Civil War and World War I despite the fact that the vast majority of banks were healthy throughout this period, and were consistently able to avoid ultimate failure.[5] Empirical studies show that the major U.S. banking panics of 1873, 1884, 1890, 1893, 1896, and 1907 were moments of heightened asymmetric information about bank risk, but not times when bank failure risk was large for the country as a whole (Calomiris and Gorton 1991; Bruner and Carr 2007).

Banking necessarily entails the delegation of decision making to bankers, who specialize in screening and monitoring borrowers and making non-transparent investments. Bankers consequently have private information about the attendant risks. During normal times, the risk premium banks pay in capital markets and money markets contains a small "opacity" premium – part of the risk depositors and bank stockholders face and charge for comes from not being able to observe the value of bank assets moment to moment – that is, not being able to mark bank portfolios to market. During the U.S. panics, the normally small opacity premium became very large, as people became aware that risks had increased and as they also were aware of what they *didn't* know, namely the incidence among banks of the probable losses that accompanied the observable increased risk.

Calomiris and Gorton (1991) show that banking panics were uniquely predictable events that happened at business cycle peaks. In the pre-World War I period (1875–1913), every quarter in which the liabilities of failed businesses rose by more than 50 percent (seasonally adjusted) and the stock market fell by more than 8 percent, a panic happened in the following quarter. This happened five times, and the Panic of 1907 was the last of those times. Significant national panics (i.e., events that gave rise to a collective response by the New York Clearing House) never happened otherwise during this period.

Bank failure rates in the years between the Civil War and World War I, even during these panic episodes, were low, and the losses to depositors associated with them were also small. In 1893, the panic with the highest failure rate and highest depositor loss rate, depositor losses were less than 0.1 percent of GDP (Calomiris 2007). *Expected* depositor losses during the panics also appear to have been small. Sprague (1910, pp. 57–58, 423–424) reports that the discount applied to bankers' cashier checks of New York City banks at the height of the Panic of 1873 did not exceed 3.5 percent, and with the exception of an initial ten-day period, that discount remained below 1 percent. A similar pattern was visible in the Panic of 1893. A 1 percent premium would be consistent with depositors in a New York City bank estimating a 10 percent chance of a bank's failing with a 10 percent depositor loss if it failed. Clearly, banking panics during this era were traceable to real shocks, but those shocks had small consequences for bank failures in the aggregate, and even at the height of the crisis those consequences were expected to be small. Historical U.S. panics teach us that even a small expected loss can lead depositors to demand their funds, so that they can sit on the sidelines until the incidence of loss within the banking system has been revealed (usually a process that took a matter of weeks).

Bank failure rates in the 1830s, 1850s, and 1920s were higher than those of the other pre-Depression systemic U.S. banking crisis episodes. The 1830s, in particular, saw a major macroeconomic contraction that caused many banks to fail, which historians trace to large fundamental problems that had their sources in government-induced shocks to the money supply (Rousseau 2002), unprofitable bank-financed infrastructure investments that went sour (Schweikart 1987), and international balance of payments shocks (Temin 1969).

The 1920s agricultural bank failures were also closely linked to fundamental problems, in this case, the collapses of agricultural prices at the end of World War I, which were manifested in local bank failures because of the lack of regional or national loan portfolio diversification (Calomiris 1992; Alston, Grove, and Wheelock 1994).

In both the 1830s and the 1920s, some states suffered more than others from waves of bank distress. In the 1830s, states that had an active role in directing the credit of their banks faired particularly badly (Schweikart 1987). Prior to both the bank failure waves of the 1830s and the 1920s, some states had enacted systems of deposit insurance in which neither entry nor risk taking was effectively constrained. These states experienced far worse banking system failure rates and insolvency severity of failed banks than did other states (Calomiris 1989, 1990, 1992).[6] Indeed, the basis for the substantial opposition to federal deposit insurance in the 1930s – an opposition that included President Franklin

D. Roosevelt, his Treasury Secretary, and the Federal Reserve – was the disastrous experimentation with insurance in several U.S. states during the early twentieth century, which resulted in banking collapses in all the states that adopted insurance, and especially severe collapses in states that made deposit insurance compulsory.

In the 1920s, state-chartered banks that participated in deposit insurance fared much worse than either national banks in those states or state-chartered banks in neighboring states. The disastrous experience of those banks reflected a combination of moral hazard and adverse selection. Moral hazard was reflected in the higher loan-to-asset ratios and lower capital-to-asset ratios of state-chartered banks in insured states. Furthermore, states that passed deposit insurance experienced substantial entry into banking by small operators in rural areas, who apparently overestimated the potential for agricultural prices (temporarily boosted by World War I) to remain high.

In contrast, in the 1920s, states that had enacted laws permitting branch banking tended to outperform unit banking states, both with respect to failure rates and failure severity (Calomiris 1990, 1992). The evidence of the stabilizing effects of even limited branch banking in the U.S. (note that branching was not permitted across states, and in many cases was constrained even when it was allowed within states) helped to produce significant relaxations of branch banking restrictions in many states and a merger wave of banks during the 1920s. From 1921 through 1931, more than five thousand banks were absorbed by acquirers. In 1910, for the U.S. as a whole, there were 292 branching banks operating 548 branches, with total loans and investments of $1.3 billion, and in 1920, there were 530 branching banks operating 1,281 branches, with total loans and investments of $6.9 billion; by 1931, there were 723 branching banks operating 3,467 branches, with total loans and investments of $20.7 billion (Calomiris 2000, p. 57).

5.2.1 U.S. bank distress during the Great Depression

The legacy of branch banking restrictions continued to destabilize banks during the Depression. Mitchener (2005) finds that states that prohibited branching had higher rates of bank failure, *ceteris paribus*. Despite these trends and evidence, the stabilizing trend toward bank consolidation and greater structural stability in the U.S. was derailed by the global macroeconomic policy disaster of the Great Depression, and its adverse political consequences for continuing bank consolidation. Most importantly, Congressmen Henry Steagall of Alabama lobbied successfully on behalf of his state's unit bankers for federal deposit insurance, which was embraced by unit bankers as a political tool to prevent competition and continuing pressure for consolidation (Calomiris and White 1994). Initially deposit insurance was passed as a temporary emergency measure limited to only cover small deposits (effectively a subsidy for small banks, for whom such deposits comprised a large fraction of their liabilities). Despite the opposition of Senator Carter Glass, the Federal Reserve System, the Treasury Department, and

President Roosevelt – all of whom were aware of the disastrous consequences of deposit insurance in the states that had experimented with it in the early twentieth century – Steagall managed to succeed in passing deposit insurance, which was soon transformed from a temporary to a permanent measure, and which now covers virtually all U.S. deposits.

Beginning in the 1880s there had been 150 attempts to introduce federal deposit insurance legislation in Congress (Calomiris and White 1994). Opponents understood and espoused the theoretical arguments against deposit insurance that are familiar today – that deposit insurance removes depositors' incentives to monitor and discipline banks, that it frees bankers to take imprudent risks (especially when they have little or no remaining equity at stake, and see an advantage in "resurrection risk taking"); and that the absence of discipline promotes banker incompetence, which leads to unwitting risk taking. Deposit insurance won the day as legislation in 1933 for political, not ideological reasons, and ironically (given Roosevelt's opposition) remains the main surviving legacy of the banking legislation of the New Deal – a stark reminder of the power of crises to change the course of banking regulation.[7]

Deposit insurance, which was very limited in coverage, and became effective only in 1934, after the banking crises of 1930–1933 had passed, had little role in stabilizing banks during the Depression of 1929–1933. Bank failures and losses were high in the early 1930s by historical standards. Recent research on the Depression has investigated the extent to which those failures reflected extremely adverse macroeconomic shocks and their consequences for bank borrowers, as opposed to excessive, panicked responses to those shocks by depositors that may have forced many solvent banks into financial distress. Recent research shows that much if not all of the bank distress of the 1930s resulted from fundamental shocks to bank assets, much like the shocks that had buffeted agricultural banks in the 1920s.

The list of fundamental shocks that weakened banks during the Great Depression is a long and varied one. It includes declines in the value of bank loan portfolios produced by waves of rising default risk in the wake of regional, sectoral, or national macroeconomic shocks to bank borrowers, as well as monetary policy-induced declines in the prices of the bonds held by banks.

Friedman and Schwartz (1963) argued that many bank failures resulted from unwarranted "panic" and that failing banks were in large measure illiquid rather than insolvent. Friedman and Schwartz's emphasis on contagion posited that bank failures mainly reflected a problem of illiquidity rather than insolvency. Illiquid but solvent financial institutions, in their view, failed purely as the result of withdrawal demands by depositors, particularly during sudden moments of panic. In contrast, an insolvent institution fails to repay depositors as the result of fundamental losses in asset value, rather than the suddenness of depositor withdrawals.[8]

Using a narrative approach similar to that of Friedman and Schwartz, but relying on data disaggregated at the level of Federal Reserve districts, Wicker (1996) argues that it is incorrect to identify the banking crisis of 1930 and the first banking crisis of 1931 as national panics comparable to those of the pre-Fed era. According to Wicker, the proper way to understand the process of banking failure during the Depression is to disaggregate, both by region and by bank, because heterogeneity was very important in determining the incidence of bank failures.[9]

Microeconomic studies of banking distress have provided some useful evidence on the reactions of individual banks to economic distress. White (1984) shows that the failures of banks in 1930 are best explained as a continuation of the agricultural distress of the 1920s, and are traceable to fundamental disturbances in agricultural markets. Declines in railroad bonds were also significant in some cases (Meltzer 2003, p. 346).

Calomiris and Mason (1997) study the Chicago banking panic of June 1932 (a locally isolated phenomenon). They find that the panic resulted in a temporary contraction of deposits that affected both solvent and insolvent banks. Fundamentals, however, determined which banks survived. Apparently, no solvent banks failed during that panic. Banks that failed during the panic were observably weaker *ex ante*, judging from their balance sheet and income statements, and from the default risk premia they paid on their debts. Furthermore, the rate of deposit contraction was not identical across banks; deposits declined more in failing banks than in surviving banks.

Calomiris and Wilson (2004) study the behavior of New York City banks during the interwar period, and in particular, analyze the contraction of their lending during the 1930s. They find that banking distress was an informed market response to observable weaknesses in particular banks, traceable to *ex ante* bank characteristics. It resulted in bank balance sheet contraction, but this varied greatly across banks; banks with higher default risk were disciplined more by the market (that is, experienced greater deposit withdrawals), which encouraged them to target a low risk of default.

Calomiris and Mason (2003a) construct a survival duration model of Fed member banks throughout the country from 1929 to 1933. This model combines aggregate data at the national, state, and county level with bank-specific data on balance sheets and income statements to identify the key contributors to bank failure risk and to gauge the relative importance of fundamentals and panics as explanations of bank failure. Calomiris and Mason find that a fundamentals-based model can explain most of the failure experience of banks in the U.S. prior to 1933. They identify a significant, but small, national panic effect around September of 1931, and some isolated regional effects that may have been panics, but prior to 1933, banking panics were not very important contributors to bank failures compared to fundamentals.

The fact that a consistent model based on fundamentals can explain the vast majority of U.S. bank failures prior to 1933 has interesting implications. First, it indicates that the influence of banking panics as an independent source of shock to the economy was not important early in the Depression. Only in 1933, at the trough of the Depression, did failure risk become importantly de-linked from local, regional, and national economic conditions and from fundamentals relating to individual bank structure and performance. Second, the timing of this observed rise in risk unrelated to indicators of credit risk is itself interesting. In late 1932 and early 1933, currency risk became increasingly important; depositors had reason to fear that President Roosevelt would leave the gold standard, which gave them a special reason to want to convert their deposits into (high-valued) dollars before devaluation of the dollar (Wigmore 1987).

As part of their bank-level analysis of survival duration, Calomiris and Mason (2003a) also consider whether, outside the windows of "panics" identified by Friedman and Schwartz, the occurrence of bank failures in close proximity to a bank affects the probability of survival of the bank, after taking into account the various fundamental determinants of failure. Calomiris and Mason consider this measure of "contagious failure" an upper bound, since in part it measures unobserved cross-sectional heterogeneity common to banks located in the same area, in addition to true contagion. They find small, but statistically significant, effects associated with this measure. The omission of this variable from the analysis raises forecasted survival duration by an average of 0.2 percent. They also consider other regional dummy variables associated with Wicker's (1996) instances of identified regional panics, and again find effects on bank failure risk that are small in national importance.

The large number of bank failures in the U.S. during the Great Depression, a phenomenon that was largely confined to small banks, primarily reflected the combination of extremely large fundamental macroeconomic shocks and the vulnerable nature of the country's unit banking system. Panic was not a significant contributor to banking distress on a nationwide basis until near the trough of the Depression, at the end of 1932. For these reasons, the Great Depression bank failure experience has more in common with the bank failures of the 1920s than the panics of the pre-World War I era.

5.2.2 Central banking and bank instability in U.S. history

Part of the microeconomic rules of the game in any banking system relate to the operations of the central bank, which include its policies for purchasing assets or lending against them, how it funds itself, and the extent to which and the ways in which it competes with other banks. In explaining Great Britain's change from a crisis-prone financial system from 1800 through 1857 to a crisis-resistant system after 1866 – the subject of Section 4 – the evolution of the Bank of England's lending policies, its financing, its competition with other banks, and the ways in which banking crises affected the evolution of these three aspects, will be central to the explanation of the stabilization of the system after 1857. But in the U.S., the role of central banking in the history of banking crises was more limited.

The first central bank, the Bank of the United States (BUS), founded in 1791 and chartered for twenty years, was the only nationally chartered institution in the country and the only one to operate in more than one state. It operated as a for-profit banking enterprise (in which the government owned one-fifth of its $10 million in initial capital stock), made loans, issued notes, and accepted deposits. It was not conceived as a tool for regulating other banks, or acting as a lender of last resort to the financial system. The BUS's most important role in the economy was as a lender to the government and as a fiscal agent for the government, managing the financial flows relating to taxes and debts.

The first panic in U.S. history, in 1792, occurred just as the BUS was gearing up its operations. As Sylla, Wright, and Cowen (2009) show, the early experience of the U.S. in dealing with the Panic of 1792 illustrates that central bankers can be sources of banking system risk as well as mitigators of those risks. The nascent BUS actually fueled the panic through an overexpansion of credit in its first months of operation. But the Treasury Secretary, Alexander Hamilton, acted as an ad hoc central banker, inventing and applying "Bagehot's (1873) rule" of lending freely on good collateral at a penalty rate eight decades before that rule would be penned.[10] Thus, although the BUS itself was not a source of stability during the panic, Secretary Hamilton and the Treasury acted as an effective ad hoc lender of last resort.

Sylla, Wright, and Cowen (2009) argue that Hamilton's success in undoing the negative effects of the BUS's destabilizing actions had significance beyond its immediate consequences for the financial system; the intervention avoided a political backlash against the Hamiltonian financial system, of which the BUS was a part. Such a backlash in response to failed financial policy innovations was more than a hypothetical possibility in 1792, given the experience of France and Britain decades earlier:

> Earlier in the eighteenth century, John Law had attempted to modernize France's financial system, but his efforts backfired when he failed to prevent the collapse of the Mississippi Bubble in 1720. At the same time, across the Channel, the collapse of the related South Sea Bubble also led to financial crisis. The British financial system, however, was more developed than that of France, as Britain had begun the modernization process in 1688, whereas France did not do so until 1715. A wounded but robust British financial system survived the shock, although legislation passed during the crisis stunted the development of Britain's corporate sector for a century.
>
> (p. 63)

This discussion illustrates two broader points: (1) the actions of central banks are not always stabilizing for the banking system, and (2) central banks' privileges can be enacted and also withdrawn. Indeed, the charter of the BUS was allowed to lapse, largely as the result of Jeffersonian objections to the concentration of financial power in a national bank.

Problems in managing fiscal affairs during the War of 1812, along with a desire to reestablish specie convertibility of state bank notes after the suspension of convertibility that had attended the War, led to the establishment of the Second Bank of the United States (SBUS), in which the government subscribed for one-fifth of its $35 million in capital stock. The SBUS was charged with assisting the government in its financial affairs, reestablishing specie convertibility of other banks' notes, and operating a general banking business. Like its predecessor it operated as the only nationally chartered bank until its charter's renewal was blocked by President Jackson in 1832. In 1836 the SBUS was granted a new charter by the State of Pennsylvania, and operated as a state bank after that date.

As Temin (1969, p. 46) points out, like its predecessor in 1792, the SBUS became overextended almost immediately after it was chartered. Its western and southern branches did not coordinate their lending with the eastern branches. Notes issued by the SBUS branches in the periphery to fund loans were presented for payment in the East, where the SBUS branches accepted them at par, thereby encouraging further note issuance and lending by its branches in the West and South. The lack of discipline in 1817–1818 extended to other banks as well. The Treasury asked the SBUS to delay the collection of balances owed to it by state banks in 1817 and 1818, which removed the SBUS as a source of interregional discipline over other banks' issuance and promoted increased leverage in the banking system. When as an act of self-preservation the SBUS finally cracked down on its branches in the West and South and on other banks, by demanding that they support their own note issues and pay their outstanding debts, a contraction of credit resulted, which according to Catterall (1902) "precipitated the panic." Gouge (1833) famously quipped that "The Bank was saved and the people were ruined." Public hostility toward the SBUS because of its role in causing the Panic of 1819 never disappeared (Temin 1969, p. 48).

The hostility toward the SBUS was further fueled by perceptions of its behavior during the financial crisis in 1825–1826, when once again it acted to limit its own credit and disciplined the state banks by demanding that they redeem their obligations. The public had expected the SBUS to prevent a financial contraction in 1825–1826. According to Hilt (2009), the SBUS was a stabilizing force during the 1825–1826 financial crisis. He argues that, despite widespread financial failures during the crisis, "there was no generalized banking crisis in the United States … in part because of the Second Bank of the United States worked assiduously with its New York branch to provide credit to the banking community there." Hilt (2009, footnote 36) also points to evidence that Nicholas Biddle (the SBUS's leader) viewed this as an important part of the mission of the SBUS. Nevertheless, such lending was limited by the SBUS's need to protect itself during the 1825–1826 contraction.

The public hostility toward the SBUS that resulted from its failure to prevent financial crises was largely misplaced. The government itself had encouraged the excessive expansion of credit in the periphery in 1817–1818, and had asked the SBUS to accommodate it. Furthermore, according to Hilt (2009), the SBUS had, in fact, been successful in preventing the financial collapse of 1825–1826 from turning into a bona fide banking crisis as the result of the assistance it provided New York banks. The SBUS's decisions to contract in 1819 and 1825–1826 were necessary for its own preservation; it was, after all, a privately owned bank, and therefore, responsible for its own survival and profitability. Most importantly, the upheavals of 1819 and 1825, like that of 1792, illustrated the limitations of the powers of the BUS and the SBUS. The BUS and SBUS lacked the full-fledged powers of a central bank to deal with crises. Indeed, some financial historians (Temin 1969, p. 45) have questioned whether the BUS or SBUS qualify to be called central banks. Unlike the Bank of England, the BUS and SBUS did not have the power to issue an unlimited supply of their own bank notes with the implied backing of the sovereign. It is hard to fault the SBUS for failing to use powers that it did not possess.

That is not to say that the SBUS was entirely powerless or unsuccessful in reducing systemic risk in the banking system, as the successful interventions in New York by the SBUS in 1825–1826 illustrate. Because of its special position as the only bank operating branches in various regions, the SBUS was large, had wide geographical reach, and played an especially important role in the bankers acceptance market for financing commerce (intermediation of the financing of trade flows via its various branches, as described in Calomiris 2000, Chapter 1) and in the market for transporting and redeeming the notes of other issuing banks. In addition to its limited powers to assist banks during crises, it could act, and did act, to stabilize the system and help avoid the risk of panics, in two ways: (1) as a source of discipline over other banks' note issuance, it limited the overextension of credit and bank leveraging during booms, and (2) as a unique interregional provider of trade credit, the SBUS reduced seasonal volatility in financial markets related to the planting and harvesting of crops. Bernstein, Hughson, and Weidenmier (2009a) find evidence in support of increased average risk, and greater seasonality of risk, after the failure to re-charter the SBUS. From 1816–1836 stock return volatility across the months of September and October (the harvesting season) averaged 2.45 percent, virtually identical to the 2.43 percent for the rest of the year. Following the SBUS's demise, from 1837 to 1860, stock return volatility rose to 6.30 percent in September and October versus 5.02 percent during the rest of the year. These volatilities rose even higher during the National Banking Period, where they were 7.30 and 5.80 percent, respectively.

Despite its stabilizing role in the financial system, the inability of the SBUS to prevent financial crises, along with various other political and ideological battles in which the SBUS and its leader, Nicholas Biddle, became embroiled, ultimately resulted in a fierce battle over the future of the bank, and Jackson's eventual veto of its re-chartering.[11]

The history of the SBUS illustrates a broader theme in the early history of central banking. Central banks, including the BUS, the SBUS, the Bank of England, and others, were chartered as for-profit companies with special privileges (in the case of the BUS and the SBUS, the special privileges had to do with their unique branching operations, and their unique relationship with the government) that also gave rise to the expectation that they would undertake special responsibilities to the public in addition to maximizing their economic value for their stockholders. That dual mandate of profitability and social responsibility implied that central banks not only had to satisfy their stockholders that they were achieving a good return and acting prudently, but also that they had to satisfy the public, through elected officials, that they were achieving their social mission. Because achieving social missions (like making markets in risky bank notes at par) tends to be costly, there has often been an inherent conflict between the private profitability of central banks and their public missions.

That conflict is precisely what makes eighteenth and nineteenth century central banks so interesting to financial historians (Goodhart 1995). Even if central bank management only cared about value maximization (a distinct possibility), bank managers had to navigate the political process that was the source of their valuable special privileges. In other words, even a selfish central banker had to find a way to optimally give services to the public – providing enough continuing service to society to prevent the central bank's privileges from being revoked. Some central bankers, like the managers of the BUS and SBUS, did not succeed in satisfying the demands for public service, and thereby lost their charters. Other central bankers, like those at the Bank of England, successfully adapted to changing circumstances (especially financial crisis in the nineteenth century) to satisfy changing public demands, and thereby managed to keep their charters and their jobs, although the nature of their privileges and responsibilities changed significantly over time as the game between the central banks and the public evolved. (We will return to that theme in Section 4's discussion of the evolving role of the Bank of England and its consequences for the stabilization of the British banking system in the nineteenth century.)

The U.S. banking system operated without a central bank from 1836 until 1913 when the Federal Reserve System was established. The establishment of the Fed was a direct reaction to the Panic of 1907, and the perception that private bankers acting as a coalition (organized to some extent through their local clearing houses, and through ad hoc efforts like those undertaken in 1907 by J.P. Morgan) had insufficient ability to preserve systemic stability. In the wake of the 1907 Panic, the National Monetary Commission was established, and it issued a voluminous and substantive report in 1910, which formed the factual and theoretical basis on which the Federal Reserve Act of 1913 was constructed, and to this day the National Monetary Commission report still contains some of the most valuable information about the operations of banks of that era throughout the world.

The Federal Reserve System, like all central banks, was a creature of a political process and compromise that balanced various competing interests, and that compromise evolved over time. The structure of the system (twelve regional Reserve Banks and a Board in Washington, with member bank ownership of the Reserve Banks) evolved into a system effectively owned by the taxpayers but still managed by a process of power sharing that gave weight to local bank and business interests (who control the Reserve Banks' boards and executive appointments), political leaders in Washington (who appoint Federal Reserve Board members and to whom the Board reports), and rural interests (who received special favors in the structuring of clearing arrangements and in the use of agriculture-related loans as collateral).

The philosophical foundations of the Fed are rather amorphous, and much of the logic that was embodied in its initial rules has been discredited by monetary economists, notably the "real bills doctrine" that was supposed to govern its lending operations. Suffice it to say for our current purposes that the Fed obtained broad powers to lend to member banks against good collateral (initially construed as high-quality commercial bills, and later, also government securities) and to engage in open market operations to control the supply of reserve holdings by member banks at the central bank.

Importantly, the Fed's charter and its powers did not envision it as a crisis manager for failing banks or as a bailout agency, and the Fed's role in causing or averting banking crises primarily revolved around the way its policies affected *market* prices and flows, rather than the affairs of particular banks. The Fed was designed to use lending and other actions to regulate the aggregate supply of reserves, money, and credit in a way that would reduce seasonal and cyclical volatility of interest rates and increase the seasonal and cyclical elasticity of reserves and loans (initially, it was expected to accomplish those seasonal and cyclical objectives while remaining on the gold standard, a goal that was temporarily put aside several times, and permanently abandoned in 1973).

The record of the Fed as a source of stability for the banking system is mixed. On the one hand, the Fed was sometimes a source of great instability in the system because the policy rules it followed for targeting monetary policy were often ill-conceived. Friedman and Schwartz (1963), and many others since, have shown that Fed monetary policy errors produced the monetary collapse that caused the economic and banking crises of the 1930s, and Calomiris and Mason (2003a) document measurable connections between the deteriorating macroeconomic and local economic environments in which banks operated and the resulting bank failures.

Wicker (1966), Brunner and Meltzer (1968), and Wheelock (1991) trace the Fed's policy errors in the 1930s and at other times to the misuse of interest rates and borrowed reserves as short-term monetary policy instruments. Ideologically, this view was related to the "real bills doctrine," the notion that the Fed's role was to accommodate commercial demand (Meltzer 2003, pp. 273–274). Wheelock (1991), in particular, argues that it was a consistently faulty monetary policy methodology, rather than a lack of leadership at the Fed following Benjamin Strong's death (which Friedman and Schwartz (1963) posit to explain Fed failures after 1929), that explains the policy errors that gave rise to the Great Depression. The monetary policy errors that caused the Great Depression show that vesting authority in a central bank can be risky; although the central bank may intend to stabilize the system, it may in fact have the opposite effect.

On the other hand, there is substantial evidence (Miron 1986; Richardson and Troost 2006; and Bernstein, Hughson, and Weidenmier 2009b) that the founding of the Fed reduced liquidity risk in the banking system, which in turn reduced the propensity for bank panics. Miron (1986) showed that the founding of the Fed was associated with reduced seasonal variability of interest rates and increased seasonal variability of lending. Miron, however, did not explain how the Fed achieved this result. Why, exactly, did Fed lending practices make the loan supply function more elastic?

Miron's (1986) findings can be explained by a variant of the deposit risk targeting model in Calomiris and Wilson (2004). In that model, the riskiness of deposits is a function of bank asset risk and bank leverage. Because total bank capital and total cash assets in the economy do not vary much over the year, a seasonal increase in bank lending (especially to finance crop harvesting and transport in the fall, which Davis, Hanes, and Rhode (2007) show was largely driven by the cotton cycle) implies a commensurate increase in bank asset risk and in bank leverage, which unambiguously means an increase in the riskiness of deposits (the actuarily fair default risk premium). This is a source of seasonal variation in the risk of deposit withdrawals, since market discipline makes the risk of withdrawal in the deposit market sensitive to increases in default risk (i.e., some depositors are intolerant of risk, and will withdraw when risk increases). A bank that increases its lending, *ceteris paribus*, faces increased deposit withdrawal risk, particularly if an adverse cyclical shock hits during a seasonal lending spike. All six of the major banking panics of the pre-World War I era happened at cyclical peaks; they were clearly responses to adverse economic shocks to banks' balance sheets (Calomiris and Gorton 1991). Furthermore, these panics all occurred either during the spring planting season or the fall harvest, at times when lending (and bank liquidity risk) was at a seasonal peak.

From the perspective of this model, the founding of the Fed provided a means of reducing liquidity risk to banks by giving them a source of liquidity to stem deposit withdrawals (making them less vulnerable to withdrawal risk at times when seasonal lending peaks coincided with cyclical downturns). The founding of the Fed thus flattened the bank loan supply function, making loans vary more over the cycle, and interest rates vary less.

Bernstein, Hughson, and Weidenmier (2009b) provide additional evidence consistent with that interpretation. They compare the standard deviations of stock returns and short-term interest rates over time in the months of September and October (the two months of the year when markets were most vulnerable to a crash because of financial stringency from the harvest season) with the rest of the year before and after the establishment of the Fed. Stock volatility in those two months fell more than 40 percent, and interest rate volatility more than 70 percent, after the founding of the Fed. Like the SBUS before it (discussed above), the Fed succeeded in reducing seasonal variations in liquidity. They also show that this result is driven by years in which business cycles peaked. In other words, the main risk that the Fed eliminated was associated with combined cyclical peaks in economic activity and seasonal peaks in lending.

Many commentators have faulted the Federal Reserve for failing to prevent bank failures during the Great Depression with more aggressive discount window lending. While it is certainly true that expansionary monetary policy, particularly in 1929–1931, could have made an enormous difference in preventing bank distress (through its effects on macroeconomic fundamentals), that is not the same as saying that more generous terms at the discount window (holding constant the overall monetary policy stance) would have made much of a difference. Discount window lending only helps preserve banks that are suffering from illiquidity, which was not the primary problem underlying large depositor withdrawals.

Indeed, in 1932, President Hoover created the Reconstruction Finance Corporation (RFC), to enlarge the potential availability of liquidity, but this additional source of liquidity assistance made no difference in helping borrowing banks avoid failure (Mason 2001). As commentators at the time noted, because collateralized RFC and Fed loans were senior to deposits, and because deposit withdrawals from weak banks reflected real concerns about bank insolvency, loans from the Fed and the RFC to banks experiencing withdrawals did not help much, and actually could harm banks, since those senior loans from the Fed and the RFC reduced the amount of high quality assets available to back deposits, which actually increased the riskiness of deposits and created new incentives for deposit withdrawals. In 1933, however, once the RFC was permitted to purchase banks' preferred stock (which was junior to deposits), RFC assistance to troubled banks was effective in reducing the risk of failure (Mason 2001).

Despite the limitations inherent in the ability of collateralized lending to prevent bank failure, there is some evidence that greater Fed assistance to banks early in the Depression could have been helpful in avoiding some bank failures. Richardson and Troost (2006) show that, despite the limited ability of Fed discount window lending to absorb credit risk, Fed provision of liquidity to member banks mitigated bank failure risk associated with illiquidity somewhat in 1930, and could have played a greater role in stemming illiquidity-induced failures if the Fed had been more willing to relax lending standards to member banks. They study the failure propensities of Mississippi banks. The Federal Reserve Act of 1913 divided Mississippi between the 6th (Atlanta) and 8th (St. Louis) Federal Reserve Districts. The Atlanta Fed championed a more activist role in providing loans to member banks experiencing troubles, while the St. Louis Fed rigidly adhered to the real bills doctrine and eschewed the extension of credit to troubled banks. Mississippi banks in the 6th District failed at lower rates than in the 8th District, particularly during the banking panic in the fall of 1930, suggesting that more aggressive discount window lending reduced failure rates during periods of panic.

5.2.3 Summary of U.S. historical experience

The unusually unstable U.S. historical experience of frequent nationwide banking panics (1819, 1837, 1857, 1873, 1884, 1890, 1893, 1896, 1907, and 1933) and a propensity for unusually severe and widespread waves of bank failures (the 1830s, the 1920s, and the 1930s) reflected a unique feature of the microeconomic structure of U.S. banking – namely the fragmented banking structure of unit banking – which made it harder to diversify lending risk *ex ante* and coordinate the management of banking system risk *ex post*.

Comparisons across regions and across states within the U.S. also reveal important cross-sectional differences in banking stability that are similarly traceable to structural features. The presence of branch banking, clearing houses, or other local institutional arrangements for collective action were stabilizing forces, but these stabilizing mechanisms were only permitted on a local or statewide basis. The presence of deposit insurance, which was advocated by unit bankers as a means of protecting them from debt market discipline, resulted in adverse selection in bank entry and moral hazard in bank risk taking, and was a destabilizing force that produced the worst localized bank failure experiences of the 1830s and the 1920s.

Early experiments with limited central banking in the U.S. resulted in the failure to re-charter central banks twice in the early nineteenth century, which reflected, in part, a difficulty in reconciling the financial limitations of a private bank of limited means with the public pressures on that bank to "pay for" its privileges by performing unprofitable services in the public interest. Although some observers accused the SBUS of contributing to financial instability through contractionary policies prior to and during both the Panic of 1819 and the financial crisis of 1825–1826, those accusations say more about unrealistic public expectations of the power of the SBUS to prevent systemic problems than they do about the desirability of rechartering the SBUS. Although neither the BUS or SBUS were equipped to act as lenders of last resort during crises, the SBUS succeeded in reducing systemic financial risk on average and over the seasonal cycle, foreshadowing the stabilizing effect of the Fed after 1913.

After the demise of the SBUS, the U.S. functioned without a central bank until the founding of the Fed in 1913. The record of the Fed vis-à-vis banking crises is mixed. On the one hand, the Fed (like the BUS in its first year of operation) could be a source of substantial risk to the system, resulting from inappropriate policy responses. The mistaken use of borrowed reserves and interest rates as monetary instruments created false impressions in 1929–1932 that encouraged monetary contraction, which precipitated the Great Depression, the real effects of which produced massive bank failures in the 1930s. On the other hand, the existence of the discount window substantially reduced systemic liquidity risk, especially the risk that banks would be caught in an illiquid position at times of seasonal peaks in lending that coincided with cyclical peaks in economic activity. Although the ability to employ the discount window to stem bank failures during the Depression was limited – since shocks buffeting banks were primarily related to solvency rather than illiquidity – there is evidence that relatively aggressive discount window lending by the Atlanta Fed during 1930 did help to prevent some bank failures.

In summary, the microeconomic rules of the banking game – the unit banking structure of the industry, the occasional reliance on destabilizing deposit insurance, and the lack of an effective lender of last resort for the pre-World War I era – all contributed to the peculiar historical instability of the U.S. banking system. The key destabilizing elements of the U.S. system – a fragmented industrial structure, the absence of an effective lender of last resort, and the occasional presence of a destabilizing deposit insurance regime – compounded one another. Canada, which avoided chartering a central bank until 1935, managed to avoid banking crises due to the stabilizing role of its branch banking system, despite the absence of a central bank. In the U.S., the fragility of the banking structure made the absence of a central bank more harmful than it otherwise would have been; likewise, the absence of an effective central bank magnified the destabilizing effects of unit banking.

5.3 A worldwide tale of two banking eras: 1875–1913 and 1978–2009

Although the U.S. was unique in its high propensity for panics (reflecting its peculiar banking structure), and it occasionally experienced high rates of banking loss, other countries sometimes experienced loss rates that exceeded that of the U.S. In the pre-World War I period (1875–1913), the highest nationwide banking system loss rate (i.e., the negative net worth of failed banks relative to GDP) for the U.S. was roughly 0.1 percent, which was the loss rate for bank failures in the panic of 1893. Other countries generally experienced even lower bank failure rates, but there were a handful of episodes in the world (between four and seven) during this period in which the negative net worth of failed banks exceeded 1 percent of GDP (a minimal severity standard used by Caprio and Klingebiel to gauge banking crises today).[12]

During the pre-World War I era, Argentina in 1890 and Australia in 1893 were the exceptional cases; they each suffered banking system losses of roughly 10 percent of GDP in the wake of real estate market collapses in those countries. The negative net worth of failed banks in Norway in 1900 was roughly 3 percent, and in Italy in 1893 roughly 1 percent of GDP, but with the possible exception of Brazil (for which data does not exist to measure losses), there seem to be no other cases in 1875–1913 in which banking losses in a country exceeded 1 percent of GDP (Calomiris 2007).

By recent standards, this record for the pre-World War I period is one of impressive banking stability, especially considering the high volatility of the macroeconomic environment during that period. In contrast, over the past thirty years roughly 140 episodes have been documented in which banking systems experienced losses in excess of 1 percent of GDP, and more than twenty episodes resulted in losses in excess of 10 percent of GDP, more than half of which resulted in losses in excess of 20 percent of GDP (these extreme cases include, for example, roughly 25–30 percent of GDP losses in Chile in 1982–83, Mexico in 1994–1995, Korea in 1997, and Thailand in 1997, and a greater than 50 percent loss in Indonesia in 1997).[13]

Loss rates in the pre-World War I period tended to be low because banks structured themselves to limit their risk of loss by maintaining adequate equity-to-assets ratios, sufficiently low asset risk, and adequate liquidity. Market discipline (the potential for depositors fearful of bank default to withdraw their funds) provided incentives for banks to behave prudently (for a theoretical framework, see Calomiris and Kahn 1991). The picture of small depositors lining up around the block to withdraw funds has received much attention by journalists and banking theorists, but perhaps the more important source of market discipline was the threat of an informed ("silent") run by large depositors (often other banks). Banks maintained relationships with each other through interbank deposits and the clearing of deposits, notes, and bankers' bills. Banks often belonged to clearing houses that set regulations and monitored members' behavior. A bank that lost the trust of its fellow bankers could not long survive.

Recent research attempting to explain the unprecedented systemic bank failures worldwide over the past three decades has emphasized the destabilizing effects of bank safety nets. This has been informed by the experience of the U.S. Savings and Loan industry debacle of the 1980s, the banking collapses in Japan and Scandinavia during the 1990s, and similar banking system debacles throughout the world. Empirical studies of this era of unprecedented frequency and severity of banking system losses have concluded uniformly that deposit insurance and other policies that protect banks from market discipline, intended as a cure for instability, have instead become the single greatest source of banking instability (see, for example, Caprio and Klingebiel 1996; Boyd *et al.* 2000; Demirguc-Kunt and Detragiache 2000; Barth, Caprio, and Levine 2006; Demirguc-Kunt, Kane, and Laeven 2009).

It is also significant that the four countries that suffered the most severe bank failure episodes of the pre-World War I era – Argentina, Australia, Norway, and Italy – had two things in common: (1) All of them suffered real estate boom and busts that exposed their financial systems to large losses; and (2) prior to these crises all of them had employed unusually large government subsidies for real estate risk taking that were designed to thwart market discipline (Calomiris 2007). In Argentina, that subsidy took the form of special mortgage guarantees issued by the government, which guaranteed holders of the mortgages repayment. Banks were licensed to originate these guaranteed mortgages, and then resold them as guaranteed liabilities in the London market, where they were traded as Argentine sovereign debts. This is akin to deposit insurance in that it makes the financing cost of the mortgage invariant to its risk, which entails the same moral hazard as deposit insurance: the guarantee makes the profitability of mortgage lending increasing in the riskiness of the mortgage portfolio, and thus encourages originators to lend to risky borrowers.

The Australian case was a bit different; financial market policies toward the private sector were not the primary means through which the government promoted the land boom that preceded the bust of 1893. The pre-1890 Australian economic expansion was largely an investment boom in which the government played a direct role in investing in land and financing farmers' investments. Government investments in railroads, telegraphs, irrigation, and farms were financed by government debt floated in the British capital market and by government-owned savings banks and postal savings banks (M. Butlin 1987; N. Butlin 1964; S. Butlin 1961; Davis and Gallman 2001).

The less dramatic banking system losses during the Norwegian and Italian land busts reflected less aggressive, more regionally focused government policies promoting land development. In Norway, that was achieved through government-sponsored lending and accommodative monetary policy; in Italy, this was achieved through liability protection for the Banca di Roma, which financed a Roman land boom at the behest of the Pope, who had lobbied for protection of the bank's liabilities (Canovai 1911). The Norwegian banks' losses amounted to roughly 3 percent of GDP, and the Italian banks' losses (which largely reflected exposures to the Roman land market) were roughly 1 percent of GDP (Calomiris 2007).

The theory behind the problem of destabilizing subsidization of risk taking has been well known for well over a century, and I have already noted that it was the basis for opposition to deposit insurance in the U.S. in 1933. Deposit insurance was seen by opponents as undesirable special interest legislation designed to benefit small banks (Calomiris and White 1994). Roosevelt, Glass, and others acquiesced for practical political reasons, to get other legislation passed, not because they wanted deposit insurance, per se. Bad economics is sometimes good politics. Similarly, Argentine mortgage subsidies were transparently intended to benefit landowners in the pampas, just as the real estate risk subsidies in Australia, Rome, and Norway were conscious attempts to support constituencies that favored real estate development.

It is worth emphasizing that all of these risk subsidizing government interventions (mortgage guarantees, liability insurance, government lending on land) were intended to overcome market discipline that had been limiting risk taking. Whatever their merits, these interventions served powerful special interests by subsidizing real estate risk, destabilized their country's banking systems, and produced substantial losses. Bank insolvency crises in the pre-World War I era fundamentally were about imprudent government policies.

Research on the banking collapses of the last three decades offers a similar message. Empirical findings uniformly show that the greater the role of government in directing credit or in providing protection to private banks through the government safety net (e.g., deposit insurance), the greater the risk of a banking collapse (Caprio and Klingebiel 1996; Boyd *et al.* 2000; Demirguc-Kunt and Detragiache 2000; Barth, Caprio, and Levine 2006; Demirguc-Kunt, Kane, and Laeven 2009). Some of this research has identified the political economy of subsidizing risk taking as a core problem, and one that would-be reformers and financial regulators have had a difficult time overcoming. Empirical research on prudential bank regulation emphasizes the inefficacy of government regulations in preventing risk taking (since they are subject to the same political forces that purposely subsidize risk), and the importance of subjecting some bank liabilities to the risk of loss to promote discipline of risk taking as the primary means of reining in excessive risk taking (Board of Governors 1999; Shadow Financial Regulatory Committee 2000; Mishkin 2001; Calomiris and Powell 2001; Barth, Caprio, and Levine 2006) – in other words, finding a means to use markets to constrain risk taking.

These studies of recent experience echo the conclusions of the studies of historical deposit insurance discussed above (Calomiris 1990, 1992), and the historical experiences of Argentina, Australia, Norway, and Italy in the pre-World

War I era. The difference is that what used to be the exception – moral hazard and adverse selection resulting from government protection that give rise to excessive risk taking – has become the rule.[14]

This evidence stands in sharp contrast to the approaches of Minsky (1975), Kindleberger (1978), and Diamond and Dybvig (1983) for explaining bank fragility. Rather than seeing market behavior, human nature, and the market-determined structure of bank balance sheets as the root cause of banking crises, this new literature argues that the solution to banking crises lies in empowering markets to rein in the risk taking that is otherwise subsidized by the government.

5.4 The political economy of central banking: the stabilization of British banking, 1800–1900

One of the most fascinating historical examples of a change from banking instability to stability occurred in Great Britain in the middle of the nineteenth century. As Capie (2009) notes, Britain experienced major banking panics in 1825, 1836–1839, 1847, 1857, and 1866, but then the propensity for panic ended for over a century (with the exception of the banking crisis that resulted from the start of World War I).[15] Scholars have traditionally credited changes in Bank of England policies with this transformation (Bagehot 1873; Andreades [1909] 1966; Hawtrey 1932, 1938; King 1936; Clapham 1944; Hughes 1960; Capie 2002, 2009). Prior to 1858, the Bank's policy was to accept a virtually unlimited amount of paper for discount at a uniform rate, both in the bubble phases leading up to financial crashes, and in the aftermath during the scramble for liquidity. In 1858 the Bank changed its discounting policies to make them significantly less generous, and over time, the Bank came to rely on variation in its discount rate and the use of open market operations as means of promoting monetary and financial stability (Hawtrey 1932, 1938). Furthermore, the decision not to assist Overend, Gurney & Co. during the crisis of 1866 was also significant, since it demonstrated that the newly announced 1858 policy change was credible. Together, policy actions in 1858 and 1866 substantially reduced problems of moral hazard in British banking.

Other changes in the microeconomic rules of the banking game, most notably greater freedom of entry into banking and expanded branching, were also complementary and helpful in stabilizing the system, partly because of how they affected the political equilibrium in which the Bank operated, and because greater banking system integration across regions reduced the demand for discounting bills.

All of these changes encouraged the evolution of the Bank from a destabilizing central bank with an uncertain future – one crippled by an inconsistent mixture of private and public missions that was forced to play a complex and uncertain political game to retain its privileges – into an institution with a relatively clear set of objectives and policies, which operated in a relatively stable financial and political environment. The combination of a well-defined understanding of the public mission of the Bank, and its success in managing systemic risk meant that public expectations of the Bank were less likely to be disappointed. The important political transition was from an early unstable political cycle of accommodation, crisis, conflict, and political reaction (over the course of each decade's financial crisis) to a political equilibrium after 1866 with a well-understood delineation of the Bank's responsibilities, effective rules to achieve those goals, and an absence of crises with political backlashes.

In addition to developing its operational tools for normal times (using variation in the discount rate and open market operations) the Bank developed a philosophy for assisting the financial system which was embodied in two incentive-compatible mechanisms of central bank assistance: (1) Bagehot's (1873) famous rule for lending during panics on good collateral at a penalty rate, and (2) risk sharing between the Bank and the London clearing banks in the provision of credit guarantees to forestall the spread of crises, which was exemplified by the agreement among London banks to stand behind Barings in 1890. As discussed further below, the "meta-rule" that subsumes both of these forms of crisis management is that central bank interventions to prevent crises should place the central bank in a senior position relative to other banks with respect to the absorption of loan losses.

This section briefly lays out the evolution of these various institutional changes, and places them in the appropriate political context. The central themes of my account are as follows: (1) The early nineteenth century propensity for panics reflected the moral hazard associated with the Bank's operations in the discount market. (2) Those operations reflected the Bank's mixed status as a private institution with a public mission; and reflected its attempt to preserve and take advantage of its special monopoly privileges and manage the political risk of a potential change in those privileges. (3) The recurring financial crises that this strategy entailed made this approach increasingly undesirable for the Bank, both because it implied large economic risks for the Bank, and because it undermined public support for the Bank. (4) The consequences of this political and economic disequilibrium produced by recurring banking crises required a combination of changes to restore economic and political equilibrium, including a diminution of the Bank's monopoly position, and changes in its discounting and lending practices. (5) That evolution restored stability to the banking system by removing the primary source of moral hazard (Bank discounting), fostering greater market competition and discipline, and encouraging the development of modern central bank practices, including Bagehot's rule, and incentive-compatible risk sharing between private London banks and the Bank in response to the threats of panics (like the Barings Crisis of 1890). The remainder of this section develops this argument in more detail.

(1) The early nineteenth century propensity for panics reflected the moral hazard associated with the Bank's operations in the discount market.

The British banking system developed a peculiar organizational structure in the early nineteenth century that encouraged financial bubbles to form. This was the result of a combination of a lack of effective prudential limits on bank leverage or the growth of risky lending, and pressures placed on the Bank of England to accommodate lending booms, which took the form of booms in the London discount market. The Bank of England was uniquely situated at the center of the financial system, with a monopoly of note issuance in London (banks outside of London could also issue a limited amount of notes, but they were not significant in size, and the Bank's notes were uniquely a legal tender). It also enjoyed barriers to bank entry that limited competition, although these were relaxed substantially over time.

Under the Bank Act of 1844 (the brainchild of the so-called "currency school"), the Bank was required to maintain 100 percent specie reserves against its note issues. That was considered a means to make the equilibrating international specie-flow mechanism more effective by linking the total supply of currency to the balance of payments. Of course, notes and specie were not the total money supply; bank deposits were widely used and bills of exchange were "the principal means of payment" used in business transactions (King 1936, p. 32), and thus the 1844 Act did not effectively constrain credit growth, deposit growth, or bill of exchange growth. In fact, credit growth and specie flows often moved in opposite directions, as in the 1850s when specie was flowing out of London (having mainly to do with bimetallic arbitrage involving France) while credit was growing dramatically (Hughes 1960, pp. 250–256). From 1852 to 1857, currency outstanding fell from 34 million to 25 million pounds, while the deposits of the five London joint stock banks rose from 17.7 million to 40 million pounds, and the average volume of bills of exchange in circulation (the asset intermediated in the London discount market) rose from 66 million pounds to an estimated 180–200 million pounds (Hughes 1960, pp. 258). The Bank's accommodative lending policies, combined with the absence of any prudential limits other than the 100 percent note reserve requirement (e.g., the absence of capital or reserve requirements relating to deposits), promoted huge growth in discounts and deposits during booms.

The precise intermediation mechanics of this remarkable growth in deposits and bills during booms is the subject of King's (1936) masterful treatise on the London discount market, which is also analyzed by Hughes (1960) in his lengthy Appendix 5. A detailed analysis is beyond our scope here.[16] Suffice it to make two points: (1) the effects of the Bank's willingness to discount bills of exchange had ramifications throughout the financial system, and this was especially visible in panic years, and (2) the London discount market's importance in the financial system reflected the limitations on bank branching at the time – the discount market operated as the primary means of redistributing financial resources from locations of surplus deposits (relative to lending opportunities) to locations of surplus loan opportunities relative to deposits. As King (1936, pp. xii–xiii) put it: "a localized banking system could function efficiently only through a sort of central pool by means of which the credit surpluses of one type of district (the agricultural areas) and the credit deficiencies of the other type of district (the industrial areas) could find their level." The London discount market was that central pool.

The Bank's accommodation of the discount market was relied upon to manage the adjustment to financial collapses by having the Bank stand ready to discount bills as needed, which it did on a widespread basis:[17]

> The deposit runs on the London discount houses and their efforts to cover their deposits led to a surge of applications to the Bank for aid during the [1857] crisis. Sanderson, Sanderman & Co., the largest London discount house to stop payment, had 3.5 million of deposits; a run on which caused Sanderson's to suspend on 11 November.... From 10 to 12 November Overend & Gurney alone were given 1.8 million. This inspired the remark after their failure in 1866 'Overends broke the Bank in 1866 because it went, and in 1857 because it was not let go.'
>
> (Hughes 1960, p. 305)

> One aspect of the crisis of 1857 which has not been given proper emphasis by historians is that the Bank's discounts and advances were given to all sectors of the business community. Too much emphasis has been given to the needs of the discount houses alone. Of the 79.4 million of accommodation given in 1857 35.8 million were given in the last three months of the year. This represents for the most part the discounts of the panic period. Of this amount, half, or 17.8 million, was direct loans and discounts to merchants. Scottish banks received 1.3 million, country banks (including joint-stock banks in London and banks outside London) had 7.1 million, and the discount houses 9.5 million. Of the country banks, those outside London received almost 6 million, while those inside the city received only about 1 million. The heaviest demand for accommodation came from the merchants, followed by the discount houses and the country bankers.
>
> (Hughes 1960, pp. 302–303)

How was the Bank able to accomplish this? Given the political imperative of promoting recovery during crises, the 1844 Act's provisions were suspended three times, during each of the three post-1844 crises, to allow the Bank of England to accommodate demand by issuing additional notes to use in discounting and lending, unconstrained by the availability of specie. Hughes (1960, p. 272) shows that the decision to relax the 1844 Act's provisions after November 12, 1857 resulted in an immediate easing in the market. As Bagehot (1873), Capie (2002) and others have emphasized, the Bank's note privileges were the key to its position as a provider of liquidity. Its ability to issue legal tender notes (after 1833), especially if unfettered by the 100 percent reserve requirement, and with the implicit backing of the state, allowed the Bank to provide substantial liquidity to the market in spite of the fact that, in theory, it was just another privately owned bank.

The fact that the government chose to amend the Bank's charter in 1833 to make its notes a legal tender indicates a conscious intention to enhance the capability of the Bank to provide credible support to the market during crises beyond the capacity of its own net worth. The lead advocate in Parliament of making Bank of England notes a legal tender, Lord Althorp, explicitly pointed to the advantage of freeing the Bank from market discipline and potential redemptions of its notes during crises (Andreades [1909] 1966, p. 260). The capacity to issue legal tender notes without limit during crises set the Bank apart from many other central banks in its capacity to act as a lender of last resort, including the previously discussed examples of the BUS and SBUS.

Why did private market discipline fail to constrain growth in deposits and discounted bills, which so predictably resulted in crises? Hughes (1960, p. 264) remarks that "[t]his inflationary bill expansion represented at any time a potential demand for payment in gold or notes even though the ability of the banking system to provide payment in gold or notes seems to have entered little or not at all into the calculations of those whose expanding credit activities were responsible for the potential demand." Why not? Hughes (1960, pp. 264–265), citing Newmarch, provides a partial answer: market participants expected to be protected by the Bank. Indeed, some of the most rapid growth in bills intermediation occurred immediately after the onset of the liquidity squeeze, indicating that the banking system continued to expand systemic risk even after the onset of problems. Newmarch argued that this reflected the fact that the public knew that bills could be presented for discount (i.e., that the Bank of England had effectively guaranteed their liquidity).

Of course, there was no explicit guarantee to convert bills to cash at the Bank of England, but there was an implicit one. David Salomon, director of the London and Westminster Bank, saw this implicit guarantee as central to the problem of credit-fueled bubbles:

> And do you think it is part of the functions of the Bank of England to discount a bill for anybody merely because the party holding the bill wishes to convert it to cash? As I said before, the Bank of England will have great difficulty in getting rid of that inconvenient idea which there is in the mind of the public, that the Bank of England is something more than an ordinary joint-stock bank.
>
> (Hughes 1960, pp. 300)

The subsidization of risk by the Bank did not follow from any attempt to undercut the market rate. In fact, the Bank's rate was above market during the 1850s (Hughes 1960, p. 301). The essence of the Bank's subsidy to the market was the put option inherent in the Bank's willingness to accommodate demand, which meant that whatever rate the bank charged, the market could comfortably discount at below that rate.[18]

(2) Those operations reflected the Bank's mixed status as a private institution with a public mission; and reflected its attempt to preserve and take advantage of its special monopoly privileges and manage the political risk of a potential change in those privileges.

The Bank of England did not want to provide risk-taking subsidies to the market, since doing so was not profitable, but the Bank was under intense pressure to do so, both in the boom periods leading up to crises and during the process of resolving the crises. King (1936, pp. 71–72) recounts how London's merchants organized protests to pressure the Bank not to constrain its discounting policies as early as 1793 and 1795. The protesting merchants issued a joint statement threatening that if the Bank were unwilling to maintain sufficient discounting, "it will be requisite that some other Public Establishment should be created to supply the Deficiency; at the same time wishing that this assistance may be derived through the old and customary Channel, the Bank of England." In other words, if the Bank of England refuses to obey the needs of the public, the public should charter a new bank to meet those needs. Later, attempts by the Bank to establish a classification system for bills, and price bills of different quality accordingly, also met with merchant opposition and were abandoned (King 1936, p. 53).

The Bank's reluctance to play the role of benefactor continued, especially during financial crises. In both 1847 and 1857, the Board of the Bank of England advised the government against suspending the 1844 Bank Act's provisions (Hughes 1960, pp. 320–321; Bagehot 1873, pp. 65–66), but to no avail. Clearly, the government saw more advantage in clearing the way for the Bank to provide assistance to the market than the Bank did.

In principle, the Bank could have refused to increase its note issuing beyond the amount of its specie reserve in 1847 and 1857, and the Bank could have refused to accommodate bills, both before and during banking crises. But that would not have been possible in practice. As Schuster (1923, p. 8) notes:

> beyond strict compliance with the Act [of 1844], no special duty is, by law, imposed upon the Bank; yet that such duties exist through an unwritten law, that they have been recognized and are acted upon, is beyond doubt. They affect our commercial life so closely and are so indissolubly connected with the functions and duties which are properly those of the State that to look upon the Bank of England merely as a private trading institution, and not as virtually the State or Government bank, is an impossibility.

At the heart of the matter is the simple fact that the Bank relied on the government, and on public opinion, to maintain its special privileges, and "an institution so dependent on the Government of the day for the continuance of valuable rights was little able, as Mr. Ricardo observed, to withstand the cajoling of Ministers" (Schuster 1923, p. 11). In this regard it is important to recall that the Bank's charter was subject to revocation by Parliament. Interestingly, the political option to revoke the charter was established as a quid pro quo in 1833 (to take effect with a twelve year lag), in the same Act of Parliament that gave the Bank's notes legal tender status (Andreades [1909] 1966, p. 262).

The responsibility of the Bank to provide accommodation was not a matter of statute. The Bank Act of 1844 clearly explained the duties of the Issue Department of the Bank, but not the implicit duties of the Banking Department (namely, to accommodate unlimited bill discounting demand at a uniform rate); nonetheless, those duties were real, and market advocates made no bones about them. Schuster (1923, pp. 21–22) summarizes the evidence from the Report of 1858 about the market's expectation of those duties:

> [According to Mr. Arbuthnot] 'There can be little doubt ... of the advantage which accrues to commerce from the employment of these funds, either directly or indirectly, in the discount of bills ... they ... find their way into the money market and are applied to the purposes of trade; but when the demands for money are great, and the rate of interest consequently high, great advantages are afforded by the resource the Bank of England affords under the system of management now pursued; such houses are assured that the funds at the disposal of the Bank will always be available for the legitimate objects of trade at the current rate of interest. Whence ensues that confidence which is derived from uniformity of system. The Bank of England has then come to be regarded as the centre and mainstay of mercantile credit.'
>
> That the Bank was so regarded is clear from the tendency of the whole of the enquiry. Witnesses were specially asked whether every house which applied, and deserved assistance, received it. From the evidence it appears that the Directors of the Bank of England went into the country to examine the accounts of banks in difficulties, in order to render assistance if they appeared to be sound.
>
> The Governor of the Bank of England was asked: 'You did not refuse accommodation to any person, even up to the time when the Act was suspended, who brought you good securities.' The answer was 'No.'
>
> 'I think you have admitted that you did not act during that time upon purely banking considerations, but that you had public considerations in view?' 'Yes.'
>
> 'You admit that the course which the relative position of the Bank took during that period is not one strictly in accordance with general banking rules?' 'Yes.'

(3) The recurring financial crises that this strategy entailed made this approach increasingly undesirable for the Bank, both because it implied large economic risks for the Bank, and because it undermined public support for the Bank.

(4) The consequences of this political and economic disequilibrium produced by recurring banking crises required a combination of changes to restore economic and political equilibrium, including a diminution of the Bank's monopoly position, and changes in its discounting and lending practices.

The public debate that ensued after the Panic of 1857 tried to come to grips with the political realities that had produced moral hazard from the Bank's accommodation policy. The Report of (July) 1858 exposed the dangers of that moral hazard and constituted a public acknowledgment that the existing accommodation policy, itself a creature of public expectation rather than law, was not good public policy. *Bankers' Magazine* and *The Economist* also decried the destabilizing effects of the discounting policy of the Bank (King 1936, pp. 202–203). All of this made it politically safe for the Bank to change policy, and its Court of Directors passed the following resolution of March 13, 1858:

> That habitual advances by Discount or Loan to Bill Brokers, Discount Companies and Money Dealers being calculated to lead them to rely on the assistance of the Bank of England for their security in time of pressure; Advances to Bill Brokers, Discount Companies and Money Dealers shall be confined to Loans made at the period of the Quarterly advances, or to Loans made under special and urgent circumstances which shall be communicated by the Governors at the earliest opportunity to the Court for its approval.
>
> (Hughes 1960, p. 305)

The put option was cancelled. But the true test of that cancellation came in the Overend, Gurney crisis of 1866, when the Bank proved in its response to the crisis that this new policy would be followed. The announced change in lending policy, and the willingness to allow Overend, Gurney to fail in 1866, credibly established the end of moral hazard.

Facilitating that change was a parallel change in the structure of the banking system – specifically, new bank entry and branching – which encouraged greater competition. Competition reduced the implicit value of the privileges the Bank enjoyed, which made the Bank less beholden to the state. Also, bank entry and branching reduced the demand for bill discounting since the discount market had evolved largely to fill gaps in a banking system that was not integrated on a national basis. In 1836, the 61 registered joint-stock banks operated 472 banking facilities; by 1870, 111 joint stock banks operated 1,127 banking facilities, and for Britain as a whole, 378 banks operated 2,738 banking facilities (Capie and Webber 1985, 576).

(5) That evolution restored stability to the banking system by removing the primary source of moral hazard (Bank discounting), fostering greater market competition and discipline, and encouraging the development of modern central bank practices, including Bagehot's rule, and incentive-compatible risk sharing between private London banks and the Bank in response to the threats of panics (like the Barings Crisis of 1890).

Once the Bank was freed from politically induced moral hazard, it was able to develop modern central banking practices, employing the discount rate and open market operations as instruments of policy, and applying rules for central bank intervention during times of financial stringency, which it did successfully to prevent full-blown panics from occurring after 1866.

The Bank developed an innovative approach to assistance in the form of a loss sharing arrangement with the other London banks during the Barings Crisis of 1890.[19] Barings' difficulties created an asymmetric-information problem for the London clearing banks, and attendant liquidity risks. Barings' losses in the Argentine bond market, and its uncertain financial links to individual clearing banks in London, created unknown risks (to depositors) in the London clearing banks, and those unknown risks created liquidity risk for all the London banks, who faced the prospect of deposit withdrawals resulting from their credit risk uncertainty. The ingenious solution devised by the Bank and the clearing banks was an insurance arrangement provided by the London banks and underwritten by the Bank of England. The London banks guaranteed Barings, and the Bank of England effectively underwrote the group's guarantee. So long as the participating banks' guarantees were adequate to meet any losses, the Bank of England would face no exposure to loss.

Given that it was apparent to depositors that Barings' losses almost certainly would not create losses in excess of the fund created by the group of banks, this arrangement resolved the asymmetric information problems facing individual depositors in their banks, and removed their incentive to run. The Bank of England's role was to provide a belt on top of the suspenders of mutual insurance within the group, and it did so with little possibility of loss, particularly as the group members paid in 17 million pounds to establish a guarantee fund in support of their endeavor (Clapham 1944, pp. 326–339; Andreades 1966, pp. 366–367).

Interestingly, like Bagehot's rule – which holds that loans from the Bank should be collateralized by good assets and provided at a higher than normal interest rate – the Barings intervention reflects the philosophy that the lender of last resort (or guarantor of last resort, in the Barings case), should take a senior position relative to other banks when assisting the financial system. By lending against good collateral, a central bank only suffers losses to the extent that the borrowing institution fails and its collateral declines in value, which places the lender of last resort in a senior position. Similarly, by requiring the London clearing banks to establish a guarantee fund for Barings, the Bank assured that they would suffer the first tier of any losses that occurred during the crisis. These incentive-compatible arrangements minimized moral-hazard problems from central bank assistance to the banking system.

5.5 The 2007–2009 crisis and historical lessons for reform

As discussed in detail in Calomiris (2009a), the subprime crisis, like the episodes of historical banking crises described above, was not just a bad accident. On an *ex ante* basis, subprime default risk was excessive and substantially underestimated during 2003–2007. Reasonable, forward-looking estimates of risk were ignored, and compensation for asset managers created incentives to undertake underestimated risks. Those risk-taking errors reflected a policy environment that strongly encouraged financial managers to underestimate risk in the subprime mortgage market. Four categories of policy distortions were most important in producing that result.

1. Lax monetary policy, especially from 2002 through 2005, promoted easy credit and kept interest rates low for a protracted period. The history of postwar monetary policy has seen only two episodes in which the real federal funds rate remained negative for several consecutive years: the high-inflation episode of 1975–1978 (which was reversed by the rate hikes of 1979–1982) and the accommodative period of 2002–2005. The Fed deviated sharply from the "Taylor Rule" in setting interest rates during 2002–2005; the federal funds rates remained substantially and persistently below levels that would have been consistent with that rule. Not only were short-term real rates held at persistent historic lows, but unusually high demand for longer-term Treasuries related to global imbalances and Asian absorption of U.S. Treasuries flattened the Treasury yield curve during the 2002–2005 period, resulting in extremely low interest rates across the yield curve. Accommodative monetary policy and a flat yield curve meant that credit was excessively available to support expansion in the housing market at abnormally low interest rates, which encouraged the overpricing of houses and subprime mortgages.

2. Numerous housing policies promoted subprime risk taking by financial institutions by effectively subsidizing the inexpensive use of leveraged finance in housing (Calomiris 2009a, 2009b). Those policies included (a) political pressures from Congress on the government-sponsored enterprises (GSEs), Fannie Mae and Freddie Mac, to promote "affordable housing" by investing in high-risk subprime mortgages, (b) lending subsidies for housing finance via the Federal Home Loan Bank System to its member institutions, (c) Federal Housing Administration (FHA) subsidization of extremely high mortgage leverage and risk, (d) government and GSE mortgage foreclosure mitigation protocols that were developed in the late 1990s and early 2000s to reduce the costs to borrowers of failing to meet debt service requirements on mortgages, which further promoted risky mortgages, and – almost unbelievably – (e) 2006 legislation that encouraged ratings agencies to relax standards for subprime securitizations.

All these policies encouraged the underestimation of subprime risk, but the behavior of members of Congress toward Fannie Mae and Freddie Mac, which encouraged reckless lending by the GSEs in the name of affordable housing, were arguably the most damaging actions leading up to the crisis. For Fannie and Freddie to maintain lucrative implicit (now explicit) government guarantees on their debts, they had to commit growing resources to risky subprime loans (Calomiris 2008; Wallison and Calomiris 2009). Due to political pressures, which were discussed openly in emails between management and risk managers in 2004, Fannie and Freddie purposely put aside their own risk managers' objections to making the market in no-docs subprime mortgages in 2004. The risk managers correctly predicted, based on their experience with no-docs in the 1980s, that their imprudent plunge into no-docs would produce adverse selection in mortgage origination, cause a boom in lending to low-quality borrowers, and harm their own stockholders and mortgage borrowers alike. In 2004, in the wake of Fannie and Freddie's decision to aggressively enter no-docs subprime lending, total subprime originations tripled. In late 2006 and early 2007, after many lenders had withdrawn from the subprime market in response to stalling home prices, Fannie and Freddie continued to accumulate subprime risk at peak levels. Fannie and Freddie ended up holding $1.6 trillion in exposures to those toxic mortgages, half the total of non-FHA outstanding amounts of toxic mortgages (Pinto 2008).

3. Government regulations limiting the concentration of stock ownership and the identity of who can buy controlling interests in banks have made effective corporate governance within large banks extremely challenging. Lax corporate governance allowed *some* bank management (for example, at Citibank, UBS, Merrill, Lehman, and Bear, but *not* at Bank of America, JPMorgan Chase, Goldman, Morgan Stanley, and DeutscheBank) to pursue subprime investments aggressively, even though they were unprofitable for stockholders in the long run. When stockholder discipline is absent, managers can set up the management of risk to benefit themselves at the expense of stockholders. An asset bubble (like the subprime bubble of 2003–2007) offers an ideal opportunity; if senior managers establish compensation systems that reward subordinates based on total assets managed or total revenues collected, without regard to risk or future potential loss, then subordinates have the incentive to expand portfolios rapidly during the bubble without regard to risk. Senior managers then reward themselves for having overseen "successful" expansion with large short-term bonuses and cash out their stock options quickly so that a large portion of their money is invested elsewhere when the bubble bursts.[20]

4. The prudential regulation of commercial banks and investment banks has proven to be ineffective. That failure reflects (a) fundamental problems in measuring bank risk resulting from regulation's ill-considered reliance on inaccurate rules of thumb, credit rating agencies' assessments, and internal bank models to measure risk, and (b) the too-big-to-fail problem (Stern and Feldman 2004), which makes it difficult to credibly enforce effective discipline on large, complex financial institutions (such as Citibank, Bear Stearns, AIG, and Lehman) even if regulators detect large losses or imprudently large risks.

The risk measurement problem has been the primary failure of banking regulation and a subject of constant academic criticism for more than two decades. Regulators use different means to assess risk, depending on the size of the bank. Under the simplest version of regulatory measurement of risk, subprime mortgages (like all mortgages) have a low asset risk weight (50 percent) relative to commercial loans, although they are riskier than those loans. More complex measurements of risk (applicable to larger U.S. banks) rely on the opinions of ratings agencies or the internal assessments of banks, neither of which is independent of bank management.

Rating agencies, after all, cater to buy-side market participants (i.e., banks, pensions, mutual funds, and insurance companies that maintained subprime-related asset exposures). When ratings are used for regulatory purposes, buy-side participants reward rating agencies for underestimating risk because that helps the buy-side clients reduce the costs associated with regulation. Many observers wrongly believe that the problem with rating agency inflation of securitized debts is that sellers (sponsors of securitizations) pay for the ratings; on the contrary, the problem is that the buyers of the debts want inflated ratings because of the regulatory benefits they receive from such ratings.

The too-big-to-fail problem involves the lack of credible regulatory discipline for large, complex banks. The prospect of their failing is considered so potentially disruptive that regulators have an incentive to avoid intervention. That *ex post* "forbearance" makes it hard to ensure compliance *ex ante.* The too-big-to-fail problem magnifies incentives to take excessive risks; banks that expect to be protected by deposit insurance, Fed lending, and Treasury-Fed bailouts and believe that they are beyond discipline will tend to take on excessive risk because taxpayers share the downside costs.

The too-big-to-fail problem was clearly visible in the behavior of large investment banks in 2008. After Bear Stearns was rescued in March, Lehman, Merrill Lynch, Morgan Stanley, and Goldman Sachs sat on their hands for six months awaiting further developments (i.e., either an improvement in the market environment or a handout from Uncle Sam). In particular, Lehman did little to raise capital or shore up its position. But when conditions deteriorated and the anticipated bailout failed to materialize for Lehman in September 2008 (showing that there were limits to Treasury-Fed generosity), the other major investment banks immediately were either acquired or transformed themselves into bank holding companies to increase their access to government support.

5.5.1 Nineteenth century Britain redux?

The mid-nineteenth century British discussions of financial reform share important features with the current debates over prudential reforms in the U.S. Many aspects of the current debate would seem familiar to nineteenth century British observers. Public resentment over the abuse of special privileges by mortgage monopolists, Fannie Mae and Freddie Mac, who fueled the subprime bubble, and whose internal emails (Calomiris 2008) show that they did so largely to preserve the special privileges conferred upon them by the government, is reminiscent of the discussion of the moral hazard produced by the Bank of England. The liquidity risk that arose from the heavy dependence on repo financing by U.S. investment banks in recent years parallels the growth of the discount brokers in London who built up huge liquidity risk in the banking system, which was the primary means of inflating bubbles during the first half of the nineteenth century in Britain. Just as the debate over financial regulation today grapples with the question of whether to impose prudential regulations on non-banks, Britain struggled with the problem of an ineffectual, narrow approach to defining prudential regulation, which was limited to the Bank Act of 1844's reserve requirement against Bank of England note issues, and did nothing to limit deposit growth or bill discounting by brokers. The concern about the "Greenspan put" and the moral-hazard consequences of the "too-big-to-fail" doctrine in the wake of the rescue of Bear Stearns, AIG, Citibank, and other large financial institutions is reminiscent of the Bank of England's struggle to cancel its put option in the London market for bills and rein in other institutions' entitlements to unlimited accommodation during crises, a practice that was ended in 1858, and proven in 1866.

This is not the place to explore in detail how to apply the lessons of the successful reform of the British banking system in the nineteenth century to the current environment (for perspectives on the reform agenda, see Calomiris 2009a, 2009b, 2009c). The important point to emphasize here is a consistent theme of the historical record: the ability to improve the financial system depends on the political environment.

The favorable outcome in Britain in the nineteenth century resulted from a political consensus that created strong political incentives to get reform right in order to stop the boom and bust cycles that had plagued the economy for decades. Reform in reaction to crisis, however, is not always so successful. Despite the advantages of creating a properly constituted central bank with a predictable and well-defined role, and with the tools necessary to execute that role, the U.S. opted to cancel the charters of its first two central banks, the BUS and the SBUS, as the result of their lack of popularity, and in the case of the SBUS that was directly related to exaggerated public perceptions that it had acted badly during the crises of 1819 and 1825. In 1933, in the U.S., public anger over the Depression was channeled by politicians into undesirable and ineffective "reforms" of the banking system, including separation of investment and commercial banking, the limitation of interest payments on deposits, and the creation of deposit insurance (Calomiris 2000, 2009a). Those political decisions had long-lasting consequences; it took more than five decades of discourse, accumulation of historical evidence and new experience to repeal Regulation Q and the separation of securities underwriting from commercial banking; deposit insurance – the last vestige of New Deal policy, and one that had no intellectual support at the time of its passage – seems destined to remain forever.

5.6 Conclusion

Banking crises properly defined consist either of panics or waves of costly bank failures. These phenomena were rare historically compared to the present. A historical analysis of the two phenomena (panics and waves of failures) reveals that they do not always coincide, are not random events, cannot be seen as the inevitable result of human nature or the liquidity transforming structure of bank balance sheets, and do not typically accompany business cycles or monetary policy errors. Rather, risk-inviting microeconomic rules of the banking game that are established by government have always been the key additional necessary condition to producing a propensity for banking distress, whether in the form of a high propensity for banking panics or a high propensity for waves of bank failures.

Some risk-inviting rules took the form of visible subsidies for risk taking, as in the historical state-level deposit insurance systems in the U.S., Argentina's government guarantees for mortgages in the 1880s, Australia's government subsidization of real estate development prior to 1893, the Bank of England's discounting of paper at low interest rates prior to 1858, and the expansion of government-sponsored deposit insurance and other bank safety net programs throughout the world in the past three decades, including the generous government subsidization of subprime mortgage risk taking in the U.S. leading up to the 2007–2009 crisis.

Other risk-inviting rules historically have involved government-imposed structural constraints on banks, which include entry restrictions like unit banking laws that constrain competition, prevent diversification of risk, and limit the ability to deal with shocks. The most important example of these structural constraints was the U.S. historical system of unit banking, which limited competition and diversification of loan risk by preventing branching, and by effectively preventing collective action by banks in the management of crises once adverse shocks had hit.

Finally, another destabilizing rule of the banking game is the absence of a properly structured central bank to act as a lender of last resort to reduce liquidity risk without spurring moral hazard. That absence contributed to instability in the U.S. prior to 1913.

Panics, whether associated with waves of bank failure or not, have been times of temporary confusion (due to asymmetric information) about the incidence of shocks within the banking system. This asymmetric-information problem was particularly acute in the U.S. Indeed, in the late nineteenth and early twentieth centuries, system-wide banking panics like those that the U.S. experienced in that period generally did not occur elsewhere. The uniquely panic-ridden experience of the U.S., particularly during the pre-World War I era, reflected a combination of the unit banking structure of the U.S. system and the absence of a proper lender of last resort. Panics were generally avoided by other countries in the pre-World War I era because their banking systems were composed of a much smaller number of banks operating on a national basis (who consequently enjoyed greater diversification, and a greater ability to coordinate their actions to stem panics *ex post*), and because they had developed incentive-compatible principles for central bank lending.[21]

The U.S. and other countries also experienced waves of bank failures unrelated to panics (most notably in the U.S. in the 1920s), which reflected the vulnerability of banks to sector-specific shocks (e.g., agricultural price declines) in an undiversified banking system. In the U.S., waves of bank failures in the 1920s were aggravated not only by the absence of branch banking but by the presence of deposit insurance in various states, which promoted moral hazard in lending and adverse selection in bank entry and which resulted in particularly severe failure experiences. In the U.S. during the antebellum period, particularly in the South, even worse failure outcomes were related to government-directed credit policies implemented through political control of banks (Schweikart 1987); Australia in 1893 suffered a similar fate.

More recent banking system experience worldwide indicates a dramatic upward shift in the costs of banking system distress – an unprecedented high frequency of banking crises, many bank failures during crises, and large losses by failing banks, sometimes with disastrous consequences for taxpayers who end up footing the bill of bank loss. This pandemic of bank failures has been traced empirically to the expanded role of the government safety net, as well as government involvement in directed credit. Government protection of banks and government direction of credit flows has encouraged excessive risk taking by banks and created greater tolerance for incompetent risk management (as distinct from purposeful increases in risk). The government safety net, which was designed to forestall the (overestimated) risks of contagion, ironically has become the primary source of systemic instability in banking.

The desirable path for reform is best illustrated by the successful adaptation that occurred in the British banking system during the second half of the nineteenth century, when it overcame its legacy of moral hazard and its high propensity for banking crises by dramatically changing the rules of the banking game to eliminate the put option in the London bill market that had been provided by the Bank of England. This transformed the Bank into an instrument of systemic stability, and encouraged greater competition in banking. Those reforms set the stage for the development by the Bank of improved mechanisms for limiting liquidity risk in the system, including Bagehot's rule and other means of incentive-compatible sharing of risk between the Bank and the coalition of private London banks.

The risk-inviting incentive problems that gave rise to the recent subprime crisis have much in common with prior experiences of unstable banking systems, and the principles for reform are similar. The key question is whether the political equilibrium will encourage favorable reforms, as it did in Britain in the nineteenth century, or unfavorable reforms as the result of populist misapprehension, as in the case of the disappearance of the BUS and SBUS, or the capture of financial reform by special interests, as was the case in the U.S. in 1933.

Notes

1 "The destruction of private wealth precipitated the fall of rank and reputation, until at last the emperor interposed his aid by distributing throughout the banks a hundred million sesterces, and allowing freedom to borrow without interest for three years, provided the borrower gave security to the State in land to double the amount. Credit was thus restored, and gradually private lenders were found." This account by Tacitus traces the crisis to government enforcement of a long-neglected usury law. Unfortunately, confusion has arisen about the origins of the Roman Panic of 33 AD due to an apparent attempt at humor by an early twentieth century American, William Stearns Davis. Davis, who was known both for historical writings and historical fiction, seems to have invented a colorful account that was informed by his knowledge of events during the US Panic of 1907. He presented it as a factual account in his 1910 treatise, *The Influence of Wealth in Imperial Rome*. Calomiris (1989) took this account seriously, as have many other scholars and journalists. Davis provided no references or footnotes; a review of Roman sources indicates no factual basis in any known source for Davis's account, and various humorous aspects of the portrayal (for example, problems in the market for ostrich feathers) add to the likelihood that the account is fictional.

2 Banking crises are also distinct from other financial crises because of their especially large social costs. Asset price collapses that are not accompanied by banking crises – such as those in the U.S. in 1987 and 2000 – did not have the severe macroeconomic consequences of the financial crises that are accompanied by banking crises (see Bernanke 1983; Calomiris and Hubbard 1989; Calomiris and Mason 2003b). Indeed, banking distress manifested in significant deposit shrinkage and loan losses, even when not associated with a banking crisis, typically poses substantial costs for the economy because of the contraction of money and loan supply. For a cross-country analysis, see Bordo and Eichengreen (2003), who study the effects of historical banking distress (broadly defined) on business cycle severity.

3 It is important to define banking panics carefully. For my purposes, panics are moments of confusion about the incidence of losses in banks that are sufficiently

severe as to create systemic withdrawal pressure on a large number of banks that is sufficient to elicit collective action by the banks and/or the government (e.g., joint issuance of liabilities, like clearing house certificates, or the undertaking of joint action, such as suspension of convertibility, or other explicit attempts to coordinate behavior to alleviate the effects of panic). This definition creates an objective standard that distinguishes true panics from less severe moments of stress that are not truly systemic in scope.

4 Bank clearing houses or informal alliances among banks to make markets in each other's deposits during crises required that members in these coalitions adhere to guidelines, and that they be able to monitor one another to ensure compliance. Not only did geography get in the way of such coordination, the sheer number of banks made collective action difficult. The benefits of one bank choosing to monitor another are shared but the monitoring and enforcement costs are borne privately; coalitions with thirty members seemed able to motivate individual banks to bear the private costs of monitoring on behalf of the coalition, but coalitions of hundreds or thousands of banks unsurprisingly were not able to structure effective monitoring and enforcement.

5 The absence of a lender of last resort, as discussed below, was also an important contributor to bank instability, but the structure of unit banking appears to be the more important influence; Canada, which operated on a branching basis, avoided panics during this era, although it did not charter a central bank until 1935.

6 The states of Indiana, Ohio, and Iowa during the antebellum period were the exceptions to this rule, as their mutual guarantee systems were limited to a small number of banks which bore unlimited mutual liability for one another, and which also had broad enforcement powers to limit abuse of that protection.

7 The other two principal measures – Regulation Q and the separation of commercial and investment banking – were essentially done away with in the last two decades of the twentieth century, although some remnants of Regulation Q remain.

8 Friedman and Schwartz attach great importance to the banking crisis of late 1930, which they attribute to a "contagion of fear" that resulted from the failure of a large New York bank, the Bank of United States, which they regard as itself a victim of panic. They also identify two other banking crises in 1931 – from March to August 1931, and from Britain's departure from the gold standard (September 21, 1931) through the end of the year. The fourth and final banking crisis they identify occurred at the end of 1932 and the beginning of 1933, culminating in the nationwide suspension of banks in March. The 1933 crisis and suspension was the beginning of the end of the Depression, but the 1930 and 1931 crises (because they did *not* result in suspension) were, in Friedman and Schwartz's judgment, important sources of shock to the real economy that turned a recession in 1929 into the Great Depression of 1929–1933.

The Friedman and Schwartz argument is based upon the suddenness of banking distress and the absence of collapses in relevant macroeconomic time series prior to those banking crises (see Charts 27–30 in Friedman and Schwartz 1963, p. 309). But there are reasons to question Friedman and Schwartz's view of the exogenous origins of the banking crises of the Depression. As Temin (1976) and others have noted, the bank failures during the Depression mainly marked a continuation of the severe banking distress that had gripped agricultural regions throughout the 1920s. Of the nearly 15,000 bank disappearances between 1920 and 1933, roughly half predate 1930. And massive numbers of bank failures occurred during the Depression era outside the crisis windows identified by Friedman and Schwartz (notably, in 1932). Wicker (1996, p. 1) estimates that "[b]etween 1930 and 1932 of the more than 5,000 banks that closed only 38 percent suspended during the first three banking crisis episodes." Recent studies of the condition of the Bank of United States indicate that it too may have been insolvent, not just illiquid, in December 1930 (Lucia 1985; Wicker

1996). Banks that considered merging with it determined at the last minute not to do so (Meltzer 2003, pp. 323–324). So there is some prima facie evidence that the banking distress of the Depression era was more than a problem of panic-inspired depositor flight.

Friedman and Schwartz omitted important aggregate measures of the state of the economy relevant for bank solvency, for example, measures of commercial distress and construction activity may be useful indicators of fundamental shocks. Second, aggregation of fundamentals masks important sectoral, local, and regional shocks that buffeted banks with particular credit or market risks. The empirical relevance of these factors has been demonstrated in the work of Wicker (1980, 1996) and Calomiris and Mason (1997, 2003a).

9 Once one disaggregates, Wicker argues, it becomes apparent that at least the first two of the three banking crises of 1930–1931 identified by Friedman and Schwartz were largely regional affairs. Wicker (1980, 1996) argues that the failures of November 1930 reflected regional shocks and the specific risk exposures of a small subset of banks, linked to Nashville-based Caldwell & Co., the largest investment bank in the South at the time of its failure. Temin (1989, p. 50) reaches a similar conclusion. He argues that the "panic" of 1930 was not really a panic, and that the failure of Caldwell & Co. and the Bank of United States reflected fundamental weakness in those institutions.

Wicker's analysis of the third banking crisis (beginning September 1931) also shows that bank suspensions were concentrated in a very few locales, although he regards the nationwide increase in the tendency to convert deposits into cash as evidence of a possible nationwide banking crisis in September and October 1931. Wicker agrees with Friedman and Schwartz that the final banking crisis (of 1933), which resulted in universal suspension of bank operations, was nationwide in scope. The banking crisis that culminated in the bank holidays of February–March 1933 resulted in the suspension of at least some bank operations (bank "holidays") for nearly all banks in the country by March 6.

From the regionally disaggregated perspective of Wicker's findings, the inability to explain the timing of bank failures using aggregate time series data (which underlay the Friedman–Schwartz view that banking failures were an unwarranted and autonomous source of shock) would not be surprising even if bank failures were entirely due to fundamental insolvency. Failures of banks were local phenomena in 1930 and 1931, and so may have had little to do with national shocks to income, the price level, interest rates, and asset prices. The unique industrial organization of the American banking industry plays a central role in both the Wicker view of the process of bank failure during the Depression, and in the ability to detect that process empirically. Because banks in the United States were smaller, regionally isolated institutions, large region-specific shocks might produce a sudden wave of bank failures in specific regions even though no evidence of a shock was visible in aggregate macroeconomic time series (see the cross-country evidence in Bernanke and James 1991, and Grossman 1994). The regional isolation of banks in the United States, due to prohibitions on nationwide branching or even statewide branching in most states, also makes it possible to identify regional shocks empirically through their observed effects on banks located exclusively in particular regions.

10 As Charles Goodhart has pointed out, Bagehot (1873) nowhere employs the phrase "penalty rate." His rule is best understood as lending at a rate in excess of the normal market rate (during non-crisis times), to prevent abuse of the option to borrow. As discussed in more detail below, a more accurate characterization of the evolution of central banking in the late nineteenth century would emphasize the development of incentive-compatible loss sharing arrangements, of which central bank lending on good collateral is one example.

11 For an excellent treatment of the ideological conflicts leading to the veto, and the gamesmanship on the part of the bank's advocates, led by Nicholas Biddle, and President Andrew Jackson during that struggle, see Schweikart (1988).

12 Two caveats are in order. First, due to the lack of existing data, there is uncertainty about whether one or more of Brazil's various pre-World War I financial crises may have produced losses in excess of 1 percent of GDP, and this accounts for the claim that the number is between four and seven. Second, the number of countries is much fewer in the historical sample than in the post-1978 sample. Nevertheless, the thrust of the comparison is still valid; the frequency and severity of bank insolvency events has increased dramatically.

13 Data is from Caprio and Klingebiel (1996), updated in private correspondence with these authors, and by subsequent additions.

14 The initial experience with federal deposit insurance in the U.S. was one of unusual stability. That experience, from World War II through the 1960s, reflected the unusual stability of interest rates, asset prices, and growth in that era, in contrast to the periods before or afterward, and even more importantly, the limited insurance of deposits in the early decades of deposit insurance (size limits were increased in phases over time; the system initially covered only a small fraction of banking system deposits, but has grown to now cover virtually all deposits).

15 For a detailed account of that crisis, see Roberts, Reading, and Skene (2009).

16 Hughes (1960, p. 306) provides a succinct analysis of the structure of intermediation detailed in King (1936): "the rise of the joint-stock banks and the transformation of the bill brokers into bill dealers who accepted money at call and discounted bills on their own accord had been complementary developments. After 1825 the London banks had given up the practice of rediscounting at the Bank and had begun employing their excess funds with the discount houses. After 1833 this practice had been given a great impetus by the bill market being granted discount facilities at the Bank. By the 1850s when the deposits of the joint-stock banks surged upwards, the practice of keeping their money at call with the discount houses had become the most important form of employing the deposits of the banks."

17 The Bank was less generous in its treatment of Scottish banks, and two large Scottish banks failed in the 1857 crisis, although Hughes argues that the Bank was right to deny credit due to the insolvency of these institutions (Hughes 1960, pp. 311–331).

18 Describing the discounting of bills as a put option is a bit of an overstatement. The Bank could, and did, raise the rate of discount during panics, so the price of the option was a moving target. Indeed, Hughes (1960, p. 371) remarks that the decision to raise the rate during the panic alarmed the market, which one could interpret as reflecting a adverse shock to market expectations. Also, the relaxation of the 1844 Act was not a certainty, so the ability to exercise the put option was subject to doubt.

19 To say that the Bank was innovative is not to say that it was uniquely innovative, or that it was the first to use this sort of technique. White (2009) shows that the Banque de France used a similar two-tiered risk sharing technique in its coordination of assistance (with French banks) for the Paris Bourse in 1882. In 1908, Jose Limantour, the finance minister of Mexico, used a guarantee approach to assist Mexican banks to float debt backed by bank loans in the wake of the Panic of 1907 (Conant 1910).

20 Although it is true that many bank CEOs lost huge amounts as their firms' stock prices plummeted, that does not exculpate them from having purposely taken on excessive risk, for two reasons: first, they may have reasonably expected a less extreme collapse than the one that occurred, and second, the game was very profitable for them while it lasted, and may have been worth playing, *ex ante*, even if they had anticipated that it would eventually end badly.

21 Of course, it was possible to have a stable banking system without a central bank, as was the case in the Canadian branch banking system, which did not establish a central bank to act as a lender of last resort until 1935.

References

Alston, Lee J., Wayne A. Grove, and David C. Wheelock (1994). "Why Do Banks Fail? Evidence from the 1920s," *Explorations in Economic History* 30, 409–431.

Andreades, A. (1966). *History of the Bank of England, 1640 to 1903*, New York: Augustus Kelley.

Bagehot, Walter (1873). *Lombard Street: A Description of the Money Market*, Reprinted by Richard D. Irwin, Homewood, Illinois, 1962.

Barth, James, Gerard Caprio, Jr., and Ross Levine (2006), *Rethinking Bank Regulation: Till Angels Govern*, Cambridge: Cambridge University Press.

Bernanke, Ben S. (1983). "Nonmonetary Effects of the Financial Crisis in the Propagation of the Great Depression," *American Economic Review* 73, June, 257–276.

Bernanke, Ben S. and Harold James (1991). "The Gold Standard, Deflation, and Financial Crisis in the Great Depression: An International Comparison," in R. Glenn Hubbard, ed., *Financial Markets and Financial Crises*, Chicago: University of Chicago Press, 33–68.

Bernstein, Asaf, Eric Hughson, and Marc D. Weidenmier (2009a). "Quasi-Central Banking and Liquidity Risk: Lessons from the Second Bank of the US," Working Paper.

Bernstein, Asaf, Eric Hughson, and Marc D. Weidenmier (2009b). "Identifying the Effects of a Lender of Last Resort on Financial Markets: Lessons from the Founding of the Fed," *Journal of Financial Economics*, forthcoming.

Board of Governors of the Federal Reserve System (1999). "Using Subordinated Debt as an Instrument of Market Discipline," Staff Study 172, December.

Bordo, Michael (1985). "The Impact and International Transmission of Financial Crises: Some Historical Evidence, 1870–1933," *Revista di Storia Economica*, 2(2) 41–78.

Bordo, Michael D. (2007). "The Crisis of 2007: The Same Old Story, Only the Players Have Changed," Working Paper, Rutgers University.

Bordo, Michael D., and Barry Eichengreen (2003). "Crises Now and Then: What Lessons from the Last Era of Financial Globalization?" in *Monetary History, Exchange Rates and Financial Markets: Essays in Honour of Charles Goodhart*, Volume 2, Cheltenham, UK: Edward Elgar, 53–84.

Bordo, Michael D., and David Wheelock (2007). "Stock Market Booms and Monetary Policy in the Twentieth Century," *Review*, Federal Reserve Bank of St. Louis, 89 (March/April).

Bordo, Michael D., and David Wheelock (2009). "When Do Stock Market Booms Occur: The Macroeconomic and Policy Environments of 20th Century Booms," in Jeremy Atack and Larry Neal, ed., *The Origins and Development of Financial Markets and Institutions*, Cambridge: Cambridge University Press, 416–449.

Boyd, John, Pedro Gomis, Sungkyu Kwak, and Bruce Smith (2000). "A User's Guide to Banking Crises," Conference Paper, The World Bank.

Bruner, Robert F., and Sean D. Carr (2007). *The Panic of 1907: Lessons Learned from the Market's Perfect Storm*, Hoboken, NJ: Wiley.

Brunner, Karl, and Allan H. Meltzer (1968). "What Did We Learn from the Monetary Experience of the United States in the Great Depression?" *Canadian Journal of Economics* 1, May, 334–348.

Butlin, Matthew W. (1987). "Capital Markets," in Rodney Maddock and Ian W. Mclean, eds., *The Australian Economy in the Long Run*, Cambridge: Cambridge University Press.

Butlin, Noel G. (1964). *Investment in Australian Economic Development, 1861–1914*, Cambridge: Cambridge University Press.

Butlin, Sydney J. (1961). *Australia and New Zealand Bank: The Bank of Australasia and the Union Bank of Australia Limited, 1828–1951*, London: Longmans.

Calomiris, Charles W. (1989). "Deposit Insurance: Lessons from the Record," *Economic Perspectives*, Federal Reserve Bank of Chicago, May/June, 10–30.

Calomiris, Charles W. (1990). "Is Deposit Insurance Necessary? A Historical Perspective," *Journal of Economic History* 50, 283–295.

Calomiris, Charles W. (1992). "Do Vulnerable Economies Need Deposit Insurance? Lessons from U.S. Agriculture in the 1920s," in Philip L. Brock, ed., *If Texas Were Chile: A Primer on Bank Regulation*, San Francisco: The Sequoia Institute, 237–349, 450–458.

Calomiris, Charles W. (2000). *U.S. Bank Deregulation in Historical Perspective*, Cambridge: Cambridge University Press.

Calomiris, Charles W. (2007). "Victorian Perspectives on the Banking Distress of the Late 20th Century," Working paper.

Calomiris, Charles W. (2008). "Statement before the Committee on Oversight and Government Reform, United States House of Representatives," December 9.

Calomiris, Charles W. (2009a). "The Subprime Turmoil: What's Old, What's New, and What's Next," *Journal of Structured Finance* 15, Spring, 6–52.

Calomiris, Charles W. (2009b). "Financial Innovation, Regulation, and Reform," *Cato Journal* 29, Winter, 65–92.

Calomiris, Charles W. (2009c). "Prudential Bank Regulation: What's Broke and How to Fix It," in Terry L. Anderson and Richard Soussa, eds., *Reacting to the Spending Spree: Policy Changes We Can Afford*. Stanford, LA: Hoover Institution Press.

Calomiris, Charles W., and Gary Gorton (1991). "The Origins of Banking Panics: Models, Facts, and Bank Regulation," in R. Glenn Hubbard, ed., *Financial Markets and Financial Crises*, Chicago: University of Chicago Press, 107–173.

Calomiris, Charles W., and R. Glenn Hubbard (1989). "Price Flexibility, Credit Availability, and Economic Fluctuations: Evidence from the U.S., 1894–1909," *Quarterly Journal of Economics*, August, 429–452.

Calomiris, Charles W., and Charles M. Kahn (1991). "The Role of Demandable Debt in Structuring Optimal Banking Arrangements," *American Economic Review* 81, 497–513.

Calomiris, Charles W., and Joseph R. Mason (1997). "Contagion and Bank Failures During the Great Depression: The June 1932 Chicago Banking Panic," *American Economic Review* 87, 863–883.

Calomiris, Charles W., and Joseph R. Mason (2003a). "Fundamentals, Panics and Bank Distress During the Depression," *American Economic Review* 93, 1615–1647.

Calomiris, Charles W., and Joseph R. Mason (2003b). "Consequences of Bank Distress During the Great Depression," *American Economic Review* 93, 937–947.

Calomiris, Charles W., and Andrew Powell (2001). "Can Emerging Market Bank Regulators Establish Credible Discipline: The Case of Argentina, 1992–99," in Frederic S. Mishkin, ed., *Prudential Supervision: What Works and What Doesn't*, 147–196.

Calomiris, Charles W., and Larry Schweikart (1991). "The Panic of 1857: Origins, Transmission, and Containment," *Journal of Economic History* 51, 807–834.

Calomiris, Charles W., and Eugene N. White (1994). "The Origins of Federal Deposit Insurance," in Claudia Goldin and Gary Libecap, eds., *The Regulated Economy: A Historical Approach to Political Economy*, Chicago: University of Chicago Press, 145–188.

Calomiris, Charles W., and Berry Wilson (2004). "Bank Capital and Portfolio Management: The 1930s 'Capital Crunch' and Scramble to Shed Risk," *Journal of Business* 77, 421–455.

Canovai, Tito (1911). *The Banks of Issue in Italy*, Washington DC: National Monetary Commission, U.S. Senate, 61st Congress, 2nd Session, Document No. 575.

Capie, Forrest (2002). "The Emergence of the Bank of England as a Mature Central Bank," in Donald Winch and Patrick O'Brien, eds., *The Political Economy of British Historical Experience, 1688–1914*, Oxford: Oxford University Press.

Capie, Forrest (2009). "Financial Crises in England in the Nineteenth and Twentieth Centuries," Working Paper, June.

Capie, Forrest, and Alan Webber (1985). *A Monetary History of the United Kingdom, 1870–1982*, London: George Allen and Unwin.

Caprio, Gerard, and Daniela Klingebiel (1996). "Bank Insolvencies: Cross Country Experience," Working Paper No. 1620, The World Bank.

Catterall, Ralph C.H. (1902). *The Second Bank of the United States*, Chicago: University of Chicago Press.

Clapham, Sir John (1944). *The Bank of England.* Cambridge: Cambridge University Press.

Conant, Charles Arthur (1910). *The Banking System of Mexico*, Washington D.C.: National Monetary Commission, U.S. Senate, 61st Congress, 2nd Session.

Davis, Joseph, Christopher Hanes, and Paul Rhode (2007). "Harvests and Business Cycles in Nineteenth Century America," Working Paper.

Davis, Lance E., and Robert E. Gallman (2001). *Evolving Financial Markets and International Capital Flows: Britain, the Americas, and Australia, 1865–1914*, Cambridge: Cambridge University Press.

Davis, William Stearns (1910). *The Influence of Wealth in Imperial Rome*, New York: Macmillan.

Demirguc-Kunt, Asli, and Enrica Detragiache (2000). "Does Deposit Insurance Increase Banking System Stability?" Conference Paper, The World Bank.

Demirguc-Kunt, Asli, Edward Kane, and Luc Laeven, eds. (2009). *Deposit Insurance Around the World*, Cambridge, MA: MIT Press).

Diamond, Douglas, and Philip Dybvig (1983). "Bank Runs, Deposit Insurance, and Liquidity," *Journal of Political Economy* 91, 401–419.

Friedman, Milton, and Anna J. Schwartz (1963). *A Monetary History of the United States, 1867–1960*, Princeton: Princeton University Press.

Goodhart, Charles A.E. (1995). *The Evolution of Central Banks*, Cambridge, MA: MIT Press.

Gorton, Gary (1985). "Clearing Houses and the Origin of Central Banking in the United States," *Journal of Economic History* 45, 277–283.

Gouge, William A. (1833). *An Inquiry into the Principles of the American Banking System*, Philadelphia.

Grossman, Richard S. (1994). "The Shoe That Didn't Drop: Explaining Banking Stability During the Great Depression," *Journal of Economic History* 54, 654–682.

Hawtrey, R.G. (1932). *The Art of Central Banking*, London: Longmans, Green.

Hawtrey, R.G. (1938). *A Century of Bank Rate*, London: Longmans, Green.

Hilt, Eric (2009). "Wall Street's First Corporate Governance Crisis: The Panic of 1826," NBER Working Paper No. 14892, April.

Hughes, Jonathan R.T. (1960). *Fluctuations in Trade, Industry and Finance: A Study of British Economic Development, 1850–1860*. Oxford: Oxford University Press.

Kindleberger, Charles P. (1978). *Manias, Panics, and Crashes: A History of Financial Crises*, New York: Basic Books.

King, W.T.C. (1936). *History of the London Discount Market*. London: George Routledge & Sons.

Lucia, Joseph L. (1985). "The Failure of the Bank of United States: A Reappraisal," *Explorations in Economic History* 22, 402–416.

Mason, Joseph R. (2001). "Do Lender of Last Resort Policies Matter? The Effects of Reconstruction Finance Corporation Assistance to Banks During the Great Depression," *Journal of Financial Services Research*, September 20, 77–95.

Meltzer, Allan H. (2003). *A History of the Federal Reserve, 1913–1951*, Chicago: University of Chicago Press.

Minsky, Hyman P. (1975). *John Maynard Keynes*, New York: Columbia University Press.

Miron, Jeffrey (1986). "Financial Panics, the Seasonality of the Nominal Interest Rate, and the Founding of the Fed," *American Economic Review* 76, 125–140.

Mishkin, Frederic S., ed. (2001). *Prudential Supervision: What Works and What Doesn't*, Chicago: University of Chicago Press.

Mitchener, Kris James (2005). "Bank Supervision, Regulation, and Instability During the Great Depression," *Journal of Economic History* 65, 152–185.

Pinto, Edward J. (2008). "Statement before the Committee on Oversight and Government Reform, United States House of Representatives," December 9.

Richardson, Gary, and William Troost (2006). "Monetary Intervention Mitigated Banking Panics During the Great Depression? Quasi-Experimental Evidence from the Federal Reserve District Border in Mississippi, 1929 to 1933," NBER Working Paper No. 12591.

Roberts, Richard, Brian Reading, and Leigh Skene (2009). "Sovereign Rescues: How the Forgotten Financial Crisis of 1914 Compares with 2008–2009," London: Lombard Street Research.

Rousseau, Peter (2002). "Jacksonian Monetary Policy, Specie Flows, and the Panic of 1837," *Journal of Economic History* 62, 457–488.

Sayers, R.S. (1976). *The Bank of England, 1891–1944*, Cambridge: Cambridge University Press.

Schuster, Sir Felix (1923). *The Bank of England and the State*, London: University of Manchester Press.

Schweikart, Larry (1987). *Banking in the American South from the Age of Jackson to Reconstruction*, Baton Rouge: Louisiana State University Press.

Schweikart, Larry (1988). "Jacksonian Ideology, Currency Control, and Central Banking: A Reappraisal," *The Historian* (November), 78–102.

Shadow Financial Regulatory Committee (2000). *Reforming Bank Capital Regulation*, American Enterprise Institute.

Sprague, Oliver M.W. (1910). *History of Crises under the National Banking System*, National Monetary Commission.

Stern, Gary H., and Ron J. Feldman (2004). *Too Big to Fail: The Hazards of Bank Bailouts*, Washington DC: Brookings Institution.

Sylla, Richard, Robert E. Wright, and David J. Cowen (2009). "Alexander Hamilton, Central Banker: Crisis Management during the U.S. Financial Panic of 1792," *Business History Review* 83, Spring, 61–86.

Tacitus, Cornelius (1996). *The Annals of Imperial Rome*, New York: Penguin.

Temin, Peter (1969). *The Jacksonian Economy*, New York: W.W. Norton.

Temin, Peter (1976). *Did Monetary Forces Cause the Great Depression?* New York: W.W. Norton.

Temin, Peter (1989). *Lessons from the Great Depression*, Cambridge, MA: MIT Press.

Timberlake, Richard H. (1984). "The Central Banking Role of Clearinghouse Associations," *Journal of Money, Credit and Banking* 16 (February), 1–15.

Wallison, Peter J., and Charles W. Calomiris (2009). "The Last Trillion-Dollar Commitment: The Destruction of Fannie Mae and Freddie Mac," *Journal of Structured Finance* 15, Spring, 71–80.

Wheelock, David C. (1991). *The Strategy and Consistency of Federal Reserve Monetary Policy, 1924–1933*, Cambridge: Cambridge University Press.

White, Eugene N. (1984). "A Reinterpretation of the Banking Crisis of 1930," *Journal of Economic History* 44, 119–138.

White, Eugene N. (2009). "The Banque de France as a Lender of Last Resort in the Nineteenth Century," Working Paper, Rutgers University.

Wicker, Elmus (1966). *Federal Reserve Monetary Policy, 1917–1933*, New York: Random House.

Wicker, Elmus (1980). "A Reconsideration of the Causes of the Banking Panic of 1930," *Journal of Economic History*, 40, 571–583.

Wicker, Elmus (1996). *The Banking Panics of the Great Depression*, Cambridge: Cambridge University Press.

Wigmore, Barrie A. (1987). "Was the Bank Holiday of 1933 a Run on the Dollar Rather than the Banks?" *Journal of Economic History* 47, 739–756.

Part III

Money and interest rates

6 Money and interest rates in the United States during the Great Depression

Peter Basile, John Landon-Lane and Hugh Rockoff

6.1 Introduction

Interest in the economics of the Great Depression has been extremely high since the 2007–2008 financial crisis. One claim that has attracted considerable attention is that the economy fell into a "liquidity trap" during the depression. Monetary policy, it is said, became ineffective and deficit spending was the only policy capable of shortening the depression. The certain sign of a liquidity trap, according to this view, is near zero rates on short-term government debt. Since these rates were close to zero in the 1930s, it follows that the economy was then in a liquidity trap. This interpretation of the liquidity trap was pushed vigorously by Alvin Hansen and other economists in the first generation of American Keynesians. An alternative view associated with Milton Friedman, Anna Schwartz, Karl Brunner, Allan Meltzer and a number of other writers – a list that ironically includes Keynes himself – is that a true liquidity trap requires that the entire spectrum of rates, including rates on long-term government debt and short-and long-term private debts, must have reached low sticking points. Finding that rates on short-term governments, or similar private assets, were near zero, in this view, is insufficient to establish a true liquidity trap. Here we reexamine this debate by exploring several rates that have been neglected in previous discussions of the liquidity trap in the 1930s: yields on corporate debt (from low risk to junk), bank lending rates, and mortgage rates. Our discussion of corporate debt, incidentally, is based on a new series of monthly junk bond yields. In general our evidence adds further support to the view that many segments of the spectrum of interest rates were flexible in the 1930s and were responsive to monetary policy. However, it must be admitted that the small segment of time in which a liquidity trap might have been present makes drawing robust conclusions difficult. The urgency for reexamining the behavior of financial markets in the 1930s is the fear that the liquidity trap is back, or as Paul Krugman might put it "baaack."[1] But the underlying issue of whether monetary policy must work through short-term government rates is important at all times.

The chapter is organized as follows. Section 2 discusses the history of thought about the liquidity trap, focusing on the early divide between Keynes and the American Keynesians. Section 3 explores a view of the transmission mechanism that underlies much thinking by economic historians about the liquidity trap: the view that monetary policy effects must spread in diminishing waves from assets that are very similar to money to assets that are very different from money. The following sections then explore the behavior of various interest rate series during the 1930s. Section 4 explores the yields on government debt. Section 5 explores the yields on corporate bonds including high-risk corporates. Section 6 explores commercial bank lending rates. The data explored in this section is well known to economic historians interested in long-term integration of banking markets, but has not been explored in relation to monetary policy. Section 7 explores mortgage lending rates. Section 8 summarizes the main findings.

6.2 Some history of thought

We will not attempt the daunting task of reviewing all of the literature on the liquidity trap in the depression. It will be worthwhile, however, to explore the basic ideas that emerged in the depression and the early postwar years. These ideas set the stage for the work that followed, and to a surprising extent drive most current policy discussions.

The idea of a liquidity trap, of course, was developed by John Maynard Keynes, who termed it "absolute liquidity preference" in the *General Theory* (1965 [1936]).[2] Indeed, while most economic ideas seem to have long and disputed pedigrees, there is wide agreement that the idea of a liquidity trap begins with Keynes. Keynes argued that the demand for money could become perfectly elastic (or almost perfectly elastic) with respect to the rate of interest, especially at very low interest rates. In those circumstances monetary policy would be ineffective.

The reason a liquidity trap could develop was derived from the role played by speculators in bond markets; a role that Keynes, himself a speculator, knew well. If most speculators believed that the current rate of interest was "normal" then any attempt by the central bank to lower it by buying government securities would be counterbalanced by the willingness of speculators to sell these securities. Since speculators believed that any increase in price produced by government purchases would be temporary, they would sell bonds at the slightest price increase, convinced that they could buy them back later at a lower price. Similarly, any attempt to raise rates would be counterbalanced by the willingness of speculators to buy bonds. Interest rates were therefore likely to be very sticky at their normal rates.

A liquidity trap could emerge at any rate that speculators believed to be normal, but it would be more likely as rates approached zero. Speculators would then be almost certain that if rates moved substantially in any direction, it would be to go higher. If the central bank attempted to lower rates further by buying bonds, speculators would be more than willing to exchange bonds that paid little interest for cash while waiting for a fall in bond prices. The implication of the liquidity trap was that monetary policy was powerless to affect interest rates, and therefore powerless to stimulate investment spending and the remainder of the economy. In Keynes's view, fiscal policy, or radical governmental controls over private investment, would have to be used to promote expansion.

In the *General Theory* Keynes (1965 [1936], 207) suggested that while a liquidity trap was an important theoretical possibility it had not yet arisen in the real world.

> There is the possibility, for reasons discussed above, that, after the rate of interest has fallen to a certain level, liquidity-preference may become virtually absolute in the sense that almost everyone prefers cash to holding a debt which yields so low a rate of interest. In this event the monetary authority would have lost effective control over the rate of interest. But whilst this limiting case might become practically important in future, I know of no example of it hitherto. *Indeed, owing to the unwillingness of most monetary authorities to deal boldly in debts of long term, there has not been much opportunity for a test* [Our emphasis].

The last line of this often quoted paragraph deserves some additional comment. Evidently, Keynes envisioned a liquidity trap not simply as a low rate on short-term government debt, but rather as low and stable rates on the whole spectrum of maturities. Until all of these rates found their sticking points, more could be done with monetary policy to lower rates, and thereby encourage investment.

By dealing boldly Keynes had in mind, we believe, direct cash purchases of debt that expanded the monetary base and the stock of money. One could imagine other sorts of operations, say conversions of one sort of debt into another, but it seems to us that Keynes probably had in mind mainly direct purchases rather than more complicated transactions. The most famous case of debt management was the British stock conversion of 1932 in which a huge government loan dating from World War I was converted into a longer-term debt with a lower coupon. A number of observers claimed that the success of this conversion lowered the whole spectrum of rates. But, as Capie, Mills, and Wood (1986) demonstrate, the effect of this conversion was to alter the slope of the term structure rather than shift the whole function to a lower level.

The story of the liquidity trap must be an American story. The depression in Britain was a much milder affair than in the United States, both in terms of financial markets and real outcomes (Capie 1990). It would have been odd to attribute a condition that we associate with depression and nonfunctioning capital markets to an economy that experienced a mild shock and showed rapid signs of improvement. But Keynes was undoubtedly aware that short-term government rates in the United States had fallen to very low levels when he wrote this passage. There is some debate about the chronological evolution of Keynes's thinking (Patinkin 1993), but it is clear that he was thinking intensively about money, interest rates, and economic activity for several years before the publication of the *General Theory* (the preface to the *General Theory* was dated December 13, 1935). Rates on U.S. Treasuries fell below one percent in May 1931 and remained below one percent (except for one month) for the remainder of the decade. Rates on short-term governments in the U.K. also fell to very low levels. If low rates on Treasuries, rates close to the "zero bound," were sufficient to constitute a liquidity trap by Keynes's definition, he would have claimed the United States and Britain as examples in the *General Theory*. Keynes never, as far as we are aware, reversed this judgment and claimed that there had been a liquidity trap during the depression (Moggridge and Howson 1974).

Although the famous passage from the *General Theory* quoted above might be referring simply to government securities, it is clear that Keynes believed that attention had to be paid to private as well as government rates. In a passage following shortly after the one quoted above, Keynes argued that even though risk free rates might be brought to very low levels by central bank monetary policies, risky rates, perhaps bank lending rates, which were relevant to investment decisions, might remain at unacceptably high levels.

> As the pure rate of interest declines it does not follow that the allowances for the expense and risk decline *pari passu*. Thus the rate of interest which the typical borrower has to pay may decline more slowly than the pure rate of interest, and may be incapable of being brought, by the methods of the existing banking and financial organization, below a certain minimum figure. This is particularly important if the estimation of moral risk is appreciable. For where the risk is due to doubt in the mind of the lender concerning the honesty of the borrower, there is nothing in the mind of a borrower who does not intend to be dishonest to offset the resultant higher charge. It is also important in cases of short-term loans (e.g. bank loans) where the expenses are heavy; – a bank may have to charge its customers 1½ to 2 per cent., even if the pure rate of interest to the lender is nil.
>
> (Keynes 1965 [1936], 208)

Keynes's belief that long-term rates could be manipulated by the government came to the fore when he advised the postwar Labour government on its cheap money policy (Howson 1987). Keynes advised the Labour government to maintain low rates on the whole spectrum of maturities. Essentially he advised the Labour government to try the experiment which in the *General Theory* he noted had not been tried during the depression. A subsequent generation of economists would worry that an expansionary monetary policy would simply raise the rate of inflation and nominal interest rates, leaving real rates unaffected, and investment unchanged. But Keynes did not worry about these long-term effects of monetary expansion on inflation and through inflation on interest rates (Wood 1989; Howson 1989).

Although Keynes did not believe that the United States had fallen into a liquidity trap in the 1930s, Keynes's American followers believed the opposite: the United States had fallen into a liquidity trap that rendered monetary policy ineffective. Alvin Hansen (1953, 132), often described as the father of American Keynesianism, thought Keynes's assertion that there had never been a liquidity trap "strange and inconsistent." In Hansen's view it was clear that, "In fact, the United States during the thirties (especially from 1934 on) was a good example [of a liquidity trap]." American Keynesians were aware, of course, that there was a broad spectrum of rates beyond short-term government rates, but they believed that these rates had been sticky and had come down too slowly to have had a significant effect on economic activity, despite the downward pressure generated by low short-term rates (Tobin 1965, 472).

The difference between Keynes's view that no economy had ever fallen into a liquidity trap and Hansen's assertion that it was obvious that the U.S. economy had, is a manifestation of Axel Leijonhufvud's (1968) distinction between *Keynesian Economics* and the *Economics of Keynes*. Keynesian economics, in Leijonhufvud's lexicon, refers to the views of economists like Hansen and his followers who believed that liquidity traps or near liquidity traps rendered monetary policy ineffective. Keynes, according to Leijonhufvud (1968, 202–203), believed something else: that it was possible for the central bank to alter crucial long rates over the long run, but that in the short run the stickiness of rates created by opinions about the normal rates might prevent the central bank from reducing rates with *sufficient speed* to restore full employment in a timely fashion.

Although there was no sign of a liquidity trap in the early postwar years, economists returned from time to time to the question of whether there had been a liquidity trap in the 1930s. Much of this literature is cited in Brunner and Meltzer (1968). One line of argument in the postwar literature pressed by advocates of monetary policy was that it is important to look at the full spectrum of securities. Only when the full spectrum, including long-term private and public securities, have reached low sticking points and have become insensitive to monetary policy can we conclude that the economy is in a liquidity trap; and by this standard, according to this school of thought, the U.S. economy had not fallen into a liquidity trap in the late 1930s.

It would be beyond the scope of this paper to document all of the references in the postwar literature to the importance of looking at the full spectrum of rates, but we can hit some of the highlights. Friedman and Schwartz (1963a, 231), in one of their first reports on their research, argued that it was necessary to go beyond the rate on short-term government bonds and consider "a much wider range of assets including not only government and private fixed-interest and equity securities traded on major financial markets, but also a host of other assets." Friedman (1971, 28), after describing Keynes's analysis of liquidity preference, claimed that the difference between monetarists and Keynesians "was less in the nature of the process than in the range of assets considered," and that he and fellow monetarists regarded "the market rates stressed by the Keynesians as only a small part of the spectrum of rates that are relevant." Indeed, Friedman would have gone so far as to include "durable and semi-durable consumer goods, structures, and other real property" in the list of assets whose prices were affected by changes in the stock of money, creating a direct link between money and real economic activity.[3]

This insight was developed in depth in the classic paper by Brunner and Meltzer (1968) on the liquidity trap to which we have already referred. This paper provided considerable theoretical and empirical evidence for rejecting the view that there was a liquidity trap in the 1930s. More recently, in response to the assertion that Japan had fallen into a liquidity trap in the 1990s, Meltzer (2003) reasserted the case against a full-spectrum liquidity trap in the 1930s in the United States or in the 1990s in Japan in a more accessible form: the idea, Meltzer declared, was "liquidity claptrap."[4]

One strategy for testing for the presence of a liquidity trap is to bypass the discussion of what was happening in financial markets and look directly for possible impacts of monetary policy on GDP and similar variables. Christina Romer (1992) in a famous paper, for example, used "multipliers" derived from pre-depression experience to show that monetary policy, rather than fiscal policy or self-correction, could explain almost all of the recovery from the depths of the depression. Other important contributions in this tradition include Athanasios Orphanides (2004) and Christopher Hanes (2006). Orphanides stressed the impact of the famous decision by the Federal Reserve to double required reserve ratios in 1936 and 1937. How could there have been a liquidity trap, if monetary policy had such powerful effects? Hanes (2006) added support for the view that there was no full-spectrum liquidity trap by showing that changes in non-borrowed reserves affected long-term government bond rates during the 1930s. Here we test the no-full-spectrum liquidity trap view by examining an array of interest rates including yields on high-grade and high-risk (junk) corporate bonds, bank lending rates, and mortgage rates, that have been bypassed in earlier discussions. In general, our results reinforce the conclusion of Friedman and Schwartz, Brunner and Meltzer, Orphanides, Hanes, and others, including Keynes, that there was no full-spectrum liquidity trap: monetary policy influenced interest rates throughout the 1930s.

6.3 A pebble in a pond or a tsunami in the sea?

One argument, particularly influential among economic historians, that supports the view that there was a liquidity trap in the 1930s, one that is particularly relevant to the empirical examples that follow, is that monetary policy must leave a greater mark on assets that are more like money. This view relies on what Peter Temin (1976, 96–103) calls the "pebble in the pond" theory of the monetary transmission mechanism. A pebble thrown into the center of a pond produces a wave of large amplitude at the spot where the pebble hits the water, which then diminishes and becomes irregular as the wave approaches the shore. In the same way, a change in the stock of money would have a large impact on the market for assets that are closest to money, for example treasury bills, but would have a diminishing impact as one moved further away – toward long-term governments, low-risk corporate bonds, high-risk corporates, stocks, and so on.

This sequence makes the most sense when the change in the stock of money is generated by open market purchases or sales of short-term governments – when the stone is in fact thrown in the center of the pond. It is one of the unique features of the 1930s that major changes in the stock of money were brought about by changes in the reserve ratios of banks, and by changes in the currency-deposit ratios of the public. Given one of these starting points, it is less obvious that government bond rates would show the first and largest effects. It is possible to imagine, moreover, adjustment paths in which monetary shocks, even shocks that begin with open market operations in treasury bills, made a smaller impression on assets similar to money and a larger impression on assets that were less similar. We might call this the "tsunami" theory of the transmission of monetary shocks because it suggests larger effects on assets that are further from money on a liquidity continuum.[5]

An example can make a tsunami effect more plausible. Suppose wealth holders view assets as lying on a continuum with cash having the highest degree of liquidity because of its short-term to maturity (zero!) and its low risk of default (zero!), deposits having the next highest degree, short-term government bonds the next highest, and so on. And suppose that the perceived liquidity of deposits declines as a result of a rising tide of bank failures. What would be the simplest way to restore the initial level of total liquidity? Rather than sell, say, \$100 of government bonds (a near money) to acquire \$100 of cash, a transaction that would have little impact on the overall liquidity position of the wealth holder, it would be more effective to sell, say, \$100 of junk bonds and acquire \$100 in government bonds or cash.

Some Keynesian economists who would agree that the economy was not in a full-spectrum liquidity trap in the 1930s would argue that rates on longer-term assets could have been forced down, but only by central bank operations in those markets. The only way, to follow the Temin analogy, to produce waves near the shore is to throw pebbles near the shore. This is the burden of the last part of the initial quote from Keynes: to lower long-term rates the central bank must *"deal boldly in debts of long term."* Evidently, Keynes believed that markets were segmented to a degree that prevented them from responding to a general increase in liquidity. This concern was raised recently by Bernanke and Reinhart (2004, 87) who argued that, even if the central bank succeeded in reducing the rates on long-term government bonds, a "disconnect" might develop between those rates and corporate bond rates. Paul Krugman seems to be in this camp. In a recent blog (*New York Times*, January 26, 2009, 3:17 pm) he agreed that we might not be in a full-spectrum liquidity trap, but suggested that the only way that monetary policy could address nonzero rates in various markets would be through "controversial measures." By this he meant, we presume, Federal Reserve purchase programs aimed at specific markets. In what follows we will be addressing two questions. The easier question is whether some rates remained high and variable despite the fall in treasury bill rates to near zero levels, the more difficult question is whether these rates remained responsive to changes in the general level of liquidity.

6.4 The yield on government debt

The basic reason for believing that there might have been a liquidity trap in the 1930s is clear in Figure 6.1, which shows the yield on 3-month treasury bills,

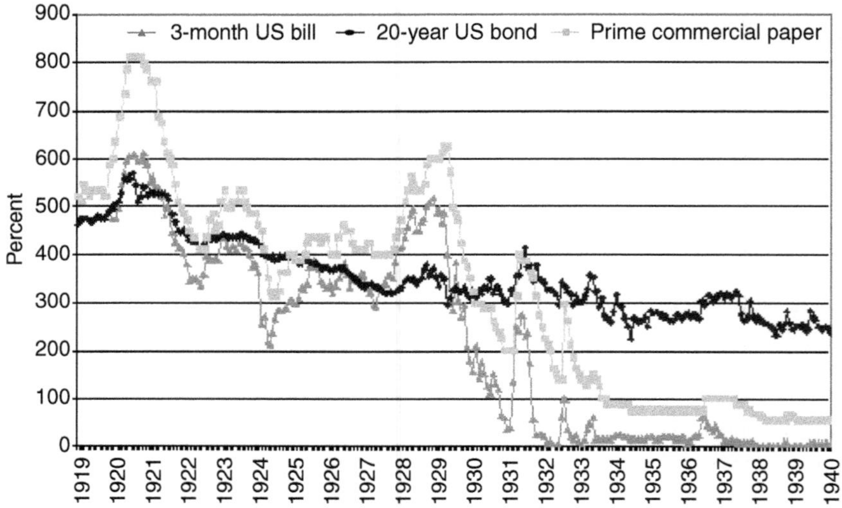

Figure 6.1 Yields on three-month U.S. Treasury Bills, 20-Year U.S. Government Bonds, and 4–6 month commercial paper, monthly, 1919–1940 (sources: U.S. Government: *Historical Statistics* (2006, series Cb56, Cb57, Cb60, and Cb61). Cb60 and Cb61 are from Cecchetti (1988, table A1). Cecchetti's series began in January 1929. We extended Cb60 backward using Cb56 but adding the average difference between Cb60 and Cb56 for the first five months of 1929. We extended Cb61 backward in the same way using Cb57. Prime Commercial Paper: *Banking and Monetary Statistics: 1914–1941* (1943 Table 120)).

the yield on 4–6 month prime commercial paper, a short-term low-risk private asset, and the yield on 20-year federal government bonds during the interwar period. During the 1920s the two short-term rates behave in a "normal" way. Both are well above zero, and both increase during postwar monetary stringencies beginning with the severe recession from January 1920 to July 1921. This recession was exacerbated by the Federal Reserve's decision to raise its discount rate to slow a postwar inflation. Both rates spike during the early 1930s. From then on, however, the two rates fall. By the end of 1934 the short-term private rate is below 1.00 percent and the short-term government is nearly zero, where they will remain for the remainder of the decade.

To be sure, the short-term rates do show a small jump during the recession of 1937–1938. This recession was also exacerbated by monetary policy: the famous doubling of required reserves. In general, however, the short-term rates remain low and stable during the second half of the 1930s. The yield on 20-year federal bonds also behaves somewhat differently in the second half of the 1930s than it did in the 1920s. The series levels off at a rate below three percent. And the response to the 1937–1938 recession is somewhat muted compared with the response in earlier periods of monetary stringency.

For many economists, this is all the proof needed to show that the economy had entered a liquidity trap: rates on safe assets were low and steady, and above all else, short-term government rates were near the "zero bound." The explanation, in simple liquidity preference terms, would be that the demand for money had remained stable and that increases in the stock of money (the stock increased rapidly in the second half of the thirties) had pushed the equilibrium interest rate down until the economy had reached the infinitely elastic portion of the liquidity preference curve.

There are other plausible reasons for the fall in the yield on low-risk debt. One, obviously, is the severity of the banking and financial crisis. Most wealth holders were looking for the safest possible place to put their savings, especially funds that they might need to retrieve quickly, and that meant liquid short-term assets or U.S. government bonds. This was true for banks, as well as other wealth holders, because banks now had to hold large liquid reserves against the possibility of a new round of bank runs. The banks that survived the crisis, moreover, were likely to have been the more conservative banks.

Friedman and Schwartz (1963b, 496) suggested some additional reasons for low interest rates in the 1930s and, especially surprising, low rates during the expansion from 1933 to 1937. One was the general anti-business environment created by the New Deal – the creation of new regulatory agencies such as the Security and Exchange Commission, Roosevelt's attacks on "economic royalists," and so on – that discouraged business investment, and hence business borrowing. On the other side of the market was the inflow of funds seeking a safe haven from political dangers in Europe. There was also an institutional change that fostered low yields on government bonds. Deposit insurance helped to stabilize the banking system and encouraged a shift back into deposits, but the prohibition of interest payments on deposits encouraged funds to flow in the other direction.[6] Much short-term lending, moreover, had traditionally been used to finance speculative positions in the stock market and had been secured by stocks as collateral. With the collapse of the stock market, this source of demand for loans dried up.

The full-spectrum school of thought, however, urges us to look at other interest rates such as yields on corporate debt before concluding that there was a liquidity trap. Deriving meaningful conclusions about the effects of monetary policy from the spreads between corporate bonds and government bonds or the spreads among corporate bonds of varying degrees of risk is fraught, as Capie and Wood (2004, 80–83) point out, with difficulties. Nevertheless, as they also point out, it is worth doing the best one can with ambiguous data when the stakes are high.

6.5 The yields on corporate bonds

Figure 6.2 shows the yields on Aaa, Baa, and junk (high-risk) corporate bonds, and the annual rate of growth of M2 monthly from January 1935 to December 1939. Money growth is, it is true, a controversial indicator of monetary policy.

For one thing, it could be argued that we should be looking at movements in the real stock of money rather than the nominal stock. Keynes, although often portrayed as assuming that prices and wages were constant, thought that one potential channel through which decreases in wages and prices could stimulate the economy was by increasing the real stock of money, which in turn would lower interest rates, although he thought that the amount of stimulation through this channel would be small (Capie and Wood 2004, 66). For our purposes, however, Figure 6.2 does not look very different when we use a real measure of the stock of money. In any case, M2 growth, which was normally positive, declined and turned negative on an annual basis in November 1937. What happened in financial markets? The rate on Aaa bonds hardly moved. If one were to look only at the Aaa rate one would conclude that the United States was in a liquidity trap, or something very close to one. If one looks at the rate on Baa bonds, however, one does see, as Meltzer (2003, 519–520) points out, an

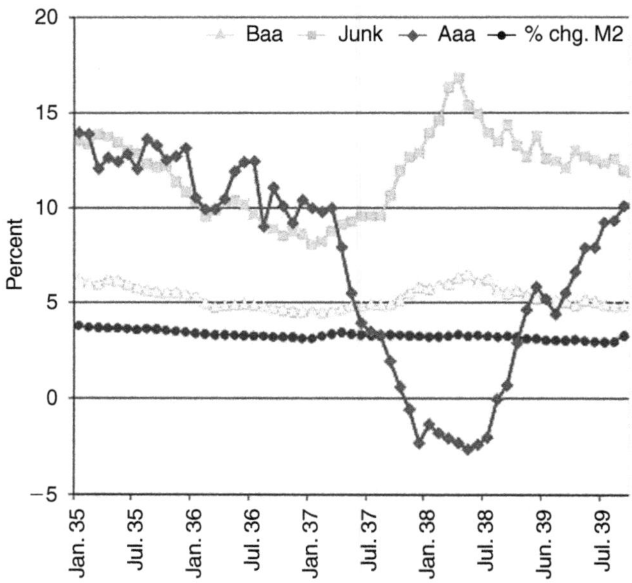

Figure 6.2 Rate of change in the stock of money and selected corporate bond yields, monthly January 1935–December 1939 (sources: Money is M2 from Friedman and Schwartz (1970, 29–35). The rate of growth of money plotted in the chart is the difference between the natural logarithm of M2 in a particular month and the natural logarithm of M2 12 months earlier multiplied by 100. The Aaa and Baa bond yields are from *Historical Statistics* (2006, series Cb58 and Cb59). Junk bond yields were prepared by the authors from individual bond yields reported in the *Wall Street Journal*. A quarterly series was reported in Basile (1989), but we prepared a monthly index for this paper. Junk bonds were defined as bonds rated B or lower by Moody's. These bonds were described by Moody's as "speculative.")

increase in rates, although an increase of only a few basis points. But if one looks at the yield on junk bonds, one sees a dramatic rise.[7] The data, in short, is consistent with the continued effectiveness of monetary policy, presuming that money can have tsunami effects on assets far removed from money on the liquidity spectrum.

This evidence, although it strengthens the case against the liquidity trap, is unlikely, to return to the point made by Capie and Wood (2004, 80–83) as to the fraught nature of such data, to end debate. For one thing, a liquidity trap is an asymmetric concept. The liquidity preference curve, as we usually picture it, is a relationship between the rate of interest measured on the vertical axis and the amount of money measured on the horizontal axis that slopes downward to the right over some normal range, but flattens out in a liquidity trap. If the economy is near the point at which the curve flattens out, decreases in the stock of money will raise rates, but increases will not lower them. Another explanation for the relationships shown in Figure 6.2 is that it was a coincidence. The recession that ran from May 1937 to June 1938 (according to the NBER chronology) was severe. Investors were afraid that 1929–1933 had returned, and the perceived probability of defaults rose. It is conceivable that nonmonetary forces produced the recession, which in turn produced the increases in Baa and junk bond yields, and that the decline in the stock of money was produced by an independent policy shock, the famous doubling of bank reserve ratios identified by Friedman and Schwartz.

Given that the main monetary event during the period in which it is alleged that there was a liquidity trap was a decrease in the stock of money and an increase in interest rates (Figure 6.2), it would not be surprising that one could find a statistical correlation between interest rates and money in monthly data. Nevertheless, we can shed some additional light on the relationship between monetary policy and bond yields by estimating a simple vector autoregression (VAR) that includes a bond yield, an indicator of monetary policy, and an indicator of general economic conditions. A formal test of the effect of a shock to monetary policy on interest rates will provide some information on statistical significance, will allow us, to a degree, to hold general economic conditions constant, and will allow us to make comparisons with other periods.[8]

We used M2 as our indicator of monetary policy. This choice goes against the grain of recent studies that use an interest rate, say the Federal Funds Rate, as the main indicator of monetary policy. A short-term rate, however, would not make much sense for the depression because short-term rates, as we have seen, were extremely low and stable. The question is whether monetary actions that clearly did not have much influence on short-term rates might have had an impact on long-term yields, including yields on risky long-term assets. M2 has the merit that it reflects changes in monetary conditions brought about by open market purchases and sales, discount loans, and reserve ratio changes. Another merit is that it emerged as the best single indicator of monetary policy in this era in the intensive testing conducted by Friedman and Schwartz. For general economic conditions we tried industrial production (IP), personal income, and department store sales. These series are frequently used in studies of the depression when a monthly indicator is required. The last two allow for movements in prices to affect rates. In principle, of course, one could include all three and many additional indicators of economic conditions – for example, indicators of total profits or wages – in the VARs. The small number of observations, however, precludes going very far in this direction.

We estimated VARs for the period from January 1934 to December 1941. This is the period when a liquidity trap was most likely to have been operating. Recall Hansen's claim: that "*especially* [our emphasis] from 1934 onward the United States was a good example [of a liquidity trap]." Demonstrating that monetary policy had an impact on junk bond rates or other yields in a sample that included other periods would not resolve the issue of whether or not there was a liquidity trap during the late 1930s.

Tests for unit roots showed that the presence of a unit root could not be rejected for IP, M2, or the yield on junk bonds. We could, however, reject the null hypothesis of a unit root in the yields on Aaa and Baa bonds. There was no statistical evidence for a cointegrating relationship among IP, M2, and junk bond yields, and no evidence of a cointegrating relationship between M2 and IP. We therefore estimated the following VARs. (1) For Aaa bonds, a VAR in first differences of M2, first differences of IP, and levels of the yield on Aaa bonds. Using information criteria we selected four lags. (2) For Baa bonds, a VAR in first differences of M2, first differences of IP, and levels of the yield on Baa bonds. Using information criteria we selected two lags. (3) For junk bonds, a VAR in first differences of M2, first differences of IP, and first differences of the yield on junk bonds. Using information criteria we selected five lags. The resulting impulse-response functions for the impacts of M2 on corporate bond yields are shown in Figures 6.3–6.5.

Each figure shows a "liquidity effect," a fall in interest rates in response to an increase in money. The difference is in the size of the effects and their statistical significance. The impact on the Aaa bond rate is very small and not statistically significant at the 5 percent level. The impact on the Baa bond rate is somewhat larger, but also not statistically significant. The impact on the junk bond rate is still larger and does reach conventional levels of statistical significance. Figure 6.5 is for a VAR in which M2 is the first variable entering the VAR and the junk bond rate is the last variable, but the impulse-response functions from other orderings are similar. The results, in other words, provide additional support for the claim advanced above that monetary stimulation remained effective, but showed up in tsunamis that left little impact on assets close to money on the liquidity spectrum but rose in magnitude as they reached the distant shores of the liquidity spectrum.

We tested the robustness of the relationships shown in Figures 6.3–6.5, particularly the effect shown in Figure 6.5, in several ways.

1 In theory increases in money could also affect nominal interest rates through income and inflation effects. Increases in money that raised income levels would raise rates by increasing the demand for credit. Increases in money that increased prices could also influence rates. Increases in income or prices

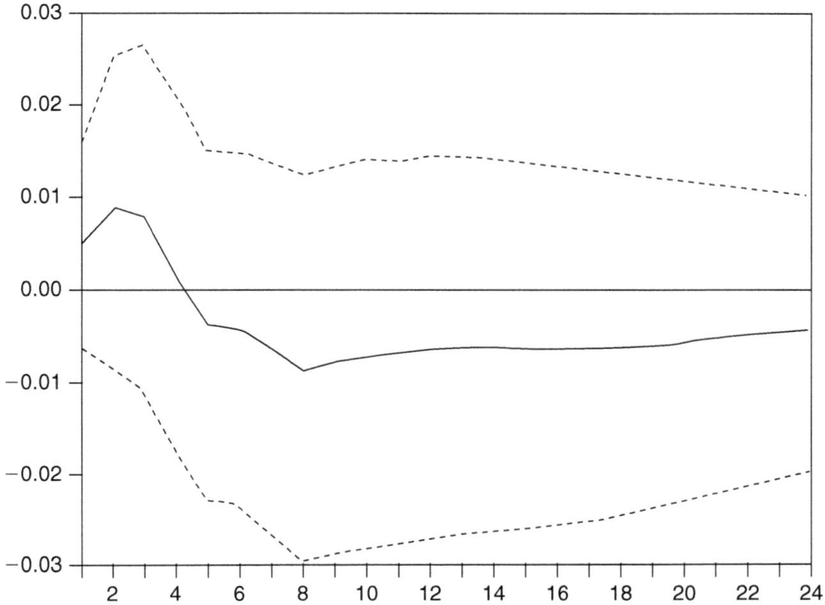

Figure 6.3 The response of the Aaa bond yield to a one standard deviation innovation in M2, Cholesky decomposition (source: see Figure 6.2).

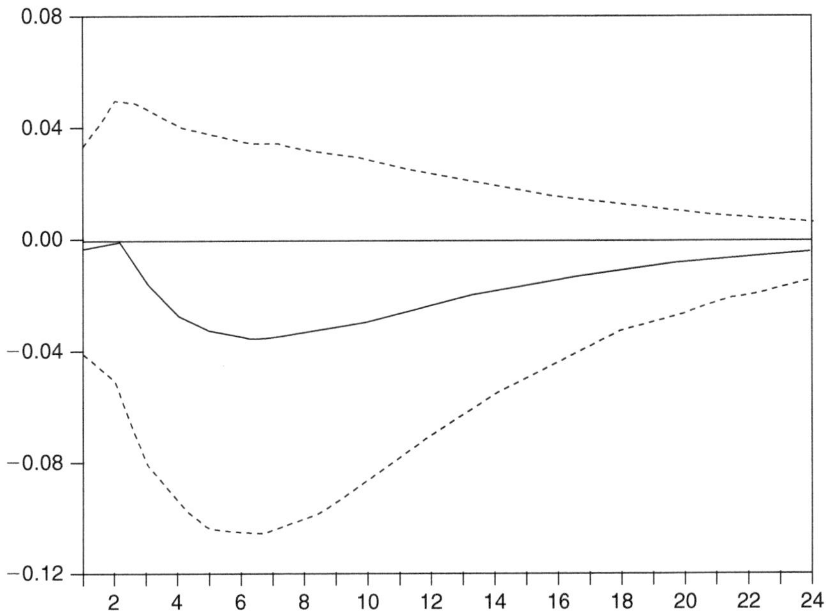

Figure 6.4 The response of the Baa bond yield to a one standard deviation in M2, Cholesky decomposition (source: see Figure 6.2).

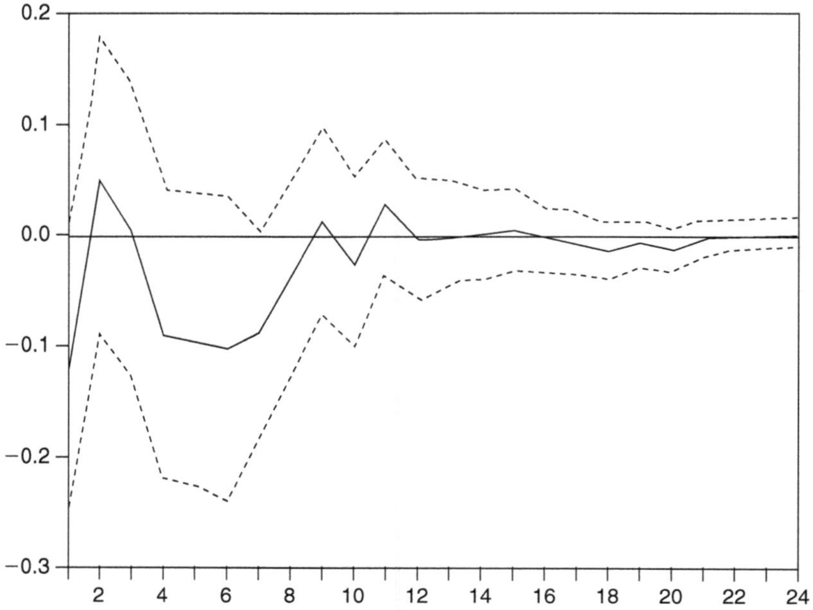

Figure 6.5 The response of the junk bond to a one standard deviation innovation in M2, Cholesky decomposition (source: see Figure 6.2).

stemming from nonmonetary forces, moreover, we should add, could also influence rates. Both Keynes and Fisher, to take two of the most astute and prominent contemporary observers, described a number of channels through which price changes might have influenced nominal rates during the depression (Capie and Wood 2004, 66–67). Prices in the United States rose during the initial recovery and then fell in the 1936–1937 recession, so it is possible that expectations of price changes may have influenced rates. We addressed this issue by trying nominal measures, department store sales, and personal income, in the VARs. Department store sales were a larger share of retail sales at that time than they are now and personal income was a larger share of GDP, so these variables were more representative of general economic conditions than they would be today. We also used these variables in combination. The impulse-response charts for the response of the junk bond rate to a monetary innovation, however, look similar no matter the variable or combination of variables used to represent general economic conditions.

2 We also tried introducing government bond rates and Aaa and Baa corporate bond rates in the VARs to see if we could still detect an effect running from money to junk bond rates when returns on governments or lower-risk corporates were allowed to affect junk bond rates. Again, the impulse-response charts showing the effect of money on junk bonds look much like Figures 6.3–6.5.

3 We also estimated the VARs over other segments of the interwar period. The period January 1919 to December 1929, the "normal" period preceding the depression, is especially useful for comparison purposes. Finding a relationship between monetary policy and junk bond yields during the 1920s would not provide much evidence against the view that there was a liquidity trap in the second half of the 1930s. But finding no relationship would raise questions about the meaning of a relationship within the liquidity-trap period. IP and department store sales are available for the 1920s. Unfortunately, monthly personal income does not begin until January 1929. Although the precise shape of the impulse-response function varies depending on the way the equation is estimated, we found similar effects in the 1920s and the second half of the 1930s.

4 We estimated similar VARs using quarterly data so that we could use nominal GNP to measure general market conditions. Again, we found effects similar to those shown in Figures 6.3–6.5. In the end we were persuaded that the evidence is consistent with the idea that changes in money produced changes in corporate yields in the late 1930s, and that the effects, especially in the junk bond market, were large enough to be taken seriously. Given the caveats noted above – the small number of observations and the asymmetrical character of a liquidity trap (decreases in money might produce increases in rates as one moved out of the liquidity trap range) – it must be conceded that room for doubt remains.

In addition to rates on assets sold on competitive national markets it is also important to look at rates set by lending institutions. These loans were an important share of total lending. In the *General Theory*, as we noted, Keynes pointed to downwardly rigid bank lending rates as a potential obstacle to reaching full employment. We will begin by examining commercial bank lending rates.

6.6 Commercial bank lending rates

The data on bank lending rates has been used mainly in studies of regional integration and has been neglected in studies of the liquidity trap. This is unfortunate because bank lending is one of the most important potential channels for monetary policy. We can take a closer look at bank lending rates based on the work of Gene Smiley (1981), who computed biannual bank lending rates by region from 1926 through 1937, and Howard Bodenhorn (1996). These rates, it must be admitted, are somewhat synthetic: they are derived from national bank earning and balance sheet data. However, Smiley and Bodenhorn did a careful job of purging the data, as much as possible, of extraneous influences. The results must come close to actual lending rates.

There is, however, another potential difficulty. Riskier borrowers were being denied loans after the depression took hold. A tighter set of lending standards was implicitly an increase in rates, but one that was not reflected in measured loan rates. Milton Friedman, writing shortly after the outbreak of the Korean

War, put it this way. "The nominal rate charged by banks or other lenders may not change but the 'quality' of loans they will make may rise; there may be what has, somewhat unfortunately, been called 'capital rationing.' Thus I shall regard the lesser availability of loans at the former rate of interest as equivalent to a rise in 'the' rate of interest" (Friedman 1951, 189). Ben Bernanke in his famous paper on nonmonetary effects of the Great Depression put it this way: "commercial loan rates reflect loans that are actually made, not the shadow cost of bank funds to a representative potential borrower" (Bernanke 1983, 264). Nevertheless, a comparison of measured loan rates across regions can provide some hints about how bank lending rates changed over the course of the depression.

Figure 6.6 shows bank lending rates in New York and Illinois, the states that contain the nation's primary financial centers, New York and Chicago. Both rates fell dramatically over the course of the depression. By 1937 they had reached a low level. Indeed, the rates in New York City and Chicago (available in Smiley's data set) were consistent with Keynes's claim, quoted above, that "in cases of short-term loans (e.g. bank loans) where the expenses are heavy; – a bank may have to charge its customers 1½ to 2 percent., even if the pure rate of interest to the lender is nil" (Keynes 1965 [1936], 208). The most likely explanation for this decline is that banks in the financial centers were able to shed their higher risk borrowers and maintain a core of very low-risk borrowers. In some cases banks in the financial centers may have been able to replace smaller firms on their customer lists with larger firms that in the twenties would have chosen to borrow on long-term capital markets. Both rates in Figure 6.6 increase between 1937 and 1938, perhaps reflecting, with some delay, the monetary contraction that influenced the bond market.

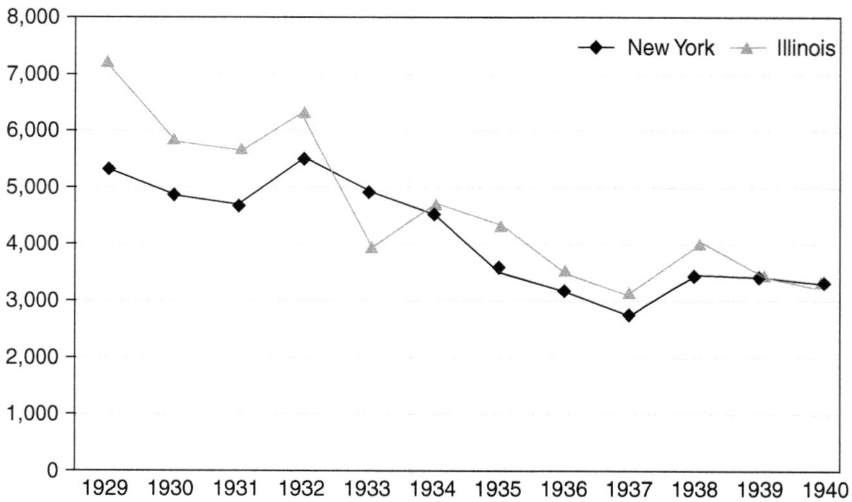

Figure 6.6 Bank lending rates in New York and Illinois, 1929–1940 (source: from the data underlying Bodenhorn (1996), courtesy of the author).

What about other parts of the country? Figure 6.7 shows bank lending rates in seven other states. These states were the most populous states (as of 1930) in the remaining census divisions. California, for example, represents the Pacific division; and Texas, the West South Central division. The pattern is somewhat mixed, but bank lending rates in five of these seven states also show the increases following the mid-depression monetary contraction. This suggests that further injections of bank reserves might have brought rates down further and faster than was the case.[9]

The national banks, which are the source of the bank lending rates explored in Figures 6.7–6.9, were forced by law to concentrate mainly on short-term commercial loans, although they did some real estate loans. The best available data for mortgage lending is the NBER's sample of mortgage loans which comes from insurance companies and other intermediaries heavily involved in real estate markets.

6.7 Mortgage rates

The NBER collected data on a large sample of mortgage loans. The most relevant variables, for our purposes, are the contract loan rate and the percentage of the purchase price that the borrower supplied from other sources, the down payment. We can refer to the latter as the buyer's equity, although in fact the purchaser may have borrowed some or all of the down payment. Other things equal, the down payment, measured as a percentage of the price, is a reasonable *ex ante* measure of the quality of loans. In the published data, at least, there does not seem to be anything else that would serve as well. Requiring a large down payment protects the lender because the price of the property can fall further before the value of the property falls below the value of the loan. On the other

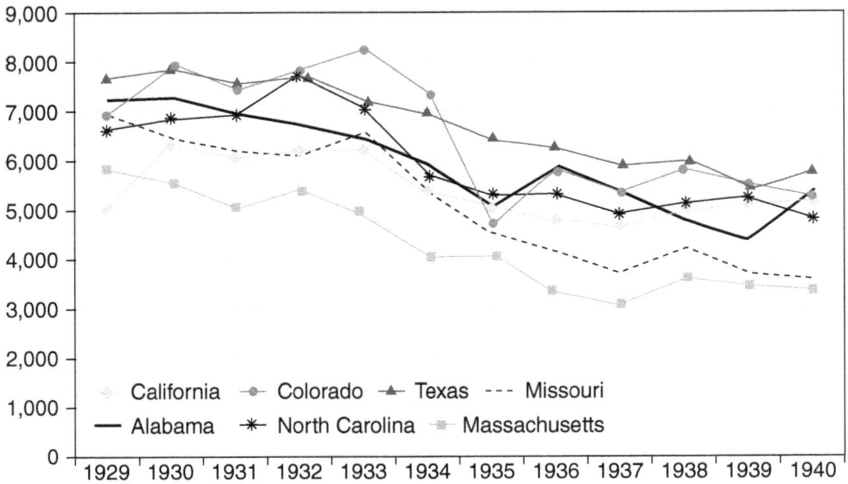

Figure 6.7 Bank lending rates in selected states, 1929–1940 (source: from the data underlying Bodenhorn (1996), courtesy of the author).

hand, requiring a large down payment is equivalent, from the point of view of the borrower, to a higher contract rate with the same down payment.[10]

Figures 6.8–6.10 show how mortgage rates and down payments changed during the depression. Figure 6.8 shows the contract rate on nonfarm mortgages made by commercial banks (measured on the left vertical axis) and the "percentage down" or equity (measured on the right vertical axis). Figure 6.9 shows the same variables for savings and loan associations, and Figure 6.10 shows the same variables for life insurance companies. As might be expected if there was arbitrage across markets, the three figures show similar patterns. The contract loan rate and down payment were stable during the 1920s for all three lenders. The loan rate and percentage required down payment rose during the financial crisis – a pattern that is clearest for the loans made by the life insurance companies.[11] Rates and down payments then fell during the remainder of the 1930s. There does not seem to have been a strong reaction to the mid-depression monetary contraction in either contract rates or required down payments. Of all the series these seem the least responsive to short-term changes in monetary policy. This was not particularly a phenomenon unique to the late 1930s; it also appears to have been true in the 1920s. Whether the fall in rates and required down payments during the second half of the 1930s was due more to the general fall in rates, and the increase in liquidity, or to the launching of New Deal mortgage programs would be difficult to determine. In either case, there was some room for mortgage rates and required down payments to decline and stimulate housing demand, although the process was drawn out over the length of the depression.

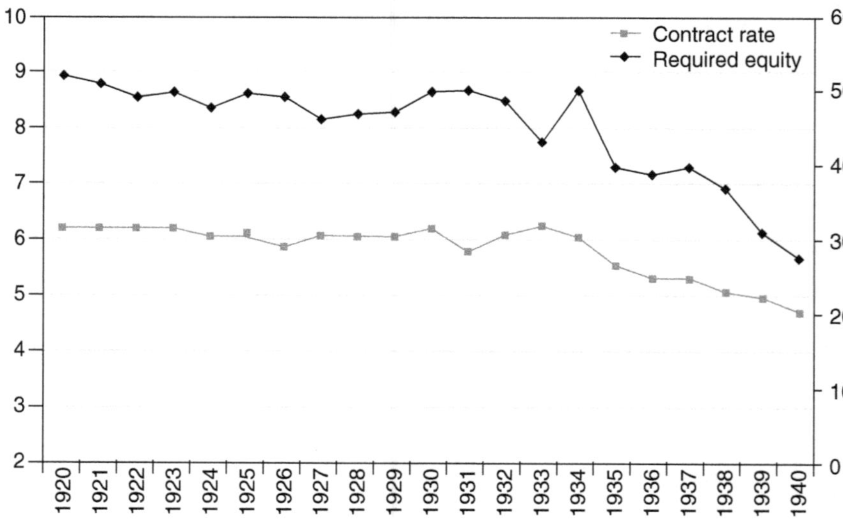

Figure 6.8 Nonfarm mortgages created by commercial banks, annual 1920–1940. The contract rate is measured as a percent along the left vertical axis, and the required down payment is measured as a percent along the right vertical axis (source: *Historical Statistics* (2006, series Dc1196 and Dc1202)).

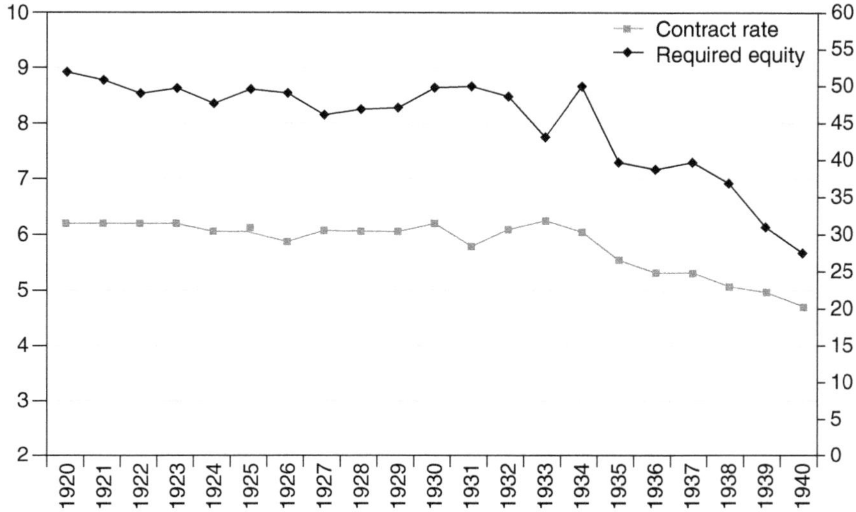

Figure 6.9 Nonfarm mortgages by savings and loan association, 1920–1940. The contract rate is measured as a percent along the left vertical axis, and the required down payment is measured as a percent along the right vertical axis (source: *Historical Statistics* (2006, series Dc1194 and Dc1293)).

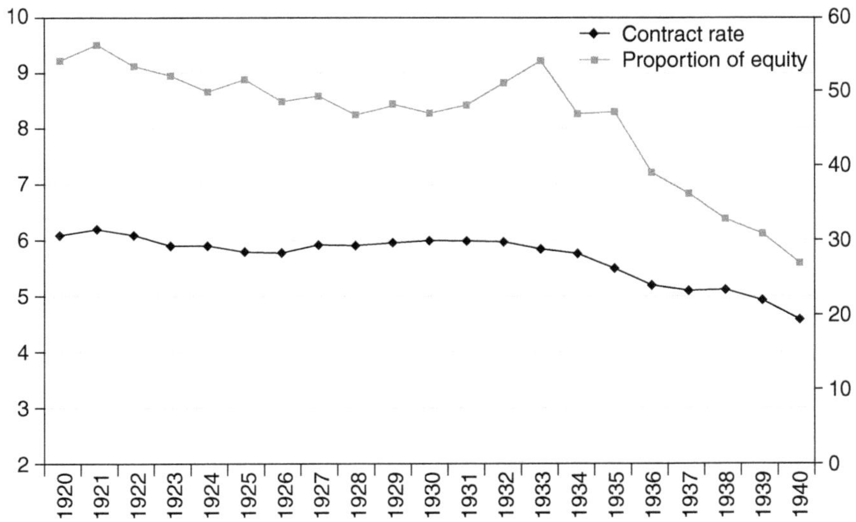

Figure 6.10 Nonfarm mortgages by life insurance companies, 1920–1940. The contract rate is measured as a percent along the left vertical axis, and the required down payment is measured as a percent along the right vertical axis (source: *Historical Statistics* (2006, series Dc1195 and Dc1201)).

6.8 Conclusions

The debate over whether there was a liquidity trap in the United States in the 1930s has continued, with varying intensity, since the concept of a liquidity trap was first developed by John Maynard Keynes in the *General Theory*. The early American Keynesians believed that the United States had fallen into a liquidity trap in the 1930s because, first of all, yields on short-term government bonds were near zero for most of the decade, and because longer-term rates seemed to adjust slowly. An alternative school of thought (which includes Keynes!) holds that even though short-term government rates were near zero, the economy had not fallen into a liquidity trap because the full spectrum of rates had not reached low sticking points. This paper provides some additional support for this view by considering a range of interest rates that have been neglected in discussions of the liquidity trap, including rates on corporate debt ranging from Aaa to high yield (junk) bonds, bank lending rates, and mortgage rates. The main finding is that as we move away from short-term government bonds on the "liquidity spectrum" we encounter rates that appear to have been sensitive to changes in monetary policy, although the mortgage rates were an exception.

These findings, even if accepted, are unlikely to end the debate over whether there was a liquidity trap in the 1930s. The period of time in which a liquidity trap was alleged to have been in effect – the 1930s as a whole, or perhaps simply the second half of the 1930s – does not provide a sufficient number of observations from which to draw robust conclusions. More importantly, the question of the transmission mechanism remains open. If we want to lower rates can we rely on general increases in the stock of money that create tsunamis throughout the whole spectrum of rates, or does lowering rates in a depression require specific measures tied to specific markets?

Notes

1 The title of an influential paper by Krugman (1998), which argued that Japan during its "lost decade" was another example of a liquidity trap, was "It's Baaack: Japan's Slump and the Return of the Liquidity Trap." Writing recently in the *New York Times* (June 14, 2009), Krugman argued that our current situation represents "the third time in history that a major economy has found itself in a liquidity trap, a situation in which interest-rate cuts, the conventional way to perk up the economy, have reached their limit. When this happens, unconventional measures are the only way to fight recession." The unconventional policies that Krugman has in mind may include Federal Reserve purchases of long-term government and possibly private securities, which would make his position close to Keynes's described below.

2 The earliest use of the term "liquidity trap" that we are aware of is Dennis Robertson (1940). The first references in a search of the economics literature on JSTOR are in reviews of Robertson by Arthur W. Marget (1941), and J.R. Hicks (1942), indicating the appeal of the term. The first reference in an article is in a critical review of Keynes's contributions by Gottfried Haberler (1946).

3 Friedman stressed the range of assets again in his "Comments on the Critics" (1972, 909–910).

4 Recently, Alan Meltzer, perhaps engaging in some hyperbole in order to drive home his point, suggested in a recent interview that all rates would have to be zero for a true liquidity trap. "... during the period of transition, long-term rates move relative to short-term rates, stock prices move relative to bond yields. And there isn't that tight relationship that would be required so that you could get a liquidity trap. *You'd have to get all those yields to zero*; we never have seen that" (Clement and Meltzer 2009).
5 A tsunami, as most of us now know, behaves differently from the wave created by a pebble in a pond. It is usually caused by an earthquake or undersea volcanic eruption (surely a better analogy for the financial crises of the 1930s than a pebble in a pond). The wave produced is barely noticeable on the surface when it is passing through deep water. As it enters the shallow water near the shore, however, the wave becomes compacted and grows in height, and can come ashore doing enormous damage.
6 An attempt to shift from deposits into bonds won't alter the total amount of deposits – the buyer's bank account will decrease by x dollars while the seller's account will increase by x dollars – but will alter the price of bonds.
7 Junk bonds were corporate bonds rated below B or lower by Moody's.
8 Garman and Fridson (1998) show that monetary factors influenced junk bond yield spreads in recent years.
9 During the depression the Federal Reserve published monthly series which they described as bank customer loan rates. These rates are available at the NBER website (www.nber.org) in their section of historical macro-data. These series do not react to the mid-depression monetary contraction. We don't have a good explanation for why these series failed to respond as did the others. Perhaps banks had shed many of their short-term customers and retained long-term customers who held very strong ideas about normal rates based on their long relationships with the banks.
10 Here is a numerical example which illustrates the relationship between loan rates and required down payments. Suppose that a borrower puts down $50 and borrows $100 in order to buy a house valued at $150. If the opportunity cost of the equity is 10 percent per year and the mortgage rate is 6 percent per year then the annual cost of the property is $11.00 per year [$11.00 = .10*50 + .06*100]. Suppose that the mortgage rate is raised to 7 percent, then the total cost would rise to $12 per year [$12 = .10*50 + .07*100]. Alternatively, the cost of the loan could be kept at 6 percent, but the borrower could be asked to make a down payment of $75. Then the cost of buying the home would still have risen to $12.00 per year [.10*75 + .06*75], the same as if the mortgage rate had risen.
11 Saulnier (1950), who presents the same series, describes it as limited to dwellings for 1–4 families.

References

Bodenhorn, Howard. "A More Perfect Union: Regional Interest Rates in the Twentieth Century United States." In *Anglo-American Financial Systems: Institutions and Markets in the Twentieth Century*, eds. Michael Bordo and Richard Sylla, 415–453. Burr Ridge, Illinois: Irwin, 1996.

Banking and Monetary Statistics: 1914–1941. U.S. Federal Reserve System, Board of Governors, September, 1943.

Basile, Peter F. "The Cyclical Variation of Junk Bond Risk Premiums in a Historical Perspective, 1910–1955," Masters Thesis, Rutgers University, 1989.

Bernanke, Ben S. "Nonmonetary Effects of the Financial Crisis in the Propagation of the Great Depression." *The American Economic Review* 73 (1983): 257–276.

Bernanke, Ben S. and Vincent R. Reinhart. "Conducting Monetary Policy at Very Low Short-Term Interest Rates." *The American Economic Review, Papers and Proceedings* 94(2), (May 2004): 85–90.

Brunner, Karl and Allan H. Meltzer. "Liquidity Traps for Money, Bank Credit, and Interest Rates." *The Journal of Political Economy* 76 (Jan.–Feb. 1968): 1–37.

Calomiris, Charles W. "Financial Factors in the Great Depression." *The Journal of Economic Perspectives* 7 (Spring 1993): 61–85.

Capie, Forrest H. "Monetary Stringency, Stock Market Crash, and the Great Depression." *European Economic Review* 34 (May 1990): 608–615.

Capie, Forrest H., and Geoffrey Wood. "Price Change, Financial Stability, and the British Economy, 1870–1939." In *Deflation: Current and Historical Perspectives*, eds. Richard C.K. Burdekin and Pierre L. Siklos, 61–90. Studies in Macroeconomic History, 2004.

Capie, Forrest H., Terry C. Mills, and Geoffrey E. Wood. "Debt Management and Interest Rates: The British Stock Conversion of 1932." *Applied Economics* 18 (Oct. 1986): 1111–1126.

Cecchetti, Stephen G. "The Case of the Negative Nominal Interest Rates: New Estimates of the Term Structure of Interest Rates during the Great Depression." *The Journal of Political Economy* 96(6) (Dec. 1988): 1111–1141.

Clement, Douglas, and Allan Meltzer. "Interview with Allan H. Meltzer." *The Region*, The Federal Reserve Bank of Minneapolis, September 2003. Available at www.minneapolisfed.org/publications_papers/pub_display.cfm?id=3356, accessed August 6, 2009.

Friedman, Milton. "Comments on Monetary Policy." *The Review of Economics and Statistics* (1951): 33(3) 186–191.

Friedman, Milton. "A Theoretical Framework for Monetary Analysis." NBER Occasional Paper 112. New York: National Bureau of Economic Research, 1971.

Friedman, Milton. "Comments on the Critics." *The Journal of Political Economy* 80 (1972): 906–950.

Friedman, Milton and Anna J. Schwartz. "Money and Business Cycles." *The Review of Economics and Statistics* 45(1) Part 2, Supplement (Feb. 1963a): 32–64.

Friedman, Milton and Anna J. Schwartz. *A Monetary History of the United States, 1867–1960*. Princeton: Princeton University Press, for the NBER, 1963b.

Friedman, Milton and Anna J. Schwartz. *Monetary Statistics of the United States: Estimates, Sources, Methods*. New York: Columbia University Press, for the NBER, 1970.

Garman, M. Christopher and Martin S. Fridson. "Monetary Influences on the High Yield Spread versus Treasuries." In *High-Yield Bonds: Market Structure, Portfolio Management, and Credit Risk Modeling*, eds. Theodore M. Barhnhill, Jr., William F. Maxwell, and Mark R.R. Shenkman. New York: McGraw-Hill, 1998, pp. 251–268.

Haberler, Gottfried. "The Place of the General Theory of Employment, Interest, and Money in the History of Economic Thought (in Keynes' *Contributions to Economics: Four Views*)." *The Review of Economic Statistics* 28 (1946): 187–194.

Hanes, Christopher. "The Liquidity Trap and U.S. Interest Rates in the 1930s." *Journal of Money, Credit and Banking* 38(1) (Feb. 2006): 163–194.

Hansen, Alvin H. *A Guide to Keynes*. New York: McGraw-Hill, 1953.

Hicks, John R. "The Monetary Theory of D. H. Robertson." *Economica*, New Series, 9 (Feb. 1942): 53–57.

Historical Statistics of the United States: Earliest Times to the Present. Eds. Susan B. Carter, Scott Sigmund Gartner, Michael R. Haines, Alan L. Olmstead, Richard Sutch, and Gavin Wright. Millennial edn. New York: Cambridge University Press, 2006.

Howson, Susan. "The Origins of Cheaper Money, 1945–7." *The Economic History Review*, New Series, 40(3) (Aug. 1987): 433–452.
Howson, Susan. "Cheap Money versus Cheaper Money: A Reply to Professor Wood." *The Economic History Review*, New Series, 42(3) (Aug. 1989): 401–405.
Keynes, John Maynard. *The General Theory of Employment, Interest, and Money*. New York: Harcourt, Brace & World, Inc, 1965 [1936].
Krugman, Paul R. "It's Baaack: Japan's Slump and the Return of the Liquidity Trap." *Brookings Papers on Economic Activity* (1998): 137–187.
Leijonhufvud, Axel. *On Keynesian Economics and the Economics of Keynes; a Study in Monetary Theory*. New York, Oxford University Press, 1968.
Marget, Arthur W. "Review of *Essays in Monetary Theory* by D. H. Robertson." *The Review of Economic Statistics* 23 (1941): 147–151.
Meltzer, Allan H. "Liquidity Claptrap." *The International Economy* (Nov./Dec. 1999): 18–23.
Meltzer, Allan H. *A History of the Federal Reserve*. Chicago: University of Chicago Press, 2003.
Moggridge, D.E. and Susan Howson. "Keynes on Monetary Policy, 1910–1946." *Oxford Economic Papers*, New Series, 26(2) (Jul. 1974): 226–247.
Orphanides, Athanasios. "Monetary Policy in Deflation: The Liquidity Trap in History and Practice." *The North American Journal of Economics and Finance* 15(1) (2004): 101–124.
Patinkin, Don. "On the Chronology of the General Theory." *The Economic Journal* 103(418) (May 1993): 647–663.
Robertson, Dennis H. *Essays in Monetary Theory*. London: P.S. King and Son, Ltd., 1940.
Romer, Christina D. "What Ended the Great Depression?" *Journal of Economic History* 52 (Dec. 1992).
Saulnier, Raymond Joseph. *Urban Mortgage Lending by Life Insurance Companies*. National Bureau of Economic Research, 1950.
Smiley, Gene. "Regional Variation in Bank Loan Rates in the Interwar Years." *The Journal of Economic History* 41(4) (Dec. 1981): 889–901.
Temin, Peter. *Did Monetary Forces Cause the Great Depression?* New York: W.W. Norton, 1976.
Tobin, James. "The Monetary Interpretation of History." *The American Economic Review* 55(3) (Jun. 1965): 464–485.
Wicker, Elmus. *The Banking Panics of the Great Depression*. Cambridge, New York: Cambridge University Press, 1996.
Wood, Geoffrey E. "A Comment on 'The Origins of Cheaper Money'." *The Economic History Review*, New Series, 42(3) (Aug. 1989): 396–400.

7 Two-and-a-half centuries of British interest rates, monetary regimes and inflation

Terence C. Mills and Geoffrey Wood

7.1 Introduction

Beginning with Henry Thornton at the turn of the nineteenth century (Thornton (1802 [1978]), the relationship between interest rates and prices, either in levels or rates of change (i.e., inflation), has provoked great interest and debate, as exemplified by Wicksell (1907), Fisher (1907, 1930) and Keynes (1930) in the early twentieth century, and Friedman and Schwartz (1982) in the late twentieth century, with Alvarez, Lucas and Weber (2001) providing a twenty-first century contribution. In this paper we re-examine this relationship across the two and a half centuries from 1750 to 2006 for which reliable British data is available, paying particular attention to changes in monetary regimes as these may lead to breaks in the relationships and to associated shifts in the stochastic structure of interest rates and prices.

Section 2 introduces the data that we use and reports initial exploratory analysis using simple graphical and regression approaches. Section 3 provides some background monetary theory. Section 4 looks explicitly at the Gibson Paradox, the relationship between the interest rate and the price level that has been thought to have been found during the gold standard regime. The behaviour of the real interest rate – in particular, the long run stability of the expected real rate – is the concern of Section 5, which also examines whether any breaks or changes in the relationship are associated with changes in the money supply regime. Section 6 provides a summary and conclusions.

7.2 Initial data analysis

The price series that we use is the composite consumer price index of O'Donoghue, Goulding and Allen (2004, Table 7.1) for 1750 to 2003. This index links together various indices to provide the longest consistent and continuous official price index for the UK yet available. As the index is the RPI from 1947, this was used to update the series to 2006. Denoting this series as P_t, the logarithms $p_t = \log(P_t)$ are plotted as Figure 7.1 and the annual rate of inflation, $\pi_t = 100\Delta p_t$, is plotted as Figure 7.2. The familiar pattern of British price level movements is clearly seen in Figure 7.1: an upward trend during the latter half of the eighteenth century, stability throughout the nineteenth century up to the outbreak of the First World War, a sharp increase at the end of the war followed by a decline throughout the interwar period, and then a continued upward trend, with various degrees of steepness, till the end of the sample period. Inflation is very volatile until the mid-1800s, although it fluctuates around zero (the median rate of inflation between 1750 and 1860 is indeed zero). Inflation fluctuations tend to decline thereafter, albeit with bouts of volatility, but average inflation becomes markedly positive. (The decline in volatility seems highly likely to be due at least in part to the broadening of the index and in particular the associated decline in the weight given to primary products.) Post-1860 median inflation is 2.4 per cent per annum, but sub-periods contain quite varied inflation rates: for example, median inflation for the sub-periods 1860–1913, 1919–1939, 1946–1967, 1968–1997 and 1998–2006 are 0 per cent, –0.6 per cent, 3.4 per cent, 6.1 per cent and 2.9 per cent respectively.

For the long interest rate we use the yield on Consols, taken from Mitchell (1998) and extended to 2006. This series, denoted R_t, is shown in Figure 7.3. For more than two centuries (1750 to 1960) the Consol yield fluctuated within the band 2.25–6 per cent. From 1965 to 1997 the yield was consistently well above this band, reaching over 14 per cent during the mid-1970s. From 1998, after (but not necessarily because) the Bank of England became independent, it has once again been below 6 per cent.

Figure 7.4 presents a scatterplot of R_t on π_t, with the 'aberrant' period from 1965 to 1997 highlighted, along with the two inflation outliers of 31.0 per cent in 1800 and –26.4 per cent in 1802. These numbers may seem large, but the price level was in fact very volatile at that time. Feinstein (1998) and Clark

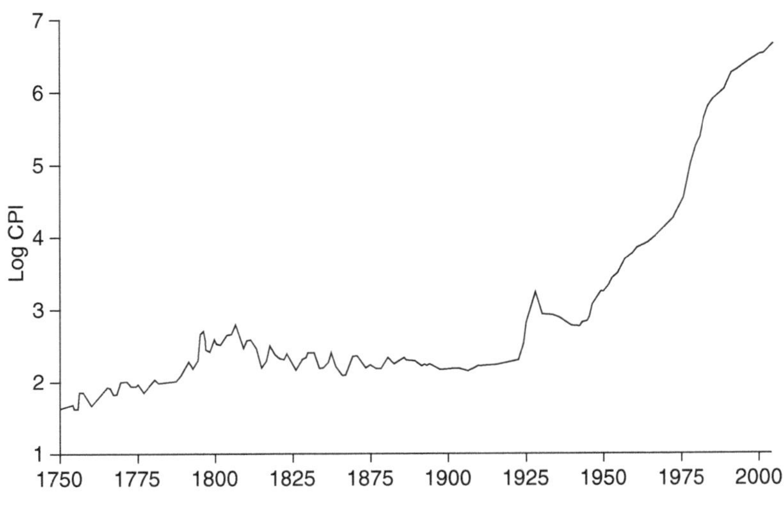

Figure 7.1 Logarithm of the cost of living index, p_t: 1750–2006.

(2001), for different measures of the price level, report price increases of 30 per cent and 29.4 per cent, respectively, for 1800 and price falls of 22.8 per cent and 24.1 per cent for 1802. The 1965 to 1997 observations appear as a distinct cluster and a regression of R_t on π_t over this sub-period produces

$$R_t = \underset{(0.436)}{6.815} + \underset{(0.050)}{0.410}\ \pi_t$$

$$R^2 = 0.685\ ;\ dw = 2.08\ ;\ T = 33\ (1965\text{–}1997)$$

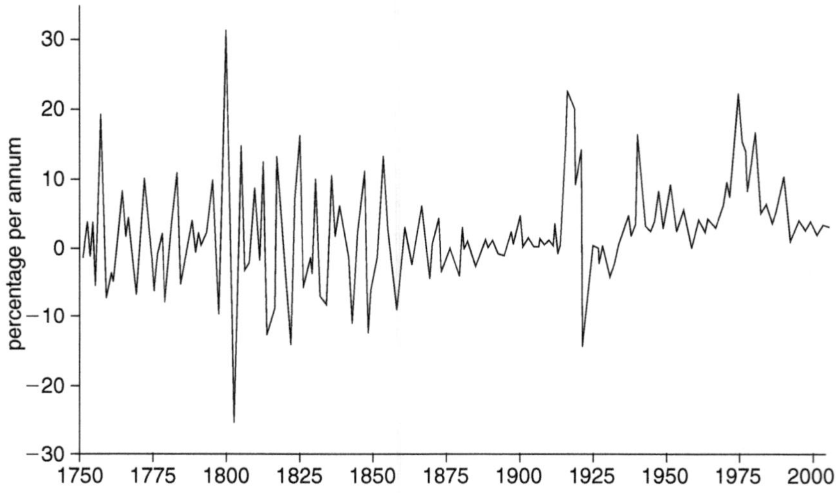

Figure 7.2 Annual inflation rate, π_t: 1750–2006.

Figure 7.3 Consol yield R_t: 1750–2006.

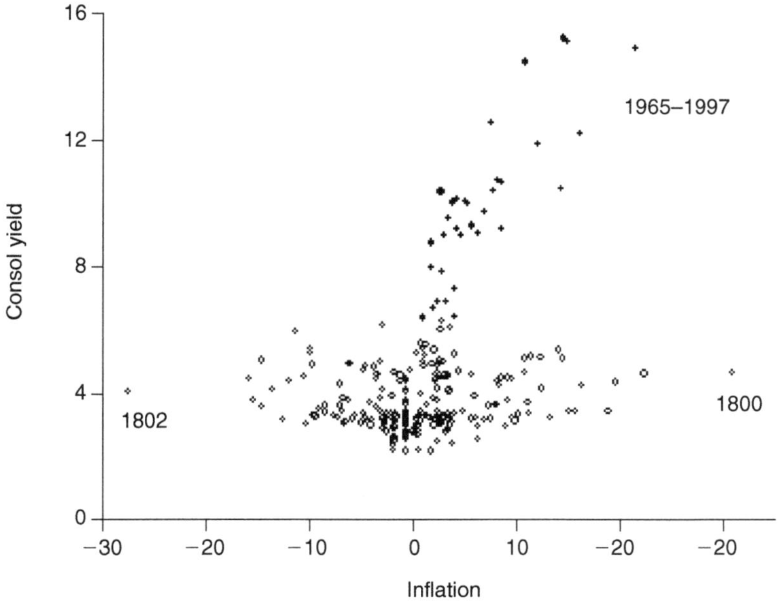

Figure 7.4 Scatterplot of R_t on π_t: 1750–2006.

Note the absence of autocorrelation and the highly significant positive coefficient on inflation (figures in parentheses are standard errors). In contrast, the corresponding regression for the remainder of the sample (1750–1964, 1998–2006) yielded

$$R_t = \underset{(0.058)}{3.724} + \underset{(0.085)}{0.083}\ \pi_t$$

$$R^2 = 0.004;\ dw = 0.18;\ T = 222\ (1750\text{–}1964,\ 1998\text{–}2006)$$

Accounting for the severe residual autocorrelation either by estimating with a first order autoregressive error process or by first differencing reduces the *t*-ratio from 1.0 to 0.3. For example,

$$\Delta R_t = \underset{(0.003)}{0.001}\ \Delta\pi_t$$

$$R^2 = 0.000;\ dw = 2.08;\ T = 221\ (1751\text{–}1964,\ 1998\text{–}2006)$$

This confirms that, for the great majority of the two and a half centuries for which we have data, there was no contemporaneous linear relationship between R_t and π_t. Neither does including lags of $\Delta\pi_t$ improve matters: adding three lags of this regressor for the 1751–1964 period only increases the R^2 to 0.012.

It is well worth remarking, however, when thinking about these results, that what we have referred to as inflation is, in this period, distinctly different from what the term is taken to mean when discussing, for example, post-1950 data. Before about 1950 prices rose and fell. It is not quite appropriate to describe these movements as price level changes, for they were not sudden steps from one level to another. They could continue for several years before more or less reversing over, usually, a similar period of time. Hence these 'inflations' are not the inexorable rise in the price level that has, in most countries, including Britain, characterised most of the years after 1950. It is important to bear this in mind when we turn to discussing measures of the real rate of interest.[1]

Barro (1987) argues that government spending has an impact on interest rates. Figure 7.5 shows the government spending ratio g_t, defined as the ratio of government spending to GNP. The large spikes in g_t associated with increased military spending during the Napoleonic and the twentieth century world wars are clearly seen, as is the rising trend throughout the twentieth century. Including g_t as a control variable produces the following regressions

$$\underset{}{R_t} = \underset{(2.142)}{1.932} + \underset{(0.047)}{0.399}\ \pi_t + \underset{(6.204)}{14.408}\ g_t$$

$$R^2 = 0.733;\ dw = 2.39;\ T = 33\ (1965\text{–}1997)$$

$$\Delta R_t = \underset{(0.0035)}{0.0006}\ \Delta\pi_t + \underset{(0.544)}{0.804}\ \Delta g_t$$

$$R^2 = 0.010;\ dw = 2.09;\ T = 221\ (1750\text{–}1964,\ 1998\text{–}2005)$$

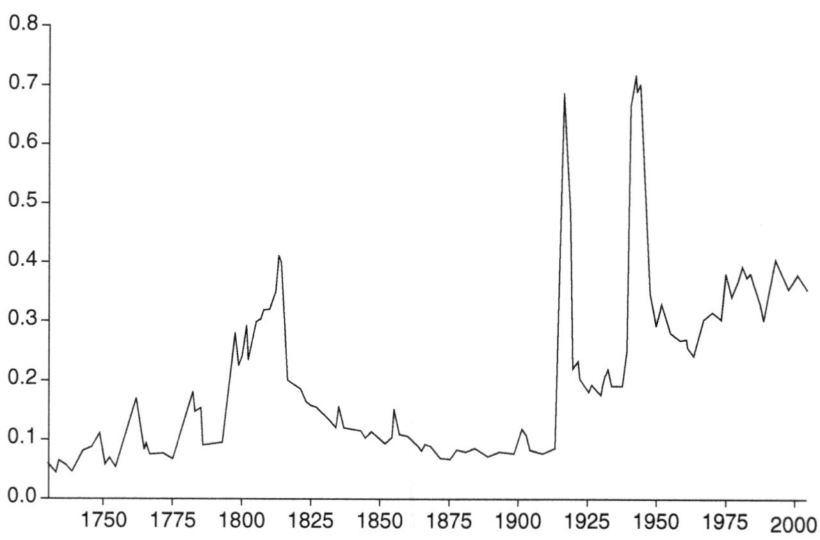

Figure 7.5 Government spending ratio, g_t: 1750–2006.

The inclusion of the government spending ratio, although it enters significantly, has no impact on the strength and direction of the relationship between consol yields and inflation. Is this evidence of no relationship a consequence of failing to distinguish between periods when Britain was on (1750–1796, 1822–1913, 1925–1931) and off the gold standard, and the price level consequently anchored or not? Figure 7.6 suggests this is not the explanation, and this is confirmed by the following regressions. Note that in the first two gold standard periods (1750–1796, 1822–1913) the government ratio of government spending to GNP, g, averaged 0.10; in the other years this average was 0.32. For the gold standard sample, we obtain

$$\underset{}{R_t =} \underset{(0.058)}{3.412} + \underset{(0.0100)}{0.0002}\ \pi_t$$

$R^2 = 0.001$; $dw = 0.18$; $T = 146$ (1750–1796, 1822–1913, 1925–1931)

$$\Delta R_t = -\underset{(0.00335)}{0.00132}\ \Delta\pi_t + \underset{(1.573)}{6.738}\ \Delta g_t$$

$R^2 = 0.114$; $dw = 2.74$; $T = 146$ (1750–1796, 1822–1913, 1925–1931)

For the periods when the gold standard was not in operation, we obtain

$$R_t = \underset{(0.105)}{4.373} + \underset{(0.0116)}{0.0070}\ \pi_t$$

$R^2 = 0.005$; $dw = 0.28$; $T = 77$ (1797–1821, 1914–1924, 1932–1964, 1998–2006)

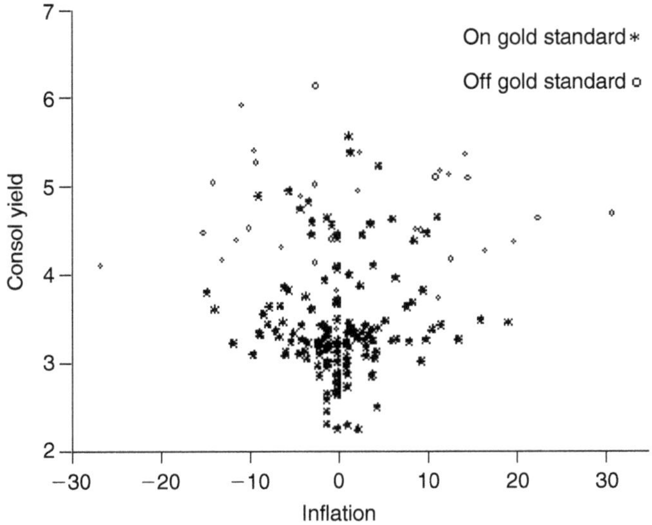

Figure 7.6 Scatterplot of R_t on π_t distinguishing between being off and on the gold standard.

and

$$\Delta R_t = \underset{(0.0068)}{0.0011}\ \Delta\pi_t + \underset{(0.798)}{0.475}\ \Delta g_t$$

$R^2 = 0.005$; $dw = 1.90$; $T = 77$ (1797–1821, 1914–1924, 1932–1964, 1998–2005)

There continues to be no relationship between R_t and π_t in any of these periods and, indeed, no relationship between R_t and g_t except under the gold standard (the possible presence of residual autocorrelation indicated by the *dw* statistic in this regression does not affect this relationship: the coefficient on g_t remains significant at less than the 0.005 level when heteroskedastic and autocorrelation consistent standard errors are used).

The difference between the gold standard periods and others may reflect the fact that Britain was very large relative to the rest of the world then, and hence government borrowing had a significant effect on rates even in an open economy with a fixed exchange rate. But this explanation leaves a puzzle. Why did not whatever produced the absence of a relationship, regardless of the exchange rate regime, outside gold standard periods not produce a similar absence when Britain was on the gold standard? This is a matter for future research.

7.3 Some theory

Before turning to the Gibson Paradox and to some further examination of our data, a brief review of the relevant monetary theory is useful. First there is the concept of a monetary (or money supply) regime. By such a regime we mean a widely understood and accepted set of rules, which may not be explicit, governing the supply of money. A modern example is Britain's inflation target for the Bank of England: another is the currency board arrangement in place between the US and the British Virgin Islands. The most famous monetary regime is the gold standard: see Bordo and Kydland (1996). The important point to note about these examples is that the regime may be internal – an inflation target; external – a currency peg; based on a commodity; or there may be no rule at all. These different types of regime may have different implications for the relationship between money and interest rates.

Our data set covers a variety of monetary regimes. In 1717 Britain became a gold standard country (inadvertently as it so happened – for details see Kindleberger 1984). It remained on the gold standard until 1793, when the standard was suspended with the start of the wars with France. The standard was resumed in 1821, and Britain then adhered to it until the suspension of 1914, which lasted until 1925. The resumed (by then gold exchange) standard lasted until 1931, and there was then a rather dirty exchange rate float. The Bretton Woods system was introduced in 1946, and retained a residual link with gold until 1971. There was then a more or less clean float from 1979 until

Britain joined the ERM in 1989. Britain was evicted from that in 1992, and has been an inflation targeting country ever since. The degree of credibility may (or may not) have increased with the granting of 'operational independence' to the Bank of England in 1997.

We next summarise very briefly the theory of the effect of money on interest rates. That prepares the way for a discussion first of the Gibson Paradox, and then for consideration of whether the money supply regime, as opposed to the money supply's behaviour, had any effect on the behaviour of interest rates. We start by setting out the effects of a shift from one steady rate of money growth to another. It is, for exposition, assumed for the moment that the price level is initially constant and that no change in money growth is anticipated.

If the price level is slower to change in response to a monetary shock than either output or interest rates (real and nominal on our price level and expectations assumption), the effects of the monetary change fall into four stages. There may be a loanable funds effect, which is then succeeded by a liquidity effect. This, in turn, is followed by an effect on output, and then by an effect on the price level. Inflationary expectations, on our assumption, change when the price level does. We describe these effects in order.

7.3.1 Loanable funds effect

Revenue accrues to the issuer of new money. If any portion of this is saved it adds to the supply of loanable funds, and thus lowers yields – on both real and nominal assets – until inflation expectations change. In addition, as the change in money growth was unexpected, realised yields on assets differ from expected yields.

7.3.2 Liquidity preference effect

This arises since we have moved, under our example, to a higher rate of growth of money, and neither income nor the price level is allowed to change at this point in the analysis. The only variable then free to move, the interest rate, must move so as to equilibrate the growing supply with the demand for money. To accommodate the ever rising money to income ratio, the nominal interest rate has to fall, and to keep on doing so until other variables start to change.

7.3.3 Income effect

We now have lower nominal and real interest rates on all types of asset. The prices of the services of assets have therefore risen relative to the prices of the assets which supply these services. Nominal expenditure then rises. This increases the quantity of real cash balances demanded at every opportunity cost, so as income rises interest rates also start to rise, thus starting to reverse the liquidity effect. (Since prices are still fixed, nominal and real rates move together.) Rates keep on rising until they are back at their pre-monetary expansion level, for only then is the stimulus to expenditure dissipated.

7.3.4 Price expectations and price change

A higher rate of money growth has been imposed on an unchanged real economy. Since no real variable changes, the only way for the continually increased money stock to be accommodated – for it to be held, in other words – is for prices to rise. They must eventually rise at the same rate as the money stock; otherwise the real supply of money will change, but that is impossible as the demand for real cash balances has not changed. When this happens price expectations must change until the inflation is fully anticipated. If they do not, real interest rates on all assets would fall again and there would be a further stimulus to expenditure.

That analysis was fully understood by writers as early as Thornton (1802 [1978]), as well as by later writers such as Irving Fisher and Alfred Marshall. It may not be surprising that Thornton was aware of it, even including the effect of inflationary expectations, for he had lived through the Napoleonic Wars, a period of considerable inflation, but it is worthy of note that Fisher and Marshall, both writing during long periods of price stability, were aware of the importance of inflation expectations in understanding economic phenomena. But aware of it they certainly were, as will become apparent when we turn to the next part of the analysis.

7.4 The Gibson Paradox

Consider Figure 7.7, which is the scatterplot of *R* on the *price level*, *p*, for the period 1750 to 1914, split (by examination of the data) into periods closely approximating the years when Britain was on and off the gold standard, i.e., 1750–1794, 1795–1820, 1821–1914. During the two 'gold standard' periods, there is clearly a positive relationship between the two variables, but there appears to be a negative relationship in the intervening years. The positive correlation between the long term interest rate and the price level, termed the 'Gibson Paradox', was regarded by Keynes (1930, page 198) as 'one of the most completely established empirical facts in the whole field of quantitative economics'. For examples of quantitative evidence concerning the Gibson Paradox, see Sargent (1973), Shiller and Siegel (1977), Benjamin and Kochin (1984), Barsky and Summers (1988) and Mills (1990), while reviews of the theoretical explanations of the Paradox may be found in Friedman and Schwartz (1982, chapter 10) and Capie, Mills and Wood (1991). That it was 'paradoxical' is clear from the above brief exposition of an aspect of standard monetary theory: any relationship between the price level and interest rates should be between the price level's *rate of change* and interest rates, and not between the price level itself and interest rates.

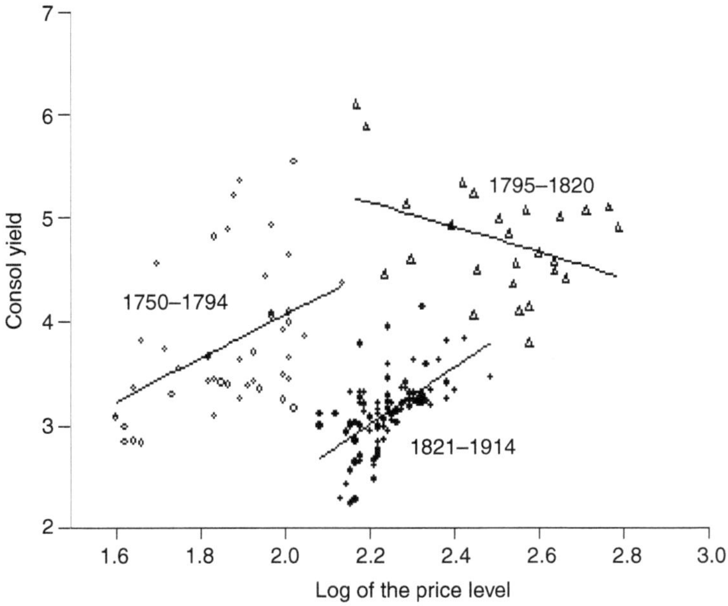

Figure 7.7 Scatterplot of R_t on p_t: 1750–1914.

The impression obtained from Figure 7.7 is confirmed by the following regressions

$$R_t = -\underset{(0.740)}{0.244} + \underset{(0.446)}{0.857}\ p_t - \underset{(0.0100)}{0.0058}\ \pi_t + \underset{(2.232)}{9.279}\ g_t + \underset{(0.123)}{0.401}\ R_{t-1}$$

$R^2 = 0.767 \qquad T = 44$ (1751–1794)

$$R_t = \underset{(1.99)}{9.71} - \underset{(0.714)}{2.773}\ p_t + \underset{(0.0080)}{0.0117}\ \pi_t + \underset{(1.802)}{6.176}\ g_t + \underset{(0.176)}{0.072}\ R_{t-1}$$

$R^2 = 0.532 \qquad T = 26$ (1795–1820)

$$R_t = -\underset{(0.476)}{1.436} + \underset{(0.239)}{0.961}\ p_t + \underset{(0.0032)}{0.0026}\ \pi_t + \underset{(0.563)}{0.195}\ g_t + \underset{(0.053)}{0.759}\ R_{t-1}$$

$R^2 = 0.864 \qquad T = 94$ (1821–1914)

Note that π_t and g_t are both included as control variables and R_{t-1} is included to model any dynamics. Their joint inclusion fails to stop p_t from remaining significant with the predicted signs. We can thus confirm the existence of the 'traditional' form of the Gibson Paradox, a positive relationship between interest rates and the price level, for the years of the gold standard *before* 1914. However, we find that there is also a relationship between these two variables when the gold standard was suspended. The relationship is, however, a negative one.

Any relationship between interest rates and the price level completely disappears after 1914:

$$R_t = \underset{(0.458)}{0.863} + \underset{(0.107)}{0.066}\ p_t + \underset{(0.025)}{0.067}\ \pi_t - \underset{(1.040)}{1.919}\ g_t + \underset{(0.052)}{0.871}\ R_{t-1}$$

$$R^2 = 0.896 \qquad T = 91\ (1915\text{–}2005)$$

Although the residuals in this regression exhibit time varying heteroskedasticity, fitting a GARCH model to them produces little change to the coefficient estimates or their significance.

As the relationship, which should not exist, obviously does, how might it be explained, and is there any way its disappearance can be explained? The explanations which have been offered can be divided into broadly three groups – sluggish expectations, real rate changes, and an absence of a link between money and prices. The last (advanced by Mathias 1983) falls down on the evidence of a clear money–price level link in the period (e.g., Friedman and Schwartz 1982). We therefore concentrate on the first two.[2]

The first explanation was advanced by Irving Fisher in several studies (1896, 1907 and 1930) and subsequently supported by Friedman and Schwartz (1982). There would be the appearance of a relationship between the price level and interest rates if inflation expectations adjusted sluggishly, only catching up with inflation after a considerable lag. If that were the case, the longer inflation persisted the higher would the price level rise, and thus the appearance of a price level–interest rate association would be produced. Hence, sluggish expectations adjustment can explain the paradox.

Wicksell (1907) and Keynes (1930) explained the observation by a decline in the marginal physical productivity of capital in the first half of the period, and a rise in the second half as the mid and far west of the US were developed. Price level movements were induced because the market rate lagged behind the natural rate.

Mills and Wood (1992) support the 'Fisherine' explanation by setting out facts that are inconsistent with all explanations except that one. (As with the results above, that paper supported the actual existence of the paradox.) The exogeneity of the growth of narrow money undermines the Wicksell-Keynes view for the UK, just as did Cagan's (1965) work on the money multiplier undermine it for the US. In addition, some further measure of support is provided by their finding shorter lag lengths than previous authors. Cagan (1972) had pointed out that the mean lags found by Fisher were a striking ten to thirty *years*. Mills and Wood (1992) found lags of a maximum length of five years, with the bulk of the effects being observed in the first three.

So there is an explanation for the finding. Is there also an explanation for its reversal and later for its complete disappearance? Empirical work on this is not possible because of the comparatively small number of observations in the first period and the extraordinary disturbances of the years after the phenomenon vanished, but a conjecture is possible.

Consider first the years when the phenomenon reversed. If it were widely accepted during the years of suspension of the gold standard that Britain would return to the standard at the same parity, then, as prices kept on rising, the expected subsequent price level fall became the greater. Hence the inverse relationship between the price level and the rate of interest.

What of the paradox's disappearance? It disappeared when the gold standard ended. If people knew that prices could then be much more variable, and the existence of the body of theory we have described surely suggests that they did, then they must have been aware of the possibility of increased price level variability, and of inflation. This increased the incentive to monitor monetary conditions, and so shortened the time lag which had produced the effect.

7.5 Modelling the real interest rate

The *ex post*, or realised, real interest rate is defined as

$$r_t = R_t - \pi_{t+1} \tag{7.1}$$

This definition of the realised real rate follows from the Fisher decomposition of the nominal interest rate as the sum of the *ex ante* real rate and expected inflation:

$$R_t = r_t^e + \pi_{t+1}^e$$

If expected inflation differs from observed inflation by a forecasting error,

$$\pi_{t+1}^e = \pi_{t+1} + \eta_{t+1}$$

then

$$r_t^e = R_t - \pi_{t+1} - \eta_{t+1}$$

This will lead to (7.1) if $r_t^\varepsilon = r_t - \eta_{t+1}$, i.e., if the 'forecast error' in predicting real interest rates offsets the inflation forecast error. From (7.1) it would seem that the stochastic properties of r_t will depend upon the stochastic properties of the observed R_t and π_{t+1}. Table 7.1 reports the conclusions on the level of integration of the respective series that we have drawn from subjecting them to a battery of unit root tests across a range of sample periods. The years from 1965 to 1997, already indicated above as 'aberrant', comprise the only period for which the variables are 'balanced' (Granger 1999, chapter 1), i.e., the price level is $I(2)$, inflation is thus $I(1)$, interest rates are also $I(1)$ and the observed real rate, being the difference between these series, is also $I(1)$. For all other periods and, indeed, for the complete sample, interest rates are $I(1)$ and inflation is $I(0)$ but real rates are also $I(0)$, whereas they should, in terms of balance, be $I(1)$.

Table 7.1 Orders of integration for p, π, R and τ for alternative sample periods. λ = var ΔR/var π

Period	p	π	R	τ	λ
1750–2006	I(1)	I(0)	I(1)	I(0)	0.010
1750–1820	I(1)	I(0)	I(1)	I(0)	0.004
1821–1914	I(0)	I(0)	I(1)	I(0)	0.001
1915–2006	I(1)	I(0)	I(1)	I(0)	0.031
1965–1997	I(2)	I(1)	I(1)	I(1)	0.119
1915–1964	I(1)	I(0)	I(1)	I(0)	0.004
1940–2006	I(1)	I(0)	I(1)	I(0)	0.082

The nonstationarity of interest rates and the apparent stationarity of inflation and the real rate can also be observed in the *spatial densities* of the three series shown in Figure 7.8 and the plot of the real rate itself in Figure 7.9. The spatial density is a concept developed in Phillips (2001, 2005) and is a generalisation of the probability distribution to nonstationary time series.[3] Phillips (2001) demonstrates that, for a stationary series, the spatial density will be fairly smooth, have quite a narrow spatial range, and will have a single mode. For a nonstationary series, the spatial density will be irregular and show substantial variation over a wide range of spatial values, providing information about the spatial points that the series has visited and the relative proportion of those visits to the full sample. The spatial densities in Figure 7.8 show, first, that interest rates, although having a mode between 3 and 3.5 per cent, also visit the regions [4.5, 5] and [8.5, 10.5] more frequently than surrounding regions, thus confirming that interest rates are nonstationary; and, second, that both inflation and real rates are concentrated in the region [0, 5], consistent with stationarity.

A resolution of the paradox is provided by the simulation experiment of Markellos and Mills (2001) and the theoretical analysis of Sun and Phillips (2004). This shows that, if the difference between an $I(1)$ and an $I(0)$ series is computed, a standard Dickey-Fuller test for a unit root would almost always reject the correct $I(1)$ null if the variance of the $I(0)$ series was much larger than the innovation variance of the $I(1)$ series. The final column of Table 7.1 reports the values for the variance ratio λ = var ΔR/var π. In most cases λ is extremely small, so that the variation in stationary inflation swamps the '$I(1)$-ness' of interest rates. In consequence real rates also appear to be stationary. This is clearly seen in Figure 7.9.

We thus continue by assuming that real rates are stationary. However, both the conditional mean and variance of r_t are autocorrelated, as seen from the sample autocorrelation functions of r_t and r_t^2 shown in Figure 7.10. After some experimentation, the AR(2)-EGARCH(1,2) model with generalised error (GED) innovations (see Nelson 1991), shown in Table 7.2, was found to adequately fit r_t for the complete sample period. This model has the following interpretation. The mean real rate is estimated to be 2.55 per cent per annum. Around this mean the real rate cycles stochastically (since the roots of the AR(2) component are complex: $0.28 \pm 0.27i$) with an average period of 8.2 years. However, this

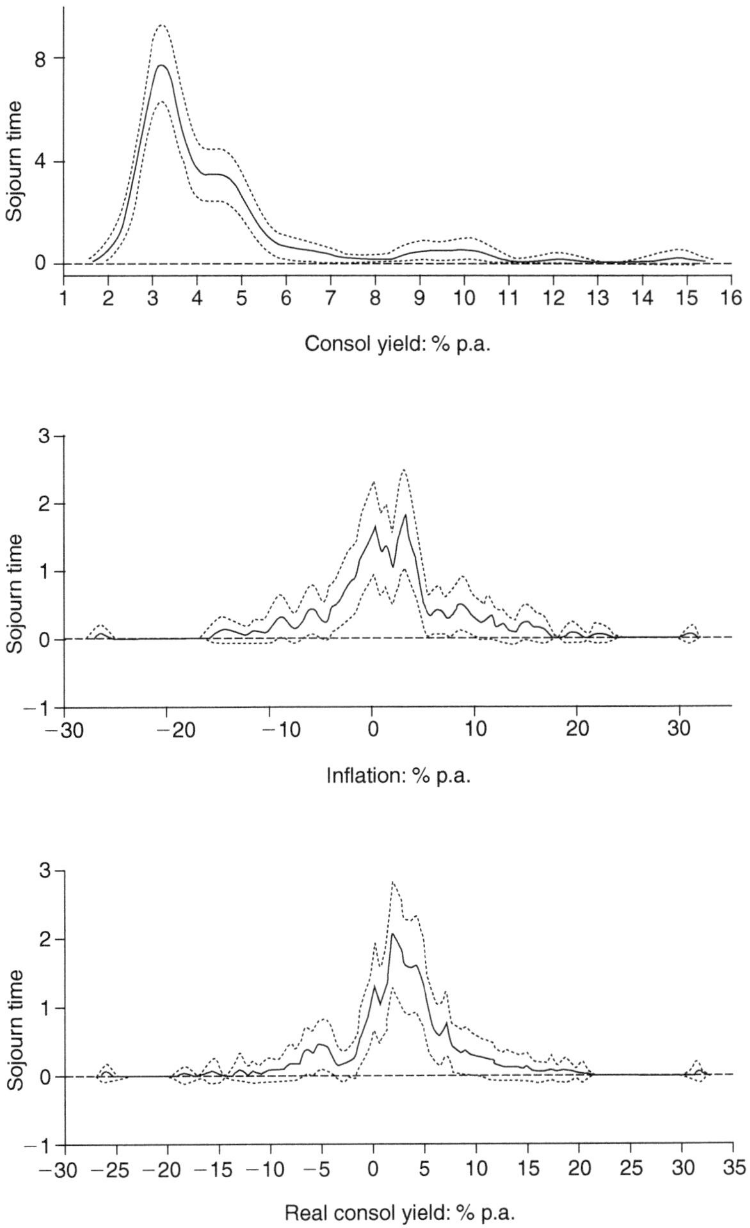

Figure 7.8 Spatial densities of R_t, π_t and τ_t: 1750–2006. Ninety-five per cent confidence bands for the spatial densities are given by the dashed lines.

Table 7.2 AR(3)–EGARCH(1, 2) model fitted to the real interest rate for 1750–2006

$$r_t = \underset{(0.280)}{2.553} + u_t$$

$$u_t = \underset{(0.064)}{0.559}u_{t-1} - \underset{(0.058)}{0.151}u_{t-2} + \varepsilon_t$$

$$\varepsilon_t = \sigma_t z_t \qquad z_t \sim GED\{1.30(0.17)\}$$

$$\log \sigma_t^2 = \underset{(0.134)}{-0.395} + \underset{(0.167)}{0.755}\,|\varepsilon_{t-1}/\sigma_{t-1}| \underset{(0.109)}{-0.366}\,\varepsilon_{t-1}/\sigma_{t-1}$$

$$+ \underset{(0.097)}{0.428}\log \sigma_{t-1}^2 + \underset{(0.104)}{0.500}\log \sigma_{t-1}^2$$

$$R^2 = 0.186 \qquad T = 254\ (1752\text{–}2005)$$

cyclical movement is rather volatile, being buffeted by drawings from a fat-tailed GED random variable (since the GED parameter is estimated to be less than 2) scaled by a time-varying σ_t, whose evolution is plotted in Figure 7.11. This is seen to be asymmetric, with rapid increases in volatility being followed by slower declines. Writing the asymmetric part of the EGARCH specification as

$$0.755|\varepsilon_{t-1}/\sigma_{t-1}| - 0.366\varepsilon_{t-1}/\sigma_{t-1} = 0.755\left(-0.485\varepsilon_{t-1}/\sigma_{t-1} + |\varepsilon_{t-1}/\sigma_{t-1}|\right)$$

enables the 'news impact' curve to be defined as

$$f(\varepsilon_{t-1}/\sigma_{t-1}) = -0.485\varepsilon_{t-1}/\sigma_{t-1} + |\varepsilon_{t-1}/\sigma_{t-1}|$$

Thus $\partial f/\partial\varepsilon_{t-1} = 0.515$ if $\varepsilon_{t-1} > 0$ and $\partial f/\partial\varepsilon_{t-1} = 1.485$ if $\varepsilon_{t-1} < 0$, showing the asymmetric response of volatility to innovations, i.e., 'news'.

Given that we have earlier identified several sub-periods showing different statistical properties, models for the real rate process were also built for those previously identified periods, namely 1750–1914, 1915–1964 and 1965–2005,

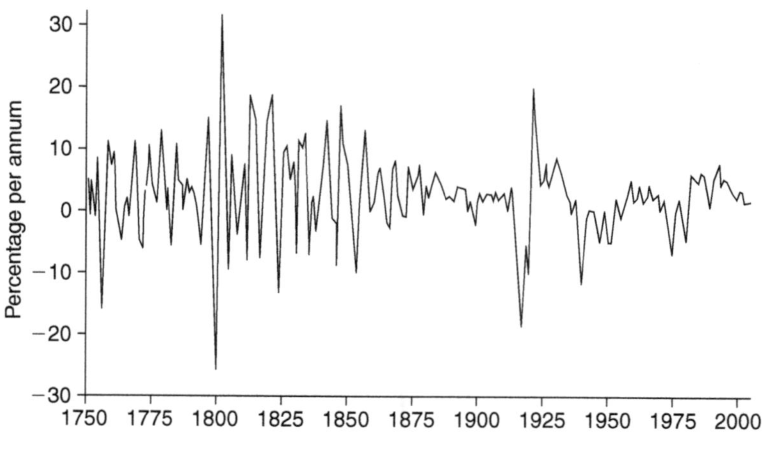

Figure 7.9 Real interest rate r_t: 1750–2005.

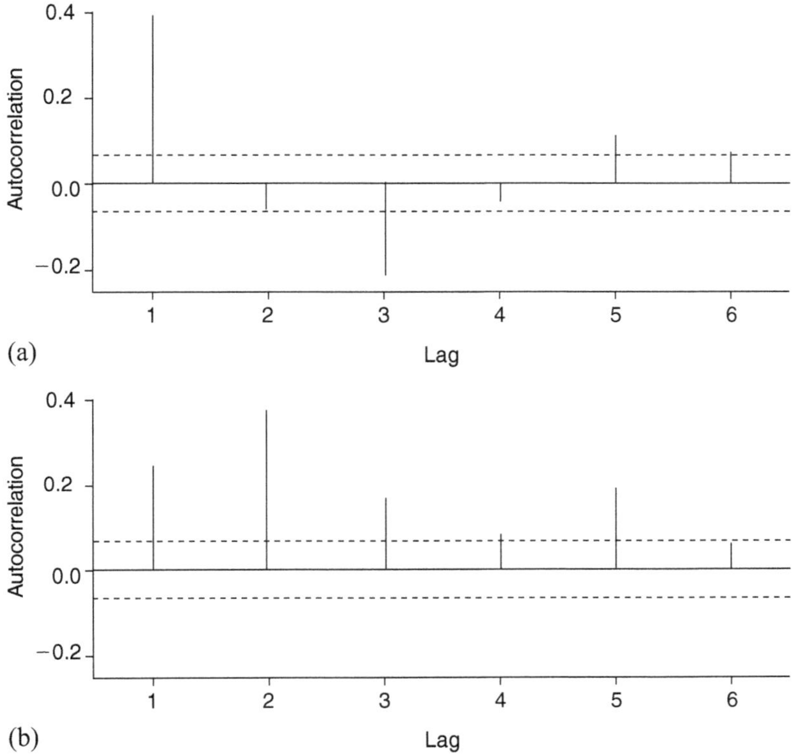

Figure 7.10 Sample autocorrelations of (a) r_t and (b) r_t^2: 1750–2005. Dashed horizontal lines indicate one standard error bounds.

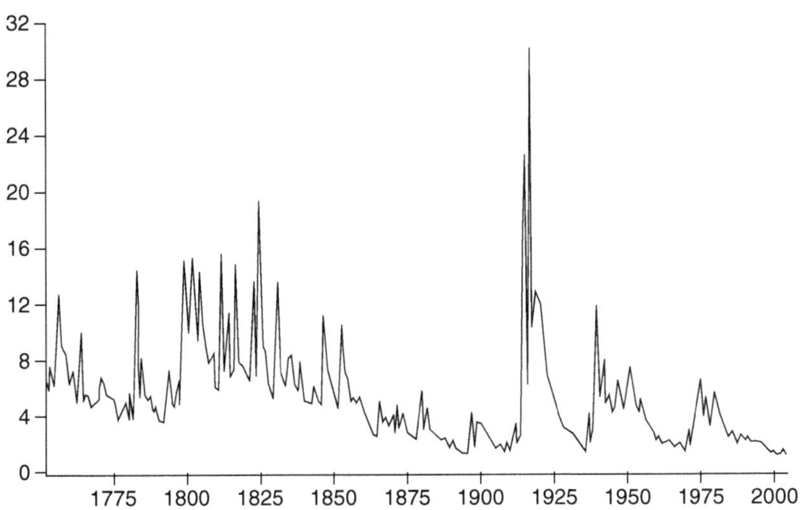

Figure 7.11 Conditional standard deviation, σ_t, of the real interest rate: 1750–2005.

so as to examine whether the real interest rate process also shifted. The fitted models are shown in Tables 7.3–7.5.

For the first period, an AR(3)-EGARCH(1,2), again with GED innovations, provided a satisfactory fit, so that the stochastic properties of the real rate for the period up to 1914 are very similar to those for the complete period. The mean real rate is 2.87 per cent per annum, around which the real rate cycles stochastically with an average period of 5.9 years (the roots of the AR(3) process are $0.35 \pm 0.62i$ and -0.47). The news impact curve is

$$f\left(\varepsilon_{t-1}/\sigma_{t-1}\right) = -0.887\,\varepsilon_{t-1}/\sigma_{t-1} + \left|\varepsilon_{t-1}/\sigma_{t-1}\right|$$

so that the asymmetry is even more marked in this sub-period than for the complete period.

Table 7.3 AR(3)–EGARCH(1, 2) model fitted to the real interest rate for 1753–1914

$$\begin{aligned}
\tau_t &= \underset{(0209)}{2.867} + u_t \\
u_t &= \underset{(0.072)}{0.236u_{t-1}} - \underset{(0.070)}{0.169u_{t-2}} - \underset{(0.066)}{0.239} + \varepsilon t \\
\varepsilon_t &= \sigma_t z_t \qquad z_t \sim GED\{1.12(0.19)\} \\
\log \sigma_t^2 &= \underset{(0.108)}{-0.294} + \underset{(0.155)}{0.371}\,|\varepsilon_{t-1}/\sigma_{t-1}| - \underset{(0.110)}{0.329}\,\varepsilon_{t-1}/\sigma_{t-1} \\
&\quad + \underset{(0.198)}{0.257}\log\sigma_{t-1}^2 + \underset{(0.203)}{0.748}\log\sigma_{t-1}^2 \\
R^2 &= 0.226 \qquad T = 162\ (1753\text{–}1914)
\end{aligned}$$

Table 7.4 AR(1)–EGARCH(1) model fitted to the real interest rate for 1915–1964

$$\begin{aligned}
\tau_t &= \underset{(0.839)}{1.937} + u_t \\
u_t &= \underset{(0.061)}{0.646u_{t-1}} + \varepsilon_t \\
\varepsilon_t &= \sigma_t z_t \qquad z_t \sim GED\{1.94(0.22)\} \\
\sigma_t^2 &= \underset{(2.970)}{6.245} + \underset{(0.639)}{0.949}\,\varepsilon_{t-1}^2 \\
R^2 &= 0.517 \qquad T = 50\ (1915\text{–}1964)
\end{aligned}$$

Table 7.5 AR(1)–EGARCH(1) model fitted to the real interest rate for 1965–2005

$$\begin{aligned}
\tau_t &= \underset{(0.823)}{2.871} + u_t \\
u_t &= \underset{(0.145)}{0.698u_{t-1}} + \varepsilon_t \\
\varepsilon_t &= \sigma_t z_t z_t \sim N(0, 1) \\
\sigma_t^2 &= \underset{(0.765)}{1.856} + \underset{(0.385)}{0.749}\,\varepsilon_{t-1}^2 \\
R^2 &= 0.447 \qquad T = 41\ (1965\text{–}2005)
\end{aligned}$$

Rather simpler models are required for the two later periods, being AR(1)-ARCH(1) processes: i.e., shocks to the real rate dissipate geometrically back to a constant mean level with the volatility process having a symmetric response to news. The mean real rate is 1.94 per cent per annum between 1915 and 1964, but is 2.87 per cent from 1965 onwards. The cyclical pattern in the real rate has therefore disappeared after 1915 and, from 1965, so has the fat-tailed GED innovations, being replaced by normality. The asymmetry in the conditional variance has also disappeared after 1915, with ARCH(1) processes being all that is required in both sub-periods. Persistence in volatility also decreases over time, since the ARCH parameter is smaller in the final sub-period.[4]

The perception thus obtained from this set of volatility models is that the expected real rate is rather stable, only slowly varying through a maximum range of 1.5 per cent to 3.5 per cent per annum. Indeed, from the GARCH models a strong claim can be made that, apart from the period from the outbreak of the First World War to the mid-1960s, when the expected real rate was just under 2 per cent, the expected real rate was constant at 2.86 per cent. Many authors (e.g., Friedman and Schwartz 1982) have commented on this stability and have, indeed, found the rate not only to be stable but to be of this order. Unfortunately there are numerous possible explanations and for most of the period insufficient data to be able to distinguish between them: is the stability due to economic openness, a highly interest elastic savings supply schedule or investment demand schedule, and so on. This matter awaits not just further study but, before that, further data.

7.6 Conclusions

Throughout the last two and a half centuries, long interest rates in Britain, as measured by the Consol yield, have been generated by a nonstationary, $I(1)$ process. The price level, on the other hand, has been stationary or nonstationary depending upon the monetary regime. Typically it has been $I(1)$, so that innovations (or shocks) to the price process are permanent and inflation – the stationary transformation of the price level – is the appropriate measure to analyse. During the gold standard era from 1820 to 1914, however, the price level was stationary, so that shocks have only a temporary impact and prices revert in time back to an underlying equilibrium level. In contrast, from the start of the stagflation era, 1965, to the beginning of Bank of England independence in 1997, the price level was $I(2)$. This implies that inflation was nonstationary and that shocks to inflation were permanent and the price process was characterised by permanent shocks to both its level and slope. Consequently, pinning down the relationship between interest rates, prices and inflation has been difficult. The Gibson Paradox, that there is a relationship between interest rates and the price level, is confirmed as holding during the gold standard, even when controlling for inflation and government spending and allowing for dynamics. Interest rates and inflation are positively related during the 1965 to 1997 period but there is no relationship between them during any other period.

The real interest rate is stationary, even though the nominal rate is nonstationary, a consequence of the excessive volatility of stationary inflation swamping the volatility of nonstationary nominal rates. It also exhibits volatility, having an asymmetric conditional volatility process driven by fat-tailed innovations, i.e., increases in volatility are more rapid than falls and these movements are driven by innovations drawn from a distribution for which the probability of obtaining large (absolute) values is much greater than for a normal distribution. The extent of this asymmetry and 'fat-tailed'-ness appears to have dissipated during the twentieth century. The expected real rate has been very stable across the entire period, being around 2.9 per cent except between 1915 and 1964, when it was about one per cent lower. Finally turning to the significance of the money supply regime, there are significant effects of being on or off the gold standard, but no other regime effects can be observed. This may, of course, be a consequence of the comparative brevity of the life of a good number of the regimes.

Notes

1 Cagan (1965) ascribed these different price level behaviours to the monetary regimes in place. We take this up below.
2 There are two other explanations which accept the money–price level connection, but fall down on other factual matters. Benjamin and Kochin's (1984) explanation depends on the paradox only holding during wars; but it also held in times of peace. Barsky and Summers (1988) depend on a fixed stock of monetary gold, but there were substantial additions to that stock in the period which drew Keynes's attention to the paradox: see, e.g., Rockoff (1984).
3 Mills (2008) provides a more detailed discussion of this concept in the present context.
4 The robustness of these results was demonstrated in Mills (2008), who uses both a two-state Markov switching process and the fitting of a nonparametric trend to obtain similar patterns of behaviour for the real interest rate.

References

Alvarez, F., Lucas, R.E., Jr. and Weber, W.E. (2001). Interest rates and inflation. *American Economic Review* 91, 219–225.

Barro, R.J. (1987). Government spending, interest rates, prices, and budget deficits in the United Kingdom, 1701–1918. *Journal of Monetary Economics* 20, 221–247.

Barsky, R.B. and Summers, L.H. (1988). Gibson's Paradox and the Gold Standard. *Journal of Political Economy* 96, 528–550.

Benjamin, D.K. and Kochin, L.A. (1984). War, prices and interest rates: a martial solution to Gibson's Paradox. In M.D. Bordo and A.J. Schwartz (editors), *A Retrospective on the Classical Gold Standard 1821–1931*, 587–604. Chicago: University of Chicago Press.

Bordo, M.D. and F. Kydland (1996). The gold standard as a commitment mechanism. In T. Bayoumi, B. Eichengreen and M. P. Taylor (editors), *Modern Perspectives on the Gold Standard*, 55–100. Cambridge: Cambridge University Press.

Cagan, P. (1965). *Determinants and Effects of Changes in the Stock of Money, 1875–1960.* New York: Columbia University Press.

Cagan, P. (1972). *The Channels of Monetary Effects on Interest Rates.* New York: NBER.

Capie, F.H., Mills, T.C. and Wood, G.E. (1991). Money, interest rates and the Great Depression: Britain from 1870 to 1913. In J. Foreman-Peck (editor), *New Perspectives on the Late Victorian Economy*, 251–284. Cambridge: Cambridge University Press.

Clark, G. (2001). Farm wages and living standards in the Industrial Revolution: England, 1670–1869. *Economic History Review* 54, 477–505.

Feinstein, C.H. (1998). Pessimism perpetuated: real wages and the standard of living in Britain during and after the Industrial Revolution. *Journal of Economic History* 58, 625–658.

Fisher, I. (1896). *Appreciation and Interest.* New York: Macmillan.

Fisher, I. (1907). *The Rate of Interest.* New York: Macmillan.

Fisher, I. (1930). *The Theory of Interest.* New York: Macmillan.

Friedman, M. and Schwartz, A.J. (1982). *Monetary Trends in the United States and the United Kingdom.* Chicago: University of Chicago Press.

Granger, C.W.J. (1999). *Empirical Modelling in Economics. Specification and Evaluation.* Cambridge: Cambridge University Press.

Keynes, J.M. (1930). *A Treatise on Money.* London: Macmillan.

Kindleberger, C.P. (1984). *A Financial History of Western Europe.* Oxford: Oxford University Press.

Markellos, R.N. and Mills, T.C. (2001). Unit roots in the CAPM? *Applied Economics Letters* 8, 499–502.

Mathias, P. (1983). *The First Industrial Nation: An Economic History of Britain, 1700–1914.* London: Methuen.

Mills, T.C. (1990). A note on the Gibson Paradox during the gold standard. *Explorations in Economic History* 27, 277–286.

Mills, T.C. (2008). Exploring historical economic relationships: two and a half centuries of British interest rates and inflation. *Cliometrica* 2, 213–228.

Mills, T.C. and Wood, G.E. (1992) Money and interest rates in Britain from 1870 to 1913. In N.F.R. Crafts and S.N. Broadberry (editiors), *Britain in the World Economy 1870–1979*, 199–217. Cambridge: Cambridge University Press.

Mitchell, B.R. (1998). *International Historical Statistics: Europe, 1750–1993*, 4th edition, Basingstoke: Macmillan.

Nelson, D.R. (1991). Conditional heteroskedasticity in asset returns: a new approach. *Econometrica* 59, 347–370.

O'Donoghue, J., Goulding, L. and Allen, G. (2004). Consumer price inflation since 1750. *Economic Trends* 604, 38–46.

Phillips, P.C.B. (2001). Descriptive econometrics for non-stationary time series with empirical illustrations. *Journal of Applied Econometrics* 16, 389–413.

Phillips, P.C.B. (2005). Econometric analysis of Fisher's equation. *American Journal of Economics and Sociology* 64, 125–168.

Rockoff, H. (1984). Some evidence on the real price of gold, its costs of production, and commodity prices. In *A Retrospective on the Classical Gold Standard, 1821–1931*, 613–646. Chicago: University of Chicago Press.

Sargent, T.J. (1973). Interest rates and prices in the long run: a study of the Gibson Paradox. *Journal of Money, Credit and Banking* 5, 383–449.

Shiller, R.J. and Siegel, J.J. (1977). The Gibson Paradox and historical movements in real interest rates. *Journal of Political Economy* 85, 891–907.

Sun, Y. and Phillips, P.C.B. (2004). Understanding the Fisher equation. *Journal of Applied Econometrics* 19, 869–886.

Thornton, H. (1802 [1978]). *An Enquiry into the Nature and Effects of the Paper Credit of Great Britain.* Fairfield, NJ: Augustus M. Kelley.

Wicksell, K. (1907). The influence of the interest rate on prices. *Economic Journal* 17, 213–220.

8 Monetary aggregates restored?

Capie and Webber revisited

Alec Chrystal and Paul Mizen

Paper prepared for the Festschrift for Forrest Capie held on 4 September 2009 at Cass Business School.

We are grateful for comments on an earlier version from David Peel and from conference participants.

The aim of this paper is to revisit the UK money supply data and test for some standard relationships between money, the price level and real GDP using (in part) data constructed by Forrest Capie and Alan Webber. We find that there is evidence of a well-determined long-run money demand function and there is a very clear long-run relationship between money, the price level and real GDP. None of this will be a surprise to those who learned their monetary economics in the 1960s and 1970s, but it may be a surprise to those trained in the 1990s and 2000s.

8.1 The love of money...

If this conference had taken place in 1989[1] instead of 2009 there would be little doubt that Forrest's major contribution to British monetary economics and economic history would have been "A Monetary History of the United Kingdom, 1870–1982" co-authored with Alan Webber (Capie and Webber, 1985, subsequently referred to as CW). This study was designed to be the UK version of Milton Friedman and Anna Schwartz's monumental "Monetary History of the United States". The latter had not just become a bible for monetarists but it also provided the evidence base for a whole new approach to economic policy (associated with Ronald Reagan and Margaret Thatcher). Twin pillars of this approach were supply side policies (including market deregulation) to stimulate growth in the real economy and (at least in the UK case) money supply targeting to provide a nominal anchor and thus to control inflation. Monetary aggregates were thus at the centre of macroeconomic policy and money supply announcements could move markets (and frequently did).

Official estimates of the money stock at quarterly and monthly frequency were only started in 1963, as a result of a plea from the Radcliffe Committee for more data. So academics and policy makers alike were hampered by an almost total lack of reliable data with which to test the relationships between money and other economic variables. When monetary targets were introduced in the second half of the 1970s there was little more than a decade of quarterly data on which to test hypotheses.[2] Enter Forrest Capie. An ESRC grant was obtained and Alan Webber was hired as the research officer. The project was instigated to take data on UK monetary aggregates back to 1870, and thus add a century of data to the decade or so of that which was extant. Annual data for the monetary base, M1 and M3 was constructed from 1871, as was monthly data for the M1 and M3 aggregates from 1922. Monthly data for the monetary base (and its components) was constructed back to 1870. The project was presumably conceived in 1979 or 1980 and work was started in 1981. The output was published in 1985.

In the 1970s, post-Competition and Credit Control (CCC), money growth in the high 20s per cent per annum led to inflation of a similar magnitude and the need to control money growth seemed self-evident. However, by the late 1980s the heyday of monetary aggregates (at least in the UK) was over. The introduction of the Corset and its abolition in 1980 led to distortions in the data. In the early 1980s (broad) money growth surged just as the economy slumped and inflation fell. The money-led boom came eventually in 1987–8 but faith in the monetary aggregates had by that time evaporated. Goodhart's Law was increasingly quoted in the 1980s as proof that monetary targeting could not work because the targeted aggregate would then change its behaviour (see Chrystal and Mizen 2003). Policy makers persisted with the framework of monetary targets for a while, but Nigel Lawson, when Chancellor, moved to an implicit exchange rate target by shadowing the DM, and the UK adopted an explicit exchange rate target in 1990 by joining the ERM.

After the UK's dramatic expulsion from the ERM in September 1992, the hunt was on for a new nominal anchor that was neither based on an exchange rate peg nor on the targeting of some monetary aggregate. The solution was to be inflation targeting. In this framework there was no intermediate target but, rather, a focus on the goal of price level stability itself. Interest rates were to be set in order to keep the inflation rate within certain bounds.

From 1992 to May 1997 the official interest rate was decided by the Chancellor on the advice of the Governor of the Bank of England (the "Ken and Eddie show"). From May 1997 the interest rate decision was given to the independent Monetary Policy Committee (MPC), which was charged with keeping inflation within plus or minus one percentage point of a specific target inflation rate.

In the inflation targeting regime there was no explicit role for monetary aggregates. Policy decisions were driven by the inflation forecast, which in turn was driven by forecasts of aggregate demand relative to potential aggregate supply. Money would have a role only if it provided information that was helpful for informing the short-term forecast of inflation. In practice the Bank of England's main forecasting model had no role for money. Monetary aggregates were certainly monitored and reported on a monthly basis to the MPC, but there are almost certainly no incidents where a policy decision was influenced by the money numbers where these were conveying a different message from the main forecast.

Much of the volatility in money growth in the late 1990s and 2000s was in the money holding of Other Financial Corporations (OFCs). There was general scepticism among MPC members and Bank staff alike that this data had anything to say about inflationary forces. Rather, its growth was more to do with financial innovation driven by bank regulation and had virtually no direct links to UK aggregate demand. Indeed, a plausible case could have been made for aggregating parts of OFCs in with the banking system and thus defining their money holding out of the official money stock entirely, just as inter-bank deposits do not get included in monetary aggregates.

The implication of all this was that the money numbers ceased to be of any interest to either policy makers or academics. Policy makers did not need them to make policy decisions and academics lost interest in topics like money demand. If policy makers are setting interest rates to control aggregate demand, the LM curve does not matter anymore. All that matters is the interest elasticity of domestic spending (the IS curve). Indeed, monetary policy seemed to be doing just fine. The decade of the Great Moderation, or the "NICE" decade, proved that inflation targeting could work very well and money numbers could remain the preserve of a few anoraks who were to be humoured but otherwise ignored.

Against this background, the historical money stock statistics proved to be of little interest. While money supply figures had moved markets in the 1970s and early 1980s, by the 1990s and 2000s they were almost never mentioned by the media and certainly had no impact on markets. Academic economists ceased to be interested in aggregate empirical relationships owing to a combination of the Lucas Critique (which suggested that all such relationships were transitory unless based on "deep parameters") and the shift in the profession toward DSGE models for some and to finance for others. The potential contribution of the newly constructed historical series failed to materialise, as attention moved elsewhere.

8.2 2007 and all that

If the Great Moderation had continued for another two years or so, we might all be feeling richer, but would certainly not be revisiting the relevance of the money numbers today. However, the financial crisis of the past two years and the associated recession has put monetary policy makers in the bind of finding that their official policy interest rates have fallen to a level where they are effectively at the lower bound of possibility and they still need to find ways to stimulate aggregate demand. The MPC solution is to adopt a policy of quantitative easing (QE) that has the ultimate goal of stimulating spending but has the intermediate goal of increasing the money stock. Hence, after two decades in the wilderness, monetary aggregates are back in business.

It is too early to analyse how successful QE has been, but it is a good time to revisit the monetary aggregates and see if they really should have been neglected or if some of the relationships which monetarists once espoused do continue to be evident in the data. Hence what we do in this chapter is revisit the monetary aggregates that Capie and Webber so meticulously constructed and test whether some rather obvious relationships hold in the data.

While CW constructed monthly data as well as quarterly averages, we focus here on the annual data. By taking the CW data from 1871 and splicing it with official data since 1963 (or 1948 in the case of GDP and the price level) we end up with a data set from 1871 to 2008 with 138 annual observations.

A similar exercise in revisiting long-run money demand functions has been undertaken by Matthews, Paya and Peel *et al.* (2004) but they replicate earlier work with data sets that do not extend beyond the 1960s and so do not face the problems of splicing with modern aggregates. They do, however, produce results that are consistent with ours.

8.3 Money, money, money?

There are a number of data issues that need to be explained before proceeding to outline and discuss our results. These mainly arise from institutional or definitional changes that make the extension of historical series problematic. CW produced data series for the monetary base, M1 and M3. Each of these would now be considered inappropriate as candidates for a measure of "the" money supply. M1 and M3 were based upon checking accounts (M1) and all deposits (M3) at banks but excluded building societies, which were permitted to convert to banks from 1988. M0 is mainly made up of notes and coin outside the Bank of England but it also includes bankers' deposits, which have been subject to big changes since the introduction, first, of the REPO market in 1996 and then the payment of interest since 2006. Narrow money has also been subject to big changes in velocity due to technical innovations in the payments system such as the introduction of ATMs and plastic payments cards.

We choose not to look at narrow money in this paper, but rather to focus on broad money. Neither M1 nor M3 can be used across the 1988/9 divide. So we base our current study on the official broad money measure, M4, back to 1963 and splice it to the CW measure of M3 for all earlier years. We do not use only the total M4 measure since 1963, as we find that the distortions created by the inclusion of OFCs render it of doubtful relevance. In an earlier study we reported the effect of using retail M4 instead of total M4 (see Chrystal and Mizen, 2003). This we use again here. However, we also use M4 excluding OFCs as one of our two preferred series.

The switch from M3 to M4 may cause some distortions but these should be small. Building societies played only a small role in the payments mechanism before the 1980s and they are included in our data from 1963. For the year when we splice the data, 1963, the CW estimate of M3 is £11,184 million, while the official figure for M4 in the same year is £14,774 million. Hence the difference between these two aggregates is not large. It is also true that OFCs were tiny in 1963, contributing only £287 million of M4 out of £14,774 million, so the fact that we exclude them in one of our money measures after 1963 but they have some presence (in M3) before is of no great significance. As we shall see, our two preferred series based on retail M4 and on M4 excluding OFCs have similar characteristics even though the latter is about 8 per cent larger than the former (in 2008). The important point seems to be that both largely exclude OFCs, which by 2008 contribute about 38 per cent of M4 deposits.[3]

This does not imply that we think OFCs are unimportant but merely that OFCs money holdings seem to behave very differently from holdings by households and PNFCs. Excluding OFCs seems to help in establishing a recognisable relationship between money, prices and real activity.

For other data series used we take official ONS GDP and RPI data series back to 1948 and we splice these onto the CW data for GNP and RPI for earlier years, which CW attribute to Feinstein (1972). We splice the CW consol rate with a long gilt rate also from 1948.

The only other data issue of importance for what follows is that we do not use any dummy variables to take out difficult observations or to force the data to deliver acceptable results. The only exception to this is where we report our replication (Chrystal and Mizen 2003) of Artis and Lewis (1984). Both of these studies started after the First World War, so avoided a period of major disruption but still used dummies for some other outliers (around the CCC period). The new data set does include all the years of the First and Second World Wars, so this is quite a severe test of the relevance of the economic relationships under consideration. However, we do concentrate on tying down the long-run relationships involved rather than worrying too much about short-run dynamics, which will vary across the many different regimes that existed between 1871 and 2008 (from gold standard to inflation targeting with Bretton Woods, ERM, monetary targeting, and various periods of direct controls, especially in wartime, mixed in). One big advantage we now have over previous studies is that 138 years is getting to be a long enough run of reasonably reliable data to be able to tie down the long-run relationships with some degree of confidence. Another advantage is that we now have available well-developed cointegration methods that help us find long-run relationships in trended data without having to worry at all about exogeneity, or otherwise, of right-hand-side variables. In this case, we are interested in what variables are moving together and not in what is causing what.

8.4 Inverse velocity

We now reproduce our main result from Chrystal and Mizen (2003, referred to as CM) which was itself a replication of Artis and Lewis (1984, referred to as AL). AL took annual data from 1920 to 1981 and showed that the log of inverse velocity was a simple function of the log of the consol rate. Using the CW data extended by use of retail M4 (which we then called M2, but the definition of M2 has now changed to include foreign currency), CM showed that the AL result still held on data extended up to 2000 when dummies were used to exclude the period immediately after CCC in the early 1970s.

The estimated equation reported in CM was:

$$\log\left(\frac{M}{Y}\right) = \underset{(0.046)}{0.305} - \underset{(0.026)}{0.538} \log R + \text{dummies} \qquad R^2 = 0.85$$

while the estimate reported by AL was:

$$\log\left(\frac{M}{Y}\right) = \underset{(0.046)}{4.717} - \underset{(0.028)}{0.536} \log R + \text{dummies} \qquad R^2 = 0.88$$

(terms in brackets in these and subsequent equations are standard errors).

The difference in the constants reflects only the scaling of the data, but otherwise these two estimates are almost identical. CM showed that when M4 itself was used rather than retail M4 it was then very clear that the relationship had broken down and the entire relationship had shifted.

Figure 8.1 shows the cross-plot of inverse velocity and the consol rate using retail M4 (with the outliers at the top being the observations dummied out of the regression), while Figure 8.2 shows how different things look using M4 itself. Clearly there was a major shift in M4 in the 1980s and 1990s that was not present in retail M4. Both figures are for the years 1920–2000.

Using our updated data set we have re-estimated the AL equation using data from 1920 to 2008, but not including any dummy variables, and we get the following result:

$$\log\left(\frac{M}{Y}\right) = \underset{(0.047)}{0.238} - \underset{(0.026)}{0.426} \log R + \text{dummies} \qquad R^2 = 0.75$$

This has a comparable overall fit. The coefficient on the consol rate is slightly smaller but it is highly significant. Replacing retail M4 with M4 leads to R^2 falling to 0.2 and the coefficient on the consol rate halving (but retaining significance with

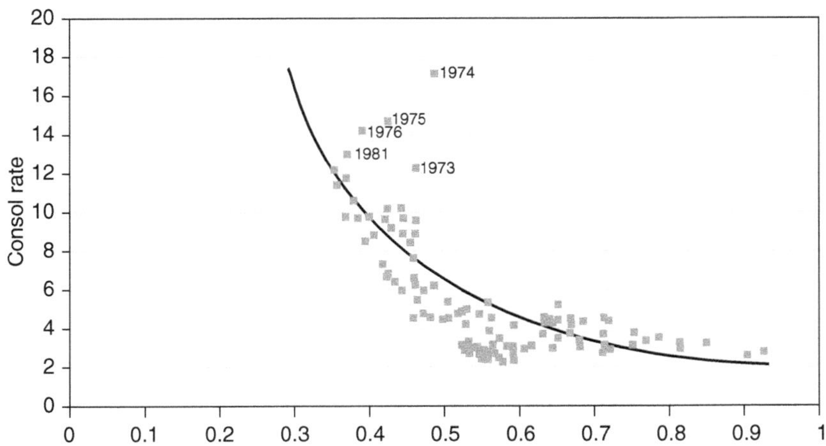

Figure 8.1 Long-run money demand, 1920–2000, using retail M4.

a t-statistic around 4). Figure 8.3 shows the fitted line and actual data using retail M4, while Figure 8.4 shows again the big shift involved when using M4.

The conclusion of this section so far is that there is a plausible and stable relationship between velocity and the long-run interest rate for the period 1920 to 2008 which is evident in the data if we use retail M4 as the modern equivalent of M3, but this relationship has clearly changed radically when M4 is involved. This is strong support for the results of Artis and Lewis (1984), even though we

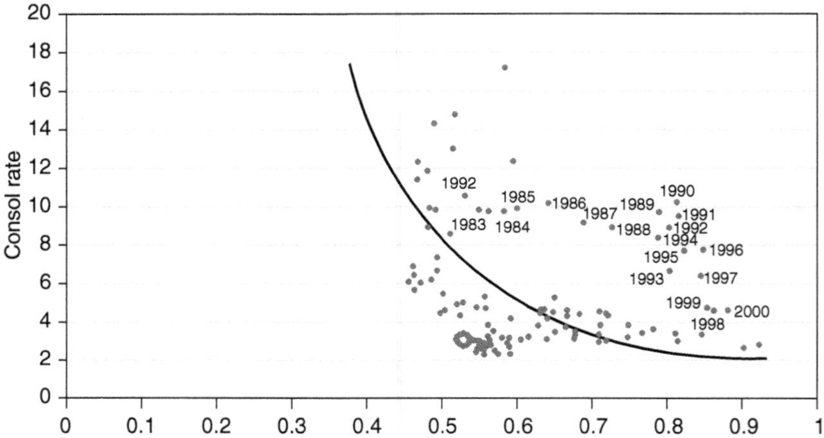

Figure 8.2 Long-run money demand, 1920–2000, using M4.

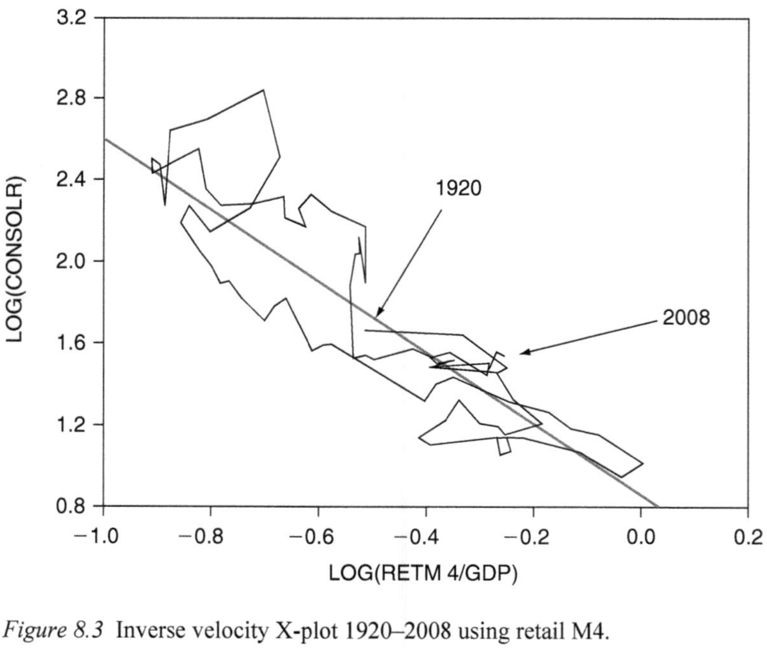

Figure 8.3 Inverse velocity X-plot 1920–2008 using retail M4.

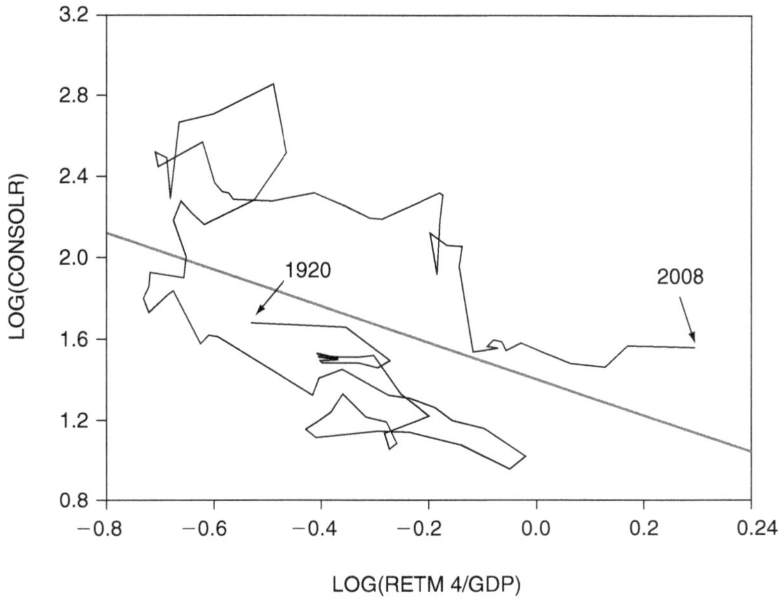

Figure 8.4 Inverse velocity X-plot 1920–2008 using M4.

have added nearly two decades of data during which financial innovation has been argued to have destroyed the relationship between money and the economy. It is notable in Figure 8.3 that the cross-plot of velocity for 2008 is very close to that for the first observation in 1920.

It could be argued that even Figure 8.4 is good news for broad money. The relationship between inverse velocity and the interest rate has clearly shifted but it has re-emerged after the shift (maybe). However, we think that the big surge in OFCs' money holding in the 2000s makes that case hard to sustain.

From this point we shall use all the data points from 1871 to 2008 and, as emphasised earlier, make no attempt to dummy out any troublesome observations. We first attempt to estimate the long-run money demand function, and we then try to identify the long-run relationship between money and the price level.

8.5 Money demand function

We now test for the existence of a conventional textbook money demand function of the form:

$$\log(\text{real money balances}) = \beta_0 + \beta_1 \log(\text{real GDP}) - \beta_2 \text{interest rate}$$

The price index we use for deflation is the RPI (spliced with the CW measure of retail prices taken from Feinstein) and the interest rate used is the consol rate (spliced with a long gilt rate). For money numbers we are interested in the properties of three different aggregate series, all of which use CW's M3 up to 1963 but then use either M4, retail M4, or M4 excluding OFCs. Note also that we do not take logs of the interest rate (as we think this is the traditional way to estimate a money demand function) so β_2 is a semi-elasticity.

The usual unit root tests indicate the obvious fact that real money balances and real GDP and (less obviously) the long interest rate are I(1) (or higher). We then test for the existence of cointegration and find that it does exist between all measures of money and the other two variables when including a constant but no trend. As we are interested only in the long-run money demand function only the cointegrating relationship from the subsequent VECM estimation is reported.

In light of our earlier discussion it should not be surprising that we do not find a satisfactory long-run money demand function using M4. Perhaps surprisingly, we do find evidence of a cointegrating vector but the ECM term does not prove to be significant. We do not bother reporting these results but they are available on request (as is the underlying data).

The main results we report are for the long-run money demand function using retail M4, which are as follows:

$$\log(\text{real money balances}) = -0.803 + \underset{(0.050)}{1.093}\ \log(\text{real GDP}) - \underset{(0.014)}{0.073}\ \text{interest rate}$$

$$\text{Error correction term}\ \underset{(0.028)}{-\ 0.062}$$

Dynamic terms in the VECM equation have been suppressed as they are not of current interest. Two lags of all variables were used. The key finding here is that interpreting the cointegrating vector as the long-run money demand function produces more or less exactly what textbooks (and the earlier money demand literature) would have us expect: that the real income elasticity of demand for real money balances is about +1 and the interest semi-elasticity is about –0.07. Importantly, the ECM term is significant in the VAR so that it does act as an attractor, albeit one where the adjustment to the long-run equilibrium is slow.

The results using M4 are less good:

$$\log(\text{real money balances}) = -1.83 + \underset{(0.055)}{1.24}\ \log(\text{real GDP}) - \underset{(0.015)}{0.075}\ \text{interest rate}$$

$$\text{Error correction term}\ \underset{(0.026)}{-0.035}$$

There are differences in the dynamic behaviour between these two equations which remain for further investigation and the error correction term is not significant. But the key point for present purposes is that they produce a very similar long-run cointegrating equation that can be re-arranged to look exactly like a classic money demand function that anybody over forty could clearly recognise as being consistent with an earlier money demand literature.

This result is robust to the choice of interest rate. Similar results can be obtained using a short rate instead of the long rate. However, there are differences in the strength of influence of the cointegrating equation between these two results which suggests that we get a much better result using retail M4 than we do with broad M4. This too requires further investigation.

8.6 Money and prices

Money demand functions are obviously of some interest, but they have one limitation in the form we have used above, which is that the price level is substituted out so that we cannot see the direct link between money and prices. Modern cointegration methods are ideally suited to estimating the long-run relationship between money and prices in a context where we have no strong prior about what is causing what. Over a time period which runs from the gold standard through pegged exchange rates to floating rates there will be some periods where money drives prices, some where prices drive money and others where third factors drive them both. We do, however, have a clear view coming from several traditions, including the quantity theory and the natural rate framework, that money and prices should be close to proportional.

Thus, while the study of money demand above has estimated an equation of the form:

$$\frac{M}{P} = f\left(\frac{Y}{P};r\right)$$

we now seek an 'inverse' relationship of the form:

$$P = f\left(M;\frac{Y}{P};r\right)$$

Again we find clear evidence of cointegration between these variables but, most importantly, find numerical values for the estimated relationship that are almost exactly what we expect. The following is the relationship using retail M4 (where only the long-run relationship is reported).

$$\log(P) = -0.00023 + \underset{(0.079)}{0.987}\ \log(M) - \underset{(0.219)}{0.992}\ \log\left(\frac{Y}{P}\right) + \underset{(0.018)}{0.109}\ r$$

$$\text{Error correction term} \quad \underset{(0.017)}{-\ 0.047}$$

Figure 8.5 shows the residuals from the above VECM equation. It is notable from the estimated long-run relationship that the coefficient on money is close to 1 and the coefficient on real GDP is close to –1. We are able to restrict these coefficients to +1 and –1 and easily accept these restrictions.

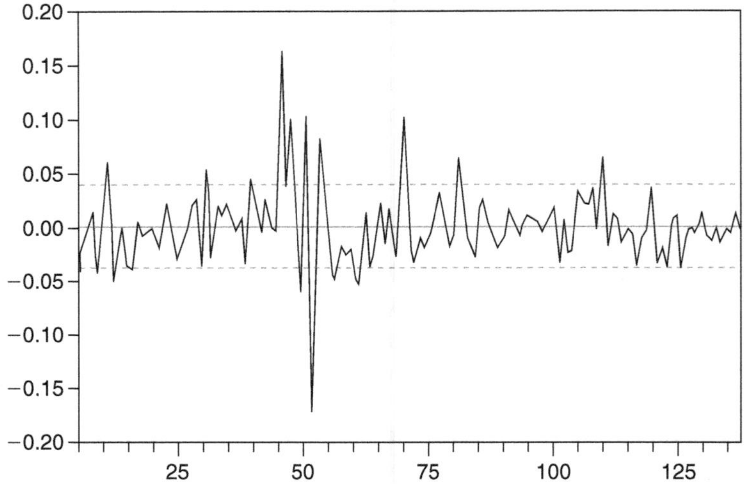

Figure 8.5 Unexplained inflation residuals from the VECM.

From the residuals it is clear that the period around the First World War was the one of worst fit (observation 50 is 1920, and observation 70 is 1940). There would thus be some improvement in overall explanatory power if the two World Wars were dummied out, but it remains of interest that the long-run relationship shines through despite the inclusion of the wars. It is also notable that the last 20 years or so fit very well when using retail M4 as the monetary aggregate.

This result is consistent with the money demand equation, but makes much clearer the long-run proportionality of money and prices. Cointegration clearly exists even though the adjustment process back towards equilibrium is slow.

The results using M4 excluding OFCs are not quite so impressive in terms of the proximity of the key coefficients to unity but they do show slightly stronger cointegration.

$$\log(P) = -0.565 + \underset{(0.084)}{0.886}\ \log(M) - \underset{(0.217)}{0.788}\ \log\left(\frac{Y}{P}\right) + \underset{(0.023)}{0.102}\ r$$

$$\text{Error correction term}\ \underset{(0.018)}{-\ 0.057}$$

However, these results are not that different from what can be obtained using M4 itself as we see below.

$$\log(P) = -0.403 + \underset{(0.070)}{0.858}\ \log(M) - \underset{(0.186)}{0.775}\ \log\left(\frac{Y}{P}\right) + \underset{(0.020)}{0.097}\ r$$

$$\text{Error correction term}\ \underset{(0.020)}{-\ 0.061}$$

This suggests that the long-run link between money and prices is sufficiently well established that even the distortions caused by OFCs have not destroyed it beyond recognition. In any event, the slow adjustment in all of these equations would render them of little use for short-term forecasting over the policy horizon of one to two years.

8.7 Causality tests

One of the nice features of using cointegration methods is that we do not have to worry about which are the exogenous variables, or about simultaneity problems. All that matters in the cointegration tests is that variables move together in the long run. We have found the long-run relationship that we expected between money and prices. However, there is no reason to expect any one-way causation between these two variables. On the contrary, with so many different regimes in the sample period, it is highly likely that there is two-way causation.

In order to test for causality, we use Granger causality tests between growth rates of variables (as the test requires stationary series) except for interest rates, which are measured as first differences (these are referred to as DLOG and D respectively in the tables below). We conduct one set of tests using two lags of annual data and another using four lags. The results using two lags are presented in Table 8.1 and the money measure reported is retail M4 (but similar results can be obtained with the other available money measures). The test results are Wald tests on the coefficients of the lagged (potentially) causing variable. To reject the hypothesis of no causation we are looking for a "prob."-value of less than 0.05, which is the usual 95 per cent level of confidence.

Table 8.1 Pairwise Granger Causality Tests using retail M4 and 2 lags of annual data, 1871–2008 (adjusted for lags).

Null Hypothesis	*Obs*	*F-Statistic*	*Prob.*
DLOG(Y/P) does not Granger Cause DLOG(P)	135	5.50083	0.0051
DLOG(P) does not Granger Cause DLOG(Y/P)		0.26739	0.7658
DLOG(M4) does not Granger Cause DLOG(P)	135	6.37775	0.0023
DLOG(P) does not Granger Cause DLOG(M4)		5.60859	0.0046
D(R) does not Granger Cause DLOG(P)	135	2.22913	0.1117
DLOG(P) does not Granger Cause D(R)		0.09839	0.9064
DLOG(M4) does not Granger Cause DLOG(Y/P)	135	1.57129	0.2117
DLOG(Y/P) does not Granger Cause DLOG(M4)		1.49815	0.2274
D(R) does not Granger Cause DLOG(Y/P)	135	3.97728	0.0211
DLOG(Y/P) does not Granger Cause D(R)		3.18883	0.0445
D(R) does not Granger Cause DLOG(M4)	135	0.43957	0.6453
DLOG(M4) does not Granger Cause D(R)		1.03578	0.3579

The strongest rejection of no causality is between money and prices, where there is clearly strong two-way causality, as expected.

We can also reject the hypothesis of no causality between the change in the interest rate and real GDP growth. The change in the long rate clearly causes GDP growth and the reverse causation is also significant. The only other strong result is that we can reject the hypothesis of no causation from real GDP growth to inflation but we cannot reject the hypothesis of no causation from inflation to real GDP growth. All other pair-wise causality tests show that the hypothesis of no causation cannot be rejected.

Granger causality tests using the same variables, but four lags, give similar results so far as money and prices are concerned but quite different results in two other important areas. First, the apparent two-way causation between the interest rate and real GDP growth disappears when four lags are used. This suggests that this dynamic relationship is not robust and thus possibly spurious. Second, there does appear to be two-way causation between real GDP growth and inflation that was not apparent with shorter lags. This is consistent with the view that inflation shocks will have real repercussions, and vice versa, but that the effects of inflation shocks on real GDP are slower to appear than the reverse effects.

The results using four lags are reported in Table 8.2.

Our conclusion from these results is that the two-way link between money and inflation is robust, there are weaker two-way links between inflation and real GDP growth, but other bi-lateral links do not appear to be present. These results for retail M4 are broadly supported when M4 and M4 excluding OFCs are used as monetary aggregates instead. The only systematic change when using these other money measures is that both of these appear to cause the long-term interest rate, though the reverse is not also true.

Table 8.2 Pairwise Granger Causality Tests using 4 lags 1871–2008 (adjusted for lags).

Null Hypothesis	*Obs*	*F-Statistic*	*Prob.*
DLOG(Y/P) does not Granger Cause DLOG(P)	133	3.37143	0.0118
DLOG(P) does not Granger Cause DLOG(Y/P)		3.46074	0.0102
DLOG(M4) does not Granger Cause DLOG(P)	133	3.84470	0.0056
DLOG(P) does not Granger Cause DLOG(M4)		4.13292	0.0035
D(R) does not Granger Cause DLOG(P)	133	2.02126	0.0955
DLOG(P) does not Granger Cause D(R)		0.34406	0.8477
DLOG(M4) does not Granger Cause DLOG(Y/P)	133	1.55612	0.1902
DLOG(Y/P) does not Granger Cause DLOG(M4)		1.27965	0.2816
D(R) does not Granger Cause DLOG(Y/P)	133	1.43933	0.2250
DLOG(Y/P) does not Granger Cause D(R)		1.09141	0.3638
D(R) does not Granger Cause DLOG(M4)	133	0.50145	0.7347
DLOG(M4) does not Granger Cause D(R)		1.94955	0.1064

8.8 Mind the gap

Our final look at these relationships is based upon creating an estimate of the (log) real GDP gap using a Hodrick-Prescott filter to extract the trend in potential GDP. We then conduct the same bilateral Granger causality tests using four lags, but replacing the growth rate of real GDP with the gap (denoted GAP).

The results are reported in Table 8.3 below. They do not show anything very different from what we found above. The same two-way causality between money growth and inflation is obviously still there as this is the same data. There is also clear two-way causation between inflation and the GDP gap. But the effect of the gap on inflation is stronger than was the effect of real GDP growth.

The gap formulation fits slightly better with a more modern way of thinking about the links between real activity and inflation but, in reality, the results using the gap formulation do not add much to what we had already found.

8.9 Conclusion

The conclusions of this study are very clear and reassuring for those of us who learned our macroeconomics in the 1960s and 1970s.

There is a stable and sensible long-run demand function for real money balances when adjustments are made to remove the distortions created by OFCs. This does not mean that OFCs are unimportant, merely that their behaviour is different from that of households and non-financial firms.

There is long-run proportionality between money and prices. This is clearest using retail M4 but the relationship is robust to changes of definition.

There is two-way causation between money growth and inflation, as there is between real GDP growth (or the GDP gap) and inflation.

Table 8.3 Pairwise Granger Causality Tests using 4 lags, 1871–2008 (adjusted for lags).

Null Hypothesis	*Obs*	*F-Statistic*	*Prob.*
DLOG(M4) does not Granger Cause GAP	133	1.72140	0.1494
GAP does not Granger Cause DLOG(M4)		1.48995	0.2093
DLOG(P) does not Granger Cause GAP	133	3.39413	0.0113
GAP does not Granger Cause DLOG(P)		3.91522	0.0050
D(R) does not Granger Cause GAP	133	1.45646	0.2195
GAP does not Granger Cause D(R)		0.82557	0.5113
DLOG(P) does not Granger Cause DLOG(M4)	133	4.13292	0.0035
DLOG(M4) does not Granger Cause DLOG(P)		3.84470	0.0056
D(R) does not Granger Cause DLOG(M4)	133	0.50145	0.7347
DLOG(M4) does not Granger Cause D(R)		1.94955	0.1064
D(R) does not Granger Cause DLOG(P)	133	2.02126	0.0955
DLOG(P) does not Granger Cause D(R)		0.34406	0.8477

Finally, it is clear that the efforts of Capie and Webber to produce the historical data have been extremely worthwhile. A policy role for monetary aggregates may be back to stay.

Notes

1 Or perhaps a year or two earlier.
2 There were other estimates of the money stock, such as Sheppard (1971) and Bordo (1981), but nothing with the detail and frequency of that to be produced by Capie and Webber (1985).
3 The Bank of England has recently been quoting an M4 series which excludes "intermediate OFCs" (a subset of the total) but this series is only available since 1997 so we have not used it in this study.

References

Artis, MJ and MK Lewis (1984) "How Unstable is the Demand for Money in the United Kingdom?" *Economica*, Vol. 51, pages 473–476.

Bordo, Michael D. (1981) "The UK Money Supply 1871–1914" *Research in Economic History*, Vol. 6, pages 107–125.

Capie, Forrest, and Alan Webber (1985) *A Monetary History of the United Kingdom 1870–1982* (London: George Allen & Unwin).

Chrystal, KA and Paul Mizen (2003) "Goodhart's Law: Its Origin, Meaning and Implications for Monetary Policy", Chapter 8 of *Central Banking, Monetary Theory and Practice: Essays in Honour of Charles Goodhart*, Volume 1, ed. Paul Mizen (Cheltenham: Edward Elgar), pages 221–243.

Feinstein, Charles H (1972) *National Income, Expenditure and Output of the United Kingdom, 1855–1965* (Cambridge: Cambridge University Press).

Friedman, Milton, and Anna J Schwartz (1963) *A Monetary History of the United States, 1867–1960* (Princeton, NJ: Princeton University Press).

Matthews, Kent, Ivan Paya and David A Peel (2004), "Alan Walters and the Demand for Money: An Empirical Retrospective" in *Money Matters: Essays in Honour of Alan Walters*, ed. Patrick Minford (Cheltenham: Edward Elgar).

Sheppard, DK (1971) *The Growth and Role of UK Financial Institutions 1880–1962* (London: Methuen & Co).

Part IV

Implications of economic integration

9 Does the euro need a fiscal union?

Some lessons from history

Michael Bordo, Lars Jonung and Agnieszka Markiewcz

Introduction[1]

The euro area is a unique form of a monetary union – with no historical precedence. The member states of the euro area have assigned the framing of monetary policy to a common monetary authority, the European Central Bank (ECB), set up as a highly independent central bank to ensure that it will be able to carry out a policy of price stability. Fiscal policy within the European Union (EU) remains the task of the national governments under a set of rules given in the Maastricht Treaty and the Stability and Growth Pact (SGP). These rules, pertaining to the Economic and Monetary Union (EMU), cover euro-area member states as well as member states that have not adopted the euro. They are monitored centrally by the Commission in a policy dialogue with the member states. This system represents the existing fiscal policy framework of the euro area that complements the monetary union and its single currency, the euro.

Ever since the plans for a single European currency were launched about 20 years ago, the institutional system for framing fiscal policies and for preserving the fiscal sustainability of the monetary union has been the subject of a heated debate – among economists as well as among policy-makers.[2] The 2007–09 global financial crisis has added new impulses to the debate about the proper fiscal policy arrangements within the EU.

Several views exist. According to one camp, the monetary union should be supplemented with an extended supranational or pan-European fiscal union to be viable and sustainable. In short, the EU should have access to a larger budget in order to design and carry its own central fiscal policies. Some go further and promote the idea of a deeper political union, like De Grauwe (2006), to ensure the success of the euro. The present debt crisis with the EMU has inspired a number of proposals for strengthening the fiscal power of the EU.

Others argue that such an extension of the fiscal powers of "Brussels" would not be accepted politically by EU citizens, threatening the political support for the monetary union in some member states, in particular in Germany. Instead, it is argued that the present institutional set-up is roughly the proper one. Some commentators propose that the monetary union is not in need of any central fiscal coordination across the member states, or at least of less coordination than presently. For them, like Mckay (2005), the fiscal policy framework should be solely the business of the member states. Another school recommends improvements in the quality of the fiscal policy process and the fiscal institutions across the EU as a promising way to go to improve fiscal policy governance in the EU.[3]

So far the debate has shown no signs of an emerging consensus.[4] Rather, it is getting more heated. One reason for the lack of unanimity is that the euro area represents a new type of monetary union. More precisely, the euro area is the first monetary union where monetary policy is set up at the central (European) level while fiscal policy is carried out at the subcentral (national) levels. Thus, the economics profession lacks historical cases to use as guidance for theoretical and empirical work. Instead, many contributions are based on either theoretical considerations or econometric calibrations and tests on data, commonly originating prior to the launch of the euro.

The aim of our study is to contribute to this debate by turning to the political and fiscal history of six federal states for an answer to the question: does the euro need a fiscal union? In short, we try to bring out the lessons from the past for the fiscal arrangements in the euro area of today. As we are primarily concerned with macroeconomic stability issues, we focus on fiscal policy as an instrument of stabilisation. We are well aware that fiscal policy-making covers many policy areas, in particular, distributional issues are closely related to questions of macroeconomic stabilisation and insurance.

We organise our study in the following way. In section 1, we give a brief overview of some key concepts and central issues. Next, in section 2, we summarise first past and then current experience of monetary and fiscal unions in six countries: the United States, Canada, Germany, Switzerland, Argentina and Brazil. In section 3, we condense lessons from our account of fiscal federalism. Section 4 contains a comparison between these lessons and the framework for fiscal policy governance in the EU. Section 5 concludes.

9.1 Fiscal federalism and fiscal policy in monetary unions: A brief overview

9.1.1 The concept of monetary and fiscal unions

A monetary union is commonly defined as a group of states sharing a single currency. In the strictest sense of the term, a monetary union means complete abandonment of regional or separate national currencies and full centralisation of monetary authority into a single joint institution. This is the case of the euro area, a subset of the Economic and Monetary Union (EMU), which covers all the 27 member states of the EU.[5]

The concept of a fiscal union entails fiscal federalism among its members, which could be either subnational (subcentral) political units or nation states. Fiscal federalism is based on a cooperative arrangement between the members of the fiscal union regarding the design and distribution of taxes and public expenditures.

There is no single definition of fiscal federalism. Sorens (2008) for example defines the "ideal type" of fiscal federalism as consisting of the following four elements: (1) subcentral political entities enjoy independence/autonomy to decide taxes and expenditures; (2) these governments face fairly hard budget constraints, that is a no-bailout rule is consistent with the ideal type of fiscal federalism; (3) there is a common market based on free trade and mobility within the fiscal union, thus there is scope for competition among subcentral governments; and (4) the system of fiscal federalism is institutionalised in a set of rules. We would like to add a fifth element to this list: (5) the common market is based on a common currency, that is, the subcentral as well as the central fiscal authorities are members of the same monetary union.

The governance structure of the EU is a challenge to put into the standard framework of fiscal federalism as there is no similar institutional set-up anywhere else in the world. The EU is different as stressed by Begg (2009): "the fact that the EU is set up as a union of citizens *and* of Member States is one of its most distinctive features." Its "federal" budget, that is the EU budget, is about 1 per cent of the national incomes of the member states. This is a much smaller ratio than the size of the federal budgets in the typical federal country. As stressed initially, the centralisation of monetary policy to ECB and the decentralisation of fiscal policy to the member states of the euro area is another unique feature of the EU. Still, in our opinion there is much in the history of fiscal federalism that can bear upon the design of EU governance in spite of the fact that EMU and the euro are unique institutions.

Musgrave (1959) provides the classical approach concerning the policy tasks of the public sector. His scheme identifies three basic policy functions: allocation/efficiency, distribution and stabilisation. These functions can be performed by different political entities within a fiscal union according to the adopted fiscal system.

The study of fiscal federalism, as defined by Oates (1999), is the study of how these roles are assigned to different levels of government and the ways in which they relate to one another through different policy instruments. The stabilisation function, that is the implementation of monetary and fiscal policies, is usually the task of the central government/central bank. The stabilisation of economic activity via fiscal policy can be achieved through two main channels. The first one refers to the role of automatic stabilisers, smoothing economic activity via the automatic response of taxes and transfer systems to the business cycle. The second channel consists of discretionary fiscal policy measures.

In this paper, we will often refer to subnational, regional, local or subcentral political entities within various federations. We will interchangeably call them jurisdictions and communities. Also, depending on the federation in question, these regions take different names; states in the United States, provinces in Canada and Argentina, Länder in Germany, cantons in Switzerland and municipalities in Brazil.

9.1.2 The normative arguments for fiscal federalism

As stated by Oates (1972), "The traditional theory of fiscal federalism lays out a general normative framework for the assignment of functions to different levels of the government and the appropriate fiscal instruments for carrying out these functions". This theory contends that the central government should have the basic responsibility for macroeconomic stabilisation and income distribution. In addition to these functions, the central government should provide national public or collective goods that service the entire population of the country such as defence.

Decentralised or lower levels of government have their *raison d'être* in the provision of public goods and services whose production and consumption is limited to their own jurisdictions. The economic argument for providing public goods at the subnational level was originally formulated in a decentralisation theorem that "...the level of welfare will always be at least as high if Pareto-efficient levels of consumption are provided in each jurisdiction than if any single, uniform level of consumption is maintained across all jurisdictions", see Oates (1972).

Thus, fiscal federalism addresses several issues. First, it has as the objective to respond to different political preferences across a country. Second, it produces positive externalities as it may generate benefits from intergovernmental competition, improve the fiscal responsibility of government, foster political participation and a sense of being a member of a democratic community and help to protect basic liberties and freedoms (Inman and Rubinfeld 1997). Finally, fiscal federalism also provides a way of maintaining the government share of GDP at a low level (Sorens 2008).

An obvious cost of federalism is the loss of autonomy by the central government. In fact, the benefits of decentralisation require that the central government's authority is limited (Rodden 2006). As a result, in highly decentralised fiscal federations, central governments might find it difficult to implement coordinated economic and other type of policies and provide federation-wide collective goods.

The conclusion that decentralised governments will provide the efficient level of public goods rests on a number of assumptions. One is that households and firms are freely mobile within the federation to generate competition between jurisdictions. If free mobility is not the case, competition among subcentral governments may lead to suboptimal outcomes. Another assumption is the lack of interdependencies between the policies of different jurisdictions. When this is not the case, competition among subnational governments may generate negative spillovers or externalities, and thus suboptimal outcomes.

If there are strong fiscal interdependencies between subnational jurisdictions policy-makers might face incentives to increase their expenditure while externalising the cost to the others. Rodden (2004, 2006) argues that this incentive is higher if the central government cannot fully commit to a no-bailout rule. Furthermore, the central government's commitment becomes less credible if sub-central governments are heavily dependent on transfers from the central authority. Intergovernmental transfers, as opposed to local taxation, change beliefs about the levels of local expenditure that can be sustained by creating the perception that the central government will ultimately provide financial help.

Transfer-dependent local governments usually face weaker incentives for responsible fiscal behaviour. For this reason, Rodden (2004, 2006) recommends a principle of subcentral sovereign debt within fiscal federations to maintain overall fiscal discipline.

9.1.3 Fiscal policy in the theory of optimum currency areas

The traditional theory of optimum currency areas (OCA), based on the work by Mundell (1961), McKinnon (1963) and Kenen (1969), also labelled by McKinnon (2004) as Mundell I, is the standard approach used by economists to evaluate and study the optimality (and thus the desirability) of monetary unions, in particular that of the euro area. This approach weighs the benefits for a country of adopting a common currency against the costs of abandoning its national currency and thus its independent monetary policy.

The benefits are higher if countries willing to join the monetary union are open economies and their trade is highly concentrated with other countries willing to join the union. On the other hand, the costs are higher when macroeconomic shocks are more asymmetric (country specific) and when other adjustment mechanisms are less effective in offsetting these shocks. These mechanisms include the flexibility of wages and prices and the mobility of labour and capital. If these mechanisms are not sufficiently developed, an appropriate fiscal policy could minimise the loss of the exchange rate channel for adjustment to asymmetric shocks.

Thus, domestic fiscal policy turns into the sole tool of stabilisation policy left for a member of a monetary union where monetary policy is carried out by a common central bank. Fiscal policy may also be organised and coordinated at the central level of the monetary union, implying a transfer of both monetary and fiscal policy to common central authorities.

While traditional OCA theory emphasises the trade and adjustment characteristics of regions/nation states willing to form a currency union, recent developments of the OCA approach, also labelled Mundell II inspired by Mundell (1973), focuses on the role of financial integration as a source of risk sharing (insurance) and consumption smoothing.

The OCA approach according to Mundell II suggests that monetary unification triggers financial market integration and the development of market-based risk-sharing mechanisms. These mechanisms may substitute for fiscal policies as they attenuate the effects of asymmetric shocks. As Eichengreen (1991, p. 17) notes, "Interregional transfers accomplished through federal taxes are justifiable only if insurance cannot be provided by the market." The Mundell II OCA theory identifies such a channel of private insurance. It is an empirical issue to what extent this channel may fully replace fiscal transfers within a monetary union.

A major weakness with the OCA approach, old as well as new, is the lack of attention paid to political and institutional factors.[6] The preferences of the public across the member states of a monetary union is the major determinant of the sustainability of monetary unification. These preferences are influenced by many factors, political as well as economic ones. Here the design of the institutional framework for fiscal policy-making – at the national as well as at the union level – comes at the centre.

9.1.4 Fiscal policy in the euro area

An extensive literature analyses the macroeconomic consequences of the institutional framework for monetary and fiscal policy-making in the EMU. In particular, it investigates the impact on inflation and debt accumulation by the existence of many independent national fiscal authorities and one single central bank.

The theoretical literature on the interaction of fiscal and monetary policies identifies various mechanisms which may lead to spillover effects across member states. For example, Dixit and Lambertini (2001) show that if monetary and fiscal authorities have different ideal output and inflation targets, Nash equilibrium output or inflation or both are suboptimal. Similarly, Chari and Kehoe (2004) find that if the central monetary authority does not commit to a future policy path, the free-rider problem leads to inefficient outcomes, i.e., excessive inflation in the whole monetary union and excessive debt issued by each member. Uhlig (2002) concludes that the existence of independent fiscal authorities and one central bank within a simple stochastic model leads, in a non-cooperative Nash equilibrium, to higher deficits of the member countries than in the cooperative equilibrium where they would be set to zero.

In line with the proposition by Rodden (2004, 2006), these studies point out that a set-up of a single monetary authority and numerous fiscal authorities requires binding fiscal policy constraints to avoid excessive deficits at the sub-central level, that is on the level of the member states in the case of the euro area.

To summarise this literature, the interplay between several fiscal and one monetary authority within a federation generates free-riding issues or common pool problems.[7] This mechanism works as follows. Each of the individual fiscal authorities sees itself only as a small player who has little impact on the common monetary policy. As a result, its fiscal policy choices would be purely driven by national interests. In equilibrium, each country free-rides and the outcome is worse than the one that could be reached in a cooperative equilibrium.

When one takes into account the medium-term and long-term costs of free-riding, the conclusions are less pessimistic. This is because the free-riding monetary union members are eventually punished for their behaviour. This mechanism is as follows. Over-expansionary fiscal policy by a member state deteriorates its relative competitive position and requires in due time costly and protracted price and wage adjustment in the medium run. Consider, for example, the case of a member state conducting a pro-cyclical fiscal policy in the euro area, leading to higher output growth and employment in the short run. Wages and prices will eventually respond to the excess aggregate demand. The ensuing deviation of price and wage inflation vis-à-vis other member states changes the relative competitive position of the member state in question. As the change in the real exchange rate stems from cumulating inflation over time, this negative competitiveness effect will dominate the expansionary fiscal policy effect after a number of years.[8]

The medium-term negative effects of lax fiscal policy do not guarantee that the member states will avoid them. This is the case because the benefits of free-riding are observable in the short run and the costs materialise only in the medium run, and hence we observe a time inconsistency policy problem.

Prior to the 2007–09 crisis, there has been little evidence either of free-riding behaviour or of any significant cross-border spillover effects within the euro area from fiscal policy. The 2007–09 crisis, however, illustrates how lax fiscal policy in a member state like Greece in the long run can build up effects that impact upon the whole euro area.

The institutional framework for fiscal policy-making and for fiscal surveillance in the EMU, that is the present fiscal union of the euro area, is likely to have contributed to this outcome. The question whether this framework will prove adequate in the long run remains. Is the present fiscal unification of the euro area sufficient to maintain price stability? To answer this question, we turn to the long-run evidence from a set of countries organised as fiscal federations.

9.2 The evolution of fiscal federalism within six monetary unions

According to Eichengreen (1991), "if a country is subject to asymmetric shocks, a system of fiscal federalism can, through regional insurance, attenuate these shocks". This proposition reflects the positive impact of fiscal federalism highlighted by theory. The argument is that a monetary union accompanied by a fiscal union is likely to operate more smoothly than a monetary union without it. A fiscal union, however, functions smoothly only if a number of assumptions, advanced in the previous section, are satisfied. History has frequently shown that the necessary conditions may not be in place. In that case, fiscal centralisation can lead to damaging fiscal policies and resulting large macroeconomic imbalances reflected in high and variable inflation and unsustainable debt developments.

To isolate the characteristics that make fiscal unions successful, we first give here an account of the historical experiences and then of the recent experience of six fiscal unions. We focus on two groups of federations: first the US, Canada, Switzerland and Germany; second Argentina and Brazil. The first group largely represents cases of successful fiscal unions, as measured by inflation and debt performance, as demonstrated in Table 9.1 which covers the period 1980–2006. The second group of Argentina and Brazil consists of less successful examples of fiscal unions. These federations are characterised by a much higher average rate of inflation than the US, Canada, Switzerland and Germany as illustrated in Table 9.1.

Table 9.1 Inflation, natural debt and interest rate performance of six fiscal federations, 1980–2006

Country	*Inflation rate*	*Inflation variability*	*Debt-to-GDP ratio*	*Debt variability*	*Nominal long-term rates for government bonds*	*Nominal interest rate variability*
US	3.9	2.6	39.0	6.6	7.6	2.8
Canada	3.8	3.0	42.2	9.9	8.4	3.1
Germany	2.4	1.7	25.7	8.9	6.4	1.8
Switzerland	2.3	1.9	17.6	5.9	4.2	1.2
Argentina	294.9	692.7	66.1	5.5	n.a.	n.a.
Brazil	403.1	856.3	40.4	8.0	23.4	9.6

Sources: OECD, World Bank, National databases.

Note

Due to lack of data for the debt-to-GDP ratio, the statistics are calculated for the period 1989–2006 for Argentina and 1991–2006 for Brazil. Long-term rates and their variability in Brazil are calculated for 1995–2006. These figures are not available for Argentina.

9.2.1 *The history of fiscal federalism*

9.2.1.1 The United States

The United States is a constitutional republic. Its government is based on a congressional system under a set of powers specified by its Constitution. The United States Congress is a bicameral legislature. The history of fiscal federalism in the United States dates back to the founding of the Union in 1789. Prior to the establishment of the federal government, the states had exercised their powers to levy taxes and provide certain public services. The tenth amendment to the US constitution explicitly reserves to "the States or to the people" all powers "not delegated to the United States by the Constitution, nor prohibited by it to the States".

During the pre-federal period, the union that existed under the Articles of Confederation constituted a league of sovereign states. It did not have the power of national taxation, or the power to control trade, and it had a comparatively weak executive. It was a "league of friendship" which was opposed to any type of national authority. Boyd and Fauntroy (1997) argue that the greatest weakness of the Articles of Confederation was that they only established state sovereignty and only delegated a few responsibilities to the central authorities. As a result, the majority of the power rested with the states. More precisely, each state had the authority to collect its own taxes, issue currency and finance its own army. The federal government's main activity was to control foreign policy and conclude treaties. As Congress, under the Articles, did not have the power to collect taxes, the central government was unable to balance its finances. It resulted in a debt of $42 million after the Revolutionary War which weakened considerably the government's economic credibility. This financial obligation was not paid off until the early 1800s.

The United States Declaration of Independence, an act of the Second Continental Congress, was adopted on 4 July, 1776. It declared that the Thirteen Colonies were independent of the Kingdom of Great Britain. The Articles of Confederation served as a "transition" between the Revolutionary War and the Constitution. In 1789, the US constitution was ratified and in 1790 the federal government assumed responsibility for the war debt, which some have called an early form of federal aid. The Tenth Amendment, added to the Constitution in 1791, protected the rights of the states and declared that all powers not expressly delegated to the central government by the Constitution were reserved for the states. This laid the foundation for the concepts of states' rights, limited national government and dual spheres of authority between state and national governments (Boyd and Fauntroy 1997).

The period from 1789 to 1901 has been termed the era of *dual federalism*.[9] It was characterised by little collaboration between the national and state governments. During this period, in particular between 1820 and 1840, the states engaged in extensive borrowing to finance their internal activities and development which resulted in high debts. Instead of introducing new taxes or adjusting their spending, numerous states demanded bailouts from the federal government. In fact, the states assumed that their debt implicitly carried a federal guarantee. However, the Congress refused to bail out indebted states and in 1840 several states defaulted on their debt and had to undertake painful adjustment measures. Thus, the federal government sent a costly but clear signal regarding the limits to its commitment to fiscal support to the states.

As a result, in the following decades, the US states developed the fiscal sovereignty that we still observe today. As Rodden (2006) puts it, states may occasionally dance around the topic of bailouts but hopes for them are not sufficiently bright that states would actually refuse to adjust while waiting for debt assumption.

Dual federalism was followed by a period of *cooperative federalism*, from 1901 to 1960.[10] This period was marked by greater cooperation and collaboration between the various levels of government.

The Great Depression played a particularly important role in the reconstruction of the relations between the central government and the states. The period from 1929 to 1941 was the most serious economic crisis in US history. Real GDP and prices fell by a third and the unemployment rate rose above 20 per cent in 1929–1933. Recovery to the 1929 level was not achieved until the start of the Second World War. The states were unable to respond effectively on their own to the economic consequences of the Great Depression leading to a major change in fiscal federal arrangements. In 1933, as a major component of his New Deal, President Franklin D. Roosevelt and the Congress greatly expanded the federal government's role in the domestic economy.

The New Deal era represented a turning point in the history of American federalism, particularly in the area of federal-state and local relations. The main change in government structure during the 1930s was the shift in expenditures from the local to the state and federal levels. Wallis (1984) argues that the emergence of "big" government in this period was a result of a change in the relative importance of federal and subnational governments rather than an increase in the growth rate of government expenditures by itself. He shows that between 1932 and 1940 the shares of government expenditures originating in federal and local governments were almost exactly reversed. Before 1932 relative shares for each level were roughly 50 per cent local, 20 per cent state and 30 per cent federal government. After 1940, 30 per cent of relative shares were local, 24 per cent state and 46 per cent federal. A major part of increasing government expenditures, 75 per cent, came in programmes administered at the federal level but in cooperation with state and local governments. Additionally, strong agricultural price supports were introduced at the federal level and were not matched by any corresponding shift in subnational expenses.

The most important modification of the US federation framework came as a new role for the fiscal policy of the central government. Before the Great Depression, the US government borrowed in time of war, and most of the time ran surpluses to pay off accumulated war debt. The possibility of using the government deficit as a tool of macroeconomic management was never considered. The Great Depression made it impossible to preserve this pattern. De Long (1996) notes that both the Hoover and the first Roosevelt administrations wished to maintain the pattern of surpluses of peacetime, but both found the austerity necessary to achieve surplus in the time of the Great Depression to be politically impossible. In the end, the US government accepted that large deficits in time of recession helped to attenuate the business cycle.

The period from 1960 to 1968 was called *creative federalism* by President Lyndon Johnson's administration. President Johnson's creative federalism, as embodied in his Great Society programme, was an important departure from the past. It further shifted the power relationship between governmental levels toward the federal government through an expansion of the grant-in-aid system and the increasing use of federal regulations.

Contemporary federalism, the period from 1970 to the present, has been characterised by shifts in the intergovernmental grant system, the growth of unfunded federal mandates, concerns about federal regulations, and continuing disputes over the nature of the federal system. There has been some devolution of programmes back to the states, reflecting, in part, dissatisfaction with the economic effects of several large federal programmes.

9.2.1.2 Canada

Canada is a constitutional monarchy and a parliamentary democracy with a federal system and strong democratic traditions. Originally a union of four provinces, Canada is now composed of ten provinces and three territories. It became a federation in 1867, which makes it the third oldest federation in the world today, after the United States and Switzerland.

Canada has a two-tiered, highly decentralised system. It can be characterised as a model of dual federalism with a coordinating central authority. Whereas federal and provincial governments are equal partners in the federation, local governments do not enjoy independent constitutional status and are simply the handmaidens of the provinces (Shah 1995). The distinct functions of the provincial legislatures and of the Parliament of Canada were established in the British North America Act, which was later renamed the Constitution Act, 1867.

The evolution of the federal system in Canada contrasts significantly with the evolution of the American federation. Both the origins of the two systems and their major developments differ. Watts (1987) argues that the Canadian federation was born in pragmatism rather than from an anti-imperial revolution sentiment. The major incentive for the unification of the Canadian colonies in 1867 was the threat of political, economic and military absorption by the United States.

Two distinctive features marked the federation created by the British North America Act. First, central powers were highly concentrated. Second, the Canadian political system combined a parliamentary form of government (similar to the British) with federalism.

Like the US, Canada suffered a major depression from 1929 to 1939. In terms of output, it was similar in both timing and magnitude to the Great Depression in the United States. Between 1929 and 1933, GNP dropped by 43 per cent and exports shrank by 50 per cent. Commodity prices fell dramatically around the world and therefore the regions and communities dependent on primary industries such as farming, mining and logging suffered the most. The economy began to recover, slowly, after 1933. However, the Depression did not end until the outbreak of the Second World War in 1939.

The Great Depression was a turning point for Canadian economic policies. Before 1930, the government intervened as little as possible, believing the free market would take care of the economy. During the Depression, the government of Canada became much more interventionist and proposed legislation that paralleled Roosevelt's New Deal agenda. In particular, it introduced high tariffs to protect domestic manufacturing, a step that only created weaker demand and made the Depression worse. It also introduced minimum hourly wages, a standard work week and programmes such as old age assistance and unemployment insurance. The Bank of Canada was created in 1934 as a central bank to manage the money supply and bring stability to the country's financial system.

In 1937, the federal government appointed the Royal Commission on Dominion-Provincial Relations, commonly known as the Rowell-Sirois Commission. Its objective was to examine issues of taxation, government spending, the public debt, federal grants and subsidies and the constitutional allocation of revenue sources. Ruggeri (2006) argues that the most important recommendation of the Commission was the payment to the provinces by the federal government of "national adjustment grants", a set of unconditional transfers aimed at equalising provincial fiscal capacity. In return, the federal government acquired exclusive jurisdiction over personal and corporate income taxes and succession duties. This new division of responsibilities between different levels of the government represented a major shift towards fiscal centralisation.

In 1938, following the Commission recommendations, the federal government for the first time consciously decided to increase spending to counteract a downturn in economic activity. In addition to fiscal expenditures the government also offered loans to municipalities for local improvements and passed a National Housing Act to encourage the building of homes. Consistent with this Keynesian approach, the government also reduced taxes and offered tax exemptions for private investors. The idea of a static and balanced budget was abandoned. In its place fiscal policy would stimulate economic recovery via government deficits and economic measures.

The budget of 1938 marks the beginning of a new concept of the role of government in Canada. Until then the federal government had concentrated on providing public services. It had now undertaken a new and significantly different responsibility: that of smoothing economic activity. It was a most radical innovation inspired by the Great Depression.

After the Second World War, the Canadian federation continued the process of centralisation, which culminated in the 1960s. Federal programme spending was almost 70 per cent larger than provincial programme spending in the early 1960s. Since then, it has declined. The enormous growth of the welfare state in the early post-war period was a joint venture with the provinces delivering the social programmes and the federal government providing conditional transfers.

The period starting in the 1980s was marked by consolidation of Canada's system of intergovernmental fiscal relations. By the mid-1990s, increasingly large deficits and debt burdens, especially those of the federal government, led to fiscal restraint that culminated in significant reductions across a wide range of federal expenditures, including transfers to provinces and territories.

Since 1983–84, provincial-territorial programme spending has declined as a share of GDP. Canadian provinces and territories were hit hard by the recession of the early 1990s, which caused a significant increase in spending on social assistance and social services. As a result, some provinces issued excessively high levels of public debt leading to an increase in risk premia and a downgrading of their bond ratings, and pressure on the federal government for a bailout. In consequence, an equalisation system was put in place whose essential features remain with us today. Starting in the mid-1990s, most provinces undertook major restructuring to reduce or stabilise their programme expenditures. The sustained job creation over the following decade has also significantly reduced provincial spending pressures in the areas of social assistance and social services. To sum up, Watts (1987) notes that since its creation the Canadian federation has evolved from a quasi-unitary structure into a federal system in which the provinces play an increasingly more important role.

9.2.1.3 Switzerland

Since the constitution of 12 September 1848, Switzerland has had a relatively complex system of three layers of government: the communes, at the local level; the cantons, at the intermediate level; and the Confederation, at the national level, interconnected by many vertical and horizontal relationships. In 2001, there were 26 Cantons and 2,880 communes.

Switzerland as a federal state is a relatively recent creation, dating from 1848, but its origins go back to the thirteenth century, when three Alpine Regions and several towns declared independence from the Habsburg and created a Confederation. Between 1798 and 1815 the country was invaded and de facto ruled by revolutionary France. The Helvetic Republic, under the 1798 constitution, lasted until 1802 and was characterised by a unitary state structure imposed by the French. The 1803 Federal Constitution set up a halfway system between a confederation and a federation, with France retaining the decisive authority.

In August 1815, the Swiss cantons regained their sovereignty from French control and re-established a confederation. The confederation was a union of 21 small sovereign states (cantons) united to, in the words of Article 1 of the Federal Treaty, "defend their freedom and independence from any foreign attack as well as preserving internal order and peace" (Church and Dardanelli 2005, p. 6). This confederation lasted until 1848, when the new Constitution established the modern federal state keeping the cantons' autonomy. Accordingly, the new federal state was still largely decentralised, with limited powers exercised at the central level. However, the need for a greater centralisation appeared. The main driving force was the desire to harmonise regulations across cantons, especially of weights and measures and of the legal codes, in order to facilitate economic activity on a country-wide basis. After a failed attempt in 1872, a wide-ranging constitutional revision was approved in 1874 giving more power to the central level, notably on matters of defence, private law, transport and the environment.

At the same time, an increase in federal expenditures took place. This increase was mainly due to the spending on the Franco-Prussian War of 1870–71. In fact, the cantons were largely responsible for military expenditure. As the mobilisation in 1870 demonstrated serious weaknesses in the largely decentralised federal system, constitutional revision in 1874 shifted most of these responsibilities to the federal government.

Another major source of expense in the early years of the confederation was a revenue-sharing scheme between the federal government and the cantons. By the beginning of the First World War, the confederation was subsidising, among other things, agriculture, hunting, education, health, science and art, road construction and public utilities; see Codding (1979). In 1913, subsidies accounted for 25 per cent of all federal expenditures. In 1910 the expenditures of the Swiss government had, for the first time, passed the one hundred million Swiss franc mark. The beginning of war was followed by even greater growth of expenditures. In 1914, they reached over two hundred million, in 1918 over five hundred million and in 1920 over six hundred million.

Between 1925 and 1930 government revenue exceeded expenditures and thus allowed for a reduction of the national debt. When the Swiss financial situation was improving, Switzerland was hit by the Great Depression, which reached its peak in 1932. This event, as in the US and Canada, forced the federal government to centralise and considerably increase its expenditure.

From the establishment of the modern federal state in 1848 until the 1970s, a continuous process of centralisation took place in the Swiss federal system. Church and Dardanelli (2005) argue that this process of centralisation was driven by two main forces: the desire to facilitate economic activity by creating a single economic area and the will to grant citizens equality of rights in the political and social spheres.

9.2.1.4 Germany

The Federal Republic of Germany consists of a federal (Bund) government, 16 Land (state) governments and numerous municipal (or local) governments. There is a formal, indirectly elected head of state, the President of the Federal Republic. All of the federal and Land governments are organised on the basis of the parliamentary system. Most Länder have unicameral legislatures, whose members are elected directly by popular vote.

Germany is a relatively recent nation state. In the mid nineteenth century, Germany was a collection of smaller states that were linked together as a German confederation. This confederation was dominated by Austria, which as an imperial power was politically and economically superior to the smaller Germanic states. In the 1860s, the dominance of Austria was challenged by Prussia and the process of unification and codification of German law began.

A gradual process of economic interdependence from the early stages of the Industrial Revolution through to the mid nineteenth century saw the Germanic states move towards economic unification. For example, the growth of the railway network in Germany led to easier access to different resources across the confederation. This helped to stimulate economic growth and meant that economic prosperity was increasingly reliant upon strong links between different member states of the German confederation.

This led to the introduction of the *Zollverein* customs union, an agreement among the German states to have preferential customs policies for member states. This economic union excluded Austria, illustrating a growing German sense of identity and a lesser dependency upon the largest of the Germanic states.

The final national unification of Germany was achieved in two steps: the creation of the North German Confederation in 1866–67 and then of the German Reich in 1871. In 1866 the arguments about the administration of Schleswig-Holstein caused a war between Austria and Prussia. The war lasted seven weeks and resulted in Prussian victory over the Austrians which led to a clearer division between Austrian and German interests. This new situation also forced the smaller states to align themselves with the Prussians, with whom they shared more economic ties due to the common *Zollverein* customs agreement.

At the same time, between 1866 and 1870, relations between Prussia and France worsened. In 1870, France declared a war that was won by Prussia. Following victories over France, in January of 1871, Prussia persuaded other German confederation members that unification was desirable. As a result, Wilhelm of Prussia was proclaimed Emperor of Germany on 18 January, 1871. The Second German Reich was born.

With unification, Prussia inherited a set of states with already highly institutionalised governance structures in place: well-developed public education systems, effective systems of public finance and stable populations; see Ziblatt (2004). After unification, the German Reich increased its spending so that the share of total government expenditures over GNP rose from 10 per cent in 1881 to 17.7 per cent in 1913 while the central government's share increased from 2.9 per cent to 6.2 per cent; Hefeker (2001).

The First World War ended in defeat for Germany. As the government financed its burgeoning deficits by the monetary printing press, saddled with enormous war debts and reparations, the economy slid into a hyperinflation in 1922–23. The hyperinflation was ended by a stabilisation package based on fiscal consolidation.

When, after the war, the Weimar Republic was founded, a drive towards a centralised state strongly dominated separatist tendencies and thus limited the possibilities for development of a federal system. The Weimar Republic is described as a "decentralised unitary state", rather than a federal state.

In early 1928, Germany's economy slipped into recession, then stabilised before turning down again in the third quarter of 1929. The decline in German industrial production during the Great Depression was roughly equal to that in the United States. Lacking adequate sources of finance, the federal government was forced to cover its budget to a large extent by issuing debt, running ultimately into a serious debt crisis. The German government did not use activist fiscal policy to attenuate the effects of the crises.[11]

In January 1933, Hitler was appointed Reich Chancellor. In terms of economic policy, the Hitler regime did not represent a radical break with past conservative policies, at least not until 1936. It increased spending for military purposes. The Nazi regime created a unitary state with all powers held by the central government while the States were relegated to administrative districts.

After the Second World War, a new type of federalism was imposed on Germany. Because of the Nazi totalitarian experience, a unitary structure for post-war Germany was ruled out. Instead a federal solution was adopted, founded on the creation of Länder. They were conceived as state units, clearly distinct from the federation, and they strongly defended their authority and financial resources against the central government. The distribution of powers between the central and Länder governments according to the Basic Law still reflects some aspects of the Weimar Republic. However, since the Second World War, the federal government has been more limited in several areas.

The system created by the Basic Law (the German Constitution) did not facilitate cooperative federalism or even the sharing of political responsibility between federation and state. The rather competitive structure of the German federation reduced the financial responsibility of the already largely transfer-dependent Länder. Although the central government officially follows the no-bailout rule, this commitment is not fully credible. There is an incentive for the Länder to borrow excessively as their taxing authority is rather limited. Indeed, the excessive debts of some of the Länder and the financial security provided by the central government, after the Second World War, demonstrate the lack of credibility and commitment of the latter.

In the immediate post-war period, the level of the public debt was rather low and evenly distributed between the three levels of the German federation. In the 1970s and 1980s, the debts of the central government and especially of the Länder rose at a sharp rate. Some of the Länder, which were particularly indebted and which were also used to receive high amounts of transfers, expected the central government to bail them out. In order to strengthen its credibility, the central government could have refused, as the US federal government did in 1840. Instead, in early 1987 the Länder of Bremen and Saarland began to receive special supplementary transfers from the central government explicitly aimed at coping with their high debts.

In 1992 the Federal Constitutional Court handed down its decision stipulating that the constitution required the Bund to make extra transfers to Bremen and

Saarland, amounting to around 30 billion DM over the period from 1994–2000; see Rodden (2004) and Heppke-Falk and Wolff (2008). Furthermore, these transfers to Bremen and Saarland have never had to be repaid.

The bailout provided by the German government was a signal of its lack of commitment, demonstrating the difficulties to commit in the existing constitutional setting, and created incentives for further irresponsible fiscal behaviour on the part of the Länder. The huge debts at the Länder level were largely responsible for Germany's breach of the Stability and Growth Pact in the early 2000s.[12] Also in a federal constitutional court ruling of 2007 on Berlin, no fundamental change of the principle of solidarity was undertaken and investors continued to price German Länder essentially similarly (Schulz and Wolff 2009). However, a similar, and significantly more severe problem, has characterised the two Latin American federations as discussed below.

9.2.1.5 Argentina

Argentina is a federal republic with 24 provinces. It has a presidential government and a bicameral legislature consisting of the Chamber of Deputies (257 seats) and the Senate (72 seats). Sturzenegger and Werneck (2006) note that while the Chamber of Deputies supposedly elects deputies in proportion to their populations, the Argentine system over-represents the participation of small provinces through a minimum number of five deputies per jurisdiction.[13] The Senate is represented by three senators from each province, two from the first majority and a third from the second party.

The Argentine state was born out of the union of colonial regions with differing economic and social characteristics. The revolution of 1810 against Spanish control led to the declaration of independence of the United Provinces of the Rio de la Plata in 1816. Independence revealed strong regional disparities which had been hidden by Spanish rule. As a result, the establishment of a national government and a constitution took almost four decades accompanied by violent struggle. Finally, in 1853 the Constitution established a constitutional federal republic. The changes in the Constitution introduced in 1860, gave the provinces priority over the central government. The provinces also gained autonomy in the administration of their territories. Despite some later modifications, the essential federalist structure of the 1853–60 Constitution remains in force today (Tommasi 2002).

By the beginning of the twentieth century, Argentina was one of the most developed countries in the world. However, after the Great Depression, it entered a path of economic decline largely reflecting a succession of poor economic policies based on populism.

The Great Depression began in Argentina in the late 1920s, even before the date of the start of the depression in the core countries of North America and Western Europe following the Wall Street crash of 1929. Like in many countries of the periphery, Argentina was exposed to commodity price shocks and, during the 1920s, its terms of trade worsened considerably. By the end of 1929, a balance of payments crisis developed, and the exchange rate was allowed to float after only two years of participation in the gold standard. Recovery began in 1931, and by 1934–35, output had regained its 1929 level.

The Argentine Great Depression was mild and short-lived by international standards. From its peak between 1929 and 1932 domestic real output fell by 14 per cent and by 1935 it had surpassed its 1929 level. Deflation was about 6 per cent in the 1929–32 period. In other gold-standard countries, such as the United States and Canada, the decline in real activity reached more than 30 per cent and price levels declined by more than 20 per cent.

Major monetary policy actions from 1929 to 1935 were responsible for accommodation of the negative shocks of the 1930s. In response to the economic difficulties, two major institutional changes in the conduct of monetary policy took place in the first half of the 1930s. The first was in 1931, when the decision was taken by the Conversion Office (a currency board established in 1910) to shift the monetary regime from a metallic regime standard based on gold to a fiduciary regime and to revalue the monetary gold stock and devalue the currency. This resulted in a more flexible monetary regime which could adapt to the economic crisis. Second, a Banco Central, a central bank, was created in 1936. This independent institution replaced the Conversion Office and abandoned its nominal anchor commitment device.[14]

During the depression, fiscal policies in Argentina remained even more conservative than in countries like the United States. The Great Depression created a sudden decrease in federal revenues. As a result, some tax collection responsibilities shifted from the subnational to the national level. The federal government started to collect taxes that were previously assigned to the provinces, invoking the "critical situation" clause in the Constitution.

Continuous growth of government in successive decades brought public expenditures to about 50 per cent of GDP in the second half of the 1990s. During the 1980s, both levels of government borrowed extensively, reflecting weak fiscal management. In addition, both levels of government accumulated large debts on payments for wages and pensions, to suppliers and for debt service. Lack of financial control prevailed in particular at the provincial level, becoming an important source of financial and macroeconomic instability.

In the late 1980s, the provinces accounted for roughly 40 per cent of the deficit of the consolidated non-financial public sector. These deficits were financed by discretionary transfers and loans from the federal government, but also by loans from the provincial banks and other parts of the financial system; see Saiegh and Tommasi (1999). The provinces borrowed from their provincial banks, who then discounted the debt at the central bank, effectively giving the provinces a share in the seignorage from inflation. This process led, by the end of the 1980s, to a hyperinflation.

By establishing a currency board arrangement, the Convertibility Law of March 1991 ended inflationary central bank financing of public sector deficits at all levels. A set of structural reforms was introduced in the 1990s.

During the period 1992–94, the federal government financed special financial rescue operations for seven provinces.[15] Nicolini *et al.* (2002) argue that one of the main sources of deficits in provincial finances was the state provincial pension system. Financial aid to provinces in difficulties took the form of issuing national treasury bonds. Using this ad hoc mechanism, the central government granted huge loans.

After a decade, Argentina returned to its historical pattern of high fiscal deficits and burgeoning debt (Tommasi 2002). In 2001 a new and much more severe debt and banking crisis occurred and the convertibility law had to be abandoned. Two fundamental problems jointly triggered the Argentinian crises of 2001–02.

First, although Argentina made many reforms in the early 1990s, it did not develop a budget policy or pass a fiscal responsibility law that controlled provincial spending. Sturzenegger and Werneck (2006) argue that the irresponsible fiscal behaviour of the provinces and the subsequent run-up in the national debt to GDP ratio was a key ingredient in the process leading to this crisis. During the 1990s, Argentina's budget deficit increased as did its mainly foreign currency denominated debt.

Second, the convertibility law tied the peso to the dollar and permitted unrestricted convertibility at a fixed exchange rate. This arrangement could not cope with an unsustainable debt on one side and an overvalued exchange rate on the other.[16]

To sum up, the history of fiscal federalism in Argentina is a case of a permanent struggle between the federal government, the provinces and the municipalities. Lack of trust and consensus across different levels of government has prevented a stable system of distribution of taxes and expenditures, in this way contributing to recurring fiscal problems (Cetrángolo and Jiménez 2004). Heterogeneity across regions and provinces, in particular the concentration of wealth to Buenos Aires, has contributed to this pattern.

9.2.1.6 Brazil

Brazil has a complex federation. Three government levels comprise the Union of 26 states plus the Federal District, and more than 5,500 municipalities. The Constitution explicitly considers municipalities to be members of the federation, giving them a much higher status and autonomy than is generally observed in other federations; see Sturzenegger and Werneck (2006).

The republic has a presidential regime and a bicameral legislature consisting of the Federal Senate and the Chamber of Deputies. Each state is equally represented in the upper chamber by three senators. Representation in the Chamber of Deputies is not strictly proportional to state constituencies. In fact, the Constitution establishes that no state may have less than eight deputies and more than 70. This leads to a disequilibrium similar to the one present in the Argentinian federation. The unpopulated Northern states are over-represented and the state of São Paulo is under-represented.

The Brazilian Federation was created along with the Republic in 1889. It was born out of the decision to divide the unitary state that prevailed during the Imperial Regime. Castanhar (2003) notes that the Federal Regime was convenient mainly for the most developed provinces of the South and Southeast, in particular São Paulo. These regions were rich in the new agricultural export products at that time. These provinces would obtain additional revenues from local taxes on these exports. In return, the less developed regions were granted political representation in the government more than proportional to their population.

This fiscal federal arrangement has undergone substantial changes over Brazil's history. During most of the nineteenth century when the country had a parliamentary monarchy a high degree of centralisation prevailed. The Proclamation of Republic in 1889 brought a general delegation of taxes and spending to the states.

During the Great Depression, Brazil, like many other commodity dependent economies, went into a deep crisis. The price of coffee (70 per cent of Brazil's exports share during the 1920s) dropped from 22.5 cents a pound in 1929 to 8 cents in 1931. As in the other federations studied by us, the economic depression accelerated expansion and centralisation consolidation of the central power. In 1929, Brazil like Argentina began to devalue its currency and as a result experienced only a relatively mild downturn and had largely recovered by 1935.

The central government was strengthened further during the authoritarian Vargas regime between 1930 and 1945. The end of the Vargas dictatorship brought a new constitution. Although the new constitution did not introduce radical changes to the tax system, it promoted significant efforts of decentralisation, giving more autonomy as well as sources of revenue to state and local governments. This decentralisation wave was interrupted by 20 years of military government, from 1964 on. The end of this regime in 1985 led to another decentralisation movement. The interests of subnational governments dominated the redesign of the fiscal federalism arrangement established by the 1988 Constitution.

As a reaction to the earlier dictatorial period, the new constitution delegated a large amount of revenue and political power towards the subnational governments, and in particular towards the municipalities. Subnational governments were directly or indirectly given a much more generous share of the aggregate taxes collected in the country. Although the Constitution already enhanced the taxing power of subnational governments, it additionally established transfers based on revenue-sharing rules; see Sturzenegger and Werneck (2006).

Soon after the approval of the Constitution and a new tax system in particular, the central government faced growing financial difficulties. In response, it undertook efforts to increase its tax revenue. As a result, inefficient taxes were introduced, i.e., various forms of turnover taxes that had been eliminated from the Brazilian tax system in the 1960s.

Brazil has experienced three major state-level debt crises between the end of the 1980s and 2000. In each of these crises, the same pattern reoccurred. The states facing unstable fiscal situations with high levels of spending on personnel and interest payments were pushed into debt-servicing crises by exogenous shocks. Rodden (2006) notes that large, indebted states like São Paulo and

Minas Gerais were aware of the fact that the centre could not let them default because of the negative spillovers onto the banking system and the country's creditworthiness. Thus, they received bailouts from the central government, and in each of the crises the federal government responded by taking measures to assume the state debts. This led to increases in the federal debt burden – fuelling a crisis.

9.2.2 Present fiscal federalism

Following the above description of the historical evolution of six federal countries, we now turn to the present situation of fiscal federal arrangements in these countries. We describe the allocation of spending responsibilities between different levels of government, intergovernmental grants and revenue sharing, budget balance requirements and borrowing constraints. Finally, we look at the size of government expenditure as a simple proxy for the influence of automatic stabilisers.

Table 9.2 summarises the degree of fiscal decentralisation in the six federations we consider. Column 1 of Table 9.2 shows a spending decentralisation index calculated as the share of subnational expenditures relative to total public expenditures. Column 2 reports the degree of fiscal independence of subnational governments measured as the ratio of the own source subnational revenue to total public sector revenue. Column 3 displays an index of transfer dependence calculated as the ratio of the sum of federal grants and revenue-sharing transfers to total revenue of subnational authorities.

Next, column 4 displays a second overall measure of transfer dependence. Tax autonomy, as shown in column 4, is calculated as the share of revenue from taxes collected at the subnational level to the total revenue of subnational governments. The index of borrowing autonomy in column 5 considers debt authorisation requirements and limits on the use of debt imposed by the central government. This variable ranges from 1 to 5, where the index equals 1 when subnational governments cannot borrow while 5 indicates maximum borrowing autonomy. For details see Rodden (2006). Finally, column 6 shows whether the central government is legally constrained by a no-bailout rule where a yes marks the existence of a no-bailout rule.

We will use Table 9.2 in our account below of the extent of fiscal federalism in our sample of fiscal federations.

9.2.2.1 United States

A detailed description of American contemporary fiscal federalism is provided by Laubach (2005). According to him, states are largely free in their choice of tax bases and rates, subject to only a few limitations imposed by the federal constitution. On the expenditure side, most major spending functions are located at the state or local government level, important exceptions being national defence, pensions and health insurance for the elderly and disabled.

Table 9.2 Characteristics of federalism (averages for the 1990s)

Country	*Expenditure decentralisation (1)*	*Fiscal decentralisation (2)*	*Transfer dependence (3)*	*Tax autonomy (4)*	*Borrowing autonomy (5)*	*No- bailout rule (6)*
USA	0.53	0.42	0.34	0.32	3.0	Yes
Canada	0.65	0.51	0.32	0.32	2.7	Yes
Switzerland	0.55	0.41	0.19	0.35	3.0	Yes
Germany	0.45	0.34	0.70	0.04	4.0	Yes
Argentina	0.44	0.18	0.56	n.a.	4.5	No
Brazil	0.41	0.28	0.36	n.a.	n.a.	No

Sources: Government Finance Statistics (GFS) Yearbook, IMF; Taxing Powers of State and Local Governments, OECD Tax Policy Studies no. 1, OECD, Paris; Rodden (2006) and Reserve Bank of India (2006).

Comments

All indices are calculated as averages over the 1990s.

Column (1): Expenditure decentralisation: subnational expenditures/total expenditures.

Column (2): Fiscal decentralisation: own source subnational revenue/total revenue.

Column (3): Transfer dependence: grants plus revenue sharing/total subnational revenue.

Column (4): Tax autonomy: subnational tax revenue/total revenue.

Column (5): Borrowing autonomy – the index of borrowing autonomy has been constructed by the Inter-American Development Bank. It considers debt authorisation requirements and limits on the use of debt imposed by the central government. This variable ranges from 1 to 5. See Rodden (2006) for details.

Column (6): No-bailout rule: a "yes" implies that the central government is legally constrained by a bailout rule and a "no" that a no-bailout rule does not exist.

Total expenditures of local governments are almost as large as those of state governments, and the sum of these two, as can be seen in column 1 of Table 9.2, is roughly equal to central government expenditure, reflecting a high degree of decentralisation in the US.

Subnational governments in the United States are, in principle, free to borrow without federal involvement. In reality, however, nearly all states have some kind of constitutional or statutory balanced-budget requirement. Indeed, according to Table 9.2, column 5, the borrowing autonomy of the subcentral governments is rather limited. The precise nature of the requirements varies considerably across states. The US federal government has followed a no-bailout policy (column 6 in Table 9.2).

In the US, there is neither overall federal-state coordination of fiscal policy nor a revenue-sharing system between the federal and state governments (Shah 1995). In fact, at the federal level, there are no transfers specifically intended to deal with subnational imbalances. The most important federal transfers are those that fund health, education and transport programmes administrated by the states. Although there is an attempt in many of these programmes to relate transfers to such indicators of need as income per capita income, there is no general system of equalisation similar for instance to the German one. Thus, the US states are not highly dependent on transfers. According to both measures reported in Table 9.2, column 3 and 4, the revenue coming from transfers accounts for around 30 per cent of the total revenue of states.

Unlike at the federal level, issues of general obligation debt require at least the approval of the state legislature, and in many states voter approval. Such debt issues are rare, with California's $15 billion bond issue, approved by voters in March 2004, the most recent example. The discipline imposed by capital markets, and the effectiveness of the budget constraints resulted almost always in positive net saving by the subnational governments.

9.2.2.2 Canada

Canadian provinces are the main providers of social programs involving public services, while the federal government is largely restricted to social programmes that involve transfers. The fact that such social programmes include a significant proportion of programme spending at both levels of government emphasises the importance of redistribution as an objective of government policy.

Since the British North American Act of 1867, the provinces have been assigned an increasing number of taxes. As stressed by Shah (1995), today they are responsible for tax collection in all areas except customs, unemployment insurance premiums and contributions to the Canada Pension Plan.[17]

Canada has a highly decentralised federal system. Subnational expenditures accounted for more than 50 per cent of total public expenditures during the 1990s (column 1 and 2 in Table 9.2). As noted by Shah (1995), in Canada there are elaborate mechanisms for federal-provincial fiscal coordination. The majority of direct programme expenditures are at the subnational level but Ottawa (i.e., the Canadian federal government) retains flexibility and achieves fiscal harmonisation through conditional transfers and tax collection agreements.

In the past several years, provincial concern has emerged over the use of federal spending power simply as a means of transferring revenues to the provinces. Canada, like almost all federations, is characterised by a vertical fiscal gap: a mismatch between the revenue means and expenditure needs. In particular, Canadian federal revenue exceeds what is required by direct and indirect spending responsibilities of the central government. Regional governments have fewer revenues than their expenditure responsibilities with the result of excess central revenue being transferred to the provinces in some form or another. Over time, the size of the vertical gap has gradually decreased, implying that provinces have gradually become more and more self-sufficient.

Much of the discipline on public sector borrowing comes from the financial sector – monitoring deficits and debt at all levels of government. Moreover financial markets, especially bond and stock markets, and provincial electorates impose a strong fiscal discipline at the subnational level. The borrowing autonomy index in Canada is the lowest in the group of countries under study (column 5 in Table 9.2). Furthermore, national policies explicitly forbid bailouts of provinces at risk of default (column 6 in Table 9.2).

9.2.2.3 Switzerland

Contemporary fiscal federalism in Switzerland can be characterised in terms of overall fiscal self-discipline and minimising the centralisation of fiscal power. Dafflon and Tóth (2005) call it "bottom-up" federalism. Constitutional arrangements, both at the federal and the cantonal levels, explain this situation. The subsidiarity principle has probably been more scrupulously respected in this country than in many other federations because of both constitutional guarantees and a traditional mistrust of nation-wide policies.[18] In addition, as Sutherland, Price and Joumard (2006) emphasise, the cantons and the communes are seen as public policy laboratories carrying out policy innovations without great risk of damaging the overall economy since the upper-level government (the confederation or the canton) will not provide a bailout (see the no-bailout rule in column 6 in Table 9.2). As a consequence, the power to decide and finance the provision of public services has remained largely in decentralised hands, that is, in the cantons or in the communes.

The cantons and the municipalities raise their own taxes and fees to finance cantonal and local expenditures. As indicated in Table 9.2 (column 4), the tax rate autonomy of the subnational jurisdictions is the highest in the studied group. These jurisdictions rely heavily on direct taxes (around 95 per cent of total tax revenue) whereas the federal government relies much more on indirect taxes (around 60 per cent of total federal tax revenue) such as VAT. The cantons and the municipalities levy the main part of the direct income taxes, although the federal government also raises its own (very progressive) income tax. The extent of the total income tax burden (including cantonal, communal and church taxes) varies considerably across the cantons.

On the expenditure side, the Swiss system is also considerably decentralised. Expenditure decentralisation exceeded 50 per cent during the 1990s (column 1 in Table 9.2). Social assistance is mostly administrated at the cantonal and local level. The cantons decide autonomously on their tax scheme. They set the rate of progression as well as the level of cantonal income taxation. In contrast, the municipalities can only levy a surcharge on the cantonal income taxes.

The extensive autonomy of cantonal and local governments for their finance is not unlimited. First, many cantons have introduced their own constitutional rules with regard to a (balanced) budget and debt limitation. Fiscal competition between jurisdictions is a second limit. However, autonomy in public expenditures, direct access to many revenue sources and, above all, differences in the cantons' economic potential have led to regional disparities, expressed in the fiscal burden of the cantons and in their financial capacity. These disparities are at the core of the Swiss equalisation policy, even though there is no claim for perfect equality between the cantons or the communes (Dafflon and Tóth 2005).

9.2.2.4 Germany

The Basic Law divides authority between the federal government and the Länder, with the general principle governing relations articulated in Article 30: "The exercise of governmental powers and the discharge of governmental functions shall be incumbent on the Länder insofar as this Basic Law does not otherwise prescribe or permit." Thus, the federal government can exercise authority only in those areas specified in the Basic Law. The federal government is assigned a greater legislative role and the Land governments a greater administrative role. The fact that Land governments employ more civil servants than federal and local governments combined illustrates the central administrative function of the Länder.

The Basic Law divides the federal government's legislative responsibilities into exclusive powers, concurrent powers and framework powers. The exclusive legislative jurisdiction of the federal government extends to defence, foreign affairs, immigration, transportation, communications and currency standards. The federal and Land governments share concurrent powers in several areas. These areas were additionally enlarged by an amendment to the Basic Law in 1969, which calls for joint action in areas of broad social concern such as higher education, regional economic development and agricultural reform.

The Länder retain no significant powers of taxation. Länder officials collect most federal taxes. The revenues provided by these taxes are very low, relative to total subnational revenue. Indeed, as indicated in column 4 of Table 9.2, tax rate autonomy is equal to 0.04, much less than in the US, Canada and Switzerland.

A key aspect of the German federal state is the solidarity between the individual Länder. However economically weak individual Länder may be, this means that no single Land has less than 95 per cent of the average per capita budgetary resources for all. The Basic Law provides for the establishment of equal living conditions throughout the country and the maintenance of legal and economic unity in the national interest. This includes the constitutionally mandated revenue sharing with the Länder from federal taxes. Virtually all of the major federal tax revenue sources are shared in this way. These constitute extensive non-discretionary unconditional transfers to the Länder.

Watts and Hobson (2000) note that in addition there are substantial intergovernmental transfers both from the federal government to the Länder, and among the Länder, which, as a result, are highly transfer dependent. When the measure of the latter includes revenue-sharing mechanisms, Länder reach the transfer dependence of 70 per cent (column 3 in Table 9.2).

On the other hand, Länder are autonomous in their borrowing activities (column 5 in Table 9.2). The central government has no power to place numeric restrictions on the borrowing activities of Länder. Nevertheless, Länder have their own laws imposing adequate restrictions. Most often, these are based on the golden rule, i.e., the loan is designated for investment purposes. However, as Rodden (2006) notes, investment is a slippery concept and many of the financial needs can be presented as investments.

In addition, the investment limits have often been breached with the argument that exceptional events have triggered expenditure needs. With the 2007–09 financial crisis leading to massively increasing deficits, the political response has been to impose further strict limits on deficits. These limits are supposed to apply to the federal as well as the Länder level.

9.2.2.5 Argentina

Provincial governments in Argentina have abundant powers to decide their own rules of governance as well as taxing and spending decisions, while municipalities report to the provincial governments. Although the Argentine Constitution establishes substantial room for subnational taxation, in practice, provinces have delegated to the national government the responsibility of raising a large share of their taxes. Sturzenegger and Werneck (2006) argue that, at the same time, the responsibility for key social functions is in provincial hands. For example, provinces have exclusive competence in primary and secondary education and in the provision of most social expenditures on education, health, poverty programmes, and housing.

As a result of expenditure decentralisation and tax centralisation, the Argentinian federal system is characterised by a high degree of vertical fiscal imbalance gap. This gap, coupled with the relatively large fraction of government services provided at the subnational level, creates a common pool problem across provinces. Tommasi (2002) argues that as a consequence some of the provincial governments are not aware of the hard budget constraint. They increase spending and reduce local tax effort relative to the values that they would obtain if they faced a hard budget constraint.

Argentina addresses its large vertical fiscal imbalance gap through a complex and extensive system of intergovernmental transfers. The transfers and other revenue-sharing proceeds account for more than half of total revenues of the provinces (column 3 in Table 9.2).[19] The most important component of this transfer system is the tax-sharing agreement called "Coparticipación", which refers to the process of reallocation by which shares of the taxes collected by the central government are reallocated to the provinces. Over time, this tax-sharing system has often been modified and several new amendments have been added to it. Furthermore, some direct transfers appear to be determined by political considerations. Its complexity and lack of transparency resulted in its description as the "fiscal labyrinth".

Within Argentina's federal structure, all levels of government are generally permitted to borrow both domestically and abroad. However, in many provinces, the provincial Constitution imposes some restrictions on the borrowing ability of the government. These restrictions are very often violated, and in many provinces they are too loose to be binding. In Table 9.2, we see that during the 1990s among the six countries studied, Argentina had the highest degree of borrowing autonomy and reached almost full borrowing autonomy.

9.2.2.6 Brazil

The decentralisation of the Brazilian federal system, initiated by the Constitution of 1988, resulted in a mismatch of the assignment of revenue and expenditure functions to subnational governments. In particular, while the assignment of revenue sources across different levels of government is clearly specified, expenditure functions are not always devolved in a clear and systematic way to subnational governments. There is no clear division of responsibilities across government levels in many areas like health care, education and social security. Furthermore, Afonzo and de Mello (2000) argue that, because of significant disparities in institutional capacity at the subnational level, even in cases where expenditure mandates are clearly defined, higher level authorities (states and federal government) do not devolve these expenditure functions to lower tiers of government for fear of disturbances in service delivery.

Brazil has a gross tax burden of more than 36 per cent; high for an emerging economy. Officially, the majority of the taxes are collected by the federal government. The states' own revenue corresponds to slightly more than 25 per cent. Municipalities are left with a share of less than 5 per cent of the total tax collection. However, once constitutional transfers are taken into account, the distribution of the aggregate tax revenue across jurisdictions differs dramatically. After all, the states remain with roughly 25 per cent and the central government receives about 60 per cent of the tax burden. The great net beneficiaries of the redistribution are the municipalities. Local governments were able to have access to an amount of resources that roughly tripled their own revenue. Although state-level governments as a whole only benefit slightly from the constitutional transfers, individual states, the poorest ones in particular, have obtained important net gains from the redistribution.

More than three-quarters of all federal transfers to subnational governments are constitutionally mandated transfers. Afonzo and de Mello (2000) claim that constitutional requirements on revenue sharing favour subnational governments to the detriment of the federal government without a clear devolution of expenditure functions to lower levels of government. Particularly important are the rules governing the sharing of the ICMS, the state-level value-added tax, which is the highest yielding source of revenue in Brazil. Discretionary, often politically motivated, grants have become much less important than in the past.

Afonzo and de Mello (2000) state that it has been widely accepted in Brazil that state debt negotiations with the federal government could be interpreted as a bailout operation unless accompanied by institutional changes aimed at imposing hard budget constraints at all levels of government.

Since the late 1990s, an important effort took place in order to provide a sound basis for macroeconomic stability. In particular, it required changes in the fiscal-federalism arrangement, in order to impose hard budget constraints on subnational governments. The recent changes in the legislation have laid the foundations for a rules-based system of decentralised federalism that leaves little room for discretionary policy-making at the subnational level. It remains to be seen how effective this new system will be.

9.3 Lessons from the history of fiscal federalism

Our account of the evolution of fiscal federalism in six countries covers also their political history. The reason for this is that all the fiscal unions evolved in close interaction with the political unions forming the ultimate basis for fiscal cooperation. Friedrich (1968) notes that federalism is not only a static pattern or design, characterised by a particular and precisely defined division of powers between governmental levels. It is a continuous process by which a number of separate political communities enter into arrangements for working out solutions, adopting joint policies and making joint decisions on common problems. Thus, each federation is an evolving entity and its structure is shaped by economic and political events.

Below we seek to identify the major driving forces behind changes in the fiscal frameworks of the six federations under study.

First, the historical account demonstrates that most of the countries created their unions for similar reasons. Many independent regions decided to found a union because of military insecurity and a consequent need for common defence or a desire to be independent of foreign powers. This was the case of the US which was founded in revolution against the British Empire. Similarly, the British North American Act established the Canadian federation in response to the threat of political, economic and military absorption by the US. The foundation of the Swiss and the Argentine federations reflected a desire to gain independence from the French and the Spanish, respectively. The union of provinces that founded the Brazilian federation was mainly driven by potential economic benefits. The creation of the German federation was driven by both potential economic gains and political reasons.

Franck (1968) argues that although factors such as a common language, similar culture, complementary economies and hope of independence, as noted above, have generally triggered the birth of federations, they are important but not sufficient conditions for the success of a federation. According to him, far more important is what Friedrich (1968) calls the "federal spirit", i.e., a commitment to the value of federalism and to compromise and adaptation. Indeed, the Canadian and Swiss cases show that in spite of the cultural differences between the original units, in particular different languages, these entities desired to unite because of such a "federal spirit".

Second, we note that institutional developments in most of the six federations were driven by exceptional events, often downturns in economic activity during deep crises. The most prominent example is the Great Depression of the 1930s which affected in a fundamental way the institutions of the six federal states. In response to the economic crisis, central governments increased their power. As a result, during and after the Great Depression, the American, Canadian, Swiss, Argentine and Brazilian federations underwent a process of centralisation. This centralisation made it easier for the governments to either introduce (as in the Canadian case) or extend (as in the US example) measures aiming at equalisation of incomes across regions. Such measures were part of the stabilisation process, since the regions which were more harmed by the recession received larger financial transfers.

In addition, in Canada and Argentina, the Great Depression resulted in the creation of central banks. These two central banks were established during the Great Depression to use monetary policy under a fiat monetary regime to help extricate the economy from the slump. Their establishment also reflected the general movement in the interwar period for independent states to have central banks.

The main policy innovation of the Great Depression was a new role for the fiscal policy of central governments. Governments increased their spending and/or cut taxes in order to stabilise the distressed economy. Later on, these policies were given an intellectual foundation by John Maynard Keynes in the *General Theory of Employment Interest and Money*. They were formalised as part of the Keynesian revolution, with its stress on the role of fiscal policy.

Third, and most important, we find a clear difference between well-functioning and poorly functioning federal states concerning inflation and debt accumulation. Those federal states that have maintained a relatively strict fiscal discipline among subnational units during recent decades like the US, Canada, Germany and Switzerland have fared better than those that have not, like Argentina and Brazil. As a rule, they have displayed lower rates of inflation, less inflation variability and less debt accumulation (see Table 9.1).

Our account of fiscal federalism demonstrates that fiscal discipline has been obtained through several techniques: explicit or implicit no-bailout clauses, constitutional restrictions and through discipline exercised by financial markets for government debt.

Once overall budgetary discipline prevails through a no-bailout rule, considerable revenue and expenditure independence of subnational governments can be maintained. This independence for regional fiscal units is thus due to a system of rules that "anchor" their budget behaviour at a sustainable path.

The present system of budgetary discipline in fiscal federations is the result of a "learning by doing" process. In the presence of moral hazard, the federal government has to give a signal of commitment to the subnational authorities. Otherwise, the latter will not learn. For example, the US government as early as 1840 gave the lesson that it would not provide bailouts to states in financial trouble. As a result, it gained credibility. Today, virtually all of the US states have their own balanced budget rules and most importantly they respect them. Today, it is the federal government that displays high deficits.

Two out of the six federations were not able to learn from their negative fiscal experiences in the past. In contrast to the US example, the Argentine and Brazilian federations during the 1980s and 1990s experienced several financial crises, which occurred because they followed an undisciplined fiscal policy. More precisely, irresponsible fiscal behaviour of the subnational authorities played a key factor in these crises. Moreover for them, the lesson has not yet been learnt. On the contrary, in each of these crises, the central government has bailed out the subnational authorities. Indeed, there is still no credible mechanism in these federations to impose fiscal discipline.

9.4 Fiscal federalism in the euro area – has the EU learnt the right lessons?

The history of successful fiscal federalism suggests four major policy lessons for the euro area. The first lesson proposes a strict no-bailout clause, preferably in combination with a system of close surveillance or monitoring of the fiscal policy and debt accumulation of subnational units, in this case of the member states. This surveillance can be carried by an institutionalised system as well as by financial markets.

Looking at the euro area, we conclude that this first lesson is well incorporated in the present system of formal rules for national fiscal policy-making. It is based on two key agreements at the European level: the Maastricht Treaty and the Stability and Growth Pact (SGP).

There is an explicit no-bailout clause in the Maastricht Treaty, which prohibits the ECB from bailing out national governments in the case of default.[20] Judging from the history of fiscal federalism, such a clause is a fundamental prerequisite for prudent fiscal behaviour among the members of a monetary union. It is not an absolute guarantee as witnessed by the debate about the credibility of this clause. Some economists argue that financial markets expect the ECB or the EU to step in to "save" a euro-area member in case of a threat of default on its government debt and that the interpretation of the no-bailout rule of the Maastricht Treaty should be "stretched" accordingly. However, the existence of the no-bail out rule has so far supported the price stability policy of the ECB.

The Maastricht Treaty also establishes criteria for fiscal convergence between the potential EMU participants. These criteria require, inter alia, annual national budget deficits to be held to 3 per cent of GDP and the gross debt-to-GDP ratio to be reduced to 60 per cent in order to ensure the avoidance of "excessive" borrowing by member states. Figure 9.1 suggests that the Maastricht criteria were overall effective in decreasing net borrowing, in particular during the run-up to the introduction of the euro in 1999.

The Treaty also includes an escape clause. In case of severe economic circumstances, the rules can be broken. Subsequently, the SGP, signed in 1997 in Amsterdam, set out the financial sanctions to be imposed on member states that violated the Maastricht budgetary guidelines after the implementation of the EMU. If a country exceeds the 3 per cent deficit requirement, it is subject to substantial fines. Later, the SGP was modified in 2005 to allow more flexibility.

The above rules basically incorporate the experience of countries with fiscal federalism. The original designers of the EU system of fiscal governance feared that some national governments would have an incentive, once they were within the monetary union, to increase their borrowing and debt levels. Consequently, countries such as Germany feared that negative externalities or spillover effects resulting from excessive borrowing would undermine the monetary union. If one country is on an unsustainable path of rising government debt, they argued, it will borrow increasingly from the EU capital markets, pushing union interest rates upwards. This, in turn, would increase the debt burden in other member states, forcing them to follow unwanted tight fiscal policies. These spillover effects could further result in undue pressure on the ECB to loosen monetary policy that could in turn undermine price stability.

The conduct of fiscal policy by EU member states is also monitored through a continuous policy dialogue between the Commission and the member states. This process of surveillance and consultations has great similarities with the IMF Article IV consultations.

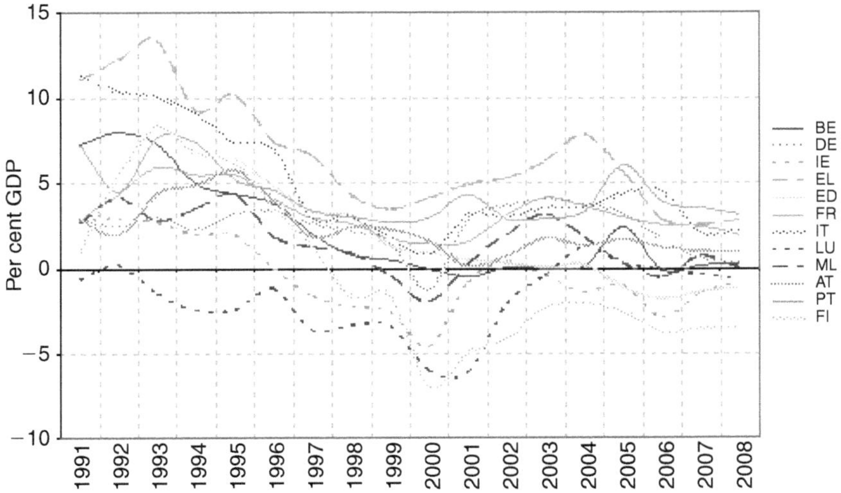

Figure 9.1 Net borrowing of general government in the euro area 12 as a percentage of GDP (source: Ameco database).

The fiscal policy of the member states is also monitored by financial markets where yield spreads for government bonds of different member states are registered. These yield spreads function as a system signalling how domestic fiscal policies are carried out. Financial markets attach a higher risk premium to countries with high borrowing and consequently create incentives for fiscal discipline.

The second lesson from history suggests that regional fiscal units can have considerable revenue and expenditure independence within a system of no bailouts from the central government. This is clearly the case of the euro area where tax and spending decisions rest with the national governments. In addition, the budget of the EU ("the European central government") is extremely limited. The member states of the euro area are considerably more dependent on their tax revenues than any subnational governments in the fiscal unions we have examined. This enforces the credibility of the no-bailout rule as there are no significant funds to obtain from the EU.[21]

The third lesson from the experience of successful fiscal unions brings out the importance of learning from and adapting to changing economic and political circumstances. Although the euro area has only existed for slightly more than ten years, the SGP was modified in 2005 after critique from major member states. We look upon this reform as a sign of necessary adaptability in the system of fiscal governance. In a similar way, we expect the present debt crisis in some euro-area members to pave the way for changes in the surveillance and monitoring system within the euro area.

This third lesson stresses that the system of fiscal federalism should properly reflect the policy preferences of the public/the voters among the jurisdictions within a fiscal union. As suggested by the literature on fiscal federalism, this is the main advantage of a federal system. By allowing for differences in policy preferences across the union, its sustainability is strengthened.

Here the present form of fiscal federalism in the EU is consistent with the current critical attitude of the public towards more "power to Brussels". The EU budget is so small – about 1 per cent of the national incomes of the member states – that this rules out any capacity to form the basis for a consistent EU-wide fiscal policy to influence aggregate economic activity in any significant way.

Since there is a strong reluctance among the member states of the euro area to abandon their tax and spending independence to a central administration, national fiscal policies also need to be considered. The large size of the public sector of the members of the euro area, measured as taxes or government revenues to GDP, suggests that national governments are well equipped to carry out fiscal policy for stabilisation purposes – through the workings of automatic stabilisers as well as through discretionary measures.[22] See Figure 9.2 and 9.3. The large size also suggests that there is room for structural reforms concerning the size of the public sector, the level and design of taxation and of government expenditures.

There are also considerable risks associated with a system of more centralised fiscal policy-making in the EU. A larger common EU budget and thus more

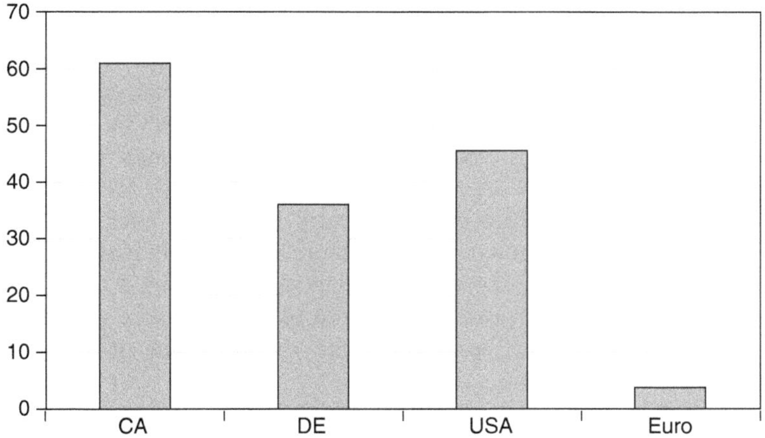

Figure 9.2 Subnational spending as a share of GDP of central government spending in Canada, Germany, the US and the euro area (average of 11 member states) in 2003 (sources: the data was kindly provided by Douglas Sutherland from the Economics department of OECD. Because of lack of data on Ireland, the euro-area average is calculated for Austria, Belgium, Finland, France, Germany, Greece, Italy, Luxemburg, Netherlands, Portugal and Spain).

Note
Spending figures exclude the transfers paid to other levels of government.

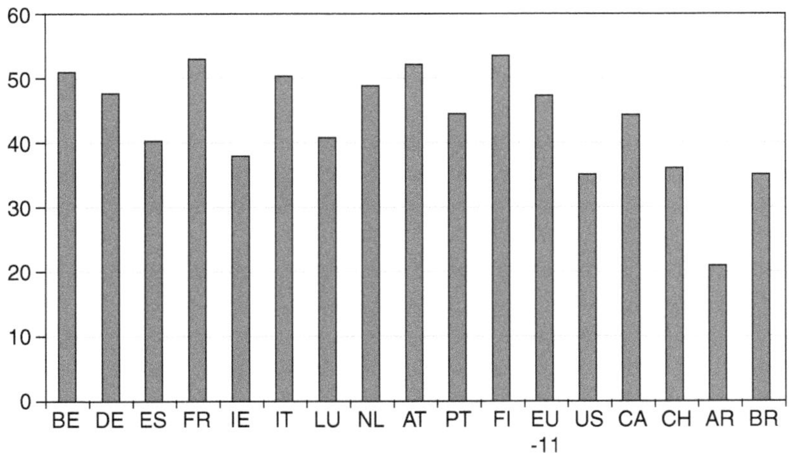

Figure 9.3 Total government spending in percentage of GDP, averages for 1990–2008 (sources: Eurostat and Economist Intelligence Unit, EU-11 is an average based on 11 euro-area members: Austria, Belgium, Finland, France, Germany, Ireland, Italy, Luxemburg, Netherlands, Portugal and Spain).

reliance on a centralised fiscal policy and support would run the risk of reducing the pressure on member states to reform. In the case a single member state is hit by a negative disturbance, it has basically two policy options. First, it can decide to improve its macroeconomic performance through various domestic measures, including structural reforms which are usually not popular among voters. Second, it can decide to ask for fiscal transfers from "Brussels" to alleviate domestic economic conditions, ignoring steps to adjust through domestic measures.

Were the EU to adopt a larger budget to carry out stabilisation through fiscal policies, the second option would appear more attractive, in particular in a short-run perspective. The prospect of receiving support during a recession from a countercyclical central fiscal policy would likely serve as a substitute for politically difficult reforms, preventing the establishment of a well-functioning EMU.

A larger EU budget would thus run the risk of creating incentives that would make it more difficult to improve the workings of the EU economy. Most likely the process would be cumulative. Once it turns out that countercyclical measures are insufficient, which is a likely outcome, there would be political pressure for more support and eventually for permanent support. This has been the case within several EU member states like Italy and Germany where regions have been hit asymmetrically by economic shocks.

A main problem of fiscal policy-making in the EU is found in weak domestic fiscal institutions in a number of member countries. Weak institutions contribute to a deficit bias and undermine the workings of the Stability and Growth Pact.[23] The solution to improve fiscal governance is then to improve these through reforms, increasing their independence, accountability and transparency – much in the spirit behind central bank reforms in the past decades. If stronger domestic fiscal institutions could be set up, the demand for a euro-area central fiscal policy would diminish.

The transfer of fiscal policy from the level of the member states to a common EU authority thus runs the risk of creating moral hazard, making member states less inclined to reform their economies and their policy-making institutions.[24]

A fourth lesson from history is that, in the face of a global economic crisis like the Great Depression, all the six countries we studied increased the fiscal capacity of the central government. This pattern suggests that the 2007–09 global crisis, which is the most severe event since the 1930s, may contribute to an increase in the central fiscal power of the EU, paving the way for larger transfers to the member states hardest hit by the crisis. Actually, the policy response of the EU in 2008–09 suggests strongly that such a movement has started, concerning inter alia the design of financial regulations, the common EU design of fiscal policies and the use of the EU Globalisation Fund.

Like the examples of the US and Canada, transfers could come via "equalisation" or other payments administered by Brussels. One possibility is to require member countries to pay a tranche of their income tax receipts to an equalisation or stabilisation fund which would be allocated to the members on some formula based on their economic performance relative to the EU average. Via such a mechanism resources would automatically be transferred from countries that have been less hard hit by the crisis to those who were harder hit. If a mechanism such as this, which is similar to that used in some of the six federations studied above, were adopted, it might mitigate the moral hazard problems described above and promote euro-area economic stability. This fiscal mechanism would complement the tasks of the ECB. Still, moral hazard would be at work unless all transfers are combined with binding rules for reform.

9.5 Conclusions: does the euro need a fiscal union?

The euro area is the first case in the history of monetary unions where monetary policy-making is centralised under one central bank while fiscal policy-making is decentralised in the hands of the national governments of the member states. This institutional framework is new for economists and policy-makers alike. Economists are thus venturing into virgin territory, which allows them to hold widely divergent views about the proper design of the fiscal union for the euro area.

With this caveat, we would like to answer the question: "Does the euro need a fiscal union?" in the following way: "Yes, the euro needs a fiscal union. And the euro area has actually such a union based on the Maastricht Treaty and the SGP." The follow-up question then emerges: "Is this type of fiscal union sufficient to sustain the euro area, that is, to support the price stability policy of the ECB?"

To answer this question, we have turned to a study of the experience of six fiscal federations. It provides us with three conditions necessary for a fiscal union to function smoothly and successfully. The first condition is a credible commitment to a no-bailout rule. The second one is revenue and expenditure independence of subnational governments reflecting the preferences of the members of the fiscal union. The third condition is a capacity to learn from past mistakes and adapt to new economic and political circumstances.

In our opinion, the state of fiscal arrangements in the euro area – at least until the 2007–09 crisis – met these three conditions, thus making the euro area appear as a properly designed fiscal union. Monetary policy can be centralised to deliver the common good, price stability, while fiscal policy-making can be left at the member state level.

The historical record for fiscal federations demonstrates, however, that in severe economic crises like the Great Depression of the 1930s, the common institutional response is to increase centralisation of fiscal policies. Since the 2007–09 global crisis, there have already been clear signs of a greater role for centralised fiscal power in the EU governance structure. The future will show to what extent the euro area will follow this crisis pattern of the past.

Notes

1 We have received constructive comments from many. We would like to thank in particular Iain Begg, Michael Bergman, Daniel Heymann, Sven Langedijk, Paul van den Noord, Jakob von Weizsäcker and Guntram Wolff.
2 For early surveys of this debate, see for example Buti and Sapir (1998) and Hallet, Hutchinson and Hougaard (1999). More recently, Buti and Franco (2005), Korkman (2005) and Wierts *et al.* (2006) among others deal with fiscal policy issues of the EMU. See also *European Economy* (2008) on the record of the first ten years of the EMU.
3 See for example Wyplosz (2005) and Jonung and Larch (2006).
4 The debate about the Stability and Growth Pact before its reform in 2005 is a striking illustration of the widely divergent views – more than 100 separate contributions – within the economics profession on the role of fiscal policy in the euro area. For a survey of these views on the proper design of the SGP, see Jonung, Larch and Fisher (2008).
5 Presently the euro area includes the following 16 countries: Austria, Belgium, Cyprus, Finland, France, Germany, Greece, Ireland, Italy, Luxembourg, Malta, Netherlands, Portugal, Spain, Slovakia and Slovenia.
6 For the shortcomings of the OCA approach, see i.a. Goodhart (1998) and Mongelli (2005). The traditional OCA theory has given a negative bias to the views of US economists on the single currency; see Jonung and Drea (2010).
7 The common pool problem arises in situations where the costs of an activity, which benefits a small group, are shared among a wider group of individuals, countries or provinces as in our case of a monetary union.
8 See for instance Deroose, Langedijk and Roeger (2004) for a discussion and illustrative model simulations on the adjustment mechanisms in EMU.
9 The term "dual federalism" was introduced by Corwin (1950).
10 The term "cooperative federalism" was extensively used by Elzar (1966).
11 Cohn (1992) notes that Germany opted for conservative fiscal policies because of its huge national debt.
12 See Heppke-Falk and Wolff (2008) for a discussion of the moral hazard problem and the issue of bailout in the German fiscal federation.
13 See for instance Sturzenegger and Werneck (2006).
14 For the details of the reforms, see Della Paolera and Taylor (1999).
15 See Nicolini *et al.* (2002).
16 On the collapse of the Argentine currency board, see also Galiani, Heyman and Torviasi (2003).
17 Sometimes Canadian provinces share the tax responsibilities with the central government.
18 Subsidiarity is the principle that a central authority should have a subsidiary function, performing only those tasks which cannot be performed effectively at a more local level.
19 See also Cetrángolo and Jiménez (2004).
20 Article 103, section 1: *The Community shall not be liable for or assume the commitments of central governments, regional, local or other public authorities, other bodies governed by public law, or public undertakings of any Member State, without prejudice to mutual financial guarantees for the joint execution of a specific project. A Member State shall not be liable for or assume the commitments of central governments, regional, local or other public authorities, other bodies governed by public law, or public undertakings of another Member State, without prejudice to mutual financial guarantees for the joint execution of a specific project.*
21 See i.a. Rodden (2004).
22 In addition, market-based risk-sharing mechanisms through financial integration seem to play an increasing role. Therefore, in due time there might be lesser need for

government interventions, both at the national and the European levels, due to the ongoing European financial integration process.

23 See Jonung and Larch (2006).

24 When the euro was launched, there was a general expectation that in due time – after a transition period – market flexibility would increase due to domestic reforms making labour markets, financial markets and markets for goods and services more open and flexible. In this way, the EMU would gradually turn into a better functioning monetary union, endogenising the OCA criteria. However, the pressure to reform has not been as high as initially expected during the first ten years of the euro. In fact, there has been a tendency for a backlash – of Maastricht fatigue.

References

Afonso, José Roberto and Luiz de Mello (2000) "Brazil: An evolving federation", paper prepared for the IMF/FAD Seminar on decentralization, Washington DC, 20–21 November. www.imf.org/external/pubs/ft/seminar/2000/fiscal/afonso.pdf.

Begg, Iain (2009), "Fiscal federalism, subsidiarity and the EU budget review", *Swedish Institute for European Policy Studies* vol. 1, Stockholm, April.

Boyd, Eugene and Michael K. Fauntroy (1997) "American federalism 1776–2000: significant events", CRS Report RL30772.

Buti, Marco and Daniele Franco (2005) *Fiscal policy in economic and monetary union. Theory, evidence and institutions*, Edward Elgar Publishing Ltd, Cheltenham.

Buti, Marco and André Sapir (1998) *Economic policy in EMU. A study*, Oxford University, Oxford.

Castanhar, José Cezar (2003) "Fiscal federalism in Brazil: Historical trends present controversies and future challenges", paper presented at VIII Congreso Internacional del CLAD sobre la Reforma del Estado y de la Administración Pública, Panamá, 28–31 October.

Cetrángolo, Oscar and Juan Pablo Jiménez (2004) "The relations between different levels of government in Argentina", *Cepal Review*, vol. 84, 115–132.

Chari, Varadarajan and Patrick J. Kehoe (2004) "On the desirability of fiscal constraints in a monetary union", NBER Working Paper no. W10232.

Church, Clive and Paolo Dardanelli (2005), "The dynamics of confederalism and federalism: Comparing Switzerland and the EU", *Regional and Federal Studies*, vol. 15, 163–185.

Codding, George A. Jr. (1979) "Financing a federal government: The Swiss example", *German Studies Review*, vol. 2, 63–87.

Cohn, Raymond L. (1992) "Fiscal policy in Germany during the Great Depression", *Explorations in Economic History*, vol. 29, 318–348.

Corwin, Edward S. (1950) "The passing of dual federalism", *Virginia Law Review* vol. 36, 1–24.

Dafflon, Bernard, and Krisztina Z. Tóth (2005) "Fiscal federalism in Switzerland: Relevant issues for transition economies in Central and Eastern Europe", World Bank Policy Research Working Paper series 3655, World Bank, Washington DC.

De Grauwe, Paul (2006) "On monetary and political union", University of Leuven, manuscript.

Della Paolera, Gerardo and Alan M. Taylor (1999) "Economic recovery from the Argentine Great Depression: Institutions, expectations and the change of macroeconomic regime", *Journal of Economic History*, vol. 59, 567–599.

De Long, Bradford J. (1996) "Fiscal policy in the shadow of the Great Depression", in Michael Bordo, Claudia Goldin and Eugene White, eds., *The defining moment: The Great Depression and the American economy in the twentieth century*, University of Chicago Press, Chicago.

Deroose, Servaas, Sven Langedijk and Werner Roeger (2004) "Reviewing adjustment dynamics in EMU: From overheating to overcooling", *European Economy*. Economic Papers No. 198, European Commission, Brussels.

Dixit, Avinash and Luisa Lambertini (2001) "Monetary-fiscal policy interactions and commitment versus discretion in a monetary union", *European Economic Review*, vol. 45, 977–987.

Eichengreen, Barry (1991) "Is Europe an optimum currency area?", NBER Working Paper no. 3579.

Elzar, Daniel J. (1966) *American federalism: A view from the States*, Thomas Y. Crowell, New York.

European Economy (2008) *EMU@10. Successes and challenges after 10 years of Economic and Monetary Union*, DG ECFIN, European Commission, Brussels.

Franck, Thomas M. (1968) *Why federations fail: An inquiry into the requisites for successful federalism*, New York University Press, New York.

Friedrich, Carl J. (1968) *Trends of federalism in theory and practice*, Praeger, New York.

Galiani, Sebastián, Daniel Heymann and Mariano Tommasi (2003) "Great expectations and hard times: The Argentine convertibility plan", *Economia*, vol. 3, 109–154.

Goodhart, Charles (1998) "The two concepts of money: implications for the analysis of optimal currency areas", *European Journal of Political Economy*, vol. 14, 407–432.

Hallet, Andrew H., Michael Hutchison and Jensen E. Hougaard (1999) *Fiscal aspects of European monetary integration*, Cambridge University Press, Cambridge.

Hefeker, Carsten (2001) "The agony of central power: Fiscal federalism in the German Reich", *European Review of Economic History*, vol. 5, 119–142.

Heppke-Falk, Kirsten and Guntram B. Wolff (2008) "Moral hazard and bail-out in fiscal federations: Evidence for the German Länder", *Kyklos*, vol. 3, 425–446.

Inman, Robert P. and Daniel L. Rubinfeld (1997) "Rethinking federalism", *Journal of Economic Perspectives*, vol. 11, 43–64.

Jonung, Lars and Eoin Drea (2010) "The euro: It can't happen, It's a bad idea, It won't last. US economists on the EMU and the euro, 1989–2002", *Econ Journal Watch* vol. 7, 4–52.

Jonung, Lars and Martin Larch (2006) "Improving fiscal policy in the EU. The case for independent forecasts", *Economic Policy*, vol. 21, 491–534.

Jonung, Lars, Martin Larch and Jonas Fischer (2008) "101 proposals to reform the Stability and Growth Pact. Why so many? A survey", *Public Finance and Management*, vol. 8, 502–560.

Kenen, Peter (1969) "The theory of optimum currency areas: An eclectic view", pp. 41–60, in Robert Mundell and Alexander Swoboda, eds., *Monetary problems of the international economy*, University of Chicago Press, Chicago.

Korkman, Sixten (2005) *Economic policy in the European Union*, Palgrave Macmillan, New York.

Laubach, Thomas (2005) "Fiscal relations across levels of government in the United States", OECD Economics Department Working Papers no. 462, OECD Economics Department.

Mckay, David (2005) "Economic logic or political logic? Economic theory, federal theory and EMU", *Journal of European Public Policy*, vol. 12, 528–544.

McKinnon, Ronald (1963) "Optimum currency areas", *American Economic Review*, vol. 53, 717–724.

McKinnon, Ronald (2004) "Optimum currency areas and key currencies: Mundell I versus Mundell II", *Journal of Common Market Studies*, vol. 42, 689–715.

Mongelli, Francesco (2005) "What is European Economic and Monetary Union telling us about the properties of optimum currency areas?", *Journal of Common Market Studies*, vol. 43, 607–635.

Mundell, Robert (1961) "A theory of optimum currency areas", *American Economic Review*, vol. 51, 509–517.

Mundell, Robert (1973) "Uncommon arguments for common currencies", pp. 114–32 in Harry G. Johnson and Alexander K. Swoboda, eds., *The economics of common currencies*, Allen and Unwin, London.

Musgrave, Richard, A. (1959) *The theory of public finance*, McGraw Hill, New York.

Nicolini, Juan Pablo, Josefina Posadas, Juan Sanguinetti, Pablo Sanguinetti and Mariano Tommasi (2002) "Decentralization, fiscal discipline in sub-national governments and the bailout problem: The case of Argentina", Inter-American Development Bank, research network working paper R-467.

Oates, Wallace (1972) *Fiscal federalism*, Harcourt Brace Jovanovich, New York.

Oates, Wallace (1999) "An essay on fiscal federalism", *Journal of Economic Literature*, vol. 37, 1120–1149.

Reserve Bank of India (2006) "Fiscal federalism. A comparative cross country analysis", Annex 4 in *State finances. A study of budgets of 2006–07*, published by A. Karunagaran for the Reserve Bank of India, Mumbai.

Rodden, Jonathan A. (2004) "Achieving fiscal discipline in federations: Germany and the EMU", paper prepared for "Fiscal policy in EMU: New Issues and Challenges", workshop organised by European Commission, Brussels, 12 November 2004. http://ec.europa.eu/economy_finance/events/2004/bxl1104/papers/rodden_en.pdf.

Rodden, Jonathan A. (2006) *Hamilton's paradox. The promise and peril of fiscal federalism*, Cambridge University Press, New York.

Ruggeri, Joe (2006) "Equalization reform in Canada. Principles and compromises", paper presented at the Conference on Fiscal Federalism and the Future of Canada, Selected proceedings, 28–29 September. www.queensu.ca/iigr/working/fiscalImb/Ruggeri.pdf.

Saiegh, Sebastian and Mariano Tommasi (1999) "Why is Argentina's fiscal federalism so inefficient? Entering the labyrinth", *Journal of Applied Economics*, vol. 2, 169–209.

Schulz, Alexander and Guntram B. Wolff (2009) "The German sub-national government bond market: Structure, determinants of yield spreads and Berlin's foregone bail-out", *Journal of Economics and Statistics*, vol. 229, 61–83.

Shah, Anwar (1995) "Intergovernmental fiscal relations in Canada: An overview", in Roy Jayanta, ed., *Macroeconomic management and fiscal decentralization*, EDI seminar series, the World Bank, Washington, DC.

Sorens, Jason (2008) "Fiscal federalism: A return to theory and measurement", working paper, Department of Political Science, University of Buffalo, SUNY. www.acsu.buffalo.edu/~jbattist/workshop/Sorens_s09.pdf.

Sturzenegger, Federico and Rogério Werneck (2006) "Fiscal federalism and procyclical spending: The cases of Argentina and Brazil", *Económica*, vol. 52, 151–194.

Sutherland, Douglas, Robert Price and Isabelle Joumard (2006) "Fiscal rules for sub-central governments: Design and impact", OECD WP(2006)/1.

Tommasi, Mariano (2002) "Federalism in Argentina and the reforms of the 1990s", Center for Research on Economic Development and Policy Reform, working paper no. 147, Stanford.

Uhlig, Harald (2002) "One money, but many fiscal policies in Europe: What are the consequences?", discussion paper no. 3296. Centre for Economic Policy Research, London.

Wallis, John (1984) "The birth of the old federalism: Financing the New Deal, 1932–1940", *Journal of Economic History*, vol. 44, 139–159.

Watts, L. Ronald (1987) "The American constitution in comparative perspective: A comparison of federalism in the United States and Canada", *Journal of American History*, vol. 74, 769–792.

Watts, L. Ronald and Paul Hobson (2000) "Fiscal federalism in Germany", mimeo. www.aucc.ca/_pdf/english/programs/cepra/watts_hobson.pdf.

Wierts, Peter, Servaas Deroose, Elena Flores and Alessandro Turrini (2006) *Fiscal policy surveillance in Europe*, Palgrave, Houndmills and New York.

Wyplosz, Charles (2005) "Fiscal policy: Institutions versus rules", *National Institute Economic Review*, vol. 191, 70–84.

Ziblatt, Daniel (2004) "Rethinking the origins of federalism. Puzzle, theory, and evidence from nineteenth-century Europe", *World Politics*, vol. 57, 70–98.

10 Making a central bank without a state

Harold James

A peculiarity of the process of European monetary integration is the way that it represents a marked contrast with almost every other known historical episode of currency unions, monetary integration, or more generally of the institutionalization of monetary arrangements.[1] To take the very striking contrast of a well-known nineteenth-century precedent, in Germany in the 1870s, Otto von Bismarck first created a political union (1871), then a common currency (1873), then a central bank (1875). In Europe at the turn of the twentieth century, there was a European Monetary Institute (1994) that laid the foundations for a European System of Central Banks, a monetary union (1999), but (as yet) no sign of political unification, despite the renaming of the European Community in the Maastricht Treaty as the European Union. In other monetary unifications, the state is at the beginning and in the center of the process; in Europe, we do not quite know where the state is.

For nineteenth-century German unification, a long-time favorite school examination question was whether Bismarck had a blueprint for German unification that he used as a strategic guide through the 1860s. Most modern historians are skeptical about the notion of a well-worked-out strategy in the case of Bismarck. For EMU and the ECB, there is no doubt about the relevance of blueprints, and two in particular were especially significant: the Werner report of 1970 and the Delors Committee report of 1989. But even before the Werner report, an institution had been created which can in some ways be regarded as the ugly chrysalis from which the beautiful butterfly of a unified currency emerged: the Committee of Central Bank Governors of the Member States of the European Economic Community.

European monetary union is a quite unique process, that has nevertheless been a subject of great fascination in other parts of the world: in the Gulf region, where there are periodic discussions of monetary unification, as well as in Asia and Latin America, where movements towards greater monetary integration also have some support but encounter a plethora of difficulties.

A large part of the fascination of the European project lies in two very particular aspects of the process: the non-state character of the integration process, and the relationship of regional changes to debates about reform of the international monetary system.

First, the European monetary union occurred outside the framework of a conventional state. The creation of money is often thought to be the domain of the state: this was the widely prevalent doctrine of the nineteenth century, which reached its apogee in Knapp's *State Theory of Money*. In the New Testament, Christ famously answers a question about obedience to civil authorities by examining a coin and telling the Pharisees, "Render unto Caesar what is Caesar's." Unlike most banknotes and coins, there is no picture of the state or its symbols – no Caesar – on the money managed by the European Central Bank. Especially in the nineteenth century, the formation of new nation-states was associated with the establishment of national moneys, which gave the new polities a policy area in which they could exercise themselves.[2]

True, there were alternative traditions, which emphasized either a natural law origin of money, or hypothesized on a contractual origin of monetary arrangements. In natural law theory, money represented an intrinsic good or value, and the theory dealt well with the problem of the interrelationship of different monetary standards in varying political structures.[3] Alternately, it is possible to conceive of money arising out of conventional agreements about the exchange of goods, between parties that are not necessarily in the same political unit. Maybe either of these theories is better situated in explaining what happened in the creation of the institutional framework for a European money. In particular, it is striking that in discussions of monetary union, there was a focus not on who was to issue a new currency, but what its characteristics should be: above all, how monetary stability could be achieved. In other words, the fundamental question of monetary sovereignty was consistently downplayed. The supranational character of a new money was often perceived as a valuable instrument in a fight against the scourge of inflation, since national moneys were too easily manipulated in accordance with national political preferences: especially in weaker or more insecure political systems. Supranational money was impossible as long as different countries had very different levels of inflation, in short as long as there was no consensus about the desirability of anti-inflationary policy. The process of monetary integration was thus accompanied by an intense reflection about what money is and what money should do.

Central banks were historically created first to manage the state's credit: this is the story of the oldest central banks, the Swedish Riksbank, the Bank of England, as well as of a newer wave of central banks that followed the example of the Banque de France: the Norwegian and Finnish banks. It was suspicion of the politics behind a designated state-oriented central bank that led to the nonrenewal of the charters, and the demise, of the First and Second Bank of the United States. In the mid-nineteenth century, a new generation of central banks was established essentially to manage payments systems, and stabilize fragile banking systems: this was the motivation behind the German Reichsbank (1875) or the Federal Reserve System of the United States (1914).

The European Central Bank was not designed as a fiscal agent of the European Community or its member states, indeed that role was played by a second institution: the European Monetary Cooperation Fund (EMCF, but often referred to by its French initials as FECOM). The EMCF began with very high ambitions, but in practice remained a rather subsidiary and shadowy institution. It was managed by the BIS, although its board was composed of the EEC central bank governors, so that it was in effect a parallel institution to the Committee of Governors. But unlike the CCBG, it was an institution of the EEC, and hence the governors regarded its institutional space with suspicion.

Neither was the ECB primarily designed as a support for an integrated but potentially vulnerable banking system. Though there were debates at the founding era in the late 1980s and early 1990s about whether it should play a central part in banking supervision and regulation, that question was answered negatively. In the wake of the 2007–8 credit crisis, the neglect of financial regulation appears as a fundamental flaw. Cross-national banks are not regulated by a European-level superviser. The head of the British FSA, Adair Turner, has concluded that there is either too much or too little Europe in banking. The most powerful European central bank, with the strongest voice in debates on monetary union, the German Bundesbank, was in general highly skeptical about arguments that the central bank should have a prominent role as an LLR. No, the ECB was designed as a non-state actor whose primary purpose was the issue of money – the kind of institution that had basically only been imagined before the 1990s by Friedrich Hayek and his wilder disciples.

The monetary arrangements for the currency union also evolved in a way that showed a striking distance from the institutions of the European Union or European Community, and have frequently been cited as an example of Europe's "democratic deficit" (while defenders argue in terms of a logic of tying hands). The Committee of Central Bank Governors of the Member Countries of the European Economic Community originated in 1964. But it was not a European Community institution, and its regular meetings were not in a member country, but rather in Basle, Switzerland, because of the location of the Bank for International Settlements. From the beginning this location meant that the institution would play with the geometry of power on the European continent, or engineer what later came to be called variable geometry. All the member countries were represented in the Committee (with the exception of Luxembourg, which was already in a monetary union with Belgium), but as the Committee began to devise monetary arrangements in the 1970s, they excluded some member countries. At the same time, the Committee devised association arrangements to work with non-EC members, notably Norway, Sweden and Switzerland, as well as with countries that were preparing for EC membership. The Treaty of Maastricht, which laid down the timetable to monetary union, did not end this peculiarity of the separation of European monetary institutions from European Community or Union constitutionalization. It only found an end in the provisions of the Lisbon Treaty.

This locational oddity (both physical and constitutional) underscores a second crucial feature of the story. The debate about an institutionalization of European monetary arrangements always took place in a wider context of discussions of the global financial system and its problems. Debates about new institutional mechanisms (such as a basket currency) that took place on the global level were also replicated with respect to European affairs. The Committee was originally created in 1964. But it had little real life until the early 1970s, when it developed into a focal point for coordinating the European response to the breakdown of the par value system. The two crucial successful surges of European monetary institutionalization both followed an acute crisis in the international system. The creation of the European Monetary System in 1979 was a self-conscious response to the rapid decline of the dollar in 1977–8 and the search for a new mechanism internationally to replace the dollar standard. Second, the process that led from the report of the Delors Committee in 1989, through the Treaty of Maastricht to the legal realization of the Euro in 1999 and the establishment of the physical currency had its origins in an attempt to devise mechanisms in the mid-1980s that would generate a more stable global exchange rate regime. The critical policy innovators, in particular the highly activist French Finance Minister Edouard Balladur, took an international answer and started to advocate its realization on the European level.

The institutional indeterminacy of the Committee makes its development a striking contrast to that of the European Economic Community, whose future was laid down by the founding document in a built-in teleology. There was no obvious blueprint to follow.

10.1 The beginnings

Since the values of European currencies were globally fixed under the terms of the 1944 Bretton Woods Agreement, and the beginning of the EEC coincided with a major and successful attempt to stabilize the French franc and to move to a general European current account convertibility, exchange rate issues played an only minor role in the initial years of the EEC. Regulation of exchange rates took place on a global, not a European, level. Later on, policy-makers, especially in France, loved to quote a prophetic remark by the French poet Paul Valéry, who in 1931 had written that "Europe visibly aspires to be governed by an American committee."[4] The IMF, which supervised exchange rate arrangements in the post-Bretton Woods world, looked to Europeans like a perfectly American committee.

The Monetary Committee of the EEC started functioning in 1958, with representatives of both central banks and finance ministries, who definitely had the upper hand. Some central bankers felt that they should establish their own institutionalized form of cooperation, as had been provided for in Article 105 of the Treaty. On November 10, 1957, the Governor of the Nederlands Bank, Marinus Holtrop, circulated a note in which he suggested that the five central banks of the EEC countries (Luxembourg had none, as it was in a monetary union with Belgium) should send identical letters to the finance ministers proposing enhanced cooperation. The Belgian, French and German governors responded skeptically, arguing that such a move would look like a concerted effort and raise national suspicions. In a subsequent discussion in Basel in January 1958, on the fringes of the monthly BIS meeting, the five men raised many of the issues that would be central to the future debates of the Committee of Central Bank Governors. The German, Karl Blessing, stated emphatically that the activities of the Monetary Committee should not be seen as central bank cooperation; the Italian, Donato Menichella, thought that the governors should not be bound by decisions of the EEC (and still less by the opinions [*avis*] of the Monetary Committee). But the outcome of the meeting produced no institutional innovation: the five simply agreed to meet again in February or March to determine whether they should hold regular meetings, and that they should inform the Council of Ministers that central bank cooperation was "well assured."[5]

That statement seems to have been accepted until an event occurred which showed that there was really not too much central bank cooperation. In March 1961, the German Mark and the Netherlands guilder were revalued, after a long period of tensions in the markets, and after a great deal of discussion within the IMF about the appropriate response to the build-up of German surpluses, but after no particular consultation with Germany's fellow EEC members. The DMark revaluation came at a sensitive time for European politics because relative prices were at the forefront of policy-makers' minds as they focused on negotiating agreements on agricultural prices. The Van Campen report to the European parliament (April 7, 1962) consequently argued that monetary policy needed to be coordinated with other aspects of economic policy.[6] It made the point that policy coordination alone would not be enough, and envisaged a federal system of monetary management analogous to the structure of the Bundesbank or the Federal Reserve System.

The EEC Commission published its Action Programme for the Second Phase of EEC on October 24, 1962, of which Part 8, inspired mostly by Robert Marjolin, focused on monetary relations and called for the establishment of a council or committee of the EEC's Central Bank Governors. The Commission's call was preceded by a sharp reminder that monetary policy was by no means a central concern of the EEC and the people who directed its fortunes at this stage: "Even though monetary policy no longer plays the almost exclusive directive role that it assumed in various epochs of the past, it still plays an essential role in the general equilibrium, even if it is only as the brake which slows down an economy threatened by inflation."[7]

The section also spoke of the desirability of a general liberalization of capital accounts, in accordance with the provisions of the Treaty of Rome. It concluded in a visionary way:

> the creation of a monetary union could become the objective of the third phase of the Common Market. The Finance or Economics Ministers of the Community, assembled in Council, would decide on conditions that should be fixed at an opportune time: the overall size of national budgets, and of the Community budget, and the general conditions of financing of these budgets. The Council of Central Bank Governors would become the central organ of the banking system of a federal type.[8]

This passage might be thought of as prophetic, in that the lines of this suggestion were followed fairly precisely in the 1990s: but there was a major difference in that by the end of the twentieth century, central banks placed a premium on devising legal guarantees of their institutional independence.

The characteristically 1960s view of central banks as a fundamental nuisance, posing a threat to growth through their interest rate policy, and requiring subordination in a general framework of economic policy direction, did not meet with a great deal of enthusiasm in the central banking community – even at that time. Central bankers in consequence devoted some imagination on how to neutralize this political initiative that would greatly extend the power of the Commission.

On November 12, 1962, the governors met again in Basel to prepare a response to the Marjolin initiative. Some national governments were skeptical. In particular, the day after the Basel meeting, an interministerial committee in France laid down some fundamental French principles: that "France has long insisted that free exchange be accompanied by a harmonization of conditions of competition." The French officials were also worried about the likely consequences of the enlargement of the EEC to include the UK, and noted that "experience shows that national imperatives are very strong in this respect."[9] Corresponding with other central bankers, the Governor of the Banque de France, Brunet, consequently insisted that "the role of governments in monetary policy be emphasized."[10]

By contrast, Karl Blessing had a rather expansive view of what central bankers might do. They should consider "not just monetary policy in the narrow sense but also all the categories of decision which could affect the general monetary situation, including the balance of payments and fiscal policy issues. On the other hand, the central bankers should not aim at a technical harmonization of policy on such issues as interest rates, minimum reserve requirements, or open market operations." Moreover, the Monetary Committee should simply act as "an organ of preparation" for Ministers' and Governors' meetings.[11]

In a note agreed by the central bank governors on December 12, 1962, they stated their wish for periodic meetings in Basel, which would "prepare" for meetings of the Ministers and Governors in the framework of the EEC Council. They would also consider public finance issues. The memorandum, however, also pointed out that some policy aspects could not be tackled at this level but required either a Treaty modification or some inter-state negotiation that could not be undertaken by central banks. Such issues included reform of the international monetary system, mutual financial support and the creation of a monetary union between the Six.[12] Brunet had been so worried by the potential ramifications of the Governors' Note that he insisted that it not be communicated to anyone apart from the Governors and the Ministers. In particular, the Note was not to be presented to Marjolin, although he explicitly asked for it in the course of a long lunch meeting with the Governors. A Banque de France minute recorded that Marjolin's exposition had indicated that he explicitly wanted to pursue other propositions which belonged to the sphere of competence of governments and not of central bankers. Marjolin had also proposed to hold two "symbolic" meetings in Brussels to emphasize the link with the EEC, a suggestion which was backed by the Belgian central bank governor, Hubert Ansiaux. The Banque de France was also basically hostile to the idea of the Note, which it considered "in a bad style, because the discussion was often delicate and some of the Governors either have an imperfect knowledge of French, or no French at all."[13] Marjolin's frustrations with the Governors clearly increased.

The Committee of Central Bank Governors was created by an EEC Council decision of May 8, 1964 in order "to hold consultations concerning the general principles and the broad lines of policy of the Central Banks, in particular as regards credit and the money and foreign exchange markets." Article 2 stated:

> The Committee shall be composed of the Governors of the Central Banks of the Member States. If they are unable to attend, they may be represented by another member of the directing body of their institution. The Commission shall, as a general rule, be invited to send one of its members as a representative to the meetings of the Committee.[14]

This 1964 decision played a crucial role in subsequent debates between the governors about the status of their committee. It was not an EEC (later European Community, and finally European Union) institution, but it had been set up by an EEC Council decision. Some German central bankers, who were particularly sensitive to the issue of the instruction of central banks by political authorities, consequently saw 1964 as "original sin" (*Sündenfall*).

The Vice-President of the EEC Commission, Robert Marjolin, who had largely been behind the initiative of creating the CCBG, also set out at the outset a bold project for its future work. Later Marjolin was profoundly disappointed. He left Brussels in 1967, convinced that the "dynamic period" in the life of the EEC had ended and that it would henceforth simply be concerned with management ("une period de gestion").[15]

The CCBG met for the first time on July 6, 1964.[16] Five Governors from the central banks of Belgium (also representing Luxembourg), France, Germany, Italy and the Netherlands sat around a table in Basel, with Alternates sitting behind them. The Governors appointed the Secretary-General of the BIS, Antonio d'Aroma, as Secretary-General of the Committee, although in practice he attended only a very few of the Committee meetings.[17] The Dutch central banker Holtrop was elected as Chairman, and continued in this position for the next three years (until he retired from the central bank) although the chair was nominally determined only for a one-year term. The EEC Commissioner with responsibility for monetary affairs, Robert Marjolin, also attended the meeting; and at the first session, seemed to play a rather dominant role.

At the initial meeting of the CCBG, Marjolin explained that "the Commission has rather ambitious views on the future of the Committee, because it believes that the Europe of the Six can also be realized in the monetary field."[18] He mentioned three particular areas of work: action to stop fluctuation in agricultural prices arising from the value of the unit of account; anti-inflationary action, since too often this was left to central banks which tightened interest rates, restricted credit, and thus confined the possibilities of investment and hence of European growth; and third, the question of capital controls used in particular by Germany to block inflows.

As an initial reaction, the Chairman of the Committee, the Netherlands central banker Marinus Holtrop, argued that there was a fundamental difference between the Monetary Committee and the new Committee:

> The former was formed by representatives of governments and experts from central banks, and is called on to advise the EEC, while the latter must above all give the possibility to the Governors of exchanging views on specific topics, for instance on the nature of measures adopted by a central bank and the influence that such measures might have on other central banks.

Otmar Emminger, a member of the board of the Bundesbank and Vice-President of the EEC Monetary Committee, spoke of a natural division of labor between the Monetary Committee, which had the principal task of promoting coordination of the policy of member countries in international monetary affairs, while the CCBG had the major mission of "coordinating the main lines of future policies of central banks."

In practice, the high hopes of the Commission and of Marjolin of finding a way of dealing with inflation without high interest rates or stop-go monetary policies were disappointed. In practice, the CCBG – because it met in Basle, at the same time as the BIS and G-10 meetings – evolved mostly into a way of formulating a common European response to the international financial and monetary problems of the day: the threats of a crisis emanating from the over-strained position of the British pound, and later from the U.S. dollar; and the discussion of a new reserve unit that might supplement or replace the dollar and provide a stable supply of international liquidity. This was also the background to the CCBG's first financial support package, which – perhaps extraordinarily – did not involve mutual support, or lending to a member country of the EEC. The European countries had to deal directly with a major flaw of the international monetary order.

On September 13, 1965, the CCBG considered the discussions that had been unfolding with the Bank of England about a support operation through the General Arrangements to Borrow (GAB). The GAB had been established by ten major countries in 1961, with the objective of providing credit of up to $6 bn., additional to the resources of the IMF. The fundamental eventuality that the G-10 might have to cope with lay in the increasing strains facing the major reserve centers: the United States and the United Kingdom. Switzerland joined this group in October 1963, although it continued to be known as the Group of Ten. For most of the 1960s, the weakest institutional link in the international monetary chain was the UK.

From August 29 to September 5, 1965, a representative of the Bank of England had visited Basel to ask for assistance from the G-10. The EEC central banks, who saw themselves increasingly as a coherent caucus within the G-10, agreed to contribute $350 m. as a three-month credit, but the Banque de France withdrew from the scheme, reducing the amount to $260 m. The Belgian central bank governor, Hubert Ansiaux, began by explaining that it did not seem likely that the U.K. would be able to repay promptly; and in fact, much larger amounts were needed ($4–5,000 m.) and Ansiaux suggested replicating something like the big stabilization loans of the 1920s, the Dawes and Young Plan bond issues, which had been used to prop up the fragile Weimar Republic, and which had (in the end) failed rather miserably. The group then discussed the British situation with Treasury Secretary Fowler, who expressed his confidence in the pound sterling ("in a manner more or less nuanced," the minutes record).[19]

A dramatic and much more significant move by the CCBG to an active lending policy occurred in July 1968. The Governor of the Banque de France, Jacques Brunet, explained that French reserve losses had required a drawing of $745 m. from the IMF, as well as gold sales to the Federal Reserve, the SNB and EEC central banks. By the beginning of July, the French reserves were nevertheless exhausted, and the Banque de France embarked on swaps of $600 m. with the Federal Reserve and with the EEC central banks. At Basel, the central bank governors resolved that the French situation met the mutual assistance conditions stipulated by Article 108 of the EEC Treaty. They agreed on a three-month $600 m. credit, with half coming from the Bundesbank, $200 m. from the Banca d'Italia and the remainder shared by the Banque Nationale de Belgique and the Nederlandsche Bank.[20] At the next meeting, the Bundesbank explained that it was prepared to extend further credit lines to the Banque de France, in order to deal with speculative pressure against the franc, and in expectation of a Mark revaluation.[21]

The European political confusion with respect to monetary arrangements was demonstrated very vividly at the Bonn G-10 summit of November 1968. The meeting took place largely at the insistence of the U.S. administration, and was exceptionally badly prepared. It took place in the very bleak modern building in Bonn occupied by the German Economics Ministry, with large quantities of beer and sparkling wine on offer, but nothing to eat but rather meagre canapés. The corridors were filled with bored officials who had been expelled from the high-level political discussions. Outside the building, demonstrators held up placards with the slogan, "Save the Mark." In the course of the negotiations, the German hosts presented a package that had been the subject of intense bargaining within the German coalition government, in which the Economics Minister Karl Schiller (SPD) wanted an alteration of the Mark parity but was in a minority. The Finance Minister, Franz Josef Strauss, of the Bavarian CSU, passionately opposed a revaluation of the Mark as it would be harmful to German export interests.

When it was clear in the meeting that, as a consequence of its complicated coalition politics, Germany would not act on the currency, the pressure shifted to France. After a telephone conversation with General de Gaulle, the French Finance Minister François-Xavier Ortoli agreed to an 11.1 percent devaluation of the French franc, but one day after the summit President de Gaulle announced that France would maintain the parity of the franc. France looked just as incapable of reaching an international agreement as Germany. It was very obvious that the G-10 mechanism was incapable of dealing with the European money muddle. In consequence, it was necessary to look for new mechanisms.

On February 12, 1969, the Commission – largely at the instigation of Raymond Barre – produced a new memorandum on monetary cooperation. The Governors were much happier to deal with this renewed effort than with the Marjolin proposals of the early 1960s. Barre proposed to establish a close link between economic policy and monetary cooperation; and Barre also discussed the possibility of coordinating cyclical fiscal policies. Monetary support would be linked with the convergence of medium-term economic objectives and coordination of short-term policies. Essentially, he proposed systematizing the support mechanism established to deal with the French case in July 1968, thus creating "the first multilateral instance to deal with the problems of a member state and offer assistance on specified conditions: composed of short term monetary support and medium term financial assistance."[22] The short-term assistance would be entirely automatic. Barre's initiative was a response to the debacle of the Bonn G-10 meeting. "It was clearly necessary to change often dilatory procedures."

Replying for the Bundesbank, Vice-President Otmar Emminger argued that Germany was suffering from inflationary pressure, and that a more expansive policy might be justified from the EEC viewpoint but not from that of Germany. It is striking that this discussion did not really focus on monetary policy adjustments: this neglect was largely the consequence of the fixed exchange rate regime, in which monetary policy tagged along. But the fixed exchange rate regime was increasingly vulnerable; and the fragility of the international order became the major theme of the following two decades. Global instability led to a European struggle to find continental solutions to world problems.

10.2 The European Monetary System

The EMS began as a very high level response to global currency chaos, and in particular to the depreciation of the dollar in 1977 and 1978, which seemed to threaten the continued reserve role of the dollar.

The outcome reflected a highly personal and originally quite secret initiative of President Giscard d'Estaing and Chancellor Helmut Schmidt. Schmidt in particular was highly skeptical about experts and central bankers, and felt that economic diplomacy, whether on the world or the European level, needed to be personalized. In the late afternoon the government leaders were separated from their advisers and from the Foreign Ministers and driven out to a dinner in Marienborg castle. Schmidt began with a plea for a wider use of the European Unit of account; and at the dinner, Giscard spoke of the dilemma of the non-Snake countries. They could either try to rejoin the Snake, or work on a different and new project. Schmidt proposed that a European Monetary Fund be created, as a regional version of the IMF and as a revival of some of the 1940s idealism that had driven the Bretton Woods conference. Countries should pool 15–20 percent of their reserves, they should increasingly use EC currencies rather than dollars in foreign exchange intervention, and there should be an enhanced use of the EUA.[23] In Schmidt's view, these proposals would move the world away from reliance on the dollar as the sole reserve currency; he even held out the prospect that OPEC members might invest a part of their surplus in the EUA, and that the EMF might issue EUA-denominated Special Drawing Rights.

> To the extent that the EUA became an alternative reserve instrument it would take the pressure off the dollar ... there is absolutely nothing anti-American in the scheme although it might lead to the EC becoming a little bit more inward-looking than in the past.[24]

Despite Schmidt's assurances about there being nothing anti-American about the plan, British Prime Minister James Callaghan called President Carter ten days after the meeting to denounce Schmidt's intentions:

> My understanding of his thoughts is that he believes the dollar is going to get into serious trouble, and we ought to try to insulate ourselves from it as much as possible. Now I don't know whether that thinking has got across to you, but with the strength of the German economy it could be extremely serious and I don't know, Jimmy, how to obviate it.... You see he knows about international finance, he understands it, he was a Minister of Finance himself, he cares about it and he believes American policy is all wrong. Now as long as that persists there's going to be trouble.[25]

In general, the British were very worried that they would be marginalized by the new scheme, and on the eve of the Copenhagen summit the cabinet secretary, John Hunt, had minuted:

> Some of the disadvantages to us are fairly clear. This could however be a move towards a two-tier community. The Prime Minister will obviously bear in mind the political and other implications if this happened and we were not in the top tier. Thus there is a case for ensuring either that this is a scheme that we can live with or that it founders.[26]

The Treasury suspected the plan as a German exercise in power projection:

> If other EEC countries stick with the mark more and with the dollar less, that helps intra-EEC German trade and also helps Germany in competition with its EEC partners in other markets ... The Germans have been much preoccupied with maintaining the competitiveness of their exchange rate and the German Government has been under strong pressure from industry on this; although that has not stopped the Germans from suggesting that any preoccupation by deficit countries with the competitiveness of their exchange rate was misguided inflationary Keynesianism.[27]

Indeed later in the year, German Finance Minister Manfred Lahnstein allegedly told Healey that Germany expected to get a competitive edge by limiting the scope for other currencies to depreciate.[28]

Schmidt's vision originally comprised three innovations: a system built around a new synthetic currency, the ECU; a new institution to manage it, the European Monetary Fund or EMF; and a rule that the EMF would apply to currency management, a divergence indicator for exchange rate fluctuations. Each of these replicated aspects of the 1944 Bretton Woods regime.

The task of working out the details was entrusted by Giscard, Schmidt and Callaghan to a group of experts: the Governor of the Banque de France, Bernard Clappier, Horst Schulmann from the Bundeskanzleramt, and the Second Permanent Secretary of the UK Treasury, Ken Couzens. In practice, however, Couzens dropped out of the negotiations at an early stage, thus greatly facilitating the task of reaching an agreement.

On December 5, 1978, meeting at Brussels, the EC Council agreed to the establishment of a European Monetary System, but it only included six member states. The UK remained outside the system, while Ireland and Italy demanded time for reflection. The core of the system became an "Agreement Between the Central Banks of the Member States of the European Economic Community Laying Down the Operating Procedures for the European Monetary System." On December 12 at Basel, the Governors agreed to recommend to the Council of Ministers to use the existing central parities of the Snake, and to derive central rates for the new EMS members from the rates at 1430 on December 29.[29]

The entry into force of the system was delayed by France, which put a reserve on the activation until there was an agreement on proposals for eliminating the MCAs (Monetary Compensation Agreements). The complex negotiations on the arrangements that followed from the interaction of monetary agreements and agricultural price support meant that it was March 13, 1979, before the EMS began to operate.

In many aspects, it was a profoundly truncated system. The ECU was in reality not at the center of the system: such a role would have required the possibility of the creation of the ECU. In the same way as the vision of an IMF as a world central bank that might create SDRs was doomed to failure, the European monetary mechanism of the late 1970s did not fulfill the aspirations of its most enthusiastic proponents. Second, the divergence indicator was of little practical use. By the time it showed a divergence, that divergence had also become clear to speculators, who could mount an attack on the exchange rate. In other words, there was already an obvious crisis – and in the early years, the result was usually a parity adjustment. In this aspect, the mechanism shared a conceptual flaw common in many attempts to establish official early warning systems: that the signals of a potential crisis become self-fulfilling. Third, the agreement provided for a further stage, the establishment of the European Monetary Fund after two years. In practice, there was no attempt to do this.

The EMS was no longer the major institutional innovation planned by Schmidt and Giscard, but an acceptance that the process of monetary coordination could most effectively be managed by central bankers. It had been designed to replace the "Snake," the DMark-based system of a small group of countries in the 1970s; it ended up by simply looking like an extended "Snake." The lesson about the limits of institutional innovation was carefully studied by Jacques Delors in the 1980s.

10.3 The Delors report

In retrospect, it appears as if the report of the Delors Committee laid down clearly and unambiguously a blueprint for the process of monetary unification that resulted in the creation of the European Central Bank and the single currency. But at the time, there were considerable doubts about the viability of the Committee's report, even (or even especially) among the members and the staff of the Committee. Even later, Karl Otto Pöhl, who as President of the Deutsche Bundesbank played a decisive role in the process, complained that the report was "a confused piece of work. There were some wild ideas in it."[30] Erik Hoffmeyer, the Danish central banker and a prominent presence on the CCBG, also turned out to be surprisingly critical in public.

There are at least three ways of thinking of the process of negotiating the steps to monetary unification: first, as the outgrowth of political entrepreneurship on the part of the Commission; second, as a struggle of interest between nation-states; and third, as the product of a global debate about rules and rule-setting in an era of increasingly apparent financial globalization.

The first tradition sees monetary union as the outcome of a series of initiatives launched by the EC Commission from Brussels. Part of the criterion determining the "success" of a Commission Presidency lay in the quality of leadership in suggesting new modes and mechanisms of integration. Presidents were expected to be policy entrepreneurs, and Jacques Delors was strikingly active in this regard. He was quite candid about the extent of his ambition. In a July 1988 speech to the European parliament in Strasbourg he stated: "We are not going to manage to take all the decisions we need between now and 1995 unless we see the beginnings of a European government."

It was an initiative of Delors that launched the committee and that guided the formulation of the report. Delors brilliantly inveigled the central bankers into his plan. The eventual success of his plan can clearly lead to a comparison of the effectiveness of different Commission presidents and initiators of policy: Marjolin's initiatives in the 1960s in the end generated only disillusion; Jenkins produced over-bold proposals that in the end were held to be unrealistic and were sidelined by Giscard and Schmidt; and Ortoli on the other hand was too sober and pragmatic in the 1970s. Delors produced just the right mixture of vision and practical sense: the vision of a bold move to realize the idea of "Union," and the pragmatic acknowledgment that only the central bankers could really remove the obstacles that lay in the way (especially the political and institutional obstacles that lay in Germany and in the particular position of the Bundesbank). Regarding the bankers as fundamentally obstructive, as the Commission did in the late 1970s, would only create an institutional impasse.

Moreover, the Commission-centered view of the integration process makes sense in a bigger way, in that many people could see the move to a single currency as a logical extension of the Single European Act of 1986 and the establishment of a unified market area in which capital would freely flow. Indeed the Commission itself adopted this position, when it set out the argument for further advances in the move to "European Union." At the start of the process, in 1985 Delors had reached the conclusion that free capital movement was essential to the realization of the 1992 program, and it was also equally apparent that the free circulation of capital would require a new approach to monetary policy.[31] In November 1986 a significant step was made when the Commission directed the transfer of a substantial group of categories of capital movement from the conditional list of 1960 to the unconditional list. By 1988, a final directive provided for a general liberalization of capital movements. Eventually, the 1989 Madrid summit acknowledged the link between capital market developments and monetary union when it determined that Stage One of monetary union would begin in July 1990 with the final removal of capital controls.

The Bundesbank began to worry that European integration was being driven unilaterally from the monetary side, without any economic convergence. The Single European Act contained no new initiatives in non-monetary areas, but pushed the capital liberalization issue, and also included an odd sub-heading in Article 20 which referred explicitly (but without any follow-up in the text) to Economic and Monetary Union. The oddity of a sub-heading that stood on its own was attributed by some to the machinations of German Foreign Minister Hans-Dieter Genscher.

The issue of whether capital market liberalization required a monetary union provoked substantial debate. As Robert Mundell had pointed out in the 1960s, free capital movements and a fixed exchange rate ruled out independent monetary policy; and in the later 1980s Tommaso Padoa-Schioppa reformulated this proposition as the "inconsistent quartet" of policy objectives: free trade, capital mobility, fixed or managed exchange rates, and monetary policy independence. This analysis of the problems of a world of capital mobility was obviously not simply restricted to the European setting.

Second, European integration has increasingly been seen as state-oriented and state-directed. Alan Millward recast the story of 1950s integration as "the rescue of the nation-state," while Andrew Moravcsik argued that the fundamental drive of later integration lay in mechanisms for reconciling domestic political integrations. It is highly plausible to apply this framework to the era in which the roadmap to monetary union was finalized. The late 1980s saw a renewed version of the long-standing clash of interpretations of European integration between France and Germany. French policy-makers, especially the President, pressed for a mechanism of asserting political control of the economy, or "economic governance," while Germans, in particular in the independently minded central bank, argued that an institutional arrangement was required which shielded a future central banking system from political interference. The Germans still repeated the "coronation theory" that played a key role in the early 1970s debates: the move to monetary union should take place only when there was a substantive economic convergence. For France, monetary union looked like a way of making a new economic policy at the community level. The debates of the 1970s between so-called "monetarists" (who held the French vision) and "economists" (the Germans) were thus revived. A conspiracy theory began to flourish around the notion that Germany was imposing a fixed and final exchange rate regime that would impose a cost disadvantage in the form of a creeping loss of competitiveness on its neighbors. To some extent, these clashes were played around the Delors Committee, and in the official French response to the Committee; but surprisingly, they were not fought out within the Committee.

Third, the debates of the late 1980s were played out not just in a European setting but on a global level. As in the later 1970s, when problems in the United States and the rapid depreciation of the dollar had summoned a European response, the most fundamental international problems did not exist on a simply European stage. Many of the problems in Europe followed from the dramatic exchange rate movements between the Deutschemark and the dollar that resulted in large part from the combination of Paul Volcker's tight monetary policy and the large fiscal deficits of the Reagan presidency (especially during the first term).

A central issue for the Delors Committee was to work out what could be done by tweaking existing institutions, and what parts of monetary integration would require profound constitutional change and a revision of the EEC Treaty. What made for an eventual success was that in the course of the discussions, the first part was "softened" – notably at the insistence of the heads of the Bundesbank and the Bank of England, which had a certain skepticism about the whole project. It was the "softening" of Stage One that made it impossible for the governments to reject the foundation of the report.

In the final report of the Delors Committee, there was a clear path mapped out for monetary union. But in its initial stage, it went through the central banks and through Basel.

The major mechanism of the transitional, pre-Treaty, phase of integration was the CCBG (section 52).

Fourth, the 1964 Council Decision defining the mandate of the Committee of Central Bank Governors would be replaced by a new Decision. According to this Decision the Committee of Central Bank Governors should:

- formulate opinions on the overall orientation of monetary and exchange rate policy, as well as on measures taken in these fields by individual countries. In particular, the Committee would normally be consulted in advance of national decisions on the course of monetary policy, such as the setting of annual domestic monetary and credit targets;
- express opinions to individual governments and the Council of Ministers on policies that could affect the internal and external monetary situation in the Community, especially the functioning of the EMS. The outcome of the Committee's deliberations could be made public by the Chairman of the Committee;

- submit an annual report on its activities and on the monetary situation of the Community to the European Parliament and the European Council.

The Committee could express majority opinions, although at this stage they would not be binding. In order to make its policy coordination function more effective, the Committee would set up three sub-committees, with a greater research and advisory role than those existing hitherto, and provide them with a permanent research staff:

- a monetary policy committee would define common surveillance indicators, propose harmonized objectives and instruments and help to gradually bring about a change from *ex post* analysis to an *ex ante* approach to monetary policy cooperation;
- a foreign exchange policy committee would monitor and analyze exchange market developments and assist in the search for effective intervention strategies;
- an advisory committee would hold regular consultations on matters of common interest in the field of banking supervision policy.

The second and third stages were much more ambitious. In Stage Two the new European System of Central Banks would absorb both the EMCF and the CCBG. It would manage the transition from the combination of monetary policies of national central banks to a common monetary policy. In the third stage, exchange rates would be locked finally and irrevocably. The ESCB would pool reserves and manage interventions with regard to third currencies. "With the establishment of the European System of Central Banks the Community would also have created an institution through which it could participate in all aspects of international monetary coordination" (Section 38), Delors emphasized that the monetary integration would need to be accompanied by a consolidation of the single market and competition policy, as well as by an evaluation and adaption of regional policies (section 56).

The Bundesbank responded directly to the Delors report. Internally, it welcomed the report as an optimal solution from its viewpoint, although subsequently a major discussion developed about whether under the new mechanism the CCBG could commit the Bundesbank to action, which would be a violation of the autonomy provisions of the central bank law. In its dealings with the German government, it set out its institutional opinion very directly. It focused on Paragraph 7 of the report, with its reference to the CCBG, and focused on the Council decision to define more extensively the competence and tasks of the CCBG. An intergovernmental conference should only be called when the preliminary work had been satisfactorily accomplished. The current progress should not be endangered by a premature fixing of exchange rates. The Bundesbank also pointed out that a fixing of exchange rates would lead to greater pressures to make transfers via the structural funds of the EC budget.

At a meeting of the EC Finance Ministers at S'Agaro (Spain), there was considerable hostility to the central recommendation of the report in paragraph 39 ("the decision to enter upon the first stage should be a decision to embark on the entire process.")

At the Madrid summit of June 26/27, 1989, however, the heads of government accepted the Delors report as "a sound basis for future work." In particular, Madrid accepted the Delors follow-up procedures (paragraphs 64–66), which entrusted more work to the European Council, as well as to the CCBG, to implement the First Stage, as well as to provide suggestions to serve as the basis for a revised treaty at an inter-governmental conference. Margaret Thatcher was furious, in that she had been outmaneuvered by Delors and betrayed by Robin Leigh-Pemberton, whom she never forgave and whom she thenceforth treated as a characteristically weak-willed and over-polite representative of Britain's effete ruling elite. The British Chancellor of the Exchequer, Nigel Lawson, had consistently argued that Stage One was desirable but that there was no need for a new Treaty for further "Stages." But Thatcher could not really disagree either with anything in the first stage, which emerged as a result of the efforts of Pöhl but also especially of Leigh-Pemberton in the "softest" possible form. Britain remained rather outside the process, even after the United Kingdom joined the exchange rate mechanism in October 1990.

Central bank cooperation appeared at Madrid – but also more generally – as a lowest common denominator on which consensus could be built. It was acceptable to governments, which could see it as a purpose-built mechanism for tackling the problem of currency stability. It was also acceptable to central banks, even to those like the Bundesbank and the Bank of England which had reservations about European visions. For those central banks, it appeared as a way of institutionalizing their independence (which the Bundesbank always worried about and which the Bank of England and the Banque de France now began to seek). Independence would not just depend on the passing whims of whatever government happened to be in power; it would be anchored in international treaties.

The European Central Bank was thus less an outcome of a European idealism driving a general movement to integration than of a search for a way of achieving central bank cooperation in a world in which currency volatility pushed cooperation up the scale of political priorities. It worked best when it was not directly dependent on state initiatives – which simply produced diplomatic impasse – and when it was not the plaything of national politicians. Oddly enough, Walter Bagehot, discussing mid-nineteenth-century plans for ambitious projects of monetary unification, had come to the same conclusion in 1869:

> We commonly think, I believe, that the coining of money is an economic function of government; that the Government verifies the quality and quantity of metal in the coin out of regard to the good of its subjects, and that Government is admirably suited to this task – that it is a very reliable verifier. But in truth, if we look at the real motives of governments, and the real action of governments, we may come to think otherwise.[32]

Notes

1 Michael Bordo and Harold James, "A Long-Term Perspective on the Euro," European Commission, EMU@10, 2008.
2 Eric Helleiner, *The Making of National Money: Territorial Currencies in Historical Perspective*, Ithaca: Cornell University Press, 2003.
3 See Benn Steil and Manuel Hinds, *Money, Markets and Sovereignty*, New Haven: Yale University Press, 2009.
4 Paul Valéry, "Notes sur la grandeur et la decadence de l'Europe," in *Regards sur le monde actuel*, Paris: Stock, Delamani et Boutelleau, 1931, p. 51. For the later use of Valéry's thought, see Michel Jobert's February 14, 1974, press conference, Aurelie Gfeller, "Re-Envisioning Europe: France, America and the Arab World 1973–1974," Princeton PhD, 2008, p. 173.
5 BdF 1489200205/46, November 10, 1957, Holtrop: Aide-Mémoire sur la Collaboration entre Banques Centrales des Pays du Marché Commun; January 13, 1958, Memorandum: Collaboration entre Banques Centrales des Pays du Marché Commun.
6 See Andre Szasz, *The Road to European Monetary Union: A Political and Economic History*, Basingstoke: Macmillan, 1999; Horst Ungerer, *A Concise History of European Monetary Integration*, Westport: Quorum Books, 1997.
7 EEC, Mémorandum de la Commission sur le programme d'action de la Communauté pendant la deuxième étape, Brussels, October 24, 1962, p. 76.
8 Ibid., p. 80.
9 BdF 1489200205/46, November 13, 1962 compte-rendu of Matignon meeting (November 9): Comité interministériel pour les Questions de Coopération Européenne.
10 BdF 1489200205/46, December 5, 1962, Guindey (BIS) to Brunet.
11 Ibid.
12 BdF 1489200205/46, December 10, 1962, Note.
13 BdF 1489200205/46, December 7, 1962, Brunet to Holtrop; December 12, 1962, Note pour le Gouverneur.
14 64/300/EEC, OJ P 77, 21.5.1964, p. 1206.
15 Robert Marjolin, *Le travail d'une vie*, Paris: Robert Laffont, 1986, p. 305.
16 The minutes (to 1978) are available at: www.ecb.int/ecb/history/archive/agendas/html/index.en.html.
17 See Guenter D. Baer, "The Committee of Governors as a Forum for European Central Bank Cooperation," in (ed.) Age Bakker, *Monetary Stability through International Cooperation; Essays in Honour of André Szász*, Dordrecht: Kluwer, 1994; David M. Andrews, "Building Capacity: The Institutional Foundations of EMU."
18 Meeting 1, July 6, 1964, Basel.
19 Meeting 8, September 13, 1965, Brussels.
20 Meeting 25, July 8, 1968, Basel.
21 Meeting 26, September 10, 1968, Rotterdam.
22 Meeting 29, Basel, March 10, 1969, Basel.
23 Peter Ludlow, *The Making of the European Monetary System: A Case Study of the Politics of the European Community*, London: Butterworths, 1982, pp. 90–92.
24 PRO, PREM 16/1615, Schmidt note on remarks at Copenhagen summit.
25 Prime Minister's telephone conversation with President Carter, April 17, 1978 at 2030, British FOI release 248745.
26 PRO PREM 16/1615, John Hunt: "Chancellor Schmidt, the Snake and Pooling Reserves," April 6, 1978.
27 PRO PREM 16/1634, June 22, 1978, DWH: European Currency Arrangements.
28 Philip Stephens, *Politics and the Pound: The Conservative's Struggle with Sterling*, London: Macmillan, 1996 p. 6; Denis Healey, *The Time of My Life*, London: Penguin, 1989, p. 438–439.

29 Meeting 128, December 12, 1978, Basel.
30 David Marsh, *Euro: The Politics of the New Global Currency*, New Haven: Yale University Press, 2009, p. 123.
31 See Rawi Adelal, *Capital Rules: The Construction of Global Finance*, Cambridge, Mass.: Harvard University Press, 2007, pp. 66–69.
32 Walter Bagehot, *A Practical Plan for Assimilating the English and American Money as a Step Towards a Universal Money*, London: Longmans Green, 1889, reprint of 1869 edition, pp. vii–viii.

11 Openness, protectionism and Britain's productivity performance over the long run

Stephen Broadberry and Nicholas Crafts

11.1 Introduction

The historical literature contains a range of views on the links between openness and productivity performance in Britain since the late nineteenth century. For one group of writers, British prosperity has been founded on participation in the international economy, with a policy of free trade seen as beneficial irrespective of any protectionist policies pursued by other countries (Imlah, 1958; Edelstein, 1982; Capie, 1983, 1994; Irwin, 1996). For others, however, the roots of British relative economic decline can be traced back to the continued adherence to liberal principles when other countries were abandoning them. Within this group, there are those such as Aaronovitch and Smith (1981) and Bairoch (1993), who see protectionism as a way of restructuring the economy onto a more favourable development path, and others who see the abandonment of free trade in Britain as a second-best policy at particular times, necessary as a response to the rise of protectionism abroad (Kitson and Solomou, 1990; Marrison, 1996). Although there are now large literatures on tariff reform before 1914 and the adoption of the general tariff in the 1930s, few writers have attempted to link these issues to the debates over de-industrialisation and "globalisation" since the 1970s. This paper uses a data set covering the long period from 1870 to 2000, adopting an explicit quantitative approach to facilitate comparisons between sub-periods. Particular attention is paid to the contribution of different sectors to Britain's comparative productivity performance, since misleading conclusions can be drawn from a consideration of only part of the economy.

Sections 2 and 3 set out the broad trends in productivity performance and the degree of openness of the British economy during the period 1870–2000. Although debates over protection often make reference to different sectors of the economy, most international comparisons of productivity work only in terms of aggregate productivity measures. Here, we draw on the data presented in Broadberry (1998) to examine the links between openness and productivity performance at the sectoral level. Although Britain was overtaken by the United States during the 1890s and by Germany during the 1960s, the sectoral patterns of changing productivity performance are very different from those emphasised in the conventional literature. In particular, we point to the importance of the later structural shift out of agriculture in the United States and Germany and to overtaking in services rather than in industry. In all three countries, trends in openness followed a U-shaped pattern with high levels of openness before the First World War and after the Second World War, separated by a protectionist interlude. However, whereas the pre-First World War level of openness was surpassed by the 1970s in Germany and by the early 1980s in the United States, this was not the case in Britain, even by 1990.

Sections 4 to 6 consider shorter periods in the light of the long-run evidence, paying particular attention to sectoral issues. First, we see that as a result of the openness of the British economy, agriculture was unusually small in nineteenth-century Britain, allowing resources to be deployed in the higher-value-added industrial and service sectors. This benefit of openness is rarely considered alongside the costs to British industry of retaining open markets when tariffs were being raised against British exports. Second, many writers criticise the cosmopolitan service sector for neglecting domestic industry. However, this ignores the importance of the outward orientation of services for service sector productivity, and the growing importance of services for productivity performance overall. Third, the trend of British industrial performance was not improved by protection when it was applied in the 1930s, despite the claims of the tariff reformers. Furthermore, protective attempts to avoid de-industrialisation after the Second World War had an adverse effect on productivity performance in industry and in the aggregate economy.

11.2 Britain's long-run productivity performance

Table 11.1 presents sectoral estimates of comparative labour productivity levels for the US/UK and Germany/UK cases over the period circa 1870–2000, derived from Broadberry (1997b; 1997c; 1998; 2006). The United States and Germany were Britain's main trading rivals during most of this period. The concept of labour productivity used here is output per person engaged. For the whole economy, labour productivity in the United States was about 90 per cent of the British level in 1870, and the United States overtook Britain as the aggregate labour productivity leader during the 1890s and continued to forge ahead to the 1950s. Since then, there has been a slow process of British catching up, but by 1990 there was still a substantial aggregate Anglo-American labour productivity gap of more than 30 per cent, which increased again during the second half of the 1990s, as US productivity surged with the diffusion of ICT (Jorgenson and Stiroh, 2000). Turning to the Germany/UK comparison, for the whole economy, German labour productivity in 1871 was about 60 per cent of the British level, and had still reached only about 75 per cent of the British level by the First World War. After a setback across the war, Germany again reached about 75 per cent of the British level by the mid-1930s. After another setback across the Second World War, Germany continued to catch-up, overtook Britain only during the mid-1960s and by 1979 had a labour productivity advantage of more than 25 per cent. However, this German advantage has been much reduced during the 1980s and 1990s.

Table 11.1 Comparative US/UK labour productivity levels by sector, 1869/71 to 1999 (UK = 100)

A US/UK

Year	*Agriculture*	*Industry*	*Services*	*Aggregate economy*
1869/71	86.9	153.6	85.9	89.8
1889/91	102.1	164.1	84.2	94.1
1909/11	103.2	193.2	107.4	117.7
1919/20	128.0	198.0	118.9	133.3
1929	109.7	222.7	121.2	139.4
1937	103.3	190.6	120.0	132.6
1950	126.0	243.5	140.8	166.9
1973	131.2	214.8	137.4	152.3
1979	156.1	186.0	137.2	145.5
1990	151.1	163.0	129.6	133.0
1999	179.6	141.4	127.9	142.5

B Germany/UK

Year	*Agriculture*	*Industry*	*Services*	*Aggregate economy*
1871	55.7	91.7	62.8	59.5
1891	53.7	99.3	64.4	60.5
1911	67.3	127.7	73.4	75.5
1925	53.8	92.3	76.5	69.0
1929	56.9	97.1	82.3	74.1
1935	57.2	99.1	85.7	75.7
1950	41.2	91.8	83.2	74.4
1973	50.8	121.1	120.1	114.0
1979	65.5	132.8	131.8	126.5
1990	75.4	111.0	134.9	125.4
1999	48.5	84.7	119.5	110.9

Sources: Derived from Broadberry (1997b, 1997c, 2006); O'Mahony and de Boer (2002).

The sectoral patterns of comparative productivity performance are quite varied. Here the nine-sector analysis provided in Broadberry (1998) has been simplified onto a three-sector basis, distinguishing between agriculture, industry and services, as in Broadberry and Ghosal (2002) and Broadberry (2005). Industry includes mineral extraction, manufacturing, construction and the utilities, while services includes transport and communications, distribution, finance, professional and personal services and government. Both Germany and the United States caught up with and overtook Britain in terms of aggregate labour productivity largely by shifting resources out of agriculture and improving their comparative productivity performance in services rather than by improving their comparative productivity performance in industry (Broadberry, 1998).

Broadberry (1993) first established that comparative labour productivity in manufacturing has remained stationary in both the US/UK and the Germany/UK cases since the late nineteenth century, and Table 11.1 shows that this result generalises to industry as a whole. By contrast, in both cases the aggregate labour productivity ratio moves broadly in line with the labour productivity ratio for services. Although both Germany and the United States have improved their labour productivity performance relative to Britain in agriculture, there has also been a dramatic decline in the importance of agriculture, which can be seen in Table 11.2. Whereas in 1870 agriculture accounted for about half of all

Table 11.2 Sectoral shares of employment in the United States, the United Kingdom and Germany, 1870–1999 (%)

A United States

Year	*Agriculture*	*Industry*	*Services*
1870	50.0	24.8	25.2
1910	32.0	31.8	36.2
1920	26.2	33.2	40.6
1930	20.9	30.2	48.9
1940	17.9	31.6	50.5
1950	11.0	32.9	56.1
1973	3.7	28.9	67.4
1990	2.5	21.8	75.7
1999	1.2	19.5	79.2

B United Kingdom

Year	*Agriculture*	*Industry*	*Services*
1871	22.2	42.4	35.4
1911	11.8	44.1	44.1
1924	8.6	46.5	44.9
1930	7.6	43.7	48.7
1937	6.2	44.5	49.3
1950	5.1	46.5	48.4
1973	2.9	41.8	55.3
1990	2.0	28.5	69.5
1999	1.9	22.9	75.2

C Germany

Year	*Agriculture*	*Industry*	*Services*
1871	49.5	29.1	21.4
1913	34.5	37.9	27.6
1925	31.5	40.1	28.4
1930	30.5	37.4	32.1
1935	29.9	38.2	31.9
1950	24.3	42.1	33.6
1973	7.2	47.3	45.5
1990	3.4	39.7	56.9
1999	2.6	29.8	67.6

Source: Derived from Broadberry (1997b, 1997c); O'Mahony and de Boer (2002).

employment in Germany and the United States, by 1999 this had fallen to under 3 per cent. The shift out of agriculture has nevertheless had an important impact on comparative productivity performance at the aggregate level. This is because in the late nineteenth century Britain already had a much smaller share of the labour force in agriculture, which has had a substantially lower value added per employee than in industry or services. Hence the large share of resources tied up in agriculture in the United States exercised a significant negative influence on the aggregate US productivity performance relative to Britain in the late nineteenth and early twentieth centuries, and as the importance of agriculture declined this negative influence was removed. Similarly, the relatively large share of resources in German agriculture had a negative effect on Germany's aggregate productivity performance relative to Britain until after the Second World War. Note that Germany in 1950 had a bigger share of the labour force in agriculture than Britain in 1871.[1]

The labour productivity differences in Table 11.1 may be explained in part by differences in capital intensity. So before we turn to measures of openness, it will be useful to provide estimates of comparative levels of total factor productivity (TFP), where TFP measures the productivity of labour and physical capital, weighted by their respective shares in income.[2] Comparing Table 11.3 with Table 11.1, we see that although capital explains a part of the labour productivity differences between the three countries, it is not sufficient to eliminate differences in TFP, some of which may be explained by openness.

For the US/UK case, trends in comparative TFP and labour productivity at the aggregate level are similar, but with TFP differences generally smaller than labour productivity differences. One point worth noting here is that whereas the United States overtook Britain before the First World War in terms of labour productivity, it was only between the wars that the United States gained a TFP advantage. This would be consistent with the emphasis of Abramovitz and David (1973, 1996) on the importance of capital rather than TFP in American economic growth during the nineteenth century. It is also consistent with McCloskey's (1970) claim that Victorian Britain did not fail, in the sense that the United States was still catching up in terms of aggregate TFP levels. In services, too, note that the US overtaking of Britain also occurred later in terms of TFP than in terms of labour productivity. For the Germany/UK case, again comparing Tables 11.1 and 11.3 we see that trends are very similar for comparative TFP and labour productivity at the aggregate level, with differences in TFP generally smaller than differences in labour productivity. Note that in industry, Germany had caught up with Britain in terms of TFP as well as labour productivity before the First World War.

11.3 Trends in openness

11.3.1 International trade and protection

The most commonly used measures of the degree of openness are the shares of imports and exports in GDP. Trade ratios can be calculated both for goods and

Table 11.3 Comparative US/UK and Germany/UK total factor productivity levels by sector, 1869/71 to 1999 (UK = 100)

A US/UK

Year	*Agriculture*	*Industry*	*Services*	*Aggregate economy*
1869/71	99.5	154.2	86.5	95.2
1889/91	123.0	139.6	64.3	83.3
1909/11	118.7	150.9	71.6	90.5
1919/20	133.1	158.3	92.1	108.2
1929	118.0	187.8	92.0	112.7
1937	119.2	161.2	89.1	105.9
1950	132.6	217.6	110.2	138.1
1973	125.9	202.2	120.6	137.4
1990	138.8	157.3	119.8	125.3
1999	129.2	130.5	123.3	125.0

B Germany/UK

Year	*Agriculture*	*Industry*	*Services*	*Aggregate economy*
1871	58.4	90.5	67.2	61.6
1891	59.8	91.6	65.5	63.2
1911	71.6	106.1	76.4	75.4
1925	57.0	92.9	83.6	74.3
1929	59.3	96.0	90.0	78.5
1935	59.6	97.1	88.8	78.2
1950	44.7	89.4	89.3	76.2
1973	48.1	105.7	127.6	108.6
1990	65.4	98.5	139.0	116.5
1999	47.5	78.8	109.9	95.4

Sources: Derived from Broadberry (1997b, 1997c); O'Mahony and de Boer (2002).

for goods and services. For the United Kingdom, the figures in Table 11.4 show a period of increasing openness before the First World War, while trade ratios declined during the period between the wars. The early post-Second World War period, although relatively open compared to the interwar period, did not match the degree of openness seen before the First World War. Even by the late 1980s, the British export trade ratios had not regained their pre-1914 levels.

Since we shall be concerned with Britain's policies and performance in an international context, it will be helpful to consider the trade ratios in the United States and Germany, Britain's main trading rivals over most of this period. In both Germany and the United States, trade ratios declined between the wars and rose again after the Second World War. In contrast to Britain, however, the pre-First World War degree of openness was decisively surpassed, by the 1970s in the case of Germany and by the 1980s in the case of the United States. This is also true for trade in goods compared with GDP in goods production which, given the rise of non-tradable services over time, is sometimes regarded as a better indicator (Feenstra, 1998).

Table 11.4 Trade ratios, 1870–1990 (% of GDP)

A United Kingdom

Year	*Imports*		*Exports*	
	Goods	*Goods and services*	*Goods*	*Goods and services*
1870	24.9	27.1	22.0	29.1
1890	26.6	28.8	22.9	29.8
1913	28.6	30.9	25.3	32.4
1925	26.0	29.2	20.3	24.9
1929	23.6	26.8	18.1	23.2
1938	15.2	18.0	10.1	13.6
1950	17.9	23.8	17.5	23.2
1970	15.7	21.4	15.7	22.2
1990	21.9	26.9	18.5	24.2

B United States

Year	*Imports*		*Exports*	
	Goods	*Goods and services*	*Goods*	*Goods and services*
1870	5.7	6.2	5.6	6.6
1890	6.5	7.2	6.9	7.2
1913	4.6	5.6	6.6	6.8
1925	4.6	5.4	5.4	5.8
1929	4.4	5.4	5.1	5.7
1938	2.6	3.3	3.8	4.5
1950	3.2	4.0	3.6	4.3
1970	4.0	5.5	4.4	5.6
1990	9.0	11.3	7.0	10.0

C Germany

Year	*Imports*		*Exports*	
	Goods	*Goods and services*	*Goods*	*Goods and services*
1880	16.6		17.3	
1890	17.5		14.1	
1913	20.5		19.3	
1925	18.5		13.8	
1929	16.9		17.0	
1938	5.6		5.4	
1950	11.7	12.7	11.9	15.1
1970	15.0	20.5	18.2	22.6
1990	22.8	26.3	26.6	32.2

Sources: United Kingdom: Feinstein (1972: Tables 3 and 15); *Economic Trends Annual Supplement*; United States: 1870–1929: Trade data from *Historical Statistics of the United States: Colonial Time to 1970*, series U2–U4 and U9–U11; GDP from Kendrick (1961) and Balke and Gordon (1989); 1929–90; Trade and GDP data from *National Income and Product Accounts of the United States, Vol. 1, 1929–58, Vol 2. 1959–88*, Tables 1.1 and 4.1 and *Statistical Abstract of the United States*; Germany: 1880–1950; Hoffmann (1965), Tables 125, 127, 248; 1950–88: *Volkswirtschaftliche Gesamtrechnungen*, 1950 bis 1990, Fachserie 18, Reihe S.15, Tables 2.2.1, 2.2.12 and 2.2.13, and *Statistisches, Jahrbuch für die Bundesrepublik Deutschland.*

It is natural to link the U-shaped pattern of the trade ratios to changes in the level of protection. Figures on the ratio of duties to total imports are given in Table 11.5. Although this ratio gives an imperfect measure of changes in tariff rates, most writers find that it captures the broad movements (Capie, 1994: 31–32). For Britain, it is necessary to exclude revenue-raising duties on tobacco and petroleum to obtain an accurate picture of the pattern of protection, particularly since the Second World War. The trend towards free trade in Britain during the nineteenth century is clearly visible, using both the total and adjusted customs revenue to import value ratios. The retreat from free trade in the interwar period is equally clear, culminating in the General Tariff of 1932. For the post-Second World War period, however, it is important to remove the customs duties on tobacco and petroleum, which should not be seen as protective (Lindert, 1991). Then the return to openness is more apparent.

For the United States, data is available on the ratio of duties to dutiable imports, as well as the ratio of duties to total imports. Although the former ratio is some-

Table 11.5 Customs revenue as a share of import values in the United Kingdom, the United States and Germany, 1820–1990 (%)

Year	*United Kingdom*		*United States*		*Germany*
	Total	*Excl. tobacco and petrol*	*Total*	*Dutiable imports*	*Total*
1820	24.0				
1830	34.3		57.3	61.7	
1840	25.4	21.9	17.6	34.4	
1850	21.7	17.6	24.5	27.1	
1860	11.6	9.1	15.7	19.7	
1870	7.1	5.0	44.9	47.1	
1880	4.7	2.7	29.1	43.5	5.8
1890	4.8	2.7	29.6	44.6	8.8
1900	4.6	2.6	27.6	49.5	8.1
1910	4.5	2.2	21.1	41.6	7.4
1913	4.4	2.1	17.7	40.1	6.3
1920	7.7	4.7	6.4	16.4	
1929	9.7	4.4	13.5	40.1	8.2
1935	24.5	10.2	17.5	42.9	30.1
1938	24.1	10.4	15.5	39.3	33.4
1940	22.7		12.5	35.6	
1945	38.2		9.3	28.2	
1950	31.2	2.9	6.0	13.1	5.4
1960	30.2	3.9	7.4	12.2	6.5
1970		3.1	6.5	10.0	2.6
1980		2.0	3.1	5.7	1.3
1990		1.4	3.3	5.2	1.3

Sources: Britain: total customs revenue from Mitchell (1988: 581–586); total import values from Mitchell (1988: 451–454); Customs revenue from tobacco and petrol from *Statistical Abstract for the United Kingdom, Annual Abstract of Statistics, and National Income and Expenditure*. Imports of tobacco and petrol from Mitchell (1988: 474–480) and *Annual Abstract of Statistics*. United States: *Statistical Abstract of the United States*. Germany: customs duties and imports from Mitchell (1975), updated from *Statisches Jahrbuch für die Budesrepublik Deutschland*.

what higher, the trend is very similar to that for the ratio of duties to total imports. A declining level of protection in the first half of the nineteenth century was sharply reversed during the Civil War decade, and although there was a further downward drift in the level during the period 1870–1913, protection remained high by international standards before the First World War. The United States remained protectionist between the wars, with the Fordney-McCumber and Hawley-Smoot tariffs of 1922 and 1930, respectively, before becoming increasingly liberal under the GATT system during the post-Second World War period.

German data on the ratio of customs duties to total imports is given in Table 11.5 for the period after the formation of the German Reich. Although there was a small increase during the 1880s, the degree of protection was much closer to the British than to the American level. Alternative data on the unweighted average level of duties confirms that the scale of the retreat from free trade in Continental Europe towards the end of the nineteenth century should not be exaggerated (Liepmann, 1938). Thus, for example, Capie (1983: 26) reports an average *ad valorem* rate of duty of 8.4 per cent for Germany in 1910. The rise of protectionism in Germany between the wars, particularly with the growth of bilateralism under the Third Reich, is clearly visible in Table 11.5. Equally clear is the firm embrace of a liberal trading policy after the Second World War. Given the strong trading links with other European countries, European integration via the EEC has resulted in very low ratios of customs duties to imports in Germany. However, Weiss (1988) offers a qualification to this view, noting the growth of subsidies to a number of German industries, thus to some extent undermining the liberal regime (Giersch Paqué and Schmieding, 1992).

11.3.2 Trade blocs

In this section we examine trends in British exports to see how Britain came to be increasingly dependent on Empire markets between the late nineteenth century and the mid-twentieth century. The key factor was the growth of protectionism in the United States and Germany during the late nineteenth century, which before the First World War culminated in a division of the world into spheres of influence by the three major manufacturing countries (Taussig, 1892; Hoffman, 1933; Schlote, 1952). A survey of many of the pre-1914 international combines is given in Plummer (1951: 4–10). The chemical industry was one of the most prone to international combination, with formal agreements in alkalis and explosives. As Reader (1970: 60) puts it,

> In deciding how to share markets, the principle generally followed in each group, was that the British member … should have the markets of Great Britain and the British Empire; the European member or members, Europe. Markets elsewhere in the world were a matter for negotiation. The USA, the richest, stood alone by reason of the formidable nature of the natives. Latin America, where both British and European connections were strong, was apt

> to be looked upon by American companies, particularly in the explosives trade, as being covered by a businessman's version of the Monroe Doctrine … For the purposes of market-sharing the Russian Empire was generally taken as a province of Europe and the Chinese as a dependency of the British.

The upshot of these trends was a clear move towards concentration by British producers on Empire markets from the late nineteenth century. Furthermore, as Schlote's (1952) data in Part A of Table 11.6 shows, this was a new departure, since there was no clear upward trend in the Empire share of British exports between 1830 and 1870. The trend towards concentration on Empire markets, particularly the Dominions of Australia, New Zealand, the Union of South Africa, Canada and Newfoundland, accelerated in the interwar period. The upheaval in the British trade data caused by the independence of the Irish Free State does not affect these trends, since the share can be calculated on both the old and the new basis in Parts A and B of Table 11.6. Continuing to 1990 in Part B of Table 11.6, the share of British exports to the original six members of the EEC as well as the share to "British countries" can be seen. Clearly the rise to dominance of Empire markets (peaking at 55 per cent in 1951) was the other side of a serious decline in the importance of Continental European markets during the interwar and transwar periods. Imperial Preference was clearly no small sideshow for the British economy in the twentieth century. Indeed, as Drummond (1974: 426) notes, imperial economic matters took up more Cabinet time than any other aspect of economic affairs between the wars. As late as 1970, more British exports were going to "British countries" than to the EEC. Since Britain joined the EEC in 1973, however, trade with "British countries" (including the Republic of South Africa and the Irish Republic) has dramatically declined in importance.

11.3.3 The protectionist period

Although the highest levels of protection for the UK economy were seen in the 1940s, it is important to recognise that protectionism was quite significant until the late 1970s. Protectionism was the order of the day throughout the years when relative economic decline was at its peak. Table 11.7 underlines the slowness of the retreat from protectionist policies in three ways. First, it is shown that in the late 1950s, virtually across the whole manufacturing sector tariffs were considerably higher than in West Germany. Second, we see that average tariff rates for UK manufacturing were still as high in the early 1960s as they had been in the 1930s. Third, a measure of trade costs relating to UK-France and UK-Germany trade flows is seen to have remained above the 1929 level until the 1970s. The 1970s fall in trade costs was driven by trade liberalisation; had this taken place earlier, for example, through accession to the EEC at the Treaty of Rome, trade costs could have been below the 1929 level much earlier.

Table 11.6 British export markets, 1830–1990

A Briish Empire share of British exports of home products

Year	*%*
1830	26.1
1840	32.3
1850	27.2
1860	32.1
1870	26.0
1880	33.7
1890	33.1
1900	32.4
1913	37.2
1925	39.6
1929	41.5
1931	38.8
1932	41.1
1933	41.2
1934	44.0

B Shares of British exports to "British Countries" and EEC6 (%)

Year	*British countries*	*EEC6*
1907	32.2	24.8
1912	36.0	22.7
1924	42.1	18.7
1930	43.5	18.3
1935	48.0	14.7
1948	52.7	9.8
1951	55.0	10.4
1954	53.0	13.0
1958	49.3	13.1
1963	37.5	20.3
1968	31.2	19.3
1970	25.1	21.7
1980	20.1	34.6
1990	16.7	41.3

Sources: Part A: Schlote (1952: Table 22); Part B: *Annual Statement of the Trade of the United Kingdom*, London: HMSO.

Notes
Part A: Old area of trade statistics after 1925 (i.e. United Kingdom of Great Britain and Ireland); Part B: "British Countries" includes the Irish Free State/Republic and the Republic of South Africa, as well as the Commonwealth.

Table 11.7 Indicators of protectionism in post-war United Kingdom

A Average tariff rates on UK manufactures (%)

1932	13.2
1935	14.7
1960	14.5
1963	12.8
1968	11.2

B Tariff rates for UK and West German manufacturing, 1958 (%)

	United Kingdom	*West Germany*
Chemicals	15	8
Leather	16	12
Rubber	21	10
Wood	15	7
Paper	13	8
Textiles	23	11
Non-Metallic Minerals	17	6
Iron & Steel	14	7
Non-Electrical Machinery	17	5
Electrical Machinery	23	6
Transport Equipment	25	12
Clothing	26	13
Instruments	27	8

C Trade Costs Index

Year	*UK–France*	*UK–Germany*
1929	100	99
1938	121	122
1950	122	142
1960	122	115
1970	110	105
1980	74	66

Sources: A Kitson and Solomou (1990), Morgan and Martin (1975); B Political and Economic Planning (1962); C Data underlying Jacks, Meissuer and Nory (2009) kindly provided by Dennis Novy.

Note
Trade costs are inferred from estimates of gravity equations and incorporate the impact of all barriers to trade including tariffs, non-tariff barriers, transport costs, communication costs, etc.

11.4 Free-trade Britain, 1870–1914

Before 1914, Britain's continued commitment to openness despite growing restrictions abroad had beneficial effects on aggregate productivity performance through the shift of resources out of low-value-added agriculture and high productivity in Britain's cosmopolitan commercial and financial service sectors. These factors are rarely given sufficient weight in the literature on British growth, which focuses on the difficulties faced by British industry as a result of tariffs faced in foreign markets and dumping by foreign producers in the British market. This section will consider in turn the situation in industry, agriculture and services before turning to an aggregate perspective.

11.4.1 Industry

The disadvantage faced by British industry in foreign markets on the eve of the First World War is easily demonstrated in Table 11.8. Part A shows *ad valorem* tariff rates on a number of British exports in 1903. The countries are listed in descending order of the degree of protection, as measured by the weighted average tariff rate across 31 commodities, using British export weights. The average tariff faced by British industrial exporters ranged from 131 per cent in Russia to 3 per cent in the Netherlands. Part B is taken from Grunzel's (1916) study of tariffs on a multilateral basis in 1913, with tariffs presented in terms of German marks per hundred kilograms. An average of tariffs on this basis would not be meaningful, but it is clear from the ordering of countries for individual commodities that the averages in Part A, based on British export prices and values, do indeed broadly reflect the multilateral situation. The United States was clearly a country with very high industrial tariffs, Germany was moderately protective and Britain was a free-trade country. Notice also from Part B that Germany had a high tariff on wheat, the key agricultural product, a theme that will be taken up in the next section.

11.4.2 Agriculture

Although the fact that free traders in nineteenth-century Britain pointed to the benefit to consumers of cheap grain prices arising from free trade in corn has been widely noted, the implications for productivity in domestic agriculture have not really been spelled out (Imlah, 1958: 145–146). In Britain, the main impact of the grain invasion from the New World was a shift of the product mix away from grain towards higher-value-added pastoral products, coupled with higher capital intensity in what remained of the British arable farming sector (Brown, 1987: 25–26, 33; Ó Gráda, 1994: 149–156). As a result, the high levels of labour productivity that already characterised British agriculture during the Industrial Revolution were raised still further, and the relatively small British agricultural sector continued to achieve output per worker levels on a par with the United States before the First World War. The highest levels of labour productivity were recorded in the parts of the New World concentrating on pastoral products, especially Australia, New Zealand and Argentina (Rostas, 1948: 80). In much of Continental Europe, however, the response to the grain invasion from the New World was an intensification of agricultural protection from the 1870s to the First World War (Bairoch, 1989: 51–69). With grain prices maintained artificially high by tariff barriers, low productivity Continental farmers were able to remain in business. Given the weight of agriculture in overall economic activity at the time, this had important consequences for aggregate productivity performance which lasted well into the post-Second World War period.

11.4.3 Services

One of the outstanding features of the period between the mid-nineteenth century and the First World War was the emergence of Britain as the centre of the world system of trade and payments. As a result, Britain's cosmopolitan service sector generated around a quarter of total exports between 1870 and 1913, as can be seen in Table 11.4. The major service sectors generating exports were transport and communications (particularly shipping), distribution (particularly wholesale merchanting) and financial services (particularly insurance and merchant banking). Imlah (1958: 70–75) provides figures on the net credits generated by these three sectors, which made a substantial contribution to the current account of the balance of payments, fluctuating between about 7 and 9 per cent of GDP. For Germany, by contrast, the much smaller and less productive service sector generated a net surplus on the current account of 2 to 3 per cent of GDP.[3]

The openness and cosmopolitanism of the British service sector has nevertheless been seen traditionally as a problem in much of the literature on British economic growth, which is heavily oriented towards manufacturing. Perhaps the most obvious manifestation of this view is the claim that the domestic manufacturing industry was starved of capital as a result of cosmopolitan financiers based in the City of London directing British savings overseas (Best and Humphries, 1986; Kennedy, 1987). While Collins (1990, 1998) provides many reasons to be sceptical of this view, we note here two points which have received insufficient attention in the literature. First, value added per employee was relatively high in financial services, so that Britain's large and specialised financial service sector made a positive direct contribution to Britain's overall productivity position. Second, the marketed services sector including finance was the one in which Britain's productivity relative to Germany and the United States was strongest in the period leading up to the First World War (Broadberry, 2006: 37, 48).

11.4.4 An aggregate perspective

A number of writers have pointed to a systematic negative relationship between openness and growth in this period (Bairoch, 1989; O'Rourke, 2000; Jacks, 2006) although this remains open to question depending on the methodology and sample used (Schularick and Solomou, 2009; Tena-Junguito, 2009). This might seem to indicate that the UK would have been well served by discarding free-trade policies in favour of the protection that was the norm in Continental Europe.

There are, however, a number of reasons to be sceptical of making this inference. First, a closer analysis suggests that, at best, it is only tariffs on manufacturing and not on agriculture that are correlated with growth (Lehmann and O'Rourke, 2008) yet the politics of protectionism in Europe was based on coalitions that protected both sectors. In Germany, agriculture was much more heavily protected than manufacturing with tariff revenue relative to imports at 12 per cent (UK = 1 per cent) compared with 5 per cent (UK = 3 per cent).

Table 11.8 Tariff rates on the eve of World War I

A *Ad valorem* tariff rates on Britain's exports in 1903 (%)

Country	*Average of 31 goods*	*Cotton yarn grey*	*Cotton fabric unbleached*	*Cotton fabric printed*	*Pig iron*	*Tin plate*	*Leather shoes*	*Caustic soda*
Russia	131	70	207	246	91	110	171	101
Spain	76	62	145	124	25	58	119	16
United States	73	48	72	88	26	50	25	36
Austria-Hungary	35	14	49	51	19	35	22	27
France	34	14	49	51	19	35	22	27
Italy	27	14	34	52	13	47	14	8
Germany	25	9	43	49	16	18	11	21
Sweden	23	9	30	50	Free	Free	38	Free
Denmark	18	7	15	60	Free	17	25	Free
Belgium	13	6	28	27	3	Free	10	Free
Norway	12	6	12	50	Free	Free	33	Free
Japan	9	7	7	11	4	9	20	11
Switzerland	7	3	4	13	1	9	5	1
Netherlands	3	Free	5	5	Free	Free	5	Free

B Multilateral tariffs in 1913, selected commodities (German marks per hundred kilograms)

Country	*Wheat*	*Cotton yarn*	*Cotton fabric unbleached*	*Cotton fabric printed*	*Laces*	*Bar iron*	*Sheet iron*	*Sewing needles*
Russia	Free	108.13	1,161.00	1,404.0	2,539.0	9.89	13.85	641.20
Spain	6.50	140.00	352.35	290.70	1,093.5	5.18	6.48	243.00
United States	3.95	67.20	51.87	103.74	45%	2.78	5.56	25%
Austria-Hungary	5.35	28.05	–	121.55	561.00	4.25	8.50	144.50
France	5.66	14.99	86.67	152.28	405.00	6.07	10.93	205.50
Italy	6.08	26.73	63.18	129.68	405.00	4.86	9.72	64.80
Germany	5.50	18.00	70.00	120.00	350.00	1.00	4.50	100.00
Sweden	4.16	22.50	56.25	123.75	450.00	Free	4.50	45.00
Denmark	Free	7.04	56.80	151.68	227.50	1.17	1.17	75.00
Belgium	Free	12.15	64.80	81.00	15%	0.81	0.81	13%
Norway	4.86	13.50	28.13	123.75	674.50	Free	Free	84.38
Japan	2.68	22.28	62.70	87.14	69.60	2.09	2.61	175.89
Switzerland	0.24	16.20	8.10	48.60	81.00	0.24	0.49	40.50
Netherlands	Free	Free	5%	5%	5%	5%	5%	5%
Great Britain	Free	Free	Free	Free	Free	Free	Free	free

Sources: A *British and Foreign Trade and Industrial Conditions*; B Grunzel (1916: 155–158).

Notes

A Average calculated using British export weights; B Percentage values refer to *ad valorem* rates.

Second, the case for protecting manufacturing was surely strongest in a context of infant industries and capital market failure. This does not fit well with the UK at this time (Michie, 1988) and, as noted above, Britain was not in fact falling behind in terms of manufacturing labour productivity before the First World War. The long-standing transatlantic labour productivity gap in manufacturing was stationary between 1870 and 1913 and no other European country was substantially ahead of Britain by 1913 (Broadberry, 1997a: 52–57). In any event, the tariff proposals that were made by Chamberlain would have tended to divert activity toward traditional sectors such as agriculture and textiles rather than new growth industries (Thomas, 1984) and tariff protection was irrelevant to the services sector which was the locus of American out-performance in productivity growth (Irwin, 2001).

Third, and most important, the long-run effects of free trade on the level of income in the UK are likely to have been substantial and positive. In the recent past the strongest evidence of a positive effect of openness on the level of income was provided by Frankel and Romer (1999), later confirmed by Feyrer (2009) in a paper which deals very well with the identification problem. Jacks (2006) found that similar but rather stronger results are also obtained for the nineteenth century. Table 11.9 reports the implications of this analysis for the UK compared with Germany, namely, that the much lower trade exposure of Germany resulting from the protectionist coalition implied a substantial income loss.

These results make sense in the context of Anglo-German productivity comparisons. As noted in Broadberry (1997c), Germany had caught up with Britain in all industrial sectors before the First World War, but German aggregate labour productivity nevertheless remained at about three-quarters of the British level. This can be explained in part by low productivity in German services, but agriculture played a more important part since: (1) the productivity gap was larger in agriculture than in services; (2) agriculture accounted for a larger share of employment than services; (3) value added per employee was lower in agriculture than in services. Openness promoted a shift out of agriculture into higher value-added services in the UK; protection obstructed this in Germany.

Table 11.9 Income gains from greater trade exposure: UK vs. Germany (% GDP)

1890	+17.0
1913	+10.6

Sources: as for Table 11.4.

Note

Trade exposure is defined as (exports + imports)/GDP and the assumed elasticity of GDP to trade exposure is 0.3; this is conservative compared with the estimates in Jacks (2006) but in line with the wider literature.

11.5 Protection and imperial preference, 1914–50

Once again, the conventional analysis focuses on industry and neglects the implications for agriculture and services. Protectionism was accompanied by a policy of imperial preference, which had a significant impact on the geographical orientation of British business activity, in services as well as in industry. This was to create difficulties of adjustment when the world economy reintegrated after the Second World War. As for the pre-1914 period, it will be useful to consider industry, agriculture and services in turn.

11.5.1 Industry

Kitson and Solomou (1990) accept the conventional view that protectionism was bad for the world economy as a whole between the wars, but make the more limited claim that the British adoption of a general tariff in 1932 was a second-best policy given the extent of protectionism abroad. One issue concerns the impact of the tariff on the level of economic activity. A cyclical recovery would be expected to have had beneficial effects on productivity in the short run, since employment lagged behind output in the economic cycle.[4] However, the more striking claim made by Kitson and Solomou (1990: 10–16) is that the tariff caused an increase in the trend rate of growth. An obvious difficulty with this argument can be seen in Table 11.10; growth of GDP was faster during the 1920s than during the 1930s.[5] Even if attention is confined to industrial production, the acceleration of growth in the 1930s is surely insufficient to warrant claims of a change in trend. However, Kitson and Solomou (1990: 12) argue that the high growth of the 1920s was just a cyclical phenomenon bringing the economy back to the trend for the period 1899–1929. So although actual growth did not increase during the 1930s relative to the 1920s, Kitson and Solomou nevertheless see an increase in trend growth during the 1930s relative to the trend for the longer period 1899–1929. This can be seen in Table 11.10 for compromise GDP as well as for industrial production. However, the argument is obviously highly dependent on the periodisation imposed on the data. If a break in trend is tested for rather than imposed, the Kitson and Solomou claim is easily rejected. For industrial production over the period 1879–1938, Greasley and Oxley (1996) find a break in trend at 1920 and crashes at 1914 and 1920, but reject a break in trend at 1929. For GDP, Mills (1991) finds a major regime shift only after the deep recession of 1921.

Table 11.10 UK growth rates, 1899–1937 (% per annum)

Period	*Compromise GDP*	*Industrial production*
1899–1929	1.00	1.54
1924–1929	2.57	2.93
1929–1937	1.96	3.28

Source: Derived from Feinstein (1972, tables 6 and 8).

Was the interwar tariff good for productivity performance in British manufacturing? Kitson and Solomou (1990) suggest that it was, at least in the short term, and they report that labour productivity growth in industries that were newly protected in 1932 showed an increase of 2.28 percentage points in 1930–35 relative to 1924–30 compared with 0.03 percentage points in the non-newly protected industries.

Table 11.11 revisits this analysis. We look at a three-way division of industries into those which were protected before 1932 through the McKenna and Key Industry duties, industries which received a new tariff of at least 20 per cent under the 1932 Import Duties Act, and industries which either received no protection or the general *ad valorem* duty of 10 per cent (and were generally not exposed to import competition) based on the information given in Hutchinson (1965) and Sebag-Montefiore (1943). We also consider longer-run differences in productivity growth by comparing 1935–48 with 1924–35 since this is likely to reveal any adverse effects of reduced competition on managerial incentives to control costs.

The results in Table 11.11 show that granting additional protection in 1932 had a positive but statistically insignificant effect on productivity growth in the short run and a negligible impact in the longer run. Interestingly, the difference in productivity growth for 1935–48 compared with 1924–35 is significantly negative for industries that had experienced a prolonged period of protection, suggesting that they may have been in the comfort zone for too long. Contrary to Kitson and Solomou (1990), there is nothing here to suggest that protection was a policy conducive to improved productivity performance.

Table 11.11 Differences in labour productivity growth, 1924–48

A Mean (standard deviation) labour productivity growth (per cent per year)

Period	*Early protected* ($N = 15$)	*Additional duties* ($N = 42$)	*Others* ($N = 33$)
1924–30	4.247 (2.576)	0.669 (2.030)	1.752 (2.771)
1930–35	4.008 (4.903)	2.722 (2.181)	2.485 (2.821)
1924–35	4.117 (2.614)	1.596 (1.343)	2.066 (1.913)
1935–48	0.891 (1.740)	0.477 (1.419)	0.838 (2.066)

B Difference-in-difference analysis

1930/35 – 1924/30 =	0.733	+	1.321 Additional	–	0.974 Early
	(1.026)		(1.384)		(–0.762)
1935/48 – 1924/35 =	–1.228	+	0.109 Additional	–	1.843 Early
	(–2.993)		(0.200)		(–2.510)

Note

Labour productivity growth calculated from Census of Production and Brown (1954). Early protected industries were silk and artificial silk, glove, chemicals, petroleum, explosives and fireworks, match, rubber, scientific instruments, musical instruments, incandescent mantles, cinematograph and film products, hardware and holloware, cutlery, motor and cycle, watch and clock.

11.5.2 Agriculture

It is worth noting that the strategic justification for protecting agriculture in peacetime so as to secure food supplies during war did not prove to be of much value during the twentieth century. As Olson (1963: 138–140) notes, it was Germany rather than Britain that succumbed to blockade during the First World War. Olson (1963: 138–139) points to the ability of the British agricultural sector to expand output on the stored-up fertility of grasslands brought back into arable use compared with the inability of German agriculture to maintain output at full stretch in the face of wartime disruption. However, Olson (1963: 146) also stresses the flexibility of the British service sector through administration as well as distribution as the decisive factor.

One factor behind the increase of arable output in Britain during the First World War was a system of guaranteed minimum prices set under the Corn Production Act of 1917. If market prices fell below the minimum for the following six years, farmers were to receive deficiency payments equal to the difference between the market and minimum prices on the volume of output that they produced (Whetham, 1978: 94–95). The system was extended for an indefinite term in the Agriculture Act of 1920, but when agricultural prices suddenly collapsed the legislation was hastily repealed in 1921 in what became known in farming circles as the "Great Betrayal" (Whetham, 1978: 139–141). Apart from a system of beet sugar subsidies introduced in 1924, there were few measures to protect agriculture during the 1920s, which continued to be a difficult time for British farmers, particularly arable producers. During the 1930s, however, a wider range of protective measures was introduced as prices collapsed still further. Although tariffs and quotas were used in some cases, support for agriculture generally took the form of subsidies and marketing schemes. This was partly as a result of government desires to keep food prices low, but it also reflected the policy of imperial preference. If Britain was to obtain access to Empire markets for industrial exports, then Empire farmers had to have access to the British market for agricultural produce. Hence Brown (1987: 118) sees protection as a great disappointment to British farmers.

As during the First World War, Britain was able to survive blockade by Germany during the Second World War (Olson, 1963: 140). During the later 1930s, as the prospect of war approached, the government made preparations for the expansion of agricultural output, and this was achieved much more rapidly during the Second World War than during the First World War (Brown, 1987: 125–146). Again, it was the possibility of expansion on the grasslands combined with the flexibility of the British service sector that proved decisive (Olson, 1963: 146).

11.5.3 Services

Most accounts of interwar British economic history emphasise the detrimental effects of the return to the gold standard at the pre-war parity in 1925. The openness and outward orientation of the financial services sector is usually seen as the driving force behind this decision, while industry is seen as bearing the costs of the overvalued exchange rate that resulted. The costs of the overvalued exchange rate have been the subject of much debate, with a number of studies attempting a quantitative evaluation (Moggridge, 1972; Broadberry, 1986). However, the benefits for productivity of an outward-oriented service sector are not usually considered in such studies; this gives the literature a bias towards industry. However, as we have seen in Table 11.1, it is the loss of productivity leadership in services that mirrors most closely Britain's overall loss of productivity leadership.

An important motivating factor behind the return to gold was a widespread belief in the City that Britain's prosperity depended on resurrecting the pre-war liberal international financial and trading systems (Pollard, 1970). The downward spiral following the onset of the Great Depression in 1929 clearly put an end to such hopes, but there were sufficient signs of a revival in the commercial bill acceptance market and new capital issues during the 1920s to suggest that such hopes were not completely without foundation (Ellinger, 1940: 374; Balogh, 1947: 249–250; Broadberry, 2006: 268–272). Furthermore, it is clear that the collapse of the liberal world economic order had a much greater negative impact on the highly globalised British economy than on either the domestically oriented US economy or the more highly protectionist German economy of the pre-1914 period. The response of the British economy to these events was a growing integration within the British Empire, which although possibly beneficial in the short run, created long-run costs of adjustment.

It should be stressed that the above argument is not intended to deny the costs imposed by the exchange rate overvaluation, which arose from a perception that the influence of the City of London would be best maintained by a return to gold at pre-war parity. However, it does suggest that *ex ante* there was also a positive side to the balance sheet, which should not be neglected. Had the return to gold been part of a successful re-establishment of a globalised world economy rather than the precursor of a globalisation backlash, Britain would have gained from expansion of its internationally oriented market services.

11.5.4 The legacy of interwar protectionism

It is important to recognise that the protectionist 1930s cast a long shadow over the post-war period in Britain. Oulton (1976: 81) claimed that "the schedule of effective tariffs in the 1960s can therefore be regarded as largely the product of the economic, social and political stresses of the First World War and the great depression" given the similarity with the 1930s. This is perhaps an overstatement but there is quite a high correlation, as Table 11.12 reveals; only in the 1970s does this evaporate completely. Clearly, once put in place, the political economy of protectionism generates persistence.

This had unfortunate implications for productivity performance through the impact that protectionism had in sustaining market power. Price-cost margins

Table 11.12 Effective protection rates, 1932, 1968, 1979 (per cent)

	1932	*1968*	*1979*
Building materials	32.0	13.7	0.2
China, glass	22.5	18.5	0.0
Coke ovens	–2.5	–7.2	–0.2
Chemicals	41.8	33.3	2.2
Soap and polishes	26.3	–0.3	–1.8
Oils and paints	16.5	–10.1/16.6	4.1
Iron and steel	34.0	32.5	2.7
Non-Ferrous metals	25.6	–3.5	0.5
Shipbuilding	–14.0	–2.4/–1.3	
Mechanical engineering	14.4	11.6	4.5
Electrical engineering	18.2	44.3	0.8
Motor and cycle	41.2	36.3	3.3
Aircraft	–7.4	–3.3	–1.0
Railway rolling stock	43.1	7.9/44.5	–0.9
Metal goods	8.7	4.7	3.0
Cotton and silk textiles	10.3	4.3	6.2
Woollen and worsted	8.8	5.9	3.5
Hosiery and lace	42.9	14.0	21.4
Other textiles	9.2	0.3	–0.8
Textile finishing	–9.6	–7.1	13.0
Leather and fur	22.1	3.6	51.1
Clothing	21.0	1.1	15.6
Food processing	26.8	–1.9	3.4
Drink and tobacco	–11.3	–6.4	6.2
Timber products	24.4	–4.5	4.4
Paper	20.1	24.0	7.7
Printing and publishing	–4.3	0.6	4.3
Rubber	13.3	8.0	1.0
Miscellaneous manufactures	22.8	33.9	12.3
Mean	17.1	8.7/10.8	5.7

Source: based on Kitson, Soloman and Weale (1991), Oulton (1976) and Greenaway (1988).

Note
Alternative estimate for oils & paints from Kitchin (1976); alternative estimate for railway rolling stock is for 1963 from Kitchin (1976).
Regression based on Oulton's estimates for 1968 gives

$$\text{ERP1968} = \underset{(0.028)}{0.098} + \underset{(3.424)}{0.501}\text{ERP1932} \quad R^2 = 0.28$$

were very high in post-war British manufacturing until the trade liberalisation of the 1970s (see Chapter 12). There is clear evidence that in the early post-war period the weakness of competition contributed to productivity problems and relative economic decline (Broadberry and Crafts, 1996; Symeonidis, 2008). This is to be expected given that UK firms were exceptionally prone to problems arising from the separation of ownership and control to which greater competition could have been an important antidote. Not surprisingly, Proudman and Redding (1998) found that openness and productivity growth were positively correlated across manufacturing sectors after 1970.

Kitson and Solomou (1990) stop their analysis at the end of the 1930s, but note in the very brief conclusion to their book that the tariff may have prevented the necessary structural change that would have accelerated economic growth after the Second World War. Quite so. The same may be said of the policy of imperial preference. We have already seen in Table 11.6 that by the end of the Second World War more than half of Britain's exports were going to Empire markets, and for some industries the Empire share of Britain's exports was more than three-quarters.[6] This may be seen as helping to maintain the level of economic activity in the short run, but creating problems of adjustment in the long run.

The trans-Second World War period saw an increase in the share of the labour force employed in agriculture and industry, which went against the trend since the mid-nineteenth century. Within the context of a controlled economy, both capital and labour inputs were directed into manufacturing, mining and agriculture on strategic grounds. Yet, as Matthews, Feinstein and Odling-Smee (1982: 235–236) point out, the increase in total factor input growth was offset by a decrease in TFP growth, suggesting a tendency to diminishing returns.

11.6 Britain in the world economy, 1950–2000

Protection for industry and agriculture continued after the Second World War. The proportion of the labour force in manufacturing continued to rise until 1960, as post-war governments sought to encourage exports and avoid balance of payments problems while maintaining a fixed exchange rate (Matthews, Feinstein and Odling-Smee, 1982: 221). Many restrictions on openness, including quotas, tariffs and exchange controls, were needed to maintain external equilibrium with the over-expanded agricultural and industrial sectors (Foreman-Peck, 1991).

As the world economy reintegrated on a liberal basis, particularly from about 1960, British industry faced major problems of adjustment. As well as an inevitable reduction in the share of the labour force devoted to industry, there were adjustment costs in switching from Commonwealth to European markets. However, the process of adjustment has had benefits as well as costs. As productivity growth in manufacturing accelerated during the 1980s, and as output and employment expanded rapidly in services, the long period of British relative economic decline came to an end. Furthermore, as the European economy became more integrated, economies of scale and standardisation helped to reduce the transatlantic productivity gaps in industry and services. Although agricultural protection has remained high under the Common Agricultural Policy, with adverse consequences for food prices, agriculture is now too small a part of the economy for this to have a major impact on productivity in the economy as a whole.

11.6.1 Industry

Matthews, Feinstein and Odling-Smee (1982: 235–236) point to the slowing down of TFP growth despite the increase in the growth of total factor input during the trans-Second World War period as evidence of diminishing returns in manufacturing. Similarly, in mineral extraction, TFP growth became negative as the movement of inputs out of the sector slowed down. It is perhaps not surprising, then, that during the early post-war period the over-extended manufacturing and mineral extraction sectors required protection. In the coal industry, import licences were granted only to the state-owned National Coal Board for use at times when home production fell short of demand (Ashworth, 1986: 47). In addition, the coal industry received substantial financial support while its major customers, the electricity supply and gas industries, were required to burn more coal than warranted by purely economic considerations (Buxton, 1978: 239). In manufacturing, the early post-war period was characterised by the widespread use of import quotas, while the rationing of key inputs such as steel helped to direct resources towards export industries (Dow, 1965: 153–162; Foreman-Peck, 1991: 159–160). As controls were removed in line with a return to a more liberal world trading environment, the British economy continually ran into balance of payments problems. In 1964 the incoming Labour government imposed a surcharge on manufactured imports in an ultimately unsuccessful attempt to avoid devaluation (Foreman-Peck, 1991: 161). They also imposed a selective employment tax (SET) to encourage labour into industrial rather than service sector employment (Cairncross, 1992: 158–159).

British industry faced additional difficulties during the early post-war period arising from the legacy of imperial preference policies adopted between the wars. Just when investment in marketing and after-sales service was becoming more important, British industry found itself oriented towards distant markets in which Britain had secured a strong position only through preferential treatment. Sometimes, the preferential treatment was rapidly withdrawn after the Second World War. In the motor vehicle industry, for example, high tariffs in Australia effectively closed off Britain's most important interwar market, while exchange controls made it difficult to invest in adequate marketing and after-sales service in Continental Europe (Whisler, 1994: 5). Since spare parts were not included in export quotas, serious damage was done to the reputation of British cars in this important market (Dunnett, 1980: 37). In Table 11.6 we see that during the 1960s there was a dramatic decline in the share of British exports going to Commonwealth markets, which were overtaken in importance by the EEC during the 1970s.

The decision to join the EEC in 1973 together with the Kennedy Round of the GATT accelerated the process of increasing openness. However, as the process of de-industrialisation also threatened to accelerate during the 1970s, governments continued to protect industry through industrial policies that effectively subsidised "lame ducks" (Millward, 1994: 163–165). The evidence regarding these interventionist policies is that they slowed down much-needed structural adjustment. The picture is that "it was losers like Rolls Royce, British Leyland and Alfred Herbert who picked ministers ... What was described as 'picking winners' appeared in practice to amount to spending large sums shoring up ailing companies" (Morris and Stout, 1985: 873).

This policy changed under the Conservative governments of the 1980s, with dramatic effects on both the size of the industrial sector and its productivity performance. As employment in manufacturing shrank by about 2 million between 1979 and 1989, labour productivity growth accelerated to 4.2 per cent per annum after stagnating at 0.7 per cent per annum during the previous cycle, 1973–79 (Broadberry, 2004). Table 11.13 shows the dramatic turnaround of British productivity performance relative to Germany in a number of industries, notably aerospace, iron and steel, and motor vehicles, the last two of which had seen heavy protection removed during the 1970s. More generally, a difference-in-differences analysis of productivity growth before and after 1979, reported in Table 11.14, suggests that the removal of such protection had a favourable impact on productivity performance.

Table 11.13 Comparative Germany/UK labour productivity levels in manufacturing (UK = 100)

	1973	*1979*	*1989*
Chemicals	103.3	127.6	102.5
Mineral oil refining	88.2	122.5	107.7
Plastic products	117.3	126.4	109.7
Rubber products	124.5	140.3	103.5
Mineral products	84.1	106.4	90.9
Ceramic goods	131.5	130.6	12.5
Glass	99.9	129.5	117.7
Iron and steel	124.8	263.4	88.9
Non-ferrous metals	80.5	119.9	112.7
Plant and steelwork	123.7	125.0	124.9
Mechanical engineering	125.9	141.9	123.7
Office machinery	100.7	107.6	86.6
Motor vehicles	148.5	186.0	123.7
Shipbuilding	144.6	143.7	105.3
Aerospace	131.2	200.4	100.9
Electrical engineering	83.5	101.9	97.6
Instrument engineering	180.5	171.6	143.6
Finished metal products	130.0	132.1	127.1
Toys, sport and musical instruments	115.4	131.8	130.4
Timber and board	95.3	110.9	105.1
Wood products	176.4	178.4	150.1
Paper and board	147.9	215.1	160.2
Paper products	164.9	174.4	169.1
Printing and publishing	158.5	189.3	145.3
Leather and footwear	93.3	84.9	104.8
Textiles	88.3	110.8	100.6
Clothing	133.5	123.5	124.2
Food	101.5	125.3	112.9
Drink	59.3	59.3	83.0
Tobacco	42.1	68.7	59.5
Total manufacturing	119.4	140.0	116.5

Source: O'Mahony and Wagner (1994: 7).

Note
Labour productivity measured as value added per hour worked.

Table 11.14 Differences in labour productivity growth, 1968–86

A Mean (standard deviation) labour productivity growth (% per year)

	Protection removed ($N = 25$)	*Others* ($N = 43$)
1968–79	2.819 (1.801)	3.569 (1.766)
1979–86	4.908 (3.174)	4.252 (2.325)

B Difference-in-difference analysis

1979/86 – 1968/79	=	0.692	+	0.397 Protection removed
		(1.381)		(1.690)

Source: Labour productivity growth from Oulton and O'Mahony (1994).

Note

Protection removed is a dummy variable based on a decrease of 10 percentage points in the effective rate of protection between 1968 and 1979 in either or both comparisons of estimates for 1968 from Kitchin (1976) and Oulton (1976) with those for 1979 in Greenaway (1988). These sectors are SIC 273, 274, 278, 279, 311, 313, 331, 332, 335, 336/7, 338, 361, 362, 363/4, 368, 369, 381, 390, 395, 411, 461, 462/3, 472/3, 484, 499

11.6.2 Agriculture

Whereas the encouragement of agricultural production during the First World War was followed by the virtual elimination of support during the "Great Betrayal" of 1921, the Second World War was followed by the reinforcement of support in the 1947 Agriculture Act (Holderness, 1985: 12–13). However, the British system of agricultural protection did not involve the sacrifice of low food prices for consumers. Building on the pre-war schemes, farmers received deficiency payments when market prices fell below guaranteed prices. This was less damaging than the variable levy system, which raises the price to consumers as well as producers (El-Agraa, 1994: 212–214). However, Britain adopted the Common Agricultural Policy of the EEC in 1973, based upon the variable levy system. The scale of support for agriculture during the 1970s and 1980s was considerable, and this can be seen in the return of Britain to self-sufficiency in many agricultural products. Even in wheat, where imports accounted for 77 per cent of consumption in 1936–39, imports had fallen to 23 per cent of consumption by 1980–81 (Holderness, 1985: 174). Nevertheless, agriculture is now such a small part of the economy that its impact on the overall level of productivity is relatively insignificant.

11.6.3 Services

As during the interwar period, the outward orientation of the financial service sector has often been seen as a disadvantage during the post-war period. Pollard (1984: 85–88) argues that during the Bretton Woods era, the desire to retain an international role for sterling led to an overvalued exchange rate, which undermined the competitiveness of British industry. This echoes his views on the interwar period, where he emphasises the costs to industry of the return to gold in 1925 at pre-war parity, but ignores the importance of high productivity in services for Britain's overall productivity performance. In fact, international financial services is one of the few sectors where Britain has retained a strong competitive position (Smith, 1992). In many other parts of the service sector Britain's performance has been undistinguished, and it is the deterioration of comparative productivity performance in services that accounts for much of Britain's relative economic decline overall. Since large parts of the service sector have been relatively closed to international competition, it is likely that, contrary to the Pollard view, it is the sheltered nature of much of the service sector rather than the openness of international financial services that has been damaging for overall productivity performance.

1.6.4 Reversing relative economic decline

From a low point at the end of the 1970s, relative British economic performance has recovered. By 2007, on the eve of the financial crisis, real GDP per person was about 9 per cent ahead of that in the West German *Länder* and 4 per cent ahead of France compared with 14 per cent and 12 per cent behind, respectively, in 1979. A long period of relative economic decline with Continental Europe had come to an end.

The evidence suggests that this has been the outcome of a move towards an economy based less on protection and regulation and more on competition than in the decades from the 1950s through the 1970s. In addition, labour market policies have been conducive to higher levels of employment. In complete contrast to the early post-war period, the UK has become an economy with relatively low levels of regulation and relatively strong competition by OECD standards (Conway and Nicoletti, 2006; Hoj *et al.*, 2007). This has been a favourable environment in which to exploit the ICT-era opportunities of new technology especially in market services (Nicoletti and Scarpetta, 2005).

11.7 Concluding comments

This chapter provides a quantitative economic analysis of the links between openness and productivity performance in Britain between 1870 and 1990, paying particular attention to sectoral issues and focusing on three sub-periods. (1) Before 1914, Britain's continued commitment to openness despite growing restrictions abroad had beneficial effects on aggregate productivity performance through the shift of resources out of low-value-added agriculture and high productivity in Britain's cosmopolitan commercial and financial service sectors. These factors are rarely given sufficient weight in the literature on British growth, which focuses on the difficulties faced by British industry as a result of tariffs faced in foreign markets and dumping by foreign producers in the British market. (2) Between the wars, given the drift into autarky in much of the world, the policies of protection and imperial preference can be seen as raising the level of domestic activity, with beneficial cyclical effects on industrial productivity in the short run. However, claims of a shift in the trend rate of growth cannot be sustained. As for the pre-First World War period, conventional analysis concentrates on industry and neglects the implications of the trade regime for agriculture and services. (3) Within the controlled wartime British economy, industry and agriculture were expanded on strategic grounds, and the expansion continued during the early post-war period for balance of payments reasons. As the world economy reintegrated on a liberal basis, however, some de-industrialisation was inevitable. The adjustment problems of industry were compounded by a need to switch from Commonwealth to European markets. However, the process of adjustment, which accelerated with the increased openness of the 1980s, has had benefits as well as costs. Dramatic improvements in Britain's industrial productivity performance and rapid expansion of output as well as employment in services have brought the long period of British relative economic decline to an end.

Acknowledgements

Stephen Broadberry gratefully acknowledges the support afforded by a period of secondment to the Centre for the Study of Globalisation and Regionalisation at the University of Warwick. Thanks also to Douglas Irwin, Andrew Marrison and Solomos Solomou for comments on an earlier draft and to Dennis Novy and Kevin O'Rourke for generously supplying us with their data.

Notes

1 Conventional shift-share analysis fails to capture the importance of structural change because it is based on the assumption that the high rates of productivity growth in the shrinking agricultural sector would still have been achieved even if labour had not left the sector. See Broadberry (1998) for an alternative calculation.

2 The share of capital declines from 0.4 before the First World War to 0.25 after the Second World War. These shares are derived from Kendrick (1961), Hoffmann (1965) and Matthews, Feinstein and Odling-Smee (1982).

3 Figures from Hoffmann (1965: 817, 825–826).

4 Although the direction of the effect is not in dispute, it is likely that Kitson and Solomou (1990) overstate its magnitude. Since the tariff was imposed after Britain left the gold standard, any improvement in the balance of trade brought about by the tariff may be expected to have caused exchange rate appreciation, offsetting the competitive gain from the tariff (Broadberry, 1986: 132–138).

5 Kitson and Solomou (1990: 11) report figures for 1925–29 rather than the conventional peak-to-peak period 1924–29; this has the effect of showing the growth rate of compromise GDP at 2.0 per cent per annum during both the 1920s and the 1930s. The explanation given for the unconventional choice of dates is that "1924 is far too close to the 1921 depression to be regarded as a peak year in economic activity" (Kitson and Solomou, 1990: 11).

6 In 1948, this was the case for fertilisers, cotton cloth, hosiery, carpets, tobacco and glass.

References

Official sources

United Kingdom

Annual Abstract of Statistics, Central Statistical Office.
Annual Statement of the Trade of the United Kingdom, HM Customs and Excise.
British and Foreign Trade and Industrial Conditions, Board of Trade.
Economic Trends Annual Supplement, Central Statistical Office.
National Income and Expenditure, Central Statistical Office.
Statistical Abstract for the United Kingdom, Board of Trade.

United States

Historical Statistics of the United States: Colonial Times to 1970, Department of Commerce, 1975.
National Income and Product Accounts of the United States, Vol. 1, 1929–58, Vol 2. 1959–88, Department of Commerce, 1993.
Statistical Abstract of the United States, Department of Commerce.

Germany

Statistisches Jahrbuch für die Bundesrepublik Deutschland, Statistisches Bundesamt.
Volkswirtschaftliche Gesamtrechnungen 1950 bis 1990, Fachserie 18, Reihe S.15, Statistisches Bundesamt, 1991.

Books and articles

Aaronovitch, S. and Smith, R. (1981), *The Political Economy of British Capitalism: A Marxist Analysis*, London: McGraw-Hill.
Abramovitz, M. and David, P.A. (1973), "Reinterpreting Economic Growth: Parables and Realities", *American Economic Review*, 63, 428–439.
Abramovitz, M. and David, P.A. (1996), "Convergence and Deferred Catch-up", in Landau, R., Taylor, T. and Wright, G. (eds), *The Mosaic of Economic Growth*, Stanford, CA: Stanford University Press, 21–62.
Ashworth, W. (1986), *The History of the British Coal Industry, Volume 5, 1946–1982: The Nationalized Industry*, Oxford: Clarendon Press.
Bairoch, P. (1989), "European Trade Policy, 1815–1914", in Mathias, P. and Pollard, S. (eds), *The Cambridge Economic History of Europe, Volume VIII, The Industrial Economies: The Development of Economic and Social Policies*, Cambridge: Cambridge University Press, 1–160.
Bairoch, P. (1993), *Economics and World History: Myths and Paradoxes*, London: Harvester Wheatsheaf.
Balke, N.S. and Gordon, R.J. (1989), "The Estimation of Prewar Gross National Product: Methodology and New Evidence", *Journal of Political Economy*, 97, 38–92.
Balogh, T. (1947), *Studies in Financial Organization*, Cambridge: Cambridge University Press.

Best, M.H. and Humphries, J. (1986), "The City and Industrial Decline", in Elbaum, B. and Lazonick, W. (eds), *The Decline of the British Economy*, Oxford: Clarendon Press, 223–239.

Broadberry, S.N. (1986), *The British Economy Between the Wars: A Macroeconomic Survey*, Oxford: Blackwell.

Broadberry, S.N. (1993), "Manufacturing and the Convergence Hypothesis: What the Long Run Data Show", *Journal of Economic History*, 53, 772–795.

Broadberry, S.N. (1997a), *The Productivity Race: British Manufacturing in International Perspective, 1850–1990*, Cambridge: Cambridge University Press.

Broadberry, S.N. (1997b), "Forging Ahead, Falling Behind and Catching-Up: A Sectoral Analysis of Anglo-American Productivity Differences, 1870–1990", *Research in Economic History*, 17, 1–37.

Broadberry, S.N. (1997c), "Anglo-German Productivity Differences 1870–1990: A Sectoral Analysis", *European Review of Economic History*, 1, 247–267.

Broadberry, S.N. (1998), "How did the United States and Germany Overtake Britain? A Sectoral Analysis of Comparative Productivity Levels, 1870–1990", *Journal of Economic History*, 58, 375–407.

Broadberry, S.N. (2004), "The Performance of Manufacturing", in Floud, R. and Johnson, P. (eds), *The Cambridge Economic History of Modern Britain, Volume III: Structural Change and Growth, 1939–2000*, Cambridge: Cambridge University Press, 57–83.

Broadberry, S.N. (2005), "Explaining Anglo-German Productivity Differences in Services since 1870", *European Review of Economic History*, 8, 229–262.

Broadberry, S.N. (2006), *Market Services and the Productivity Race, 1850–2000*. Cambridge: Cambridge University Press.

Broadberry, S.N. and Crafts, N.F.R. (1996), "British Economic Policy and Industrial Performance in the Early Post-War Period", *Business History*, 38(4), 65–91.

Broadberry, S.N. and Ghosal, S. (2002), "From the Counting House to the Modern Office: Explaining Comparative Productivity Trends in Britain and the United States since 1870", *Journal of Economic History*, 62, 967–998.

Brown, E.C. (1954), "Industrial Production in 1935 and 1948", *London & Cambridge Economic Bulletin*, December, pp. v–vii.

Brown, J. (1987), *Agriculture in England: A Survey of Farming, 1870–1947*, Manchester: Manchester University Press.

Buxton, N.K. (1978), *The Economic Development of the British Coal Industry: From the Industrial Revolution to the Present Day*, London: Batsford.

Cairncross, A. (1992), *The British Economy since 1945: Economic Policy and Performance, 1945–1990*, Oxford: Blackwell.

Capie, F. (1983), *Depression and Protectionism: Britain Between the Wars*, London: Allen & Unwin.

Capie, F. (1994), *Tariffs and Growth: Some Insights from the World Economy, 1850–1940*, Manchester: Manchester University Press.

Collins, M. (1990), *Banks and Industrial Finance in Britain, 1800–1939*, London: Macmillan.

Collins, M. (1998), "English Bank Development within a European Context, 1870–1939", *Economic History Review*, 51, 1–24.

Conway, P. and Nicoletti, G. (2006), "Product Market Regulation in Non-Manufacturing in OECD Countries: Measurement and Highlights", OECD Economics Department Working Paper No. 530.

Dow, J.C.R. (1965), *The Management of the British Economy, 1945–60*, Cambridge: Cambridge University Press.

Drummond, I. (1974), *Imperial Economic Policy, 1917–1939: Studies in Expansion and Protection*, London: Allen & Unwin.

Dunnett, P.J.S. (1980), *The Decline of the British Motor Industry: The Effects of Government Policy, 1945–1979*, London: Croom Helm.

Edelstein, M. (1982), *Overseas Investment in the Age of High Imperialism: The United Kingdom, 1850–1914*, London: Methuen.

El-Agraa, A.M. (1994), *The Economics of the European Community*, fourth edition, London: Harvester Wheatsheaf.

Ellinger, B. (1940), *The City: London Financial Markets*, London: Staples.

Feenstra, R.C. (1998), "Integration of Trade and Disintegration of Production", *Journal of Economic Perspectives*, 12(3), 31–50.

Feinstein, C.H. (1972), *National Income, Expenditure and Output of the United Kingdom, 1855–1965*, Cambridge: Cambridge University Press.

Feyrer, J. (2009), "Trade and Income: Exploiting Time Series in Geography", NBER Working Paper No. 14910.

Foreman-Peck, J. (1991), "Trade and the Balance of Payments", in Crafts, N.F.R. and Woodward, N.W.C. (eds), *The British Economy Since 1945*, Oxford: Clarendon, 141–179.

Frankel, J. and Romer, D. (1999), "Does Trade Cause Growth?", *American Economic Review*, 89, 379–399.

Giersch, H., Paqué, K.H. and Schmieding, H. (1992), *The Fading Miracle: Four Decades of Market Economy in Germany*, Cambridge: Cambridge University Press.

Greasley, D. and Oxley, L. (1996), "Discontinuities in Competitiveness: The Impact of the First World War on British Industry", *Economic History Review*, 49, 82–100.

Greenaway, D. (1988), "Effective Protection in the United Kingdom", *Oxford Bulletin of Economics and Statistics*, 50, 313–324.

Grunzel, J. (1916), *Economic Protection*, Oxford: Carnegie Endowment for International Peace and Clarendon Press.

Hoffman, R.J.S. (1933), *Great Britain and the German Trade Rivalry*, Philadelphia, PA: University of Pennsylvania Press.

Hoffmann, W.G. (1965), *Das Wachstum der deutschen Wirtschaft seit der Mitte des 19. Jahrhunderts*, Berlin: Springer-Verlag.

Hoj, J., Jiminez, M., Maher, M., Nicoletti, G. and Wise, M. (2007), "Product Market Competition in OECD Countries: Taking Stock and Moving Forward", OECD Economics Department Working Paper No. 575.

Holderness, B.A. (1985), *British Agriculture Since 1945*, Manchester: Manchester University Press.

Hutchinson, H. (1965), *Tariff-Making and Industrial Reconstruction*. London: Harrap.

Imlah, A.H. (1958), *Economic Elements in the Pax Britannica: Studies in British Foreign Trade in the Nineteenth Century*, Cambridge, MA: Harvard University Press.

Irwin, D.A. (1996), *Against the Tide: An Intellectual History of Free Trade*, Princeton, NJ: Princeton University Press.

Irwin, D.A. (2001), "Tariffs and Growth in Late Nineteenth-Century America", *The World Economy*, 24, 15–30.

Jacks, D.S. (2006), "New Results on the Tariff-Growth Paradox", *European Review of Economic History*, 10, 205–230.

Jacks, D.S., Meissner, C.M., and Novy, D. (2009), "Trade Booms, Trade Busts, and Trade Costs", NBER Working Paper No. 15267.

Jorgenson, D.W. and Stiroh, K.J. (2000), "Raising the Speed Limit: US Economic Growth in the Information Age", *Brookings Papers on Economic Activity*, 1, 125–211.

Kendrick, J.W. (1961), *Productivity Trends in the United States*, Princeton, NJ: National Bureau of Economic Research.

Kennedy, W.P. (1987), *Industrial Structure, Capital Markets and the Origins of British Economic Decline*, Cambridge: Cambridge University Press.

Kitchin, P.D. (1976), "Effective Rates of Protection in UK Manufacturing for 1963 and 1968", in Artis, M.J. and Nobay, A.R. (eds), *Essays in Economic Analysis*. Cambridge: Cambridge University Press, 193–207.

Kitson, M. and Solomou, S. (1990), *Protectionism and Economic Revival: The British Interwar Economy*, Cambridge: Cambridge University Press.

Kitson, M., Solomou, S. and Weale, M. (1991), "Effective Protection and Economic Recovery in the United Kingdom during the 1930s", *Economic History Review*, 44, 328–338.

Lehmann, S.H. and O'Rourke, K.H. (2008), "The Structure of Protection and Growth in the Late Nineteenth Century", NBER Working Paper No. 14493.

Liepmann, K. (1938), *Tariff Levels and the Economic Unity of Europe*, London: Allen & Unwin.

Lindert, P.H. (1991), *International Economics*, Homewood, IL: Irwin.

McCloskey, D.N. (1970), "Did Victorian Britain Fail?", *Economic History Review*, 23, 446–459.

Marrison, A. (1996), *British Business and Protection, 1903–1932*, Oxford: Clarendon Press.

Matthews, R.C.O., Feinstein, C.H. and Odling-Smee, J.C. (1982), *British Economic Growth, 1856–1973*, Oxford: Clarendon.

Michie, R. (1988), "The Finance of Innovation in Late Victorian and Edwardian Britain: Possibilities and Constraints", *Journal of European Economic History*, 17, 491–530.

Mills, T.C. (1991), "Are Output Fluctuations in the UK Transitory or Permanent?", *Manchester School*, 59, 1–11.

Millward, R. (1994), "Industrial and Commercial Performance Since 1950", in Floud, R. and McCloskey, D. (eds), *The Economic History of Britain Since 1700, Second Edition, Volume 3: 1939–1992*, Cambridge: Cambridge University Press, 123–167.

Mitchell, B.R. (1975), *European Historical Statistics, 1750–1970*, London: Macmillan.

Mitchell, B.R. (1988), *British Historical Statistics*, second edition, Cambridge: Cambridge University Press.

Moggridge, D.E. (1972), *British Monetary Policy, 1924–1931: The Norman Conquest of $4.86*, Cambridge: Cambridge University Press.

Morgan, A.D. and Martin, D. (1975), "Tariff Reductions and UK Imports of Manufactures, 1955–1971", *National Institute Economic Review*, 72, 38–54.

Morris, D.J. and Stout, D. (1985), "Industrial Policy", in D.J. Morris (ed.), *The Economic System in the UK*. Oxford: Oxford University Press, 851–894.

Nicoletti, G. and Scarpetta, S. (2005), "Product Market Reforms and Employment in OECD Countries", OECD Economics Department Working Paper No. 472.

Ó Gráda, C. (1994), "British Agriculture, 1860–1914", in Floud, D. and McCloskey, D. (eds.), *The Economic History of Britain Since 1700, Second Edition, Volume 2: 1860–1939*, Cambridge: Cambridge University Press, 145–172.

O'Mahony, M. and de Boer, W. (2002), "Britain's Relative Productivity Performance: Has Anything Changed?", *National Institute Economic Review*, 179, 38–43.

O'Mahony, M. and Wagner, K. (1994), "Changing Fortunes: An Industry Study of British and German Productivity Growth Over Three Decades", Report Series No. 7, National Institute of Economic and Social Research, London.
O'Rourke, K.H. (2000), "Tariffs and Growth in the Late 19th Century", *Economic Journal*, 110, 456–483.
Olson, M. (1963), *The Economics of the Wartime Shortage: A History of British Food Supplies in the Napoleonic War and in World War I an II*, Durham, NC: Duke University Press.
Oulton, N. (1976), "Effective Protection of British Industry", in Corden, W.M. and Fels, G. (eds), *Public Assistance to Industry*, London: Macmillan, 46–90.
Oulton, N. and O'Mahony, M. (1994), *Productivity and Growth*, Cambridge: Cambridge University Press.
Plummer, A. (1951), *International Combines in Modern Industry*, London: Pitman.
Political and Economic Planning (1962), *Atlantic Tariffs and Trade*, London: George Allen & Unwin.
Pollard, S. (1970), "Editor's Introduction", in Pollard, S. (ed.), *The Gold Standard and Employment Policies between the Wars*, London: Methuen.
Pollard, S. (1984), *The Wasting of the British Economy: British Economic Policy 1945 to the Present*, second edition, London: Croom Helm.
Proudman, J. and Redding, S. (1998), "A Summary of the Openness and Growth Project", in Proudman, J. and Redding, S. (eds), *Openness and Growth*, London: Bank of England, 1–29.
Reader, W.J. (1970), *Imperial Chemical Industries: A History, Vol. 1: The Forerunners, 1870–1926*, Oxford: Oxford University Press.
Rostas, L. (1948), *Comparative Productivity in British and American Industry*, Cambridge: Cambridge University Press.
Schlote, W. (1952), *British Overseas Trade: From 1700 to the 1930s*, Oxford: Blackwell.
Schularick, M. and Solomou, S. (2009), "Trade and Economic Growth: Historical Evidence", Cambridge Working Paper in Economics No. 0936.
Sebag-Montefiore, M.J. (1943), *Trade Regulations and Commercial Policy of the United Kingdom*, Cambridge: Cambridge University Press.
Smith, A.D. (1992), *International Financial Markets: The Performance of Britain and its Rivals*, Cambridge: Cambridge University Press.
Symeonidis, G. (2008), "The Effect of Competition on Wages and Productivity: Evidence from the United Kingdom", *Review of Economics and Statistics*, 90, 134–146.
Taussig, F.W. (1892), *The Tariff History of the United States*, New York: Putnams.
Tena-Junguito, A. (2009), "Bairoch Revisited: Tariff Structure and Growth in the Late Nineteenth Century", LSE Department of Economic History Working Paper No. 121.
Thomas, M.F. (1984), "An Input-Output Approach to the British Economy, 1890–1914", D. Phil thesis, Oxford.
Weiss, F.D. (1988) (ed.), *Trade Policy in West Germany*, Tübingen: Mohr.
Whetham, E.H. (1978), *The Agrarian History of England and Wales, Volume VIII, 1914–1939*, Cambridge: Cambridge University Press.
Whisler, T.R. (1994), "The Outstanding Potential Market: The British Motor Industry and Europe, 1945–75", *Journal of Transport History*, 15, 1–19.
Wren, C. (1996), "Grant-Equivalent Expenditure on Industrial Subsidies in the Post-War United Kingdom", *Oxford Bulletin of Economics and Statistics*, 58, 317–353.

12 The price–cost mark-up in the UK

A long-run perspective

Nicholas Crafts and Terence C. Mills

12.1 Introduction

Since the seminal paper by Nickell (1996), the role of competition in promoting good productivity performance has come to be generally recognised, especially in economies which are 'close-to-frontier', i.e. those which have technology levels near to those of the leading economies (Aghion and Howitt, 2006). Competition is likely to be especially important where the separation of ownership and control leads to agency problems within firms and/or where successful innovation means that incumbent firms can prevent a loss of rents to new entrants. In this context, the key to market power is not market structure per se but the strength of the threat of potential entry. In an open economy, this points to the relevance of trade policy and, more generally, trade costs, to the strength of competition and thus to productivity outcomes.

This has considerable resonance for the UK and its relative economic decline during the twentieth century. From being virtually a free-trade country prior to the First World War, high levels of protection on manufactures were adopted after 1932 which prevailed through the early 1960s, at which point nominal tariffs were about twice the levels prevailing in West Germany (see Chapter 11). It is generally believed that in this period product-market competition was relatively weak (Hannah, 1983) and the separation of ownership and control in UK business became exceptionally pronounced (Cheffins, 2008). As is well known, by the 1970s the UK had fallen behind major continental economies in terms of real GDP per person. There is certainly evidence that weak competition adversely affected productivity in firms without a dominant external share-holding (Nickell, Nirolitsas and Dryden, 1997) and that, on the one occasion when competition policy was seriously strengthened, productivity improved (Symeonidis, 2008). It is also generally accepted that, in the recent past, the 'second wave' of globalisation and initiatives such as the European Single Market have intensified competition and reduced price-cost margins (Gorg and Warzynski, 2006).

Yet, persuasive as this narrative may sound, a key piece of information is missing, namely, a measure of the evolution of market power over the long run. Traditionally, in the era of the structure–conduct–performance paradigm in industrial economics, it was assumed that this would be correlated with developments in average domestic concentration ratios. Here the evidence suggested that, in manufacturing, these were increasing through the end of the 1970s before starting to decline in the 1980s (Clarke, 1993). Adjusting these measures for imports modifies this picture a bit and suggests that the peak was in the late 1960s and that, by the late 1970s, failing to adjust for import competition significantly exaggerates the extent of industrial concentration (Utton, 1982). But, if potential entry is what counts rather than market structure, these measures may be misleading. Moreover, barriers to entry by imports cannot be judged simply by reference to the chronology of protectionist policies since these are only part of trade costs, which also reflect the impact of technological change and fuel prices on transport and communication costs and a variety of other non-tariff barriers to trade (Anderson and van Wincoop, 2004).

Recent assessments of the strength of competition focus on mark-ups of price over cost, notably in the research of the OECD (Hoj *et al.*, 2007), and the most convincing empirical analyses of the impact of competition on investment, innovation and productivity are based on the mark-up as a key to the transmission mechanism from policies to outcomes (Griffith and Harrison, 2004; Griffith, Harrison and Simpson, 2006). This suggests that, in looking at the evolution of market power in the UK, it would be helpful to look at long-run trends in the aggregate mark-up in the economy.

A preliminary attempt to do this was made by Ellis (2006) as a by-product of an attempt to develop an improved econometric methodology for predicting mark-ups for use by monetary policymakers. In this paper, we build on this work through use of an improved data set and refinements to the econometric techniques. In particular, we examine the chronology of the price-cost mark-up more carefully in the context of nineteenth-century globalisation, the interwar protectionist backlash, and subsequent trade liberalisation through the GATT and European integration. Previous literature suggests that, over time, the aggregate price-cost margin has followed an inverted U-shape and, given the evolution of trade costs to new lows in the recent past (Jacks, Meissner and Novy, 2008), it might be hypothesised that by the early twenty-first century it was lower than at any time in the previous century and a half. We investigate the validity of these claims as a contribution to understanding the role that trade openness has played in the competitive environment in the UK over the long run.

12.2 Theory

We begin, as does Ellis (2006), by utilising the conventional neoclassical model in which mark-ups play a key role in the long-run relationships resulting from the first-order conditions for capital and labour for a profit-maximising firm. Assuming a constant returns to scale (CRS), constant elasticity of substitution (CES) production function with labour augmenting technical progress η, output Y is defined as

$$Y^S = \left(\alpha K^{-\theta} + (1-\alpha)\left(Ne^{\eta}\right)^{-\theta}\right)^{-1/\theta} \tag{12.1}$$

where K denotes capital, N denotes labour, α is the distribution parameter governing the allocation of income between capital and labour, and $1/(1 + \theta) = \sigma$ is the elasticity of substitution between capital and labour in production. If we also assume a constant elasticity demand curve,

$$Y^D = P^{-\varepsilon} \tag{12.2}$$

where P is the price of output and ε the elasticity of demand, the first-order conditions for a profit-maximising firm with respect to the two factor inputs K and N may be derived. The first-order condition for labour yields

$$\frac{\partial}{\partial N}\left(Y^{1-\frac{1}{\varepsilon}}\right) = W \tag{12.3}$$

where W denotes the cost of employing labour. The solution to (12.3) is

$$W = P\left(1-\frac{1}{\varepsilon}\right)(1-\alpha)e^{-\theta\eta}\left(\frac{Y}{N}\right)^{1+\theta} \tag{12.4}$$

which, on taking logarithms and rearranging, yields the standard factor pricing equation for labour:

$$w - p = -\mu + \log(1-\alpha) + \frac{\sigma-1}{\sigma}\eta + \frac{1}{\sigma}(y-n) \tag{12.5}$$

Here w, p, y and n denote the logarithms of W, P, Y and N, respectively, and μ is the (log of the) mark-up, defined as

$$\mu = \log\left(\frac{\varepsilon}{\varepsilon-1}\right) \tag{12.6}$$

Since the mark-up is a function of the elasticity of demand ε, any change in the mark-up will reflect a change in this elasticity or, equivalently, a change in competition. Equation (12.5) can be rewritten as the factor-demand equation for labour

$$y = n - \sigma(p-w) + (1-\sigma)\eta - \sigma\log(1-\alpha) + \sigma\mu \tag{12.7}$$

Subject to the capital accumulation identity

$$K_{t+1} = (1-\delta)K_t + \tag{12.8}$$

the factor-demand equation for capital is derived as

$$y = k + \sigma r - \sigma\log\alpha + \sigma\mu \tag{12.9}$$

where r is the (log of the) real user cost of capital (RCC). The labour and capital factor-demand equations should hold in long-run equilibrium: note that from the assumption that technical progress is labour-augmenting the latter equation does not contain η.

A simple transformation of (12.7) yields

$$\mu = (p-w)+(y-n)+\left(\frac{1-\sigma}{\sigma}\right)(y-n-\eta)+\log(1-\alpha) \tag{12.10}$$

With α assumed to be fixed, this equation has the simple interpretation of

$$\textit{markup} = \textit{inverse labour share} + \left(\frac{1-\sigma}{\sigma}\right)\times(\textit{labour productivity} - \textit{technical progress})$$

In a steady state the mark-up and labour share will not vary over time and technical progress may be interpreted as 'trend' labour productivity. When labour productivity is above (below) this trend, the mark-up is then rising (falling) (conditional on the labour share). The lower σ is (the harder it is to swap between capital and labour in production) the bigger any change in the mark-up will be.

However, the mark-up itself is an unobserved variable. While it is often assumed to be constant when models of this type are estimated, this obviously imposes steady-state behaviour. As an alternative, μ might be modelled by including other variables such as capacity utilisation or import prices, essentially 'adding on' these variables to a constant. As there is, in general, no reason to believe that movements in the mark-up must correspond exactly to movements in these variables, a less restrictive approach in which the mark-up is allowed to vary over time in a non-dependent framework would be attractive. Similar considerations would also apply to technical progress. Such time dependencies must obviously be related to the behaviour over time of the observed variables in (12.7) and (12.9), the (inverse) labour-output and capital-output ratios, $y - n$ and $y - k$, the price to labour cost ratio $p - w$ and the real cost of capital, r, which naturally leads us on to a discussion of the available data.

12.3 Data

The data covers the period from 1855 to 2007. Indices for real output, the volume of capital and labour inputs were constructed both for the whole economy and for the manufacturing sector. Indices for the price level, money wage rate and price of capital goods were constructed for the whole economy and also used in the model for the manufacturing sector. Data for the post-war period is readily available from ONS sources and was spliced to estimates from Feinstein to extend back to 1855. The main problem here concerns the war years, where interpolation is required. For details, see the data appendix.

Two points are worth highlighting. First, with regard to capital inputs, the series for 1950 to 2007 are based on estimates of the volume of capital services (VICS) recently developed by ONS, where the innovation is that aggregation is based on rental prices rather than asset prices, as described by Wallis and Dey-Chowdhury (2007). This gives a faster growth of capital inputs during the last 25 years or so but seems to make little difference before then. Second, labour inputs are measured in terms of hours worked rather than persons employed. Over the long run, this is important because annual hours worked per person employed have fallen markedly; for example, compared with 100 years ago employment is now about 70 per cent greater but total hours worked are about the same. This also matters for the construction of the money wage series, which is obtained by dividing labour income by total hours worked.

The real user cost of capital is defined as

$$RCC = \frac{P_K}{P}\left(i + \pi^e + \rho - \delta\right)$$

in which P_K is the capital goods price and i is the long-term interest rate. The expected inflation rate, π^e, is calculated as the trend component from the Hodrick-Prescott filtered observed rate of inflation, while ρ is a risk premium set at 4 per cent, following the approach proposed by Tevlin and Whelan (2003). Based on Feinstein (1972) and O'Mahony (1999), the depreciation rate is defined as

$$\delta = \begin{cases} 2.7\% & \text{for } 1855\text{–}1913 \\ 3.7\% & \text{for } 1914\text{–}1945 \\ 9.4\% & \text{for } 1946\text{–}2007 \end{cases}$$

12.4 Modelling the mark-up

The various series for the whole economy required for estimation of equations (12.7) and (12.9) are shown in Figure 12.1 (note that *RCC* rather than its logarithm is shown for ease of interpretation).

It is clear from these graphs and from more formal unit root tests that $y - n$ and $p - w$ are drifting I(1) processes while $y - k$ is a drift-free I(1) process. There is some degree of uncertainty as to whether the logarithm of *RCC*, r, is stationary or not. What is clear, however, is that standard tests of cointegration show neither the pair $y - n$ and $p - w$ nor the pair $y - k$ and r to be cointegrated. These findings have the implication that, in (12.9), the 'drift-free I(1)-ness' of $y - k$, irrespective of whether r is stationary or a drift-free I(1) process, must imply that a time-varying mark-up must be a drift-free I(1) process as well. Consequently, the 'non-cointegrated drifting I(1)-ness' of $y - n$ and $p - w$ must translate itself into a time-varying technical progress variable that is a drifting I(1) process.

These considerations suggest that the empirical counterpart of the system (12.7) and (12.9) should take the form

$$\begin{aligned} y_t - n_t &= \beta_0 + \sigma\big(\mu_t - (p_t - w_t) - \eta_t\big) + \eta_t + e_{1t} \\ y_t - k_t &= \beta_1 + \sigma(r_t + \mu_t) + e_{2t} \\ \mu_t &= \mu_{t-1} + \lambda_t \\ \eta_t &= \gamma + \eta_{t-1} + \varphi_t \end{aligned} \tag{12.11}$$

where $\beta_0 = -\sigma \log(1 - \alpha)$, $\beta_1 = -\sigma \log \alpha = \beta_0(\alpha - 1)/\alpha$ and the innovations are assumed to have zero means, constant variances σ_1^2, σ_2^2, σ_λ^2 and σ_ϕ^2, and to be individually and mutually uncorrelated. Thus the mark-up is a drift-free random walk while technical progress is a random walk with a drift of γ.

The system (12.11), as it is in state space form, could be estimated by using the Kalman filter, with the unobserved components μ_t and η_t then being obtained using an appropriate filtering operation. Unfortunately, the cross-equation restrictions imposed by the specification proved to be too severe to enable sensible results to be obtained, thus forcing a modified approach to be undertaken.

On writing the mark-up and technical progress equations as $\Delta\mu_t = \lambda_t$ and $\Delta\eta_t = \gamma + \phi_t$, respectively, where Δ is the difference operator, the first equation of (12.11) can be rewritten as

$$\Delta(y_t - n_t) = \gamma(1-\sigma) - \sigma(p_t - w_t) + (1-\sigma)\varphi_t + \Delta e_{1t} \tag{12.12}$$

Since the composite error $(1 - \sigma)\phi_t + \Delta e_{1t}$ can be written as a first-order moving average process, (12.12) can be estimated by least squares on incorporating this moving average error. This yields an estimate of the elasticity of substitution of $\sigma = 0.574$ and this value was then imposed on the system (12.11). The system was then estimated via the Kalman filter and the unobserved mark-up calculated using the accompanying smoothing filter. The estimated mark-up is shown in Figure 12.2 and is found to be oscillatory up to the beginning of the First World War and declining after the Second World War. The two wars saw a rapid increase in the mark-up, which declined substantially in the interwar period.

Of course, both the effect of the wars and the assumption that the elasticity of substitution was fixed at $\sigma = 0.574$ for the entire 150-year period must be cause for concern. The exercise was therefore repeated for the pre-First World War and the post-Second World War periods. For 1855–1913, we obtained $\sigma = 0.394$ and, for 1946–2007, $\sigma = 0.063$. The resulting mark-up series are also shown in Figure 12.2 and continue to follow the evolution of the mark-up calculated for the entire sample period.

The system (12.11) was also fitted to the manufacturing sector data shown in Figure 12.3 using the same approach. The estimated elasticity of substitution was found to be $\sigma = 0.030$ and the estimated mark-ups for manufacturing and the whole economy, now accompanied by two standard error bounds, are shown in Figure 12.4, while Figure 12.5 is the manufacturing sector counterpart of Figure 12.2.

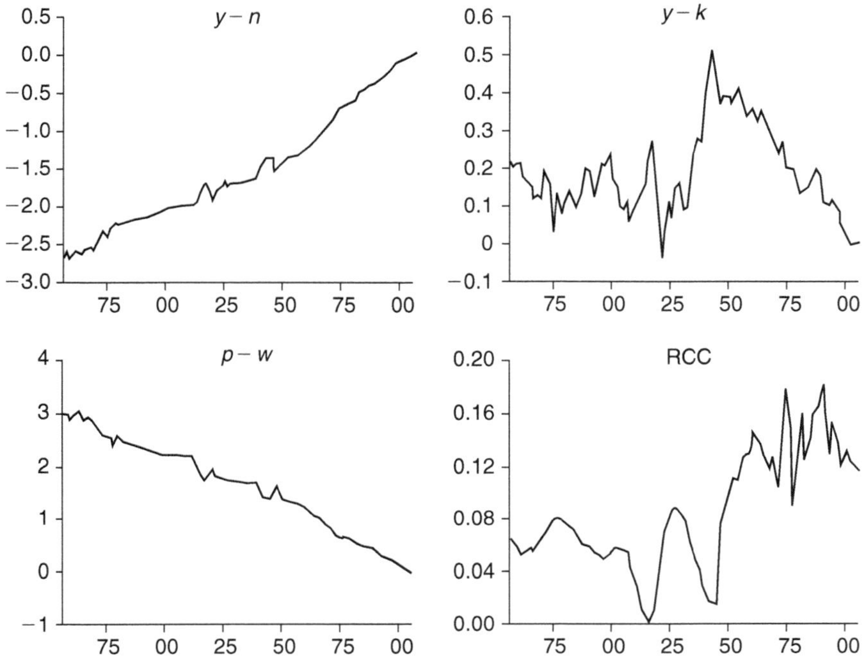

Figure 12.1 Labour productivity ($y - n$), capital–output ratio ($y - k$), price to labour cost ratio ($p - w$) and real cost of capital (RCC) for 1855 to 2007.

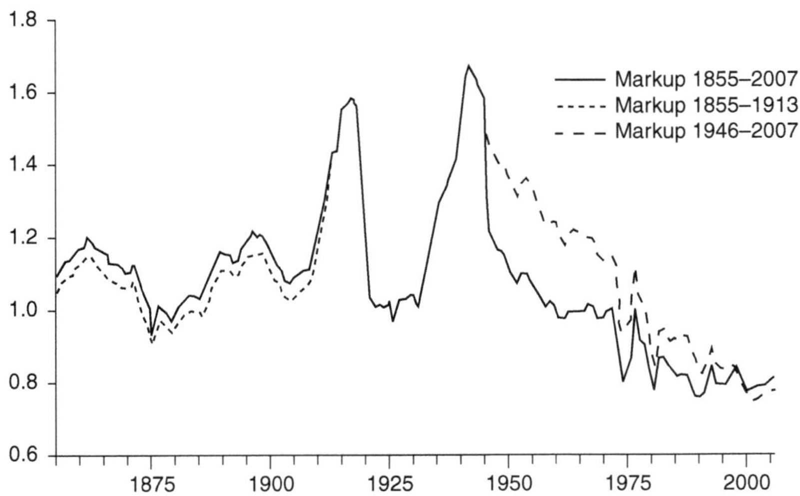

Figure 12.2 Estimated mark-up conditional upon (a) $\sigma = 0.574$: 1855–2007; (b) $\sigma = 0.394$: 1855–1913; (c) $\sigma = 0.063$: 1946–2007.

12.5 Discussion

The estimates of the price-cost mark-up displayed in the last section offer an interesting picture of market power in the UK over the long run. Looking at the whole economy in Figures 12.2 and 12.4, several points stand out from the results obtained for the whole period from 1855 to 2007. First, the suggestions that the mark-up describes an inverted-U-shape through time is not really borne out, although there do appear to be spikes associated with the wartime periods. The evidence is that the price-cost mark-up in the 1950s was much the same as in the mid- or late nineteenth century. Second, in the period since the late 1970s

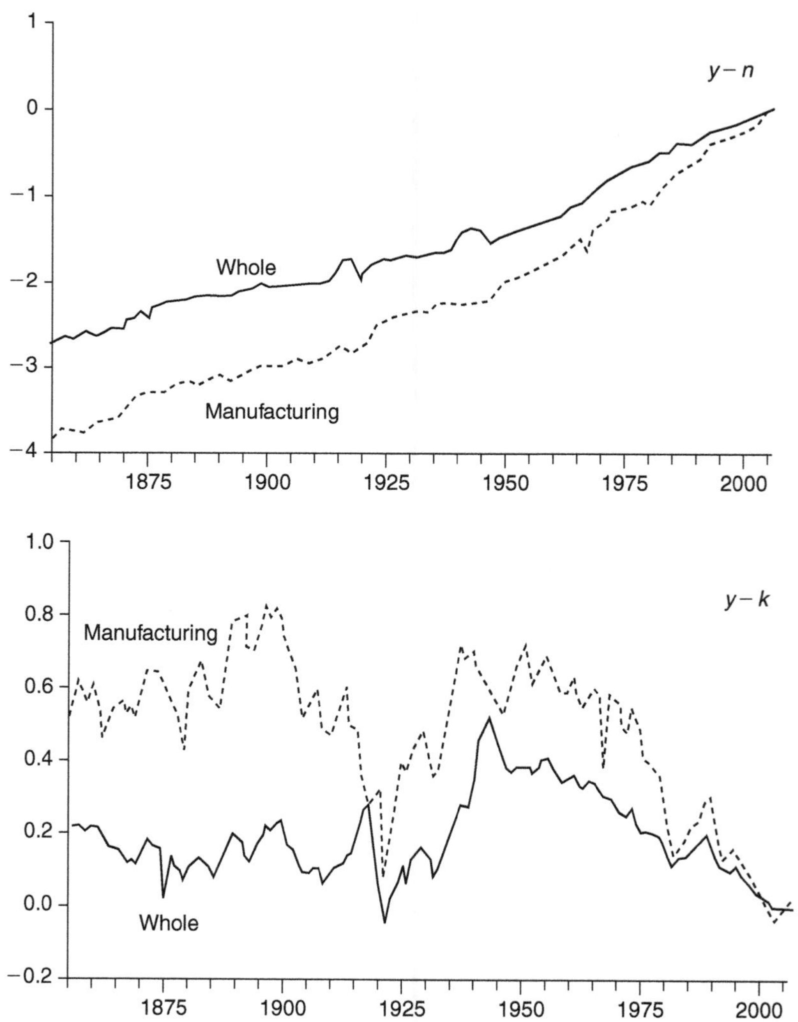

Figure 12.3 Manufacturing sector labour productivity ($y - n$) and capital–output ($y - k$) ratios with whole economy ratios for comparison.

the mark-up has been at an historically low level, with the point estimate being about 20 per cent lower than the level prevailing in the early 1970s. Third, the decrease in the mark-up occurred quite rapidly during a 15-year interval.

These findings are broadly consistent with the results obtained by restricting the estimation to shorter periods, cf. Figure 12.2, which can be regarded as a sensitivity analysis. The main differences are that these results are a bit kinder to the inverted-U hypothesis, with mark-ups noticeably higher relative to the base year of 1971 in the 1950s but appreciably lower in recent years. The estimated elasticity of substitution underlying these results is rather low relative to those found elsewhere in the literature (for example, Barrell and Pain, 1997) and we are inclined to place more weight on the whole-period estimates.

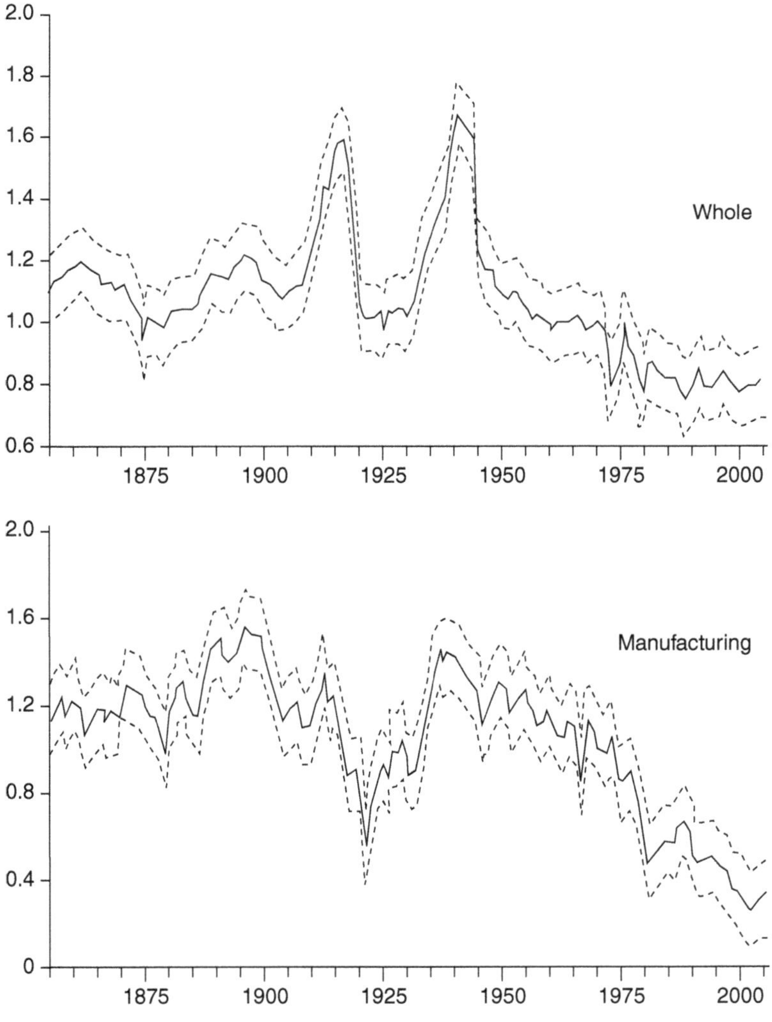

Figure 12.4 Estimated sectoral mark-ups with two standard error bounds.

Turning to the estimates for the manufacturing sector (Figures 12.4 and 12.5) we find that there is relatively little difference between whole-period and shorter-period estimates of the mark-up. Once again, the 1950s looks quite similar to the later nineteenth century and we do not see the inverted-U shape that might be expected if mark-ups followed the trajectory of domestic concentration ratios. Here, too, since the late 1970s the mark-up has been at a new low level but, compared with the whole economy, the fall by the mid-1980s is about twice as big and continues beyond then. Clearly, the pressure on mark-ups in UK manufacturing since the end of the long post-war boom has been much greater than in other parts of the economy.

The change in manufacturing price-cost margins is quite substantial and implies that they must have been high prior to the 1970s. The magnitude and timing of the estimated decrease is very similar to that estimated in an earlier paper (Crafts and Mills, 2005). Taking 1971 = 1, this paper estimates 1958 = 1.1, 1985 = 0.6 and 1995 = 0.5; the estimates in our 2005 paper, which used a completely different estimation technique, were 1958 = 1, 1985 = 0.5 and 1995 = 0.48.

A plausible reason for these recent reductions in price-cost margins is increasing actual or potential entry by imports. This would be consistent both with the sectoral impact, much greater for manufacturing with a much greater internationally tradable component than services, and the timing. The sharp decrease in mark-ups occurred at the same time as the UK experienced a major reduction in trade costs. According to the new estimates made by Jacks, Meissner and Novy (2009), trade costs, measured in terms of tariff-equivalents and inferred from estimated gravity equations, decreased by about 35 per cent for UK-France and UK-Germany during the 1970s (cf. Figure 12.6) and, at last, fell below the 1929 level.

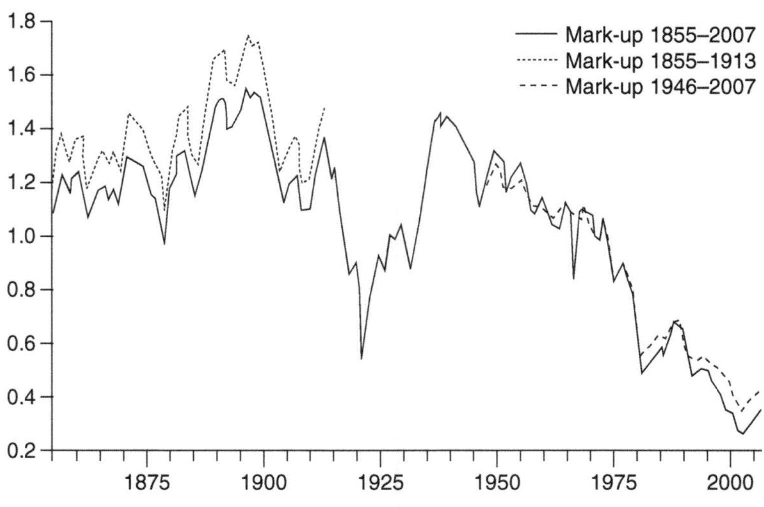

Figure 12.5 Manufacturing sector mark-up, conditional upon (a) $\sigma = 0.030$: 1855–2007; (b) $\sigma = 0.014$: 1855–1913; (c) $\sigma = 0.052$: 1946–2007.

Declining trade costs in the 1970s did not reflect reductions in transport costs, which were pushed up by fuel price increases which outweighed technological progress (Hummels, 2007). They should, rather, be seen as the result of trade liberalisation both through the GATT and from the entry of the UK into the EEC. The average effective protection rate fell from 9.3 per cent in 1968 to 1.2 per cent in 1986 (Ennew, Greenaway and Reed, 1990).

This suggests that, had the UK pursued policies of greater trade openness early in the post-war period, for example by joining the EEC at the outset, mark-ups would have been considerably reduced, especially in manufacturing. This counterfactual of a more competitive environment for business would have been an important antidote to principal-agent problems. Nickell, Nicolitsas and Dryden (1997) estimated that, for firms without a dominant external shareholder (the norm for big British firms at this time), a reduction in supernormal profits from 15 to 5 per cent of value added would raise total factor productivity growth by 1 percentage point. This points to the protectionist legacy from the interwar period, from which the UK was slow to escape, as a significant factor in relative economic decline.

By contrast, the free-trade environment before the First World War was an era in which mark-ups were high compared with those that we now observe in the second wave of globalisation, even though by the early twentieth century transport costs were probably no higher than in the 1950s. The implication is that potential import competition was a less powerful restraint on market power. The reasons for this deserve greater scrutiny.

12.6 Conclusions

Forrest Capie has always been sceptical of those who advocate protectionism as a way of improving economic performance (Capie, 1994). This paper adds support to this general line of argument by focusing on the importance of

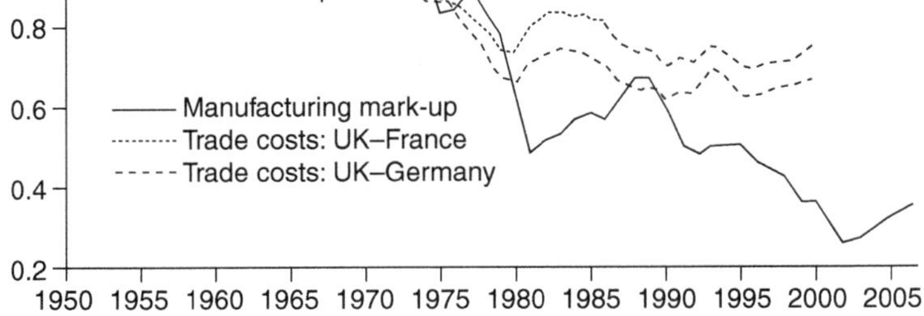

Figure 12.6 Manufacturing sector mark-up and trade costs post 1950.

potential entry by imports as a restraint on the exercise of market power in the domestic economy.

The main results of the paper are that the mark-up of price over cost in the UK economy has fallen substantially in recent decades and is now lower than at any time in the last 150 years. The trend has been more marked in the manufacturing sector which is more exposed to international competition than the economy as a whole.

The timing of the decline after the early 1970s suggests that the major reason for it was a marked decrease in trade costs associated with the trade liberalisation that accompanied the UK's entry into the EEC and the Kennedy Round of the GATT rather than falling transport costs. The implication is that market power in the UK could have been quite effectively addressed by trade policy in the early post-war decades.

Failure to do so had implications for productivity performance. Weak competition permitted the survival of inefficient firms and working practices. By intensifying competition, trade liberalisation could have played an important part in improving supply-side policy and in promoting better productivity outcomes.

Data appendix

The sources used to construct the database used in estimation were generally taken from the Office of National Statistics (ONS) for the post-war period and linked to the work of Charles Feinstein for earlier years. The details are as follows.

Whole economy

Real Output: 1855–1947: Feinstein (1972), pp. T14–16; 1948–2007: *UK Economic Accounts*, Table 1.01.

Capital Input: 1855–1920: Feinstein (1988), pp. 452–453; 1921–49: Feinstein (1972), p. T97; 1950–2007: based on VICS estimates at www.statistics.gov.uk/statbase/product.asp?vlnk=14205.

Labour Input: measured in terms of hours worked based on annual hours per person employed × civil employment. 1855–1949: employment from Feinstein (1972), pp. T125–127 and annual hours based on Matthews, Feinstein and Odling-Smee (1982), pp. 70–71 and 566; 1950–2007 from the Conference Board, Total Economy Database June 2009.

Output Price: based on the GDP deflator. 1855–69 derived from Mitchell (1988), p. 832, 838; 1870–1947 from Feinstein (1972), pp. T132–133.

Capital Goods Price: 1855–1920: Feinstein (1988), pp. 470–471; 1921–49: Feinstein (1972), p. T133; 1950–2007: derived from ONS series CIXM and GUCJ for capital stocks in current and constant prices.

Money Wage Rate: based on income from employment in the national accounts divided by hours worked as above. 1855–1948: Feinstein (1972), pp. T4–6 treating income from self-employment as suggested by Matthews, Feinstein and

Odling-Smee (1982), pp. 164–170 and Tables 6.1, 6.3; 1950–2007: from *UK Economic Accounts*, table 1.04 assuming half of 'other income' accrues to labour.

Manufacturing

Real Output: 1855–1947: Feinstein (1972), p. T111–112; 1948–2007: *UK Economic Accounts*, Table 1.10.
Capital Input: 1855–1920: Feinstein (1988), pp. 452–453; 1920–49: Feinstein (1972), p. T99; 1950–2007: based on VICS estimates at www.statistics.gov.uk/statbase/product.asp?vlnk=14205.
Labour Input: hours worked as for whole economy. Employment: 1855–1920 derived as in Broadberry (1997), pp. 42–43; 1920–49: Feinstein (1972), p. T129; 1950–96: O'Mahony (1999), p. 86, 96; ONS, Economic and Labour Market Review, Table 2.06.

Acknowledgements

We are very grateful to Dennis Novy for supplying data on trade costs used in Figure 12.6 and to Gavin Wallis for his assistance regarding VICS estimates of capital inputs.

References

Aghion, P. and Howitt, P. (2006), 'Appropriate Growth Theory: a Unifying Framework', *Journal of the European Economic Association*, 4, 269–314.
Anderson, J.E. and van Wincoop, E. (2004), 'Trade Costs', *Journal of Economic Literature*, 42, 691–751.
Barrell, R. and Pain, N. (1997), 'Foreign Direct Investment, Technological Change and Economic Growth within Europe', *Economic Journal*, 107, 1770–1786.
Broadberry, S.N. (1997), *The Productivity Race*. Cambridge: Cambridge University Press.
Capie, F. (1994), *Tariffs and Growth*. Manchester: Manchester University Press.
Cheffins, B.R. (2008), *Corporate Ownership and Control*. Oxford: Oxford University Press.
Clarke, R. (1993), 'Trends in Concentration in UK Manufacturing, 1980–9', in M. Casson and J. Creedy (eds.), *Industrial Concentration and Economic Inequality*. Aldershot: Edward Elgar, 121–142.
Crafts, N. and Mills, T.C. (2005), 'TFP Growth in British and German Manufacturing, 1950–1996', *Economic Journal*, 115, 649–670.
Ellis, C. (2006), 'Elasticities, Mark-Ups and Technical Progress: Evidence from a State-Space Approach', *Bank of England Working Paper* No. 300.
Ennew, C., Greenaway, D. and Reed, G. (1990), 'Further Evidence on Effective Tariffs and Effective Protection in the UK', *Oxford Bulletin of Economics and Statistics*, 52, 69–78.
Feinstein, C.H. (1972), *National Income, Expenditure and Output of the United Kingdom, 1855–1965*. Cambridge: Cambridge University Press.

Feinstein, C.H. (1988), 'National Statistics, 1760–1920', in C.H. Feinstein and S. Pollard (eds), *Studies in Capital Formation in the United Kingdom, 1750–1920*. Oxford: Clarendon Press, 257–471.

Gorg, H. and Warzynski, F. (2006), 'The Dynamics of Price-Cost Margins: Evidence from UK Manufacturing', *Revue d'OFCE*, 304–318.

Griffith, R. and Harrison, R. (2004), 'The Link between Product Market Regulation and Macroeconomics', *European Commission Economic Papers* No. 209.

Griffith, R., Harrison, R. and Simpson, H. (2006), 'Product Market Reform and Innovation in the EU', *Institute for Fiscal Studies Working Paper* No. 06/17.

Hannah, L. (1983), *The Rise of the Corporate Economy*. London: Methuen.

Hoj, J., Jimenez, M., Maher, M., Nicoletti, G. and Wise, M. (2007), 'Product Market Competition in OECD Countries: Taking Stock and Moving Forward', *OECD Economics Department Working Paper* No. 575.

Hummels, D. (2007), 'Transportation Costs and International Trade in the Second Era of Globalization', *Journal of Economic Perspectives*, 21(3), 131–154.

Jacks, D.S., Meissner, C.M. and Novy, D. (2008), 'Trade Costs, 1870–2000', *American Economic Review Papers and Proceedings*, 98(2), 529–534.

Jacks, D.S., Meissner, C.M. and Novy, D. (2009), 'Trade Booms, Trade Busts, and Trade Costs', *NBER Working Paper* No. 15267.

Matthews, R.C.O., Feinstein, C.H. and Odling-Smee, J.C. (1982), *British Economic Growth, 1856–1973*. Stanford: Stanford University Press.

Mitchell, B.R. (1988), *British Historical Statistics*. Cambridge: Cambridge University Press.

Nickell, S.J. (1996), 'Competition and Corporate Performance', *Journal of Political Economy*, 104, 724–746.

Nickell, S.J., Nicolitsas, D. and Dryden, N. (1997), 'What Makes Firms Perform Well', *European Economic Review*, 41, 783–796.

O'Mahony, M. (1999), *Britain's Productivity Performance 1950–1996: an International Perspective*. London: NIESR.

Symeonidis, G. (2008), 'The Effect of Competition on Wages and Productivity: Evidence from the United Kingdom', *Review of Economics and Statistics*, 90, 134–146.

Tevlin, S. and Whelan, K. (2003), 'Explaining the Investment Boom of the 1990s', *Journal of Money, Credit, and Banking*, 35, 1–22.

Utton, M.A. (1982), 'Domestic Concentration and International Trade', *Oxford Economic Papers*, 34, 479–497.

Wallis, G. and Dey-Chowdhury, S. (2007), 'Volume of Capital Services: Estimates for 1950 to 2006', *Economic and Labour Market Review*, 1(12), 37–47.

Appendix

Forrest Capie's publications

1972

"British and New Zealand Trading Relationships, 1841–1853" *Economic History Review* (with K.A. Tucker)

1976

"Consumer Preference: Meat in England and Wales, 1920–1938" *Bulletin of Economic Research*

1977

"The Depression in Perspective" *The Banker* (with M. Collins)

"The World Recession in the 1930s and 1970s" *The Banker* (with M. Collins)

1978

"Australian and New Zealand Competition in the British Market, 1920–1939" *Australian Economic History Review*

"The First Export Monopoly Control Board" *Journal of Agricultural Economics*

"The British Tariff and Industrial Protection in the 1930s" *Economic History Review*. Reprinted in C.H. Feinstein (ed.) *Essays in British Economic Policy and Performance since 1930* (OUP 1983)

1979

"Britain and Empire Trade in the Second Half of the Nineteenth Century" in D. Alexander and R. Omner (eds) *Volume not Value* (Memorial University).

1980

"The Extent of British Economic Recovery in the 1930s" *Economy and History* (with M. Collins)

"The Pressure for Tariff Protection in Britain, 1917–1931" *Journal of European Economic History*

"The British Market for Meat, 1850–1914" *Agricultural History* (with R. Perren)

1981

"Shaping the British Tariff Structure in the 1930s" *Explorations in Economic History*

"Invisible Barriers to Trade: Britain and Argentina in the 1920s" *Inter-American Economic Affairs*

"Long Waves in Economic Development" *CUBS Annual Monetary Review*

"Tariffs, Prices and Elasticities in Britain in the 1930s" *Economic History Review*

"The British Empire before 1914" in M. Falkus and J. Gillingham *An Historical Atlas of Britain* (Random House)

1982

"Concentration in British Banking, 1880–1914" *Business History* (with G. Rodrik-Bali)

1983

"Total Coin and Coins in Circulation in the UK, 1868–1914" *Journal of Money Credit and Banking* (with A. Webber)

The British Economy Between the Wars (MUP) (with M. Collins)

Depression and Protectionism, Britain between the Wars (George Allen & Unwin) Paperback, 1985; Reprinted 1994

"Tariff Protection and Economic Performance in the Nineteenth Century" in J. Black and D.A. Winters (eds) *Economic Policy and Trade Performance* (Macmillan)

1984

"Bank Deposits and the Quantity of Money in the UK, 1870–1921" *Research in Economic History* (with A. Webber)

"Economic Recovery in the United Kingdom in the 1930s" Bank of England Panel Paper (with M. Beenstock and B. Griffiths)

1985

"The Money Adjustment Process in the United Kingdom, 1870–1914" *Economica* (with G. Rodrik-Bali)

Monetary History of the United Kingdom, 1870-1982: Data Sources & Methods (George Allen & Unwin) (with A. Webber) Reprinted 1995

"The Demand for Meat in England and Wales between the Wars" in D. Miller and D. Oddy (eds) *Diet and Health in Modern Britain* (Croom Helm)

1986

"Conditions in Which Hyperinflation Has Appeared" in K. Brunner and A. Meltzer (eds) Carnegie-Rochester Public Policy Series. Reprinted in F. Capie (ed.) *Major Inflations in History*

"Debt Management and Interest Rates: The War Loan Conversion of 1932" *Applied Economics* (with T.C. Mills and G.E. Wood)

Financial Crises and the World Banking System (Macmillan) (ed. with G.E. Wood)

"What Happened in 1931" in F. Capie and G.E. Wood (eds) *Financial Crises and the World Banking System* (with T.C. Mills and G.E. Wood)

"Unemployment and Real Wages between the Wars" in S. Glynn and A. Booth (eds) *The Road to Full Employment* (George Allen & Unwin)

"Long Run Behaviour of the Money Multiplier" *CUBS Economic Review* (with G. Rodrik-Bali)

1987

"Two Devaluations Compared: British Economic Policy in 1931 and 1945" in D.R. Hodgman and G.E. Wood (eds) *Making Monetary Policy* (Macmillan) (with G.E. Wood)

1988

"Structure and Performance in British Banking before 1939" in D.E Moggridge and P. Cottrell (eds) *Money and Power* (Macmillan)

"Prices and Price Controls: Are Controls a Policy Instrument?" in D.R Hodgman and G.E. Wood (eds) *Macroeconomic Policy and Interdependence* (Macmillan) (with M. Pradhan and G.E. Wood)

1989

Monetary Economics in the 1980s: Some Themes from Henry Thornton (Macmillan, ed. with G.E. Wood)

"Anna Schwartz's perspective on British Economic History" in M. Bordo (ed.) *Money, History and International Finance* (Chicago University Press) (with G.E. Wood)

1990

"Monetary Stringency, Stock Market Crash and Economic Activity" *European Economic Review*

A Directory of Economic Institutions (ed.) (Macmillan)

"The Evolving Regulatory Framework in British Banking in the Twentieth Century" in M. Chick (ed.) *Government Industry Relations* (Gower)

"Banking Structure and Banking Stability after 1992" in D.E. Fair and C. de Boissien (eds) *Financial Institutions in Europe Under New Competitive Conditions* (Kluwer) (with G.E. Wood)

"Asset Bubbles" in E.N. White (ed.) *Crashes and Panics: The Lessons from History* (McGraw-Hill)

1991

"Money and Business Cycles in the US and UK, 1870–1913" *Manchester School* (with T.C. Mills)

"Tariff Policy and Economic Recovery in Britain in the 1930s" *Economic History Review*

"Central Banks and Inflation in Historical Perspective Part I" *Central Banking* (with G.E. Wood)

"Finance and Economic Activity in Britain, Some Preliminary Observations" *Chiba Journal of Commerce* (with M. Collins)

Unregulated Banking: Chaos or Order (Macmillan) (ed. with G.E. Wood)

Major Inflations in History (ed.) (Edward Elgar)

"Financial Structure in a Changing Regulatory Environment: Europe after 1992" in Scheld (ed.) *Game Plans for the 1990s* (with G.E. Wood)

"Money, Interest Rates, and the Great Depression" in J. Foreman-Peck (ed.) *New Perspectives on the late-Victorian Economy* (CUP) (with T.C. Mills and G.E. Wood)

"Major Inflations in History: An Introductory Essay" in F. Capie (ed.) *Major Inflations in History* (Edward Elgar)

"Money and Business Cycles in Britain 1870-1913" in K. Velupillai and N. Thygesen (eds) *Business Cycles: Theories, Evidence and Analysis* (Macmillan)

"Free Banking in the French Revolution" in F. Capie and G.E. Wood, *Unregulated Banking* (Macmillan)

1992

"Money and Business Cycles in the US: A Re-examination of Friedman and Schwartz" *Explorations in Economic History* July (with T.C. Mills)

"Central Banks and Inflation in Historical Perspective Part II" *Central Banking* (with G.E. Wood)
Did the Banks Fail British Industry? (IEA) (with M. Collins)
Trade Wars: A Repetition of the Inter War Years? (IEA)
"British Economic Fluctuations in the late Nineteenth Century" in S. Broadberry and N. Crafts (eds) *Essays in Trade and Finance* (CUP)
Protectionism in the World Economy (ed.) (Edward Elgar)
"European Payments Union" in *New Palgrave Dictionary of Finance* (Macmillan)
"Window Dressing" in *New Palgrave Dictionary of Finance* (Macmillan)

1993

Central Bank Independence: What is it and what will it do for us? (IEA) (With T.C. Mills and G.E. Wood)
Monetary Regimes in Transition (CUP) (ed. with M. Bordo)
A History of Banking (ed.) (Pickering and Chatto) 10 volumes
"Inflation in Britain in World War II" in G. Mills and H. Rockoff (eds) *Economic History of World War II: An International Perspective* (Iowa Press) (with G.E. Wood)
"Explaining Monetary Regime Change" in M. Bordo and F. Capie (eds) *Monetary Regimes in Transition* (CUP) (with M. Bordo)
"The Evolution of Modern Banking, 1650–1850" in F. Capie (ed.) *History of Banking* (Pickering and Chatto)

1994

Tariffs and Growth (MUP)
The Future of Central Banking (CUP) (with C. Goodhart, J. Fischer and N. Schnadt)
"Money in the British Economy, 1870–1939" in R. Floud and D. McCloskey (eds) *Economic History of Britain* (CUP) (with G.E. Wood)
"Commercial Bank Historiography in Britain and Scandinavia" in M. Pohl (ed.) *The Writing of Bank History* (Scholar Press)
"Central Bank Independence: Some Exploratory Analysis" in P. Siklos (ed.) *Monetary Regimes* (Kluwert) (with T.C. Mills and G.E. Wood)
"The Evolution of Financial Institutions and Markets in the UK in the Twentieth Century" in G. Feldman (ed.) *Financial Institutions and Markets in the 20th Century*

1995

"British Commercial Bank Conservatism" *Explorations in Economic History* (with T.C. Mills)
"Central Banks, Macro Policy and the Financial System" *Financial History Review* (with C. Goodhart)
"Money and Prices in the Long Run" *Economic Affairs*
"The Bank of England after WW II" in M. Leboyer (ed.) *Banking in Europe since the War* (Ministry of Finance, Paris)
"Commercial Banking in Britain Between the Wars" in C. Feinstein (ed.) *Banking Currency and Finance in Europe Between the Wars* (OUP)
"Money, Finance and the Great Depression" in *Festschrift for Luigi de Rosa* (Rome)
A European Lender of Last Resort" in J. Reis (ed.) *International Monetary Systems* (Macmillan) (with G.E. Wood)
"Prudent and Stable: but Inefficient? English Banks" in M. Bordo and R. Sylla (eds) *Anglo American Financial Systems*

1996

"Debt Deflation and Economic Policy" *Review of Policy Issues* (with G.E. Wood)
"English Banks and Customer Distress 1850–1914" *Business History* (with M. Collins)
Monetary Economics in the 1990s (ed.) (Macmillan) (with G.E. Wood)
"Protectionism in Europe before 1939" in R. Tilly and P.J.J Welfens (eds) *European Economic Integration* (Springer)

1997

Asset Prices and the Real Economy (ed.) (Macmillan) (with G.E. Wood)
"Trade Policy and Economic Growth in Europe, 1850 to 1950" in J. Davis and P. Mathias (eds) *International Trade and British Economic Growth* (Blackwell)
"Deficient Suppliers? English Commercial Banks" in P.L. Cottrell, A. Teichova and T. Yuzana (ed.) *Finance in the Age of the Corporate Economy* (Aldgate) (with M. Collins)
"The Demand for Money under the Gold Standard" in B. Eichengreen and T. Bayoumi (eds) *Modern Perspectives on the Gold Standard* (CUP) (with G.E. Wood)
"Introduction" in *Assets Prices in Real Economy* (Macmillan) (with G.E. Wood)
"Central Banking in Economies in Transition" in G. Caprio (ed.) *Reforming Financial Systems* (CUP)
"Central Bank Independence: The Historical Dimension" in E. Hochreiter (ed.) *Credibility of European Monetary Policy* (Austrian National Bank)
"The Sources of British Protectionism before 1932" in A. Marrison (ed.) *Freedom and Trade* (MUP)
"Great Depression 1873–96" in *Encyclopaedia of Business Cycles* (with G.E. Wood)
"British Trade Cycle 1929–37" in *Encyclopaedia of Business Cycles* (with G.E. Wood)
"1914 Crisis" in *Encyclopaedia of Business Cycles* (with G.E. Wood)

1998

"Can There Be an International Lender of Last Resort?" *International Finance* (Reprinted in C. Goodhart ed. *Reader on Lender of Last Resort* (OUP))
"Long-run Relationship Between Money and Prices" in G.E. Wood (ed.) *Money Prices and the Real Economy* (Elgar)
"The Emergence of Central Banking in Europe", in R. Sylla, R. Tilly, G. Tortella (eds) *The State and the Financial System* (CUP)
"Dangers Ahead for the Euro" *European Journal*

1999

"The Place of the Euro in the International Monetary System" *Open Economies Review*
"Banks, Industry and Finance 1850–1914" *Business History* (with M. Collins)
"Organisation and Control in English Banking" *Revista de Historia Economica* (with M. Collins)
"The IMF as Lender of Last Resort" *Journal of International Bank Regulation* (with G.E. Wood)
Banking History in Nineteenth Century Texts (ed.) (Routledge) (with G.E. Wood)
The Development of Monetary Theory in the 1920s (ed.) (Routledge) (with G.E. Wood)
"Dangers Ahead for the Euro" in M. Fratianni and D. Salvatore (eds) *The Future of the International Monetary System* (Kluwer)

2000

"Electronic Money: The Last Frontier" *Economic Trends* (Finland) (with Y. Gormez)

"Price Stability and Financial Stability" (World Gold Council) (with G.E. Wood)

"What Kind of Stability Helps Industry? Contrasting Experiences with British and German Banking" (with G.E. Wood) in S. Frowen and F.P. McHugh (eds) *Financial Competition, Risk and Accountability* (Palgrave Macmillan)

"Recent Crises in Historical Perspective" in *Financial Crises for Ever?* Austrian National Bank.

2001

"The Birth, Life, and Demise of a Currency" *Economic Journal* (with G.E. Wood)

"Prices, Financial Fragility, and Stabilization Proposals" *Journal for Financial Services Research*

"Profitability in English Banking in the Twentieth Century" *European Review of Economic History* (with M. Billings)

"Price Controls in War and Peace: A Marshallian Conclusion" *Scottish Journal of Political Economy* (with G.E. Wood)

"Accounting for Profitability in British Banking" *Journal of Accounting and Financial History* (with M. Billings)

"Regulation in British Banking: From Crisis to Stability" *Bankhistorisches Archiv*

"Monetary Unions: Economic Criteria, History and Prospects" *Greek Economic Review* (with G.E. Wood)

Liberalization in the World Economy in Historical Perspective (RIIA)

Capital Flows and Capital Controls (IEA)

Monetary Policy in the Late Twentieth Century (ed.) (Routledge) (with G.E. Wood)

"A Future for Private Money" *Scottish Journal of Institute of Bankers*

"The Origins and Development of Stable Monetary and Fiscal Institutions in England" in M. Bordo and R. Cortes-Conde (eds) *Transferring Wealth and Power from the Old World to the New* (CUP)

2002

"Does Fiat Money Have a Future?" *Revue bancaire et financiare* (with G.E. Wood)

Monetary Unions (ed.) (Macmillan) (with G.E. Wood)

"Protectionism and the International Economic Order between the Wars" in H. James (ed.) *The Interwar Depression in an International Context* (Oldenbourg Verlag)

"Monetary Unions: Evidence from the Past" in F. Capie and G.E. Wood (eds) *Monetary Unions* (Macmillan) (with G.E. Wood).

"Financial Crises and the Business Cycle" in *Actas del il congresso internacional sobre ciclos economiecos* (with G.E. Wood)

"Can EMU Survive Unchanged?" in A. El-Agraa (ed.) *The Euro and Britain* (Pearson)

"The International Financial Architecture in the Second Half of the Twentieth Century" in M. Oliver (ed.), *Essays in Honour of D.H. Aldcroft* (Ashgate) (with G.E. Wood)

"Can There Be an International Lender of Last Resort?" in C. Goodhart and G. Illing (eds) *Financial Crises Contagion and the Lender of Last Resort* (OUP)

"The Emergence of the Bank of England as a Mature Central Bank" in D. Winch and P.K. O'Brien (eds) *The Political Economy of British Historical Experience, 1688–1914* (British Academy and OUP)

2003

"Deflation in the British Economy, 1870–1939" *Journal of European Economic History* (with G.E. Wood)
"The Federal Reserve, 1914–1951" Review article *Central Banking*
"The History of British Taxation, 1800–1970" Review article *Business History Review*
"Comment on Bordo, Eichengreen, and Schwartz" in P. Mizen (ed.) *Monetary History, Exchange Rates, and Financial Markets* (Elgar)
"The World Economy: 50 Years of Change" in J. Hirst (ed.) *The Challenge of Change* (Profile Books)
"Central Banking" in J. Mokyr (ed.) *Encyclopaedia of Economic History*
"Tariffs" in J. Mokyr (ed.) *Encyclopaedia of Economic History*

2004

"Competition in English Banking, 1920–1970" *Financial History Review* (with M. Billings)
"Foreign Direct Investment: Flows, Attitudes and Implications" *Journal of Interdisciplinary Economics* (with G.E. Wood)
"The Development of Management Accounting in the UK Clearing Banks, 1920–1970" *Accounting Banking and Financial History* (with M. Billings)
"Markets and Governments" in R. Michie and P. Williamson (eds) *The British Government and the City of London in the Twentieth Century* (CUP)
"Money and Economic Development in England in the Eighteenth Century" in L. Prados de la Escosura (ed.) *Exceptionalism and Industrialisation; Britain and its European Rivals, 1688–1815* (CUP)
"Price Change, Financial Stability and the British Economy, 1870–1939" in R. Burdekin and P. Siklos (eds), *Deflation: Current and Historical Perspectives* (CUP) (with G.E. Wood)
"George Rae" in *Dictionary of British Economists*

2005

"Foreign Direct Investment in Britain" in H. Huizinga and L. Jonung (eds) *Internationalisation of Asset Ownership in Europe* (CUP) (with G.E. Wood)

2006

"Gold as a Hedge Against the Dollar" Journal of *International Financial Markets, Institutions and Money* (with T.C. Mills and G.E. Wood)
"Illusion versus Reality: A Comparison of Governance and Outcome in British and German Banking" *Journal of Interdisciplinary Economics* (with G.E. Wood)
"Asset Prices, Financial Stability, and the Role of the Central Bank" (with G.E. Wood) in K. Matthews and P. Booth (eds) *Issues in Monetary Policy* (IEA)
"Modelling Institutional Change in the Payment System" in S. Schmitz and G.E. Wood (eds) *Institutional Change in the Payment System and Monetary Policy* (Routledge) (with D. Tsomocos and G.E. Wood)
"Inflation" in *Encyclopaedia of Twentieth Century Europe*

2007

"Capital in British Banking, 1920–1970" *Business History* (with M. Billings)
The Lender of Last Resort (ed.) (Routledge) (with G.E. Wood)
"Inflation in the Twentieth Century" in M. Oliver (ed.) *Great Disasters of the Twentieth Century*

"Some Historical Perspective on Financial Regulation" in D. Mayes and G.E. Wood (eds) *The Structure of Financial Regulation* (Routledge)

"E-barter vs Fiat Money: Will Central Banks Survive?" in E. Drandakis, D. Glycopantis and G. Stamatis (eds) *Essays in Honour of T Benos* (Kritiki)

"International Monetary Co-operation after WWII: A British Perspective" in H. James and J.C. Martinez Oliva (eds) *International Monetary Cooperation Across the Atlantic* (European Association of Banking History)

2009

"Scattered Thoughts from History on the Design of Central Banks" in D. Mayes and G.E. Wood (eds) *Designing Central Banks* (Routledge)

2010

The Bank of England 1950s–1979 (CUP)

Index

For Product Safety Concerns and Information please contact our EU
representative GPSR@taylorandfrancis.com
Taylor & Francis Verlag GmbH, Kaufingerstraße 24, 80331 München, Germany

www.ingramcontent.com/pod-product-compliance
Ingram Content Group UK Ltd.
Pitfield, Milton Keynes, MK11 3LW, UK
UKHW020020200926
475702UK00014B/1975
9780415749947